Cultural Theory

Cultural Theory

Edited by Tim Edwards

SAGE Publications
Los Angeles ▪ London ▪ New Delhi ▪ Singapore

First published 2007

SAGE Publications Ltd
1 Oliver's Yard
55 City Road
London EC1Y 1SP

SAGE Publications Inc
2455 Teller Road
Thousand Oaks, California 91320

SAGE Publications India Pvt Ltd
B 1/I 1 Mohan Cooperative Industrial Area
Mathura Road, Post Bag 7
New Delhi 110 044

SAGE Publications Asia-Pacific Pte Ltd
33 Pekin Street #02-01
Far East Square
Singapore 048763

British Library Cataloguing in Publication data

A catalogue record for this book is available
from the British Library

ISBN 978-0-7619-4862-9
ISBN 978-0-7619-4863-6

Library of Congress control number available

Typeset by C&M Digitals (P) Ltd., Chennai, India
Printed on paper from sustainable resources
Printed in India at Replika Press Pvt Ltd

Contents

● ● ● ● ● ● ● ●

• • • Contents • • •

Notes on Contributors

•••••••••

Peter Beilharz is Professor of Sociology and Director of the Thesis Eleven Centre for Critical Theory at La Trobe University, Australia. He is author of *Trotsky, Trotskyism and the Transition to Socialism* (Croom Helm 1987); *Labour's Utopias* (Routledge 1992); *Postmodern Socialism* (Melbourne University Press 1994); *Transforming Labour* (Cambridge 1994); *Imagining the Antipodes* (Cambridge 1997); and *Zygmunt Bauman – Dialectic of Modernity* (Sage 2000); and is editor of fifteen books. He is working on a book on Australia, to be called *The Unhappy Country*.

Ann Brooks is author of *Academic Women* (Open University Press, 1997); *Postfeminisms: Feminism, Cultural Theory and Cultural Forms* (Routledge, 1997); *Gender and the Restuctured University: Changing Management and Culture in Higher Education* (with Alison Mackinnon) (Open University Press, 2001) and *Gendered Work in Asian Cities: The New Economy and Changing Labour Markets* (Ashgate, 2006). Ann is currently Head of Sociology Programmes at SIM University, Singapore and was previously a Senior Lecturer in Sociology at Massey University, New Zealand. Her latest project is a book for Routledge entitled *Intimacy, Reflexivity and Identity: The Gendered Self in Chinese Diasporic Communities*.

Eamonn Carrabine is Senior Lecturer in the Department of Sociology at the University of Essex. His teaching and research interests lie in the fields of Criminology and Cultural Studies. His books include *Crime in Modern Britain* (with Pamela Cox, Maggy lee, and Nigel South, Oxford UniversityPress, 2002), *Criminology: A Sociological Introduction* (with Paul Iganski, Maggy Lee, Ken Plummer, Nigel South, Routledge, 2004) and *Power, Discourse and Resistance: A Genealogy of the Strangeways Prison Riot* (2004). He is currently working on a book on *Crime and the Media: Interrogating Representations of Transgression in Popular Culture*.

Douglas Kellner is George Kneller Chair in the Philosophy of Education at UCLA and is author of many books on social theory, politics, history, and culture, including works in cultural studies such as **Media Culture** and **Media Spectacle**; a trilogy of books on postmodern theory with Steve Best; a trilogy of books on the Bush administration, including **Grand Theft 2000, From 9/11 to Terror War**, and his latest text **Media Spectacle and the Crisis of Democracy**. His website is at www.gseis.ucla.edu/facullty/kellner.

Tim May is Professor and Director of the Centre for Sustainable Urban and Regional Futures (www.surf.salford.ac.uk). Tim is the author of works on urban and science policy, universities, social theory, research methodology and methods, philosophy of social science and organisational change. He has recently edited special editions of journals (with Beth Perry) on universities and academic production, science and regional policy and urban sociology and is writing a book on social science and reflexivity. He is also series editor of *Issues in Society* for McGraw-Hill/Open University Press. Tim is undertaking research for various clients on knowledge production and transfer, science and cities and regional and urban policy. He also works for universities advising them on intellectual, organisational and strategic developments and is a member of 'The Transatlantic Forum on the Future of Universities' (http://www.einaudi.cornell.edu/sshen/index.asp).

William Merrin is a lecturer in media and communications at the University of Wales, Swansea, specialising in media theory, new media and cyberculture and media history. He is the author of *Baudrillard and the Media: A Critical Introduction* (Polity, 2005), and *New Media: Key Thinkers* (Polity, forthcoming) as well as a range of articles on media theory and history and is a member of the editorial board of the on-line *International Journal of Baudrillard Studies*.

Maggie O'Neill is Senior Lecturer in the Deptartment of Social Sciences at Loughborough University. Committed to interdisciplinarity her work is situated at the crossroads of sociology, feminist theory, cultural and critical criminology and social policy. She co-edited *Sociology* (with Tony Spybey): the journal of the British Sociological Association from 1999–2002. Her books include *Adorno, Culture and Feminism* (Sage, 1999); *Prostitution and Feminism: Towards a Politics of Feeling* (Polity, 2001); *Prostitution: A Reader* with Roger Matthews (Ashgate, 2002); *Gender and the Public Sector* with Jim Barry and Mike Dent (Routledge, 2002); *Sex Work Now* with Rosie Campbell (Willen 2006). She is currently convening a regional network underpinned by the principles of PAR and funded by the AHRC 'making the connections: arts, migration and diaspora – www.makingtheconnections.info and a board member of the global human dignity and humiliation studies network (HDHS) – www.humiliationstudies.org

Jason L. Powell is Senior Lecturer in Sociology at the University of Liverpool. His research interests are in social theory, Foucauldian approaches to ageing and social policy. He has published extensively and most recently is author of *Social Theory and Ageing* as part of Charles Lemert's distinguished book series on 'New Discursive Formations' (2006, Rowman and Littlefield, Lanham); *Rethinking Social Theory and Later Life* (2006, Nova Science Press, New York) and edited (with Dr. Azrini Wahidin)

Foucault and Aging (2006, Nova Science Press, New York). He also serves on several editorial boards notably *Sociological Research On-Line* and *Journal of Sociology and Social Welfare*. His current work focuses on understanding relationship of discourse and subjectivity to performance of ageing identity in public spaces.

Derek Robbins is Professor of International Social Theory in the School of Social Sciences, Media and Cultural Studies at the University of East London where he also is Director of the Group for the Study of International Social Science. He is the author of *The Work of Pierre Bourdieu* (1991) and of *Bourdieu and Culture* (2000); the editor of two 4-volume collections of articles on Bourdieu in the Sage Masters of Contemporary Social Thought series (2000 and 2005) and of a 3-volume collection of articles on Lyotard in the same series (2004). His *On Bourdieu, Education and Society* was published by Bardwell Press in July, 2006, and he was the editor of the special number of *Theory, Culture and Society* on Bourdieu (23, 6, November, 2006). He is currently writing *The Internationalization of French Social Thought, 1950–2000* for publication by Sage.

Chris Rojek is Professor of Sociology & Culture at Nottingham Trent University. His most recent books are *Celebrity (2001), Stuart Hall (2003), Frank Sinatra (2004)* and *Leisure Theory: Principles and Practice (2005).*

John Scott is Professor of Sociology at the University of Essex, having previously been Professor at the University of Leicester. Specialising in social stratification, economic sociology, and social theory, his most recent books include *Power* (Polity Press, 2001), the *Oxford Dictionary of Sociology* (editor, Oxford University Press), and *Sociology* (with James Fulcher, Third Edition, Oxford University Press, 2007), and he has edited *Sociology: The Key Concepts, Fifty Key Sociologists: The Formative Theorists,* and *Fifty Key Sociologists: The Contemporary Theorists* (Routledge, 2007).With Sage he has published *Social Theory: Central Issues in Sociology* (2006).

Nick Stevenson is a Reader in Cultural Sociology at the University of Nottingham. His recent publications include *Understanding Media Cultures* (2002) for Sage, *Cultural Citizenship* (2003) for Open University Press and more recently *David Bowie* (2006) for Polity Press. He is currently working on the question of European identity in the context of cultural and political change.

Acknowledgements

•••••••••

I would sincerely like to thank all at Sage, and particularly Chris Rojek, for their support and assistance, and all the contributors for their work and patience.

Introduction

Tim Edwards

Recent decades have witnessed an almost ever-increasing attention to questions of culture, cultural theory and the cultural turn, yet what this means is still not entirely clear. In this collection, a range of authors, both well established and new, address these questions in a variety of ways. While literatures on cultural theory, including large edited collections, are now profuse, if not perhaps even profligate, this collection is unique in two senses. First, rather than acting as a 'round-up' of previously published readings, it brings together a series of original papers by authors, both time-honoured and recent; and, second, instead of asking the question, what is the significance of the impact of cultural analysis and theory for or upon sociology and social science, it asks, what is the legacy of sociology and wider social scientific inquiry in understanding the significance of culture, cultural practice, or cultural theory? It is perhaps a rather odd sleight of hand that manages to reinvent history so that cultural inquiry almost appears to precede the immense significance of over a century and a half of sociological theory and social investigation of concepts, practices and phenomena that clearly had much to do with culture, however defined. In this brief introduction, then, I have two intentions: first, to outline what constitutes and defines 'cultural theory' in this particular instance and, second, to summarize some of the findings of the authors in this particular collection at this particular moment of time, space and culture.

The term cultural *theory* is something of a misnomer here for the original title of cultural *sociology,* thus directly informing an understanding of the cultural significance of sociology and the sociological significance of culture. Understandings of cultural theory must necessarily reflect, and indeed depend upon, definitions of culture *per se*. As is now well known across the social sciences, these tend to split into two: the first definition centred on notions of art, style and more widely the visual, and the second definition simply defined as ways of life (see, for example, Williams, 1988). Of course, this is precisely where the perceived conflict between cultural studies and or more 'culturalist' poststructural and postmodern theory and social science and sociology, particularly its nineteenth-century classical traditions, can perhaps be seen to originate. Sociology and social science have always been concerned with culture as ways of life – that is precisely what makes any of it 'social' – yet understandings of visual culture have tended to reside under the auspices of the arts. The rise of studies of popular culture, media theory, visual analysis, and so on – following their growing importance throughout the western world and beyond in the twentieth century – started to force these two previously separate disciplines, and even worlds, to collide, leading to what is now commonly recognized as the 'turn to culture'. This is perhaps most succinctly defined by Stuart Hall in his essay on the centrality of the cultural (Hall, 1997). Here, Hall defines the cultural turn according to two key dimensions: first, the substantive turn to culture in terms of empirically demonstrable developments in the media, economy, technology and most significantly globalization; and, second, the epistemological turn to culture in terms of the more philosophical break with Marxism and the rise of poststructural theory centred on new, and much more fluid, notion of language – and indeed culture – in particular. This somewhat dualist sense of the turn to culture also informs the collection of essays here which are divided into three parts: the first focusing on the legacy of sociological theory, the second considering some more contemporary theorists, and the third concerned with more empirical, or at least topical, dimensions of contemporary theory.

The first five chapters focus on the legacy of the classical tradition in sociology and the importance of the Frankfurt School in understanding more contemporary cultural theory more particularly. Key within this is the supposed 'break' with Marxism that is commonly seen to lead to the formation of cultural studies yet this is variously demonstrated to be as mythical as it is real. John Scott's chapter on Humanist Marxism in particular pulls apart the so-called rupture between cultural studies and Marxist theory and focuses on the continuities. Starting with the work of Lukács, Scott shows how the Frankfurt School acted as a forerunner for more contemporary notions of the cultural economy, particularly in its perception of the need to complement economic analysis with cultural study. Chris Rojek, in Chapter 2, while berating the belated and uneven legacy of the work of Simmel for cultural studies, also argues strongly that Simmel's work on money and the metropolis, as a form of what Frisby calls 'sociological impressionism', not only constitutes one of the most important analyses of modernity but a primary 'entrée' or route into more contemporary cultural analysis (Frisby, 1981). One might also cite the growing sociology of consumption as one example of such a legacy. Similarly, in keeping with Scott's trajectory, Kellner, in Chapter 3, re-evaluates the significance of the Frankfurt School and the work of Walter Benjamin more particularly as potential forerunners of contemporary media studies. Indeed, in illustrating their influences upon work as diverse as that of the Birmingham School for Contemporary Cultural Studies and Raymond Williams, Todd Gitlin and Jürgen Habermas, Kellner shows how the break with Marxism is often misplaced, and that this centres more upon the rise of a more particular form of poststructural and postmodern theory. This is a theme picked up in the following two chapters which consider a couple of more particularly British traditions in sociology. Rojek's direct consideration of the work of Stuart Hall and the Birmingham School for Contemporary Cultural Studies, in Chapter 4, follows Kellner's logic in detecting a linguistic turn rather than a cultural turn as critical in causing the drift away from more directly Marxist theorizing. Hall's influential essay on en/decoding is pivotal here in highlighting the growing significance of anti-essentialist theorizing, often influenced in turn by the rise of identity politics such as feminism and anti-racism (Hall, 1980). The name of Anthony Giddens is not the first that springs to mind when considering cultural theory, yet in Chapter 5 John Scott argues that culture is central to Giddens' analysis on two fronts: first, culture as structure in relation to his consideration of rules, norms and dispositions and, second, culture as lifeworld in relation to ways of life. Thus, Scott argues, Giddens' analysis of culture informs his influential theory of structuration and his wider sociology of modernity although he critiques Giddens' lack of interrogation of the role of material resources.

In Part II, our attention shifts more towards the contemporary terrain of cultural theory yet a continuing emphasis upon social structure and patterns of inequality informs Peter Beilharz's consideration of Bauman, in Chapter 6, where he argues that culture for Bauman is primarily a 'structuring activity'. Through a wide-ranging analysis of the influences upon Bauman's work from Marxism and Freud through to Foucault, Beilharz interrogates Bauman's *Culture as Praxis*, ultimately returning to Bauman's dialogue with anthropology, and the work of Lévi-Strauss specifically, arguing that this is most fundamental in understanding Bauman's work on culture (Bauman, 1999). No work on cultural theory would be complete without reference to the seminal influence of French social science, and the work of Foucault most particularly. Powell and May's analysis of Foucault in Chapter 7 is driven most strongly by a consideration of his work on the philosophy of knowledge and his theorizing of subjectivity. Key within this is Foucault's anti-essentialist, and one might also say anti-realist, stance that refutes the 'reading off' of culture from deeper structures and his rearticulation of the role of culture in relation to wider – and more dynamic – historical and societal contexts, including medicine, sexuality and the role of the state. His attention to questions of power is a theme taken up in Chapter 8 in Robbins' consideration of the work of Bourdieu who, he argues, sees culture as a form of power relations or perhaps stratification, while still attempting to refute the concept *per se*. Robbins is particularly sensitive to what one might call the 'uses and abuses' of the work of Bourdieu and the significance of Anglo (mis)interpretation of specifically French philosophy and theorizing. Finally, in Chapter 9, Will Merrin considers the work of the on occasions near sociological *persona non grata* of Baudrillard. In conducting a particularly thorough review of his work, Merrin argues that Baudrillard – like Bourdieu – is subject to much misunderstanding and misuse when his work, and particularly his reformulation of semiotics or what Merrin calls his 'Durkhemian radicalism', are of enormous and continuing relevance to understandings of culture.

In summary to these more directly theoretically driven chapters, we are perhaps presented with three strongly interlinked key themes or points: first, that the supposed and oft-quoted break of contemporary cultural theory with early or more classical sociology, and particularly Marxism, is – to say the least – often overstated; second, significant continuities as well as conflicts exist between apparently diverse and contrasting strains of theorizing and analysis; and third, that those contrasts that do still exist are often contextually based and, more specifically, related to differing traditions of Anglo-American and European thought.

Following this point, in Part III, our attention shifts to more applied and topical dimension of contemporary cultural theory. In Chapter 10, Ann Brooks shows how feminist work and debates concerning subjectivity and identity intersect with and inform issues of transnationalism and transculturalism. Within this she considers two examples: the Chinese diaspora and the 'politics of veiling' or Islam and feminism. Through a wide-ranging discussion, often placing a heavy emphasis upon questions of feminist praxis, she concludes that neither the traditions of sociology nor cultural studies alone are wide enough to incorporate the complexities of contemporary culture. Implicit within this and a recurrent theme through Part III is an engagement with interdisciplinarity or, more basically, an argument for what one might call subject hybrids combining and drawing on an array of disciplinary backgrounds. O'Neill's Chapter 11 on feminist epistemology and the role of participatory action research is complementary here. Interestingly, once again, she also returns to reconsider the legacy of the Frankfurt School and phenomenology more widely for contemporary feminist praxis. In his chapter on pop music, Eamonn Carrabine provides an effective survey of a wide range of theorizations of music from Adorno's work on jazz through to McRobbie's critique of Hebdige, concluding that pop music is indeed a hybrid topic in need of equally hybrid theorizing and understanding. Stevenson's final chapter on citizenship is perhaps the most wide-ranging of all and the one that opens up, and yet also concludes, the discussion of cultural phenomena. In opening up the politics of the cultural through an analysis of the increasing conflation of citizenship and consumption, Stevenson steers a deft course through the contested terrain of the cultural and the economic concluding that more attention is needed to address the increasing social divisions emerging from neo-liberal politics and practice, suggesting that the work of Raymond Williams may form the basis for such an engagement.

At the start of this Introduction, I pointed to a perceived conflict or tension between cultural theory and sociology. The chapters collected here, however, in a wide diversity of ways point to the falsity of any such division and the need for greater – and mutual – engagement between such disciplines and indeed many others. The challenge, then, is to put this into effect not only individually or in one direction but collectively across disciplines and with the mutual recognition of the enormity of contributions of sociology and sociologists past and present for cultural analysis and cultural practice.

References

Bauman, Z. (1999) *Culture as Praxis*. 2nd edn, London: Sage.
Frisby, D. (1981) *Sociological Impressionism*. London: Heinemann.
Hall, S. (1980) 'Encoding and decoding', in S. Hall, et al. (eds) *Culture, Media, Language*. London: Hutchinson.
Hall, S. (1997) 'The centrality of culture: notes on the cultural revolutions of our time', in K. Thomson (ed.) *Media and Cultural Regulation*. London: Sage.
Williams, R. (1988) *Keywords: A Vocabulary of Culture and Society*. London: Fontana.

PART I

THE LEGACY
OF SOCIOLOGY

CHAPTER ONE
●●●●●●●●

Cultural Analysis in Marxist Humanism

John Scott

Marxist humanism, in its broadest sense, can be traced back to some of the earliest attempts to combine a Marxist approach to philosophical issues with Hegelian and interpretivist ideas. It involves the attempt to construct a philosophical standpoint that begins from real, conscious human beings and explores the ways in which their self-conscious knowledge enters into the constitution of the world in which they live and act. History is seen as an outcome of those creative human actions through which people both produce a social world and give meaning to it. Glimpsed during the 1890s, this attempt has continued to the present day. Understood as a more specific approach to cultural analysis, however, Marxist humanism has a much shorter history. Systematic cultural analyses from a Marxist humanist standpoint were a specific product of the 1920s and flowered in the 'critical theory' of the Frankfurt School of social theory. It virtually disappeared as a distinct and active strand of cultural theory with the demise of this critical theory and the absorption of its key ideas about culture into very different philosophical and sociological frameworks.

A quite specific framework of cultural analysis was built and elaborated by these writers, though certain of their themes were echoed by a wider group of theorists. Most of their central arguments, however, were later accepted, even though the origin of these ideas is not often recognized.

In view of the criticisms levelled against Marxism, this point is worth emphasizing. The growth of new approaches to culture within cultural studies has been associated with a rejection of what is seen as the crude materialism of mainstream Marxism (e.g., Hall, 1977). These approaches have, paradoxically, drawn much of their inspiration from the work of Gramsci (1929–35), a Marxist who owes much to the same Hegelian tradition that has also shaped the forms of Marxist humanism. Similar points can be made about the work of such postmodernists as Baudrillard (1981), Jameson (1991), and Bauman (1991a). Their works on the contemporary cultural condition are widely seen as pointing social analysis in a new direction, with a greater sensitivity to the plurality and diversity of cultural responses. Jameson, however, presents his work as a cultural complement to the economic logic central to Marxism, reiterating precisely those points made by the writers under consideration here. In the case of Baudrillard and Bauman, the connection is even clearer. The early work of both writers (Baudrillard, 1972; Bauman, 1976) was firmly rooted in the work of the critical theorists who formed the core of Marxist humanism. The growing recognition of the centrality of the media of mass communications has simply enlarged and extended ideas already apparent in that work.

In this chapter, I will focus on the products of the relatively short history of Marxist humanism. The early work of Lukács and the ways in which his ideas were taken up by Horkheimer, Adorno, and Marcuse will be considered. Some of the contours of their wider acceptance will be discussed, but I will not explore this work in any detail. It is important, nevertheless, to indicate some of the contemporary work that falls firmly within the tradition of Marxist Humanism. I will, therefore, sketch the ways in which the broad philosophical framework of Marxist humanism has persisted, especially in Eastern Europe, where it provided a continuing critical current to the once-dominant Soviet orthodoxy.

Orthodoxy and Western Marxism

At the time of his death, Karl Marx was known principally for his political writings, such as *The Communist Manifesto* (Marx and Engels, 1848), and for the broadly materialist interpretation of history that underpinned these writings. Marx had been working on the economic theories that were central to this materialism for many years, but he had managed to publish only a very small part of his voluminous research. Of his projected multi-volume *Economics*, only the first of the volumes on *Capital* had appeared. In the years following his death, others struggled to complete the unpublished works that formed his intellectual legacy, aiming to demonstrate their continuing relevance for understanding contemporary conditions.

Central to this task was Friedrich Engels. Despite undertaking important work of his own before he began working with Marx, Engels can properly be considered 'the first Marxist' (Carver, 1981: 31). He saw his life's work as promoting and popularizing the ideas of Marx by casting them in a systematic and more rigorously 'dialectical' framework. It was in Engels's hands that 'Marxism' came to be systematized as a positivistic science formulating law-like generalizations. His Marxism comprised an economistic view of history that gave little autonomy to cultural phenomena.

Engels's efforts were closely linked to the development of Marxism in Europe. Franz Mehring and Karl Kautsky in Germany and George Plekhanov in Russia were the most important theorists of what came to be known as 'orthodox' Marxism or, by its critics, 'vulgar Marxism'. 'Revisionists' such as Eduard Bernstein and the Fabians, who pioneered the attempt to revise Marxism to take account of the growing monopolization of capitalist production and of imperialist expansion, did not significantly challenge the economic focus and deterministic framework of orthodox Marxism. This economism was also apparent in the more radical attacks levelled against both orthodoxy and Revisionism by Rosa Luxemburg and the Austro-Marxists (Renner, 1904; Hilferding, 1910).

These radical attacks did, however, begin to raise questions about the ability of orthodox Marxism to understand political and cultural factors and about the part played by conscious human action in the development of these elements of the 'superstructural'. Some years earlier, the Italian Marxist Antonio Labriola had rejected the strong deterministic arguments of his compatriots Loria and Ferri. Drawing on Hegel, he stressed that Marxism posits action – praxis – as the crucial link between economic conditions and cultural life, and that 'social psychology' is a crucial element in historical explanation. However, Labriola's influence on other Marxists was limited, and he did not go on to construct a systematic social theory of either politics or culture.

It was only in the 1920s that the economism and determinism of established forms of Marxism were seriously challenged. The philosophical reconsiderations that have come to be known as 'western Marxism' laid the real foundations of Marxist humanism (Anderson, 1976). Karl Korsch and Georg Lukács, in particular, worked through a larger body of philosophy and provided the basis on which the later work of the critical theorists in Frankfurt was built. Writing from within the Marxist tradition, they looked back to the roots of Marxism itself, and particularly to its philosophical roots in Kant and Hegel. They sought to reconstruct Marxism on a new philosophical basis that would take account of the sociological work of Weber and Simmel and the psychological work of Freud. It was this novel mix of ideas that shaped the emerging framework of Marxist humanism.

Born in Hungary, Georg Lukács attended Simmel's lectures in Berlin and became a member of Simmel's private seminar group. A fellow member of this group, Ernst Bloch,[1] took Lukács to Heidelberg to hear Rickert's lectures, and in Heidelberg they both became members of Max Weber's academic circle. Lukács's primary interests lay in aesthetic theory and literature, which he approached from the standpoint of the *Geisteswissenchaften* and he began to read Hegel and the 'Young Hegelians' of the 1840s. An especially important influence on his work, however, was Kierkegaard, whose ideas were concurrently being intensively examined by other important thinkers: while Lukács was drawing out the Hegelian dimension in Kierkegaard's work, Heidegger and Jaspers were using it to forge their existential phenomenology.

Lukács's aim in his earliest books had been to interpret the symbolic structures through which literary works are produced. In *Soul and Forms* (Lukács, 1910)[2] he used Simmel's idea of 'form' (Simmel, 1900; see also Simmel, 1908) to analyse literary expression, while in *The Theory of the Novel* (Lukács, 1914–15) he adopted more explicitly Hegelian ideas. To these arguments, however, he added the Marxist view that cultural products of all kinds had to be seen as originating in specific social classes (Arato and Breines, 1979). All cultural production, he argued, occurs within a capitalist division of labour and must be seen as involving a process of 'objectification' that separates the products from their creative human producers. The cultural sphere, then, comes to appear as if it were an objective and impersonal sphere of intellectual forms detached from any subjective human meaning. The task of cultural analysis is to show that cultural products can be understood only if they are related back to the meanings and interests of their producers, understood as class members.

Drama and novels, together with other forms of modern art, Lukács argued, are to be seen as bourgeois productions in which there has been a separation of the cultural forms from the personalities of their producers. He saw the central values of the bourgeoisie, centred on individualism and an ascetic sense of duty, reflected in the 'tragic' vision in literature. The bourgeoisie, however, was a declining social class, and its cultural products show the evidence of its decline. Contemporary social conditions could no longer sustain audiences for the classic bourgeois forms of art. Contemporary audiences seek out mass entertainment, and they find it increasingly difficult to exercise any reflective judgement on the social conditions responsible for their cultural preferences. Lukács clung to the hope that the proletariat might still be a source of creative cultural renewal and historical understanding, but he believed that the class consciousness of the German proletariat, as it currently existed, was inadequate. It had been distorted by bourgeois concerns that resulted from their structural subordination within capitalist production. It was these reflections on class consciousness that led Max Weber famously to commend this 'talented author's' views.

Lukács's early political and economic ideas were not based on a wide reading of Marxist works, and on his return to Hungary he set about remedying this. Together with Arnold Hauser and Karl Mannheim, he formed a study group that aimed to reconcile the approach of the *Geisteswissenchaften* with Marxist economic theory. Lukács wanted to incorporate Marxist views on cultural production into his developing framework of ideas. His engagement with Marxist theory, and his rejection of the particular materialist philosophy that underpinned orthodox Marxism, became the central element in his thought when he began to work on the series of essays that were brought together in his famous work, *History and Class Consciousness* (Lukács, 1923). This book was intended as a provisional and programmatic statement of ideas, rather than a definitive solution to his philosophical concerns, and Lichtheim has correctly remarked that it is a rather uneasy amalgam of neo-Hegelian philosophy with economic and political analyses derived from Luxemburg and Lenin (Lichtheim, 1970: 20).

Karl Korsch, at the same time, was developing similar ideas. An active member of the German Communist party (the KPD) from 1920, Korsch for some years combined membership of the Reichstag with his university work. Korsch was a Leninist in politics, but he rejected the conventional philosophical basis of Leninism. In *Marxism and Philosophy* (Korsch, 1923), he argued that knowledge of the social world was not the mere 'reflection' of an independent, external world but was directly constitutive of that world. There could be no sharp line drawn between an external reality and our consciousness of it. This implied the radical thesis that the forms of consciousness that comprise what was conventionally regarded as the 'superstructure' are directly constitutive of the social relations that comprise the 'base'.

History and Class Consciousness, too, aimed to defend the politics of orthodox Marxism against revisionism and reformism, while challenging its philosophical distortions. Like Korsch, Lukács rejected the naïve representational realism of Engels and Lenin and sought to recapture the Hegelian dimension that had been lost in the building of orthodox Marxism. By stressing the importance of Hegel – and, beyond him, of Kant – Lukács re-opened the whole question of the relationship between knowledge and the nuomenal world of things-in-themselves.

Culture, Totality, and Reification

These philosophical considerations were put to work in a systematic examination of the ideas of class consciousness and ideology. The orthodox Marxist view of base and superstructure saw all artistic expressions as mere epiphenomena of an economic base. Lukács rejected this, seeking to recognize the autonomy of cultural production and all forms of social consciousness. This was combined with a reconsideration of the role of Marxist parties in forging proletarian class consciousness. His key aim was to develop a new philosophical and theoretical basis for what remained an essentially Leninist view of politics.

The crucial idea in Marxism, Lukács argued, was not the idea of the base and the superstructure, but that of the whole and its parts. The parts have always to be grasped in relation to the whole or *totality* in which they are bound. The idea of the totality is central to the dialectical method of thinking and is the core of what Lukács took from Hegel. According to Hegel, the concepts used by people can provide only a partial perspective on the world, and each partial perspective has to be seen as a 'moment' of a larger truth. Each particular point of view gives a limited and one-sided picture, but the whole contains all of these limited representations of it and so is superior to any of them considered separately. Partiality can be overcome through the constant criticism – or 'negation' – of intellectual ideas, reconstructing them and so moving them closer to an overall picture of the totality.

Lukács agreed that the meaning of all observed facts derives from the whole of which they are mere parts and that each particular fact is an analytically isolated aspect or moment of the whole. The process of relating part to whole is a process of 'mediation' (Mannheim, 1929), a creative act of 'synthesis'. In historical study, 'social being' is the relevant whole and is logically prior to the forms of consciousness and social institutions that form its various parts. A social totality is, moreover, a dynamic totality. It is constantly in process of change and development, and all social facts and events must be seen in relation to the past, the present, and the future of the social totality of which they are parts.

The 'method of totality' does not follow the natural science method followed in positivism and orthodox Marxism. There is, as Dilthey and Rickert argued, a funda-mental difference between the natural sciences and the historical sciences. With Weber, Lukács saw values as the bases from which concepts are constructed in the historical sciences. However, he held that all consciousness and knowledge is socially located and that values, therefore, had to be related back to their social origins. From Marx he took the idea of the centrality of class location, and concluded that all knowledge of the social, historical world is constructed from the standpoint of par-ticular class positions. There can be no 'detached' or external form of knowledge.

The method of totality that characterizes his Marxism, Lukács argued, is rooted in the class position of the proletariat. It is the standpoint of the proletariat that, uniquely, makes possible an explicit adoption of the method of totality. The synthesis sought by Hegel can be achieved only from a proletarian standpoint; all other standpoints offer only limited or partial points of view. Marxism, therefore, must be seen not as a neutral and detached scientific description of the world, but as an expression of the consciousness of the proletariat. It does not, however, correspond to the actual consciousness of the proletariat as it might exist in any particular place or time. The proletariat as it exists in a particular society may be in a condition of false consciousness and so its members may misunderstand their own position and prospects. What is important for Lukács is the theoretical consciousness of a mature proletariat that has come to a full understanding of its own position in history and of the actions necessary to advance its further historical development. To achieve this state of consciousness, Lukács concluded, proletarian consciousness must be guided by a Communist Party whose leaders have a sure grasp of the real situation faced by the class. Communist intellectuals are able to formulate the revolutionary will of the proletariat in a rational form as they move towards a grasp of the totality. A superior intellectual understanding of the social world is built inside a Communist Party, and so it can truly act as the vanguard of the proletariat.

There is an obvious contradiction in this position, which Lukács failed to resolve. On the one hand, he argued, true science must be informed by the proletarian standpoint. On the other hand, however, he saw this standpoint as non-existent in most real situations, and actual proletarians must be guided by a scientifically informed vanguard of intellectuals. If, however, intellectuals can grasp the totality before members of the proletariat have achieved this consciousness, a justification for their knowledge must be made on grounds closer to those of orthodox 'scientific' Marxism and positivism: and if this is the case, what then differentiates Marxism from any other intellectual position?

Lukács's early work had been concerned with the cultural products of art and literature, but the arguments of *History and Class Consciousness* were concerned with culture in the broader sense of the practical consciousness and experiences of particular social groups. It is not simply novels and dramas that derive from class standpoints, it is whole ways of life. It was in developing this particular view of culture that Lukács introduced the idea of 'reification'. He used this concept of reification to explore the false consciousness of actual proletarians, and in doing so he virtually reinvented the early Marx's work on alienation. The concept, in fact, had its origins in Marx's analysis of 'commodity fetishism' in *Capital*, and Lukács effectively reconstructed the Hegelian basis of Marx's mature work. Marx had argued that the personal characteristics of people in a capitalist society are irrelevant to their role in the process of production. Workers are treated as mere quantities of labour power that can be bought or sold in the market and so can be subjected to a process of rationalization, a specialization and fragmentation of work tasks. As a result, relations between people appear simply in the form of the value relations among commodities and money. Their human character and meaning are lost and they are reified, seen as 'things'. This was the insight that never figured in bourgeois economics and that had been lost sight of in orthodox Marxism. Lukács's work aimed to return an awareness of the human character of social products to their producers.

Lukács held that bourgeois thought is necessarily confined to these reified appearances. The particular class standpoint of the bourgeoisie limits its perspective on the world, and does not allow it to penetrate beyond the ways that things appear externally. Bourgeois intellectuals cannot escape their limited standpoint and so bourgeois knowledge necessarily emphasizes the properties of particular isolated and thing-like phenomena. This is shown clearly in the categories and theorems of classical economic theory, Lukács argued, where all social phenomena are reduced to value relations that can be explored through calculation and precise prediction.[3] Proletarian thought, as grasped by its vanguard thinkers, can penetrate beyond appearances and so can overcome this reification. Those intellectuals who adopt the proletarian standpoint are able to point the way to a more adequate understanding of contemporary social conditions. True proletarian consciousness has to be seen as the self-knowledge of the commodity, of the specific commodity that is human labour power. When workers understand how they have come to be a commodity and how their emancipation depends on their transcending the knowledge and conditions of bourgeois production, they will have achieved a self-knowledge that will guide them in their revolutionary practice.

Lukács had, then, restored to Marxism many of the ideas set out by Marx in 1844–45, though this became apparent only after Marx's early works were prepared for their first publication in the 1930s. Orthodox Marxists, in the 1920s, saw the incorporation of a Hegelian dimension into Marx's work as dangerous and heretical, and *History and Class Consciousness* caused a fierce storm in Marxist circles. Like Korsch, Lukács had been active in Communist politics, and this made it inevitable that, along with Korsch's *Marxism and Philosophy*, his own book would be denounced. Thus, Zinoviev and Bukharin, the leading activists and theorists of the Communist International, criticized it for its abandonment of the scientific principles of Marxism. Lukács toyed with the idea of publishing an answer to his critics, but – however strategically – he left his response unpublished and reverted to a more orthodox position.[4] Korsch refused to abandon his views and went on to elaborate them further. As a result of this and his expulsion from the KPD, his work (Korsch, 1936) was not widely read in Marxist circles.[5]

Lukács published a more orthodox study of *Lenin* (Lukacs, 1924), and became increasingly committed to the Stalinist political line of those who had denounced him. In 1929, he even recanted his earlier theoretical 'aberrations' and re-stated his commitment to a reflectionist view of truth and his commitment to Soviet orthodoxy and the Soviet regime. Lukács moved to Moscow to work in the Marx archives and, apart from a brief visit to Berlin, he remained there until the end of the Second World War. His work in the Marx archives involved a study of the still unpublished early manuscripts of Marx, and it must have been galling for him to discover their great similarities with his own, now denounced and rejected, work.[6]

Lukács's most creative period ended at precisely the time that other Marxists were beginning to see his Hegel-influenced work as an important contribution to the reconstruction of Marxism. Lukács himself played no part in this and espoused a generally orthodox position. Indeed, Lichtheim has remarked, only a little unfairly, that his work on aesthetics and literary theory during the 1930s (Lukacs, 1937, and various essays later published as Lukacs, 1946) 'are the work of a man who had performed a kind of painless lobotomy upon himself, removed part of his brain and replaced it by slogans from the Moscow propagandists' (Lichtheim, 1970: 83–4).

Lukács returned to Hungary in 1945, and the main works that he published after his return were studies that he had been preparing through the 1930s and 1940s. These were a study of Hegel (Lukács, 1948), and a massive history of German thought since Schelling (Lukács, 1953), in which he criticized Heidegger, Jaspers, and the German sociological tradition in the name of Lenin's representational realism. He also produced a study of modernism (Lukács, 1958), and, in the early 1960s, a two-volume study of aesthetics. These works were attempts to rebuild the approach to aesthetics that he had set out in his very earliest works, but from a more orthodox Marxist basis. His final work, the outcome of his reflections on the implications for Marxism of Marx's early manuscripts and Lenin's philosophical notebooks, was *The Ontology of Social Being*, which was published only after his death (Lukács, 1971a).[7]

Marxist Humanism at Frankfurt

The core ideas of Marxist humanism as a method of cultural analysis were set out in Lukács's key work. It was developed in its classic form, however, by a group of German academic Marxists who took up Lukács's ideas and enlarged them into a systematic social theory. These were the theorists of the Institute of Social Research at the University of Frankfurt.

The Institute was formed in 1923 with an institutional existence quite separate from the Department of Sociology (then headed by Franz Oppenheimer) and the other academic departments of the university.[8] Formed with funding from Felix Weil, the son of a wealthy merchant, its aim was to carry out and promote radical social research. Weil, a committed Marxist who had helped to finance the publication of Lukács's *History and Class Consciousness*, promoted the Institute in order to further Marxist research on socialism and the labour movement. Karl Korsch, then at Jena but soon to be enmeshed in the controversies surrounding his and Lukács's work, actively supported the Institute's research. Under its first Director, Carl Grüneberg, this interdisciplinary group of Marxist scholars had a distinctly Austro-Marxist focus: Grüneberg had studied at Vienna under both Hilferding and Renner. Its members and work in the early years included Henryck Grossman on the economics of monopoly and finance capital,[9] Karl Wittfogel on Chinese society, Franz Borkenau on feudal and bourgeois world-views, and Friedrich Pollock on the Soviet planned economy. Members of the Institute of Social Research worked closely with Ryazanov's editing of the Marx archives in Moscow.

Grüneberg's retirement in 1929 precipitated a shift in focus for the Institute, which became both more philosophical and more concerned with cultural issues. The intellectual centre of gravity at the Institute began to shift from Austro-Marxism to Marxist humanism. The new director, Max Horkheimer, initiated this change of direction. He recruited Herbert Marcuse, Erich Fromm, and Franz Neumann to the Institute, and worked closely with Theodor Adorno, then a member of the Philosophy Department. Others associated with the Institute in this period included Leo Löwenthal and Walter Benjamin, both of whom were working on literary theory.

Horkheimer's ideas were firmly rooted in Austro-Marxism, but his association with Adorno led him to take a greater interest in cultural issues. Adorno's principal interests were in aesthetic theory and the analysis of music, and he had furthered his studies of musical theory and practice in Vienna, where he studied under Schönberg's pupil, Alban Berg. Adorno wrote a number of philosophical pieces while in Vienna, but on his return to Frankfurt in 1926 he applied himself to completing a habilitation thesis on the irrational and the unconscious in Freud's *Introductory Lectures* (Freud, 1915–17).[10] Influenced by Horkheimer, Adorno began to draw on Marxist ideas, seeing irrationalism as an ideological expression of bourgeois thought that took its most extreme form in fascism. His use of Marxism did not impress his examiners, however, and he did not secure an academic position. He began to spend more time in Berlin, where both he and Horkheimer were members of an intellectual circle that included Walter Benjamin, Ernst Bloch, and many of the artistic avant garde. The intellectual focus for the circle's discussions at this time was Lukács's *History and Class Consciousness*, and Ernst Bloch provided a direct link back to Simmel's discussion group that had stimulated Lukács's explorations into cultural forms. Adorno worked with Benjamin on a reconsideration of Kantian ideas, and in 1931, when his philosophical expertise could no longer be denied, he joined the Philosophy Department – but not the Institute – at Frankfurt.

A prominent member of the Institute from 1930 to 1939 was Erich Fromm, who had studied for his doctorate under Alfred Weber in the 1920s and had then moved into psychoanalysis. Fromm sought to integrate psychoanalysis with Marxism, He became the leading researcher in the newly established Psychoanalytical Institute at Frankfurt, where he began work on a number of general psychoanalytic studies (published after he left the Institute) and collaborated with the Institute of Social Research on a study of German workers (Fromm, 1939). Another member in the 1930s, Herbert Marcuse, used Lukács's ideas in his aesthetic theory, but he broadened the base of his philosophy when he became a teaching assistant to Heidegger. He had also begun to study Hegel, and when Marx's early manuscripts appeared in the year before he joined the Institute, Marcuse saw them as providing the key for his own work (Marcuse, 1941).

Following the Nazi consolidation of power, state control over intellectual life grew, and many Jewish intellectuals were forced out of the universities and into exile. Karl Mannheim, Norbert Elias, and Hans Gerth of the Sociology Department left Frankfurt for Britain and the United States. The Institute of Social Research – its staff both Jewish and Marxist – was closed down and its property seized. Members of the Institute moved to Switzerland in 1933 and its intellectual activities were then transferred to Columbia University in New York and, a little later, to California. It was during this period of exile that Adorno became a full member of the Institute. He joined Horkheimer to produce a series of 'philosophical fragments' that were later published as *Dialectic of Enlightenment* (Adorno and Horkheimer, 1944), which Horkheimer then popularized in a book of his own (Horkheimer, 1947). Adorno, meanwhile, brought together much of his work on music for publication as a book (Adorno, 1949). Horkheimer returned to Frankfurt in 1950 to re-establish the Institute and to become Rector of the University, and he secured a Chair in the Philosophy Department for Adorno in 1953. Marcuse, who had left the Institute in 1942 to take up some work for the US government, chose to remain in the United States when Horkheimer failed to support his return to an academic post at Frankfurt.

Horkheimer did little to develop his own ideas following his return to Frankfurt, and he taught only on the history of philosophy. While Adorno chose to concentrate much of his attention on aesthetics, he did continue to develop his wider philosophy (Adorno, 1951; 1955; 1966) and his sociology of culture, and he became heavily involved in methodological debates on the character of empirical research in sociology. The bulk of the Institute's work at this time was contract research of an uninspiring kind, and Adorno withdrew from empirical research after the mid-1950s.

I will look at the ideas of the Frankfurt Marxist humanists in the following sections. I will look, first, at their views on knowledge and its relation to the social position of the knowing subject. Then their accounts of rationality and technological domination and of the culture industry will be explored. Finally, the investigations into socialization and social control, which were central to the more general concept of culture that they were developing, will be discussed.

Standpoints, Knowledge, and Critique

Hegel's view of knowledge was the fundamental point of reference for virtually all philosophical debate in Germany, and its influence led many sociologists to see their main, or exclusive, concern as being the construction of a sociology of culture (Weber, 1920–21). These issues were hotly debated in the Philosophy and Sociology Departments at Frankfurt University, and the ideas of Horkheimer and Adorno developed, in particular, in relation to the arguments of Max Scheler and Karl Mannheim. These writers thought it essential to see how sociology could escape the inherently partial and relative character of all socially bound knowledge, and they explored this in what they called a sociology of knowledge.

Scheler, who moved to Frankfurt shortly before his death in 1928, argued that a transcendental realm of objective truth lay behind the historical relativity of actual values and ideas, and he saw his task as defining this objectivity in the face of cultural relativism. Mannheim, on the other hand, rejected any view that postulated movement towards absolute truth: there simply was no sphere of absolute truth. He did, however, try to steer a course that also rejected any radical relativism while, at the same time, recognizing what he called the 'relational' or perspective-bound character of knowledge (Mannheim, 1925; 1929). Mannheim focused on the role of intellectuals in the production of knowledge. In doing so, he was drawing on the cultural sociology of Alfred Weber and the Marxism of Lukács, as both writers had sought to distinguish the knowledge produced by intellectuals from the everyday knowledge of other social actors. Intellectuals had the necessary education and training to engage in social research, and the universities could give them a base of relative autonomy from practical interests and concerns that allowed them to detach themselves from practical struggles and work towards a knowledge of the larger context within which people are bound. They can produce a knowledge that is, necessarily, 'relational', but which is not merely 'relative' to a given social location (see Scott, 1998).

Both Horkheimer and Adorno shared this assumption that the production of knowledge that escapes the limited perspectives of everyday knowledge, however partially, is a task that can be pursued only by an intellectual minority working under appropriate social conditions. Horkheimer (1935) took a similar position to Mannheim, holding that all truth must be recognized as limited and tentative. Social scientists, he argued, are engaged in a critical reconstruction of the knowledge and ideas of particular historical groups. This is a practical, progressive movement towards a view of the social whole from within which these particular ideas originate. This view of the whole remains, nevertheless, a tentative product of particular individuals and groups. While it is superior to the unreflective partial perspectives from which it is built, it is still a partial view. At the same time, however, the social whole is constantly changing. Change occurs through the practical activities of the individuals and groups that compose it, which are informed by their particular ideas. The partial knowledge possessed by social groups informs their actions, which bring about social change in the totality that shapes their knowledge. Social scientists who achieve a critical reconstruction of the whole are aiming at a moving and constantly changing target. Horkheimer, therefore, agrees with Mannheim that any 'synthesis' of partial perspectives must be a 'dynamic' synthesis that is constantly moving towards a better and more adequate knowledge of the whole, but can never be fixed as a definitive statement of absolute truth.

Adorno agreed that historically objectified knowledge is perspectival in character, and he adds that the plurality of such knowledge in any society highlights the contradictory character of social reality itself. The aim of historical understanding, Adorno argued, is to grasp the contradictory character of the world by disclosing the structural elements that organize it and showing how each perspective or standpoint 'negates' all others. These contradictions cannot be overcome or unified in the kind of 'synthesis' sought by Hegel. They exist within complex social wholes that have no overall, essential unity. Cultural analysis involves an identification of the elements or parts of the whole and an imaginative recombination of them in such a way as to disclose their contradictions, oppositions, non-identities, and negations. These contradictions cannot simply be thought away, but must be retained as integral to the character of the whole.[11] The model for such an analysis is Marx's analysis of commodity exchange, which identified the forces and the relations of production as the parts and recombined them into a model of a mode of production in which their contradictions explained the observable pattern of market relations and predicted the future course of economic change.

These ideas were explored in Horkheimer's discussion of class consciousness, and of proletarian consciousness in particular. He saw the German proletariat as marked by a sharp division between an employed fraction and the submerged and deprived fraction of the unemployed. This class division fragmented the labour movement and undermined its chances for political unity. The employed section of the working class in Germany, for example, had allied with the reformist tendencies in the SPD and other moderate parties, while the unemployed, with no capacity for political organization or class consciousness, were naïve and uncritical supporters of the KPD.

Horkheimer saw Marxist intellectuals as able to generate a critical reconstruction of the partial perspectives found in the fraction of the working class, but he was more pessimistic about actual proletarian consciousness than Lenin and Lukács. The proletariat had become subject to ever-stronger ideological forces of domination that strengthened its false consciousness. Its objective conditions push it towards truth, but ideology limits and restricts it. Parties become agents of this ideology and so cannot be regarded as reliable sources of revolutionary change. A properly progressive and critical theory, therefore, has to be developed by intellectuals with an autonomous base, independent of both party and state. It can be produced by a small circle of intellectuals, united by their common commitment to developing a theory that will contribute to the elimination of exploitation and oppression. Horkheimer saw intellectuals such as himself developing their ideas through dialogue and debate with the most 'advanced' sections of the working class. The theoretical consciousness that corresponds to the proletarian standpoint, then, can be developed only *outside* the proletariat and taken to them from this autonomous, external base. The intellectuals of the Institute of Social Research were able, in principle, to use their ideas, to bring the two sections of the German proletariat into a political unity in which their differences are recognized and understood but are subordinated to their common opposition to the bourgeoisie.

To understand the role of Marxist intellectuals, Horkheimer drew a distinction between their 'critical theory' and the bourgeois forms of 'traditional theory' (Horkheimer, 1937). Traditional forms of theorizing, such as positivistic science, obscure the practical interests that organize them, hiding them behind a mask of objectivity and absolute impartiality. In representing particular interests as if they were universal, they are ideological. By contrast, critical theorizing, in demonstrating the partiality of all perspectives, exposes and articulates the links between knowledge and interests. It shows the limitations inherent in traditional theorizing by showing how its results can be placed within a larger practical context. What gives critical theory its progressive character is its orientation towards the emancipation of people from all forms of domination – from domination by market relations and from the political relations of totalitarian control that have become such a marked feature of contemporary capitalism. Unlike Lukács, Horkheimer does not see the adoption of this emancipatory interest as requiring that intellectuals actually take the standpoint of the proletariat. Critical theory, he argued, must retain its independent commitment to the achievement of a rational form of society that will achieve full human potential. Liberation from class relations is one, albeit central, aspect of this process of emancipation.

Marcuse most explicitly forged links between a critical theory and the heritage of Hegel's idea of negative, critical thinking (Marcuse, 1941; see also Marcuse, 1936 and 1937). Marcuse argued that Marxism was the true inheritor of the critical tendencies of the early works of Hegel, of his so-called Jena system of philosophy. He drew specific parallels between the treatment of the early works of both writers. These early works were, in each case, unpublished when written. Only in the 1920s and 1930s had scholars discovered this work and made it available: Hegel's earliest works were first published in 1923 and in 1931–32, while Marx's early manuscripts were published in 1932. Marcuse saw himself and the other Frankfurt theorists as recovering the critical Hegelian dimension in Marx's thought that had been denied by orthodox and revisionist Marxism.

This emphasis on critical theory continued into the 1950s and 1960s. Adorno, working mainly on aesthetics and philosophy rather than the sociology of culture, engaged in a series of debates and discussions on methodology. Faced with the challenge posed by the growth of non-Marxist sociology in the post-war period, Adorno and others at the Institute attempted to clarify the distinctive character of critical theory and its relationship to 'bourgeois' sociology. With other members of the Institute he produced a series of papers on methodology (Adorno, 1957; 1962b), a collectively authored textbook (Horkheimer et al., 1956), and a series of introductory lectures (Adorno, 1968). The context for much that he wrote was the so-called 'positivist dispute'. This was a debate around the nature of social science method in which Adorno defended the idea of critical theory in the face of the claim by Popper and some interpreters of Weber that sociology was doomed unless it rigorously and systematically followed the methodology of the natural sciences. Adorno pointed to the distorting and destructive consequences of this 'positivism' and stressed, once again, the importance of negativity for critical thinking.

Substantively, however, Adorno's social theory had much in common with orthodox sociology and with the classical German sociology of Simmel and Weber. He sought to integrate these ideas with contemporary American work, while also showing that their conclusions had to be grounded in the framework that only critical theory could provide. Orthodox sociology, like orthodox economics, remained too closely bound to superficial appearances, failing to see them as the expressions of deep-seated contradictions that had their basis, ultimately, in the relations and forces of production. 'Society', like the parallel concept of the 'economy', reified realities that have their foundations in the sphere of production. Critical theory, then, was not a simple alternative to conventional sociology but an extension and deepening of it that approached more closely the character of the social whole.

Technology, Organization, and Domination

The substantive work carried out by the key members of the Frankfurt Institute during the period of exile was organized around a fundamental insight: that the economic analyses undertaken by Marx and Marxists had to be complemented by a cultural analysis that gave appropriate autonomy to the cultural sphere. The most general formulation of this argument was Adorno and Horkheimer's jointly produced *Dialectic of Enlightenment* (Adorno and Horkheimer, 1944). They documented a process of rationalization, which they saw in Weberian terms as an expansion of the deliberate and systematic technical orientation towards and control over the natural world, other people, and our own selves. This rationalization was spreading through all areas of social life. They found the origins of this in the philosophy of the Enlightenment.

The Enlightenment had begun a process of liberation from myth and fear through its ongoing 'disenchantment' and demythologization. It continually undermined the claims of religion, custom, and tradition in favour of promoting a rational, instrumental knowledge of the world through the systematic accumulation of rational, scientific knowledge. It was the product of a self-conscious group of intellectuals committed to rational social change, and the major early achievements of this 'Enlightenment project' were the rational organizational structures of capitalism and industrialism. Contemporary society, Adorno and Horkheimer argued, had taken this rationalization to a particularly high level, producing an increased centralization of economic and political power and a growth in state intervention in the economy.

This trend was apparent in all capitalist societies, but it had reached its most extreme form in German fascism during the 1930s and 1940s. Views differed within the Institute as to whether this marked a new and more stable form of society. According to Neumann (1942), National Socialism was a combination of monopoly capitalism and a command economy in which all subordinate classes were fragmented and all intermediate groups had been destroyed. The proletariat had been transformed into a dependent and subordinate 'mass' that was tied directly into the state through its autocratic bureaucratic structures. As it remained a form of capitalism, however, Neumann argued that fascism would eventually be undermined by its internal contradictions. For Pollock (1941), on the other hand, state intervention marked the emergence of a new phase of 'state capitalism'. The authoritarian or totalitarian form of state capitalism found in fascism was marked by the dominance of a new ruling group of industrial and state managers. State capitalism had resolved the economic contradictions of private capitalism and had achieved a non-socialist form of political stability.

There was, however, a common recognition that the expansion of human powers of technical control had, at the same time, undermined human autonomy by subjecting people to ever-stronger relations of power. This was most apparent in the fetishism of commodities, through which human social relations of exchange had been transformed into abstract monetary relations among things. Such domination was spreading through all areas of life. All aspects of modern life tend to become commodified or administered, and human beings become subject to ever more intensive forms of domination. Whole areas of social life, outside the economy and the political system, were subject to this same process of rationalization. The principles and mechanisms of 'society' were assimilated to those of the political economy, and the political and economic systems themselves acquire greater power over more purely 'social' and cultural processes. The power relations of the economy and the state had an objectivity and impersonality that made them appear to be necessary and inescapable. Acceptance of these reified constraints made the idea of human freedom appear to be a merely utopian fantasy.

This was the 'dialectic' of the Enlightenment. In promising human liberation through rational knowledge, it had, in fact, produced systems and principles that denied and undermined real freedom. The Enlightenment project was contradictory in its consequences, producing a social whole that combined rational technique with the distortion of human creativity and autonomy: 'With the extension of the bourgeois commodity economy, the dark horizon of myth is illumined by the sun of calculating reason, beneath whose cold rays the seed of the new barbarism grows to fruition' (Adorno and Horkheimer, 1944: 32).

The Frankfurt Marxist humanists, then, saw capitalism as having developed into a system that was capable of sustaining growth and full employment and that was less likely to be undermined by its internal economic contradictions. Even Marcuse was pessimistic about the likelihood of spontaneous change in the short or medium term. Through the capitalist consolidation of instrumental rationality, he argued, technocratic forms of consciousness were coming to prevail. People believed that their actions were governed by technical necessity – by 'laws' – but this was simply a reification: power relations appeared as relations between things that are subject to objective and impersonal laws. Under these circumstances, there is little likelihood that people will develop any critical consciousness of their own subjection (Marcuse, 1964a).

The Culture Industry

Horkheimer and, especially, Adorno saw music as central to contemporary and historical cultures, and they felt that an analysis of the state of musical production and consumption would say a great deal about wider social conditions. Lukács, it will be recalled, saw literature in much the same way, and there are many parallels in their concerns. Adorno's earliest works in this area drew on his own experiences in studying and composing music. He saw music, like all forms of art, as social production that originates in particular social classes. In capitalist societies, the prevailing musical forms were bourgeois products, and Adorno, using ideas from Schönberg, extended this simple Marxian insight.

It was Schönberg's view that music is a rational, intellectual articulation of objective cultural truths; it is not a mere expression of subjective emotions. Musical intellect is exercised through its specific forms of expression, and musical creativity involves the use of the 'grammatical' forms of a particular musical language in innovative ways. The musical forms of a society change over time, and Schönberg, in his own compositions, sought to go beyond the long-established classical forms and to develop and work within new, atonal forms. Adorno suggested that the classical forms – principally tonal composition and the sonata form – had arisen with the bourgeoisie and that their decline was linked to the transformation of this class.

This analysis of music carried forward the argument of the early Lukács that the specifically bourgeois literary forms were those of narrative realism and characterization found in the novel and modern drama. Adorno added that there were parallel bourgeois forms in pictorial art – most notably linear perspective and representationalism. In all areas of culture, Adorno argued, the established bourgeois forms were disintegrating, and avant garde artists were exploring the possibilities this opened-up for artistic expression. In music, the progressive avant garde comprised Schönberg, Berg, Webern, and Mahler; in literature it included Kafka and the 'stream of consciousness' literature of Joyce, Proust, and Woolf; while in art it included Picasso, Braque, and Kandinsky. Their forms of artistic expression, Adorno claimed, embodied a critical intent and so could grasp the truth of the subject's condition under contemporary conditions.

These progressive features in art music contrasted sharply with the cultural trends that Horkheimer and Adorno identified in popular music, where the rationalization of social life had especially marked consequences. These consequences they diagnosed in their exploration of what they called the 'culture industry'.[12] The cultural sphere is one in which escape from domination should be possible, but it is increasingly subject to the same process of rationalization as all other spheres of social life. Instead of offering an escape from rational domination, cultural activity was itself becoming an industrialized process of production that drew people ever more deeply into the rationalized system and gave them only a false idea of escape and freedom. Artistic culture was more and more difficult to sustain as an autonomous activity, as cultural productions were becoming available to people only in commodity form.

In the stage of liberal capitalism, the producers and consumers of popular culture had retained a degree of autonomy over their own cultural activities. In the monopoly stage of capitalism, however, this is no longer the case. Popular culture, as it developed within monopoly capitalism, is the product of a culture industry that produces cultural items as commodities. Both leisure and consumption are organized along capitalist lines: they are locked together with work and production into a single system dominated by the instrumental rationality of capitalist production. Cultural development is not shaped by performers and their audiences, but by the finance capitalists and managers who run the various branches of the culture industry. They are integral elements within the larger capitalist system. The directors of the cultural monopolies are fused with company directors and owners in steel, petroleum, electricity, chemicals, and banking as part of a single system of finance capital. Within this complex, the cultural controllers are a relatively weak and subordinate part, and the system as a whole is dominated by banking and big business considerations (Adorno and Horkheimer, 1944: 122).

Thus, cultural items in modern capitalism are not supplied to meet the spontaneous wishes of a public but on the basis of what the culture industry itself wants to supply to the market. The passive masses are not active producers of the culture that they consume.[13] The differentiation of cultural commodities is organized around a classification and labelling of consumers, with market research and advertising being geared to ensuring that the consumers do actually buy them. Rationalized market processes have ensured that the rise of the culture industry results in a cultural uniformity. Cultural commodities are shaped by a standardizing, commercial logic, rather than by purely aesthetic considerations. Films, radio, magazines, and other cultural forms are homogeneous, standardized, and uniform in all important respects. The products of the culture industry are produced to standard formulas that reflect the need to package them and to sell them in calculable ways. Mass-produced soap operas, songs, films, and so on, as items of 'entertainment', are embedded in a system of advertising that integrates mass cultural meanings with other commodities such as cars, cigarettes, and food. One implication of this, Horkheimer and Adorno argue, is that the boundaries between cultural representations and everyday life break down: 'Real life is becoming indistinguishable from the movies' (Adorno and Horkheimer, 1944: 126). The aim of film producers, for example, is to ensure that people see the world outside the cinema as continuous with the film. It is what Baudrillard (1981) would see as 'hyperreal'.

Cultural products are geared to amusement and entertainment, but their claims to make people happy rest on the fulfilment of false pleasures rather than real ones. This analysis tends to conflate scientific description and aesthetic judgement, and Adorno's distaste for all popular culture is apparent in the tone and language of his writing. For Adorno, a standardized and mass-produced culture is, inevitably, an inauthentic and second-rate one that bears no comparison with 'true' artistic achievement. The culture of the masses accords only with their alienated needs (Adorno, n.d.; see also Adorno, 1984).

One of Adorno's earliest applications of his ideas was a study of jazz (Adorno, 1937) in which he attempted to decompose and reconstruct this particular musical form. In improvising, he argued, a jazz soloist appears to be departing from the established pattern but is, in fact, conforming to a larger structure. The soloist follows rules that are specific to the musical form of jazz. Adorno, however, was no aficionado of jazz, as is apparent in his view that syncopation – anticipating the beat – is akin to premature ejaculation and so signifies not musical power but musical impotence. Such negative aesthetic judgements on popular music remained an important part of Adorno's cultural analysis throughout his life.

Taking up some of the ideas from his discussion of jazz, Adorno sought to draw a sharp distinction between the factors influencing the development of serious, art music and the popular music produced by the culture industry. Popular music, he argues, is characterized by standardization and pseudo-individualization. The basic structural elements of popular songs are standardized and interchangeable, but they are differentiated in minor and peripheral ways in order to enhance their market appeal. This reflects trends in the mass production of all commodities. Henry Ford had famously said of the first Ford cars that purchasers could have any colour they liked, so long as it was black. By contrast, present-day Ford cars are built from standard components and to standard specifications but are differentiated by body colour, internal fabrics, fascia design, wheel trims, and so on. Such variation gives the consumer the illusion of real choice. Similarly, argues Adorno, the standardized

12-bar and 16-bar structures and song forms of popular music are obscured by minor variations in vocal styling, instrumentation, recording effects, and so on.

Even art music is not immune to these cultural trends. Adorno would, no doubt, see the recent trend of packaging certain forms of classical music for radio performance and CD compilation ('Beethoven's Greatest Hits') as a further sign of commodification, but he recognized a deeper impact of rationalization on serious music. He had initially seen Schönberg's music as expressing the modern condition and posing a challenge to it, as standing in the same relation to the bourgeois musical forms of classicism as his own philosophy stood in relation to bourgeois philosophy. In his later work, however, he saw Schönberg's chromaticism as overly rationalized and as destroying the possibility of individual expressivity (Adorno, 1962a).

The cultivation of individual expression through serious music – something that Adorno tried to pursue in his own compositions – should be a form of critique, a search for truth that poses a political challenge to rationalization and to the culture industry that it has spawned. What is apparent here, in Adorno's emphasis on 'truth', is his cognitive or intellectualist view of artistic expression. He saw music, like philosophy, as an attempt at a cognitive or intellectual understanding of the world, albeit in non-verbal form. There is no recognition of any cathartic or emotional role for music that is not tied to ideological distortion and its orientation to rationalized domination. Emotionality in music is a manifestation of alienation and a denial of its progressive, critical role in social life.

In the sphere of popular culture and all that comes within the orbit of the culture industry, genuine artistic expression is extinguished and individuals are subjected ever more deeply to oppression and alienation. Their oppression takes a cultural form, as ideological domination. This undermines their ability to act as autonomous subjects by manipulating their desires and channelling them around the false needs whose pursuit sustains the capitalist system. Culture, then, becomes central to the reproduction of capitalism through encouraging the consumption of commodities and through forming a standardized mass consciousness.

Adorno's aesthetic rejection of popular cultural products and his view of the masses as oriented by false needs did not lead him to see consumers as mere dupes of the culture industry. They are its victims, but they are victimized by a lack of choice rather than by a false consciousness: 'The triumph of advertising in the culture industry is that consumers feel compelled to buy and use its products even though they see through them' (Adorno and Horkheimer, 1944: 167)

Just as popular music adopts standardized forms that inhibit thought and restrict people to false pleasures, so other aspects of popular culture move in the same direction. Film stunts the imagination because movies are so designed that the need to follow the plot rules out any sustained thought. Writing in the 1940s, when television was in its early stages, Horkheimer and Adorno saw it as bound to intensify this process. These cultural trends reinforce social authority by eliminating alternative viewpoints. Immediate wishes linked to consumption and emotional desires are easily fulfilled and channelled into safe forms of expression, and any drive to challenge or to alter things is defused. Potential opposition is defused and depoliticized.

Herbert Marcuse explored the specifically political dimensions of these cultural changes. This was most powerfully expressed in his *One Dimensional Man* (Marcuse, 1964b), where he traced the new forms of alienation and need repression generated in the contemporary 'totalitarian' form of organized capitalism prevailing in both the United States and the Soviet Union (Marcuse, 1958). The capitalist system, he argued, had developed to the point at which basic human needs could be satisfied and new 'false needs' created. False needs are those that are imposed on individuals as a means for their repression – and Marcuse instances the need to consume commodities in the ways that they are presented in advertisements. In such a situation, people become oriented to the needs generated by the forms of cultural production of the mass media, and so their needs come to be determined by external powers over which they have no control. Although individuals may identify with these needs – regarding them as their own true needs – they are, in fact, products of ideological domination: they are repressive needs, from which individuals must be liberated. The cultural sphere is marked by 'desublimation', by a destruction of the truths previously found in the sublimations of a truly artistic culture. Commodification of cultural products ensures that people lose the ability to think critically about their own society and are socialized into the 'Happy Consciousness' (Marcuse, 1964b: 79) of the new conformism: the existing world is seen as a rational world that delivers the desired goods and is, therefore, to be welcomed.

This conformist orientation and the lack of any critical potential are seen by Marcuse as indicative of the 'one-dimensional thought' that characterizes contemporary capitalism. Rationalization consists not simply of the application of rational knowledge, but also of the extension of a systematically rational pattern of mind and behaviour. Positive, technical knowledge is ideological, a source of domination. In these circumstances, no effective challenge to economic, political, and cultural domination can be mounted from within contemporary capitalism itself. The primary challenge must come from those outside the system, from the subordinate masses of the Third World and the marginalized, poor, and excluded sections of the western proletariat who have not been incorporated into the happy consciousness of their affluent and conformist compatriots.

Authoritarianism, Socialization, and Culture

The rationalization of economics, politics, and culture was seen as producing social stability by defusing the critical consciousness of those who live in contemporary capitalist societies. An important theme in the writings of the Frankfurt School, therefore, was the exploration of the psychological processes that complemented the social processes of rationalization and homogenization. It is through their socialization into its culture that people come to identify with the system that oppresses them, and Institute members turned to psychoanalytical ideas for insights into this.

Much work on developing this integration of Freud with Marx was done by Erich Fromm and Herbert Marcuse. Fromm produced many ideas that contributed to the

Institute's analysis of authoritarianism, but his main investigations into the links between the early Marx and Freudian psychoanalysis (Fromm, 1942; see also Fromm, 1961) date from after he left the Institute in 1939. Marcuse's early explorations into pleasure and motivation (Marcuse, 1938) were also important, but his main engagement with Freud dates from the 1950s. It was Adorno, however, who was principally responsible for the Freudian dimension to the Institute's work in the 1940s.

The Institute sponsored a number of investigations into the psychological sources of authoritarianism and support for fascism during the early years of its exile, with fieldwork carried out in France and Switzerland. Fromm's research on German working-class consciousness (Fromm, 1939)[14] was one of a series of studies that he supervised at the Institute during the 1930s. The focus of this work (Horkheimer and others, 1936) was the link between authority relations within families and structures of domination in the wider society. The initial publication was a rather poorly integrated combination of theory and empirical data, but it set the agenda for the continuing work. Its basic assumption was that the bourgeois family form – a family form found in the proletariat and the petty bourgeoisie as well as in the bourgeoisie itself – generates a submissiveness that is central to the stability of organized capitalism in its totalitarian form. This authoritarian character type embodies both the capitalist spirit of acquisitiveness and the anal personality attributes studied by Freud. It is worth noting the emphasis, once again, on the 'forms' of social life that Lukács and the Frankfurt School have consistently regarded as the major insight that their work derived from the sociology of Simmel and Weber. It is through the artistic forms that artistic creativity is able to express itself, or can be denied, and the family form plays a similar part in relation to the expression of domestic and political individuality.

During the Second World War, some broader research into anti-Semitism was undertaken, some of this jointly with Robert MacIver at Columbia University. A number of specialist publications were produced, including an account of the famous 'f-scale' of authoritarian (or fascistic) personality attributes, and the core ideas were eventually presented in *The Authoritarian Personality* (Adorno et al., 1950). This work set out the underlying character traits expressed in fascist, anti-Semitic, and other authoritarian forms. Underpinning these arguments were specific psychological arguments that connected the emphasis on authoritarianism, the analysis of the culture industry, and the biological basis of human action.

Marcuse's argument shared many of the concerns of the 'culture and personality' approach, but he re-emphasized the Freudian recognition of the importance of biology and, in particular, of instinctual drives. In his *Eros and Civilization* (1956), Marcuse built on this psychoanalytical perspective to explore the deeper bases of social stability. Freud had argued that repression is a necessary consequence of technical civilization, but Marcuse took issue with this. He argued that the link between civilization and repression is such that repression always takes historically specific forms. He drew the conclusion that there could be non-repressive forms of civilization: technology has the potential to liberate people from the class-specific forms of repression that mark contemporary capitalist societies.

Freud had seen the instincts as destructive unless they are channelled and controlled by culture. Left to their own devices, the instincts operate according to the 'pleasure principle' as largely unconscious driving forces through which people orient themselves towards their world. The rational deliberations of the ego are geared towards achieving instinctually driven goals and, therefore, to forming a representation of the world through which the instinctual demands of the id can be controlled and co-ordinated. Cultural control over the instincts works through a 'reality principle', and this underpins the conformity of individuals to the demands of civilization. People learn that their instincts cannot be immediately and fully satisfied, and so they also learn to renounce and restrain them so that they can be satisfied – at least in part – over the longer term. The effects of parental socialization within the family reinforce conscious control by the ego. It is through this socialization that a superego is formed as external demands are 'introjected' as a moral conscience. The superego is, then, the sediment of a person's past experiences. The moral controls imposed by the superego may run counter to the potentialities for instinctual gratification that are possible under present conditions.

Civilization, therefore, tends to involve the cultural domination of the ego and the superego over biological needs and instincts. Where Marcuse differs from Freud is that he pointed to the possibilities that conscious actions have for eliminating extraneous and unnecessary barriers to gratification. The impact of culture on human needs is not fixed and completely determined, and, under appropriate conditions, it can be a means of liberation and instinctual expression. Through conscious action and the application of reason, Marcuse argued, it is possible to create social conditions that maximize opportunities for instinctual gratification. Culture and technical civilization, then, have the potential to channel instincts in both negative and positive ways. They can deny and suppress them totally, replacing them with false needs and desires that can be satisfied only from within the existing form of society; or they can create the conditions under which, as far as possible, individuals can exercise a true freedom in the expression and satisfaction of their instincts.

Marcuse's diagnosis of contemporary conditions in the advanced capitalist societies is that the rationalization of culture has, through processes of socialization and ideological incorporation, established a conformist character type that is unable to challenge structures of domination and is, indeed, unaware of the extent of its own domination. The institutionalization of the 'performance principle', as the specific form taken by the reality principle, leads people to adopt a calculative and acquisitive orientation towards their work, emphasizing its alienated form (Marcuse, 1956: 45). Indeed, they come to accept this technological domination as normal and natural. At the same time, however, the performance principle enhances productivity and rational control, thus creating the preconditions for an alternative, and non-repressive, reality principle. Recognition of this liberating potential is what gives Marcuse's theory its critical dimension. It has the power to explain the social forms that are associated with the cultivation of false needs and the denial of instincts, and it is thereby able to show the conditions under which people can liberate themselves from those social forms by building alternatives that allow a more authentic expression and satisfaction of their needs.

Personal differences between Marcuse and his former colleagues (rooted in minor jealousies about his independence of thought) meant that Marcuse's work was not published under the auspices of the Institute. Nevertheless, *Eros and Civilization* and his later books, were almost the only significant works of the 1950s and 1960s that embodied the substantive ideals of critical theory and that articulated any deepening of the Marxist humanist account of culture.

The Legacy of Marxist Humanism

While the critical theorists were first developing their ideas, other Marxists were also setting out related ideas, though none of these achieved the impact enjoyed by those of the Frankfurt theorists. Henri Lefebvre's work *Dialectical Materialism* (Lefebvre, 1934–35) was poised somewhere between Lukács and Horkheimer. It was based largely on Marx's early manuscripts, which Lefebvre had translated for publication in France. Lefebvre's work was rejected by the Communist Party orthodoxy, and he remained a marginal figure. It was not until much later that his application of these ideas to every-day life and urban structures began to have a wider influence (Lefebvre, 1968; 1973). Franz Jakubowski, from Danzig, studied under a former member of the Frankfurt Institute and drew on Marx's early manuscripts when writing his thesis on the idea of base and superstructure (Jakubowski, 1936). Although this thesis was published in 1936, the Nazis imprisoned Jakubowski and his book had no real impact at the time.[15]

In Italy, Gramsci was working on a related set of ideas. A Communist activist in the 1920s, Gramsci had been sentenced to prison for 20 years in 1926. Though this cut him off from any active political participation, it did give him an unsought opportunity to develop his own theoretical ideas. Drawing, in particular, on Labriola's 'philosophy of praxis', Gramsci used the Hegelian ideas of Croce to develop an account of the cultural and political hegemony that he saw as an integral aspect of ruling class power and of the part played by intellectuals in the formation of a proletarian counter-hegemony. The surviving manuscripts from this period, now known as the 'Prison Notebooks' (Gramsci, 1929–35), were incomplete, unedited, and unpublished when Gramsci died in his prison clinic. As a result, his ideas began to have a significant influence only after others had established the framework of Marxist humanism.

The Marxist humanism that developed in the works of Lukács and the critical theorists themselves provided a remarkably powerful approach to cultural analysis. Many of their central tenets, therefore, have been incorporated into the mainstream of cultural sociology and have often found a place in work that is neither Marxist humanist nor even Marxist. It is a sign of their success that their key concepts, along with the more recently discovered ideas of Gramsci, have figured in the works of structural Marxists, postmodernists, symbolic interactionists, and many others. They have, for example, been central to influential arguments in cultural studies concerning cultural hegemony in contemporary society (e.g., Hall et al., 1978; Clark et al., 1979) The corollary of this intellectual success, however, is the virtual exhaustion of Marxist humanism itself as a distinctive paradigm for cultural analysis. The deaths of Horkheimer, Adorno, and Marcuse brought an obvious end to their work, though the former two had long since ceased to make or attempt any novel contributions to a critical theory of culture.

Despite this diffusion of ideas and the dissipation of the paradigm, some have continued to try to develop a distinctively Marxist humanist approach. Even among these writers, however, the most powerful and influential ideas have come from those who have moved beyond Marxist humanism and have integrated the concerns of Lukács and the Frankfurt School with wider theoretical arguments.

The most direct inheritor of the Frankfurt tradition of critical theory is Jürgen Habermas, one-time teaching assistant to Adorno in the 1950s. His early work (Habermas, 1962; 1965; see also Schmidt, 1962) is in the direct line of Frankfurt theory, but he broke away from this during the late 1960s (Habermas, 1968; 1971). His work now draws heavily on functionalism, systems theory, linguistic philosophy, and symbolic interactionism (Habermas, 1981a; 1981b) and, for all its analytical power, can no longer be regarded as distinctively Marxist humanist. Indeed, many have argued that it should not even be regarded as distinctively Marxist. This theoretical work has, however, helped to generate the very important works of writers such as Wellmer (1971), Offe (1970), and Eder (1993).

The most notable follower of Lukács was Lucien Goldmann, who studied under the Austro-Marxist Max Adler and discovered the work of Lukács in the 1930s. Many of his central concepts were taken from *History and Class Consciousness* and Lukács's later work on the novel (Lukacs, 1937), but Goldmann also took ideas from Piaget's structuralism. He set out some early methodological reflections on class consciousness and the role of the intellectual (Goldmann, 1952) and he traced the development and transformation of bourgeois class consciousness in French literature during the seventeenth century (Goldmann, 1956; 1964).[16]

Lukács also influenced a significant group of Hungarian writers. These included Istvan Meszaros (1970; 1989; see also Meszaros 1971b and 1971a), Ferenc Feher (1983), and Agnes Heller (1974; 1983). Of these, the most important is Heller, who has developed her work in a very similar direction to the way in which Habermas developed the critical theory of Horkheimer and Adorno. She has, in particular, drawn on a neo-Parsonian systems theory that borrows extensively from Niklas Luhmann, and has gone well beyond Marxist humanism to look at what she calls the dynamic of modernity (Heller 1982; 1984; 1990).

In Poland, Marxist humanist philosophical ideas were developed by Leszek Kolakowski (1968; and see Kolakowski 1978) and Adam Schaff (1963). Kolakowski particularly stressed the importance of individual and collective action in history and the moral responsibility that individuals have for their actions. Influenced by theses ideas, Zygmunt Bauman (1991b; 1991a; 2001) developed a powerful and independent form of social analysis that now has similarities with the work of Habermas and Heller and, like them, is not distinctively Marxist in character.[17]

Karl Kosik in Czechoslovakia set out similar views to Kolakowski and Schaff (Kosik, 1976), but the most vibrant tradition of Marxist humanist philosophy was that of the 'Praxis' group in Yugoslavia.[18] From 1964 to their suppression in 1975, and heavily influenced by the arguments of Erich Fromm (1965), they developed ideas from the young Marx, especially in relation to alienation and freedom (Marković and Petrovic, 1979). Most important among these was Mikhael Marković (1974; Marković and Cohen, 1975). Marković wrote specifically on culture, though his main contribution was to restate the arguments of Galbraith (1967) rather than make any specifically novel Marxist contribution. Golubović (1972), however, did set out a general view of culture that explored the relationship between 'elite' and 'mass' culture and applied this to the situation of intellectuals in 'actually existing socialism'.

Marxist humanism, then, is no longer sustained as a strong research tradition, and it is doubtful whether it can, any longer, form the basis of a viable research programme. It proved highly successful at a time when the main currents of Marxism gave little attention to cultural matters and sociology was, for the most part, failing to produce comprehensive explanations of the social organization of culture. Having successfully put cultural analysis on the agenda, its ideas were rapidly adopted by others and put to use in alternative research programmes. It is now difficult to see how the sociology of culture could be anything other than a central part of sociological analysis, but it is equally difficult to see how a Marxist humanism could, any longer, provide the sole intellectual basis for this.

Notes

1 Bloch's first book (Bloch, 1918) was on music and art, drawing on Simmel's ideas but seeing these artistic forms from the standpoint of the utopian (the 'not yet'). In the 1920s, he became a Marxist, supporting the Soviet Union and Stalinism.

2 *Soul and Forms* consists of essays written in Budapest between 1907 and 1910. They were first published in book form in 1910 and were expanded in 1911.

3 Central to Lukács' ideas on reification were the arguments of Simmel in his analysis of money (Simmel 1900).

4 Lukács prepared a response to some of his orthodox critics (Lukács 1925) but he left it unpublished and seems never to have referred to it again. Not until the 1990s, long after his death, was the manuscript found in the CPSU archive in Moscow, having narrowly escaped destruction in 1941. It was published for the first time in 1996 and was translated into English in 2000.

5 Korsch lost his professorship with the rise of the Nazis, moving to Denmark and then to England and the United States. He remained in the US until his death in 1961.

6 Following the Russian revolution, the Marx archives were centralized in Moscow, where David Ryazanov at the Marx-Engels Institute began a systematic publication of the collected works (the so-called *M.E.G.A.*). For a time, this became the focus of a reconsideration of Marx's ideas. The Institute of Social Research worked closely with Ryazanov during the 1920s, and Lukács worked on the *Economic and Philosophical Manuscripts* (Marx, 1844) in Moscow to ready them for their publication, for the first time, in 1932. Karl Löwith's review of the manuscripts immediately argued that they vindicated Lukács's book and his use of Hegelian ideas. Henri Lefebvre translated these manuscripts into French in 1933. Developments in Russia, however, brought this to a virtual end: Ryazanov was purged by

Stalin in 1931, and even the relatively orthodox Bukharin was tried and executed in 1938. The eventual publication of the *Grundrisse* (Marx, 1858) in 1939–41 helped to show the crucial link between Marx's early work and his mature economic theory.

7   It is likely that the manuscript of this book was completed during the 1960s. The English translation is a partial translation of the Hungarian text, which includes further sections on reproduction, ideology, and alienation. An autobiography was discovered and published after his death (Lukács, 1971b).

8   Useful discussions of the history of the Institute and the development of critical theory can be found in Jay (1973) and Held (1980).

9   Similar ideas to Grossman's were later set out in the United States by Paul Sweezy (1942).

10   A useful account of the development of Adorno's work can be found in Buck-Morss (1977).

11   Adorno began to use the term 'negative dialectics' in the 1950s to describe this grasping of contradictions. The position was fully articulated in his book of that title (Adorno, 1966).

12   Adorno first set out these ideas in a paper of 1938 (Adorno, 1938), subsequently developing it in the later part of *Dialectic of Enlightenment.*

13   In a later paper, Adorno notes that he introduced the term 'culture industry' in preference to 'mass culture' precisely in order to emphasize that popular culture did not 'arise spontaneously from the masses themselves' (Adorno, 1964: 85).

14   When Fromm left the Institute, his plans for the publication of his book on the German working class were abandoned. The book was published posthumously in 1980, and translated into English in 1984.

15   After his family secured his release from prison, he moved to the United States and lived under the name Frank Fisher until he died in 1971.

16   A general statement of his ideas can be found in the posthumous volume on *Cultural Creation* (Goldmann, 1970).

17   Bauman's earlier ideas on culture can be found in his *Culture as Praxis* (Bauman, 1973).

18   I do not here consider the Marxist humanism of Dunayevskaya (1973), a Marxist who moved to the United States in 1920 and worked as secretary to Trotsky. Although inspired by Marx's early manuscripts and Lenin's philosophical notebooks, she is a humanist writer in a different tradition from those considered in this chapter.

References

Adorno, T. (1937) 'On jazz', in T. Adorno, *Essays on Music*. R. Leppert (ed.). Berkeley, CA: University of California Press.

Adorno, T. ([1938] 1991) 'On the fetish character of music and the regression of listening', in T. Adorno, *The Culture Industry*, J. Bernstein (ed.). London: Routledge.

Adorno, T. ([1949] 1973) *Philosophy of Modern Music*. London: Sheed and Ward.

Adorno, T. ([nd., 1950s] 1991) 'The schema of mass culture', in T. Adorno, *The Culture Industry*, J. Bernstein (ed.). London: Routledge.

Adorno, T. ([1951] 1974) *Minima Moralia*. London: New Left Books.

Adorno, T. ([1955] 1967) *Prisms*. New York: Spearman.

Adorno, T. ([1957] 1976) 'Sociology and empirical research', in T. Adorno et al. (eds) *The Positivist Dispute in German Sociology*. London: Heinemann.

Adorno, T. ([1962a] 1976) *An Introduction to the Sociology of Music*. New York: Seabury Press.

Adorno, T. ([1962b] 1976) 'On the logic of the social sciences', in T. Adorno et al. (eds) *The Positivist Dispute in German Sociology*. London: Heinemann.

Adorno, T. ([1964] 1991) 'Culture industry reconsidered', in T. Adorno, *The Culture Industry*. J. Bernstein (ed.). London: Routledge.

Adorno, T. ([1966] 1973) *Negative Dialectics*. London: Routledge and Kegan Paul.

Adorno, T. ([1968] 2000) *Introduction to Sociology*. Cambridge: Polity Press.

Adorno, T. (1984) *Aesthetic Theory*. London: Routledge and Kegan Paul.

Adorno, T., Frenkel-Brunswick, E. Levinson, D.J. and Sanford, R.N. (1950) *The Authoritarian Personality*. New York: Harper.

Anderson, P. (1976) *Considerations on Western Marxism*. London: New Left Books.

Arato, A. and Breines, P. (1979) *The Young Lukács and the Origins of Western Marxism*. London: Pluto Press.

Baudrillard, J. ([1972] 1981) *For a Critique of the Political Economy of the Sign*. St. Louis, MO: Telos Press.

Baudrillard, J. ([1981] 1983) *Simulations*. New York: Semiotext(e).

Bauman, Z. ([1973] 1999) *Culture as Praxis*. London: Sage.

Bauman, Z. (1976) *Towards a Critical Sociology*. London: Routledge and Kegan Paul.

Bauman, Z. (1991a) *Intimations of Postmodernity*. London: Routledge.

Bauman, Z. (1991b) *Modernity and Ambivalence*. Cambridge: Polity Press.

Bauman, Z. (2001) *Liquid Modernity*. Cambridge: Polity Press.

Bloch, E. ([1918] 2000) *The Spirit of Utopia*. Cambridge: Cambridge University Press.

Buck-Morss, S. 1977. *The Origin of Negative Dialectic*. Hassocks: Harvester.

Carver, T. (1981) *Engels*. Oxford: Oxford University Press.

Clark, J., Critcher, C. and Johnson, R. (eds) (1979) *Working Class Culture: Studies in History and Theory*. London: Hutchinson.

Dunayevskaya, R. (1973) *Philosophy and Revolution*. New York: Delacorte.

Eder, K. (1993) *The New Politics of Class: Social Movements and Cultural Dynamics in Advanced Societies*. London: Sage.

Feher, F. Heller, A. and Markus, S. (1983) *Dictatorship Over Needs*. New York: St Martin's Press.

Freud, S. ([1915–17] 1974) *Introductory Lectures on Psychoanalysis*. Harmondsworth: Penguin.

Fromm, E. ([1939] 1984) *The Working Class in Weimar Germany*. Leamington Spa: Berg.

Fromm, E. (1942) *Fear of Freedom*. London: Routledge and Kegan Paul.

Fromm, E. ([1961] 1990) *Marx's Conception of Man*. New York: Continuum.

Fromm, E. (ed.) (1965) *Socialist Humanism*. Garden City, NY: Anchor Books.

Galbraith, J. K. (1967) *The New Industrial State*. London: Hamish Hamilton.

Goldmann, L. ([1952] 1969) *The Human Sciences and Philosophy*. London: Jonathan Cape.

Goldmann, L. ([1956] 1964) *The Hidden God*. London: Routledge and Kegan Paul.

Goldmann, L. ([1964] 1975) *Towards a Sociology of the Novel*. London: Tavistock.

Goldmann, L. ([1970] 1977) *Cultural Creation*. Oxford: Basil Blackwell.

Golubović , Z. ([1972] 1979) 'Culture as a bridge between utopia and reality', in M. Marković and G. Petrović, (eds) *Praxis*. Dordrecht: D. Reidel.

Gramsci, A. ([1929–35] 1971) *Selections From The Prison Notebooks* London: Lawrence and Wishart.

Habermas, J. ([1962] 1989) *Structural Change in the Public Sphere*. Cambridge, MA: MIT Press.

Habermas, J. ([1965] 1971) 'Technology and science as "ideology"', in J. Habermas (ed.) *Towards a Rational Society*. London: Heinemann.

Habermas, J. ([1968] 1972) *Knowledge and Human Interests*. London: Heinemann.

Habermas, J. ([1971] 1974) *Theory and Practice*. London: Heinemann.

Habermas, J. ([1981a] 1984) *The Theory of Communicative Action*, Vol. 1: *Reason and the Rationalisation of Society*. London: Heinemann.

Habermas, J. ([1981b] 1987) *The Theory of Communicative Action*, Vol. 2: *The Critique of Functionalist Reason*. London: Heinemann.

Hall, S. (1977) 'The "political" and the "economic" in Marx's theory of classes', in A. Hunt (ed.) *Class and Class Structure*. London: Lawrence and Wishart.

Hall, S. Critcher, C. Jefferson, T. Clarke, J. and Roberts, B. (1978) *Policing the Crisis: Mugging, the State and Law and Order*. London: Macmillan.

Held, D. (1980) *An Introduction to Critical Theory*. London: Hutchinson.

Heller, A. ([1974] 1976) *The Theory of Need in Marx*. London: Allison and Busby.

Heller, A. (1982) *A Theory of History*. London: Routledge and Kegan Paul.

Heller, A. (ed.) (1983) *Lukács Revalued*. Oxford: Basil Blackwell.

Heller, A. (1984) *Everyday Life*. London: Routledge and Kegan Paul.

Heller, A. (1990) *Can Modernity Survive?* Cambridge: Polity Press.

Hilferding, R. ([1910] 1981) *Finance Capital*. London: Routledge and Kegan Paul, 1981.

Horkheimer, M. ([1935] 1995) 'On the problem of truth', in M. Horkheimer, *Between Philosophy and Social Science: Selected Early Writings*. Cambridge, MA: MIT Press.

Horkheimer, M. ([1937] 1972) 'Traditional and critical theory', in M. Horkheimer (ed.) *Critical Theory*. New York: Herder and Herder.

Horkheimer, M. (1947) *Eclipse of Reason*. New York: Oxford University Press.

Horkheimer, M. et al. (1936) *Studien über Autorität und Fámilie*. Paris: Félix Alcan.

Horkheimer, M. and Adorno, T.W. ([1944] 1979) Dialectic of Enlightenment. London: verso.

Horkheimer, M., Adorno, T. and The Institute of Social Research, ([1956] 1973) *Aspects of Sociology*. London: Heinemann.

Jakubowski, F. ([1936] 1976) *Base and Superstructure*. London: Allison and Busby.

Jameson, F. (1991) *Postmodernism, or the Cultural Logic of Late Capitalism*. London: Verso.

Jay, M. (1973) *The Dialectical Imagination*. London: Heinemann.

Kolakowski, L. (1968) *Towards a Marxist Humanism* (also entitled: *Marxism and Beyond*). New York: Grove Press.

Kolakowski, L. (1978) *Main Currents in Marxism,* Vol. 3. Oxford: Oxford University Press.

Korsch, K. ([1923] 1970) *Marxism and Philosophy*. London: New Left Books.

Korsch, K. ([1936] 1938) *Karl Marx*. London: Chapman and Hall.

Kosik, K. (1976) *Dialectics of the Concrete*. Dordrecht: D. Reidel.

Lefebvre, H. ([1934–35] 1968) *Dialectical Materialism*. London: Cape.

Lefebvre, H. ([1968] 1971) *Everyday Life in the Modern World*. Harmondsworth: Penguin, 1971.

Lefebvre, H. ([1973] 1976) *The Survival of Capitalism*. London: Allison and Busby.

Lichtheim, G. (1970) *Lukács*. Glasgow: Fontana.

Lockwood, D. (1964) 'Social integration and system integration', in Zollsdran S. and Hirseb, W. (eds) *Explorations in Social Change*. New York: Houghton Mifflin.

Lukács, G. ([1910] 1974) *Soul and Form*. London: Merlin Press.

Lukács, G. ([1914–15] 1978) *The Theory of the Novel*. London: Merlin Press.

Lukács, G. ([1923] 1971) *History and Class Consciousness*. London: Merlin Press.

Lukács, G. ([1924] 1997) *Lenin*. London: Verso.

Lukács, G. ([1925] 2000) *A Defence of History and Class Consciousness: Tailism and the Dialectic*. London: Verso.

Lukács, G. ([1937] 1976) *The Historical Novel*. Harmondsworth: Penguin.

Lukács, G. ([1946] 1972) *Studies in European Realism*. London: Merlin Press.

Lukács, G. ([1948] 1975) *The Young Hegel*. London: Merlin Press.

Lukács, G. ([1953] 1980) *The Destruction of Reason*. London: Merlin Press.

Lukács, G. ([1958] 1963) *The Meaning of Contemporary Realism*. London: Merlin Press.

Lukács, G. ([1971a] 1978) *The Ontology of Social Being,* Vol. 1: *Hegel,* and Vol. 2. *Marx*. London: Merlin Press.

Lukács, G. ([1971b] 1983) *Record of a Life*. London: Verso.

Mannheim, K. ([1925] 1952) 'The problem of a sociology of knowledge', in K. Mannheim, *Essays on the Sociology of Knowledge*. London: Routledge and Kegan Paul.

Mannheim, K. ([1929] 1936) 'Ideology and utopia', in K. Mannheim, *Ideology and Utopia*, London: Routledge and Kegan Paul.

Marcuse, H. ([1936] 1968) 'The concept of essence', in H. Marcuse, *Negations*. New York: Beacon Press.

Marcuse, H. ([1937] 1968) 'Philosophy and critical theory', in H. Marcuse, *Negations*. New York: Beacon Press.

Marcuse, H. ([1938] 1968) 'On hedonism', in H. Marcuse, *Negations*. New York: Beacon Press.

Marcuse, H. ([1941] 1954) *Reason and Revolution*. 2nd edn. New York: Humanities Press.

Marcuse, H. (1956) *Eros and Civilization*. London: Routledge and Kegan Paul.

Marcuse, H. (1958) *Soviet Marxism: A Critical Analysis*. London: Routledge and Kegan Paul.

Marcuse, H. ([1964a] 1968) 'Industrialization and capitalism in the work of Max Weber', in H. Marcuse, *Negations*. New York: Beacon Press.

Marcuse, H. (1964b) *One-Dimensional Man*. London: Routledge and Kegan Paul.

Marković, M. (1974) *From Affluence to Praxis*. Ann Arbor, MI: University of Chicago Press.

Marković, M. and Cohen, R. (eds) (1975). *Yugoslavia: The Rise and Fall of Marxist Humanism*. Nottingham: Spokesman Books.

Marković, M. and Petroviæ. G. (eds) (1979) *Praxis*. North Holland: D. Reidel.

Marx, K. ([1844] 1959) *Economic and Philosophical Manuscripts*. London: Lawrence and Wishart.

Marx, K. ([1858] 1973) *Grundrisse*. Harmondsworth: Penguin.

Meszaros, I. (1970) *Marx's Theory of Alienation*. London: Merlin Press.

Meszaros, I. (ed.) (1971a) *Aspects of History and Class Consciousness*. London: Routledge and Kegan Paul.

Meszaros, I. (1971b) *Lukács' Concept of Dialectic*. London: Merlin Press.

Meszaros, I. (1989) *The Power of Ideology*. London: Merlin Press.

Neumann, F. ([1942] 1963) *Behemoth: The Structure and Practice of National Socialism*. New York: Octagon Books.

Offe, C. ([1970] 1976) *Industry and Inequality*. London: Edward Arnold.

Pollock, F. ([1941] 1978) 'State capitalism: its possibilities and limitations', in A. Arato and E. Gebhardt (eds) *The Essential Frankfurt School Reader*. Oxford: Basil Blackwell.

Renner, K. ([1904] 1928) *The Institutions of Private Law and their Social Function*. rev. edn. London: Routledge and Kegan Paul.

Schaff, A. (1963) *A Philosophy of Man*. London: Lawrence and Wishart.

Schmidt, A. ([1962] 1971) *The Concept of Nature*. London: New Left Books.

Simmel, G. ([1900] 1978) *The Philosophy of Money*. London: Routledge and Kegan Paul.

Simmel, G. ([1908] 1968) *Soziologie: Untersuchungen über die Formen der Vergesellschaftung*. Berlin: Düncker und Humblot.

Scott, J. (1998) 'Relationism, ubism and reality: beyond relationism', in May, T. and Williams, M. (eds) *Knowing the Social World*. Buckingham: Open University Press.

Sweezy, P.M. (1942) *The Theory of Capitalist Development*.

Weber, A. ([1920–21] 1939) *Fundamentals of Culture-Sociology: Social Process, Civilization Process and Cultural Movement*. New York: Columbia University Press.

Wellmer, A. ([1971] 1974) *Critical Theory of Society*. New York: Seabury Press.

Georg Simmel

CHAPTER TWO

●●●●●●●

Chris Rojek

Recognition of Simmel's (1858–1918) importance in the study of culture has been belated and uneven. There are four reasons for this. First, the Birmingham School, which is widely regarded as the crucible of modern Cultural Studies, never engaged seriously with his work. To some extent, this neglect was a matter of the paucity of translations of his publications during the hay-day of the Birmingham School in the 1970s. But Simmel was also never an overly political author. Hence, on *a priori* grounds, he was an irretrievably marginal figure on the Birmingham horizon.[1] It would be wrong to infer that the Birmingham School set the agenda for the development of Cultural Studies. Other influences have been feminism, techno-cultural studies, poststructuralism and postmodernism, especially identity politics. Nonetheless, the Birmingham approach was a particularly important training ground for graduates who went on to gain influential academic positions in the UK and US: Phil Cohen, Hazel Corby, Paul Gilroy, Dick Hebdidge, Larry Grossberg, Angela MacRobbie, David Morley and Paul Willis. None of these engaged seriously with Simmel's work. The emissaries who have done most to demonstrate Simmels' relevance to the study of culture are David Frisby in the UK and Donald Levine in the USA, both of whom are career sociologist's, and hence would not be regarded by most people in Cultural Studies as mainstream figures. Similarly, while his influence in the philosophy of culture is significant, encompassing such major figures as Ernst Bloch, Ernst Cassirer, Arnold Gehlen, Martin Heidgegger Siegfried Kracauer, Georg Lukacs and Heinrich Rickert, this whole Germanic tradition has tended to be eclipsed by later developments in Sociology and Cultural Studies. The result is that Simmel's contribution has been further obscured.

Second, even within the discipline of sociology, Simmel is regarded as an ambivalent figure. He is seldom recognized as a 'founding father' of the discipline. His view of sociology was that it is a subject dealing with reciprocity, interaction and process. These are abstract phenomena, omnipresent in their effect but approached by Simmel in a peculiar, multi-layered way which is strangely elusive about orthodox sociological considerations such as causal chains and discrete consequences. While Simmel's work regularly examines them in their concrete instantiations, its drive is toward figuring the concrete as an expression of the abstract. This exacerbates the problem of elusiveness. Simmel always returns to the reciprocity of action and the manifold processes of circulation and exchange that encompass modern experience. This is at odds with more powerful and, in terms of contemporary academic power hierarchies, and it must be added, more successful, traditions that frame the discipline either as the study of social institutions, or commit to some version of action sociology.[2] In both traditions a preference for testing propositions in concrete social and historical settings is accentuated. In contrast, as Siegfried Kracauer (1995: 225) noted, Simmel's sociology shows little interest in situating social interaction in its appropriate historical context. It engages with other figures and positions in the social sciences in a fleeting manner, and virtually ignores the natural sciences. Nor is there any commitment to test propositions via fieldwork. 'He has no interest,' writes Kracauer (1995: 257) 'in grasping a phenomenon in terms of its obvious meaning, but instead wants to allow the entire plenitude of the world to pour into it.' This creates obvious difficulties both in terms of secondary interpretation and pedagogy.

Third, despite his insistence on the value of a *scientific* approach to society and culture, he never elucidated a compelling methodology setting out principles of research for others to follow. Frisby (1981) gets it right when he characterizes Simmel's approach as *sociological impressionism*. His methodology involves opening-up analytical consciousness to the complexity and subtlety of the manifold, ever-changing processes of circulation, exchange and interaction. So mush so that in a book like *The Philosophy of Money* (1900), Simmel's *magnum opus,* the reader is occasionally overwhelmed by the erudite, multi-layered analysis. Simmel seems to notice everything and make highly original connections between circulation, exchange and consciousness. It is probably correct to view him as a sociological virtuoso, much like Goffman later in the twentieth century, whose insights and style of analysis are frequently breath-taking, but whose originality cannot be readily emulated. Imitators of Simmel and Goffman have generally achieved little other than to reveal the inimitability of their masters. There are no schools of Simmel of Goffman as there are, for example, of Marx, Durkheim, Weber and Parsons. By definition, the virtuoso in Sociology and Cultural Studies is a one-off and this presents transparent difficulties in developing the sociological heritage left by these writers.

Fourth, Simmel was badly served by his American tribunes, especially Albion Small. They represented him as a formal sociologist, the academic chronicler of the 'dyad', the 'triad', 'group subdivisions', 'hierarchy', 'ritual' and so on. But these formal concepts are actually secondary to his paramount interest in reciprocity, interaction, circulation and exchange. In Simmel we get an early, unusually sophisticated sense of the contingent, interrelated, tumultuous character of Modern experience and its relationship to consciousness. It is this sense that makes it so hard to conceive of his sociology as a contribution to theories of social policy or character. There is indeed, no obvious action sociology to be extrapolated from Simmel's work, save perhaps a commitment to patiently accumulate scientific knowledge. Instead, the balance of his work is in developing a critical sympathy with the rhythms of Modernity, so as to separate its distinctive elements from traditional society and to better understand the character of the times. If Marx was the premier sociologist of capitalism,

Durkheim, the sociological *savant* of the division of labour and organic solidarity, and Weber, the best sociologist of rationalization and the disenchantment of the world, Simmel is the first and greatest sociologist of Modernity.

Modernity

What does it mean to be a sociologist of Modernity? Other sociological approaches focus on the transition between traditional and modern institutions. For example, Marxism examines the process of modernization as a transition between Ancient, Feudal and Capitalist society. Durkheim, basing his view in a more anthropological and legalistic view of collective life, distinguishes between mechanical and organic solidarity and seeks to clarify the contrasting dominant institutions and agents in both formations. Weber's work on religion, the work ethic and the nation-state produces a formidable historical analysis of the sequential changes that led to the rise of legal–rational bureaucratic society.

Simmel's approach is different in as much as it eschews history and concentrates on the *experience* of modernity. The principal motifs of this experience are fragmentation and ephemerality. For Simmel, unlike social formations wedded to the hereditary principle and religious cosmology, Modernity presents a material and mental universe of contingent relations, cultural relativism and breaking boundaries. This universe is directly expressed in aesthetics, which is one reason why Simmel, unusually for sociologist's of his day, took fashion, art, adornment and subjective culture so seriously. The metropolis is a constantly changing landscape of people, vehicles, exhibitions, advertisements and to put it concisely, *gross stimuli*, that accentuate the position of visual culture in modern experience.

Simmel's sociology presents the experience of Modernity as flux, as intense, unremitting consciousness of diverse, forms in motion. It is an approach that logically carries with it an enhanced recognition of the transitory nature of relationships, the arbitrary form of external cosmology and the conditional character of identity. Arguably, this recognition was only fully developed later in the twentieth century in the development of symbolic interactionism and poststructuralism.

To a degree that would today be regarded as unusual, and arguably insufficiently global, Simmel's view of Modernity reflected his status as a citizen of Berlin. For most of his adult life he taught sociology and philosophy at the University of Berlin. As such he experienced at first hand, Bismarck's ferocious attempts to weld the German peoples into a German Empire under Prussian hegemony, and the eventual collapse of the German Empire in military defeat, economic disintegration and counter-revolution in 1918. He was 13 when Bismarck defined the new German nation-state after the Franco-Prussian war of 1870, and 56 when the Whilheminian era propelled the nation into World War. The intervening 43 years witnessed the utter transformation of Berlin. Simmel directly observed the extraordinary expansion of the city, the tearing down of old buildings and the raising-up of new ones; the incorporation of villages, hamlets as suburbs through new rapid tansit rail and road links; the expansion in population and subcultures; and the emergence of new retail outlets, notably the department store and the shopping arcade. In these years Berlin established itself as the centre for both the power elites of old Prussia and the new financial centres, mass media, organized interests and political parties (Sturmer 2000: 81–2). The revolutionary pace of change in Berlin presented Simmel with the experience of an unusually white-hot concentration of urban and cultural transformation. From its midst money and the metropolis were irresistibly suggested as central metaphors of Modernity. The money economy both contributed to and represented the sense of increasingly indirect relations between people while the rapid rate of expansion in the city produced a melting pot of new stimuli in the form of amalgamated German national cultures, immigrant communities, international finance and modernist retail commerce.

Simmel's sociology was also a product of the crisis in intellectual life associated with these deep changes. As befits Modernity, he lived at a time when traditional verities were overturned overnight and revolutionary new ideas on identity, association and practice cascaded into society at a pell-mell pace. Nowhere was this more acutely expressed than in science. Simmel was certainly influenced by the *methodenstreit* debate in German sociology in the late nineteenth century. This was a dispute between *neo-Kantians* who held that the natural and cultural sciences are different in kind and hence require distinctive methodologies, and the *Naturalists* who held the view that a single scientific methodology is appropriate to the study of culture and nature. The methods of hermeneutics and verstehen emerged from this conflict.[3] A parallel debate between the historical and neo-classical schools in Economics focused on the question of the role of value judgements in scientific research and introduced the concepts of value freedom and value neutrality.[4]

Simmel did not take a direct stance on either of these debates, although his work clearly reflects their ramifications. In particular, the questions of the distinction between subjective and objective culture and the dilemma of how to intellectually encapsulate flux in worthwhile ways is stressed. There is no doubt that he believed in the possibility of a *scientific* comprehension of the culture of Modernity and that this was in fact, the object of his work. As he (1900: 102) proposed:

> The goal of our thoughts is to find what is steadfast and reliable behind ephemeral appearances and the flux of events; and to advance from mutual dependence to self-sufficiency and independence. In this way we attain the fixed points that can guide us through the maze of phenomena, and that represent the counterpart of what we conceive ourselves as valuable and definitive.

His analysis of modern experience constantly returns to the notion of the 'levelling' effect of ceaseless change and the 'colourlessness' of reciprocal relations with others. Yet it also recognizes substantive distinctions, nowhere more so than in the distinction between the superficial attachment to everyday life and a scientific attachment that is capable of producing durable insights and forms of knowledge. Positivism and empiricism are foreign to his sociology. However, Simmel is enough of a counter-Modernist to acknowledge science as offering a route out of the vicious circle of cultural relativism and psychological disturbance unleashed by Modernity.

Mentality

What is the mentality of Modernity? For Simmel, *Modernism* is distinct from traditionalism by the replacement of essence with form as the central category of popular consciousness. Traditional society regarded identity, place and culture to be held in place by essential, immemorial hereditary principles and Deistic necessity. The law of the monarch and his Court elicited in human form, the God-given universe. On this reading, culture is an allotment of fixed and pure essences, expressed most implacably, in the concept of immemorial hereditary hierarchy and the greater glory of God. It is a closed system in which the room for manoeuvre between position, status and community is tightly constrained. In contrast, Modernity is a much more open system in which the experience of upward and downward mobility is more widely distributed and the allocation of status and reward by hereditary principles is openly challenged by contest systems. The meritocratic ideal flourishes under Modernism. It may not be evenly reproduced in the culture of everyday life, but its presence sets the tone of the relations of everyday life, especially when these relations meet the obstructions of hereditary might and custom. In Simmel's view culture is form, in the sense that it refers to the synthesizing categories that transform raw experience into determinate unities. He differentiates this from 'content', which he understands to refer to the nuclei of social life which, as Levine (1971: xv) put it cannot 'be apprehended by us in their immediacy'. The study of form may reveal content, but the situation is complicated under Modernity by the tumultuous character of form.

Simmel encapsulates these arguments in the proposition that the transition between Traditional and Modern society involves the domination of objective culture over subjective culture. Under Modernity objective culture is not imposed upon individuals by a dominant social formation as is the case, for example in traditional *monarchical*, *court* and *class* rule. Of course, Simmel recognizes the existence of hierarchies in Modernity and acknowledges that some of these carry the vestiges of the hereditary principle. On the other hand, the accent in his analysis is upon the crystallization of objective culture deriving from interaction between constellations of actors. By the term, *objective culture*, Simmel means above all, the spirit (*Geist*) of rational calculability, technological innovation and scientific authority which permeates everyday life. The corresponding term, *subjective culture*, refers to the realm of the emotions, localized practices, conventions and attachments, personal daydreams and imaginary relations. The division between these two levels of culture was a very prominent theme in nineteenth century *fin de siecle* German sociology. It reached its zenith in Max Weber's rationalization thesis with its forlorn, eerie metaphor of the encroaching, implacable disenchantment of the world.

Simmel's sociology places the lion's share of causality behind this process in the division of labour and the money economy. These two institutions contribute to the distancing effect in human relations which, on the level of common experience, is expressed in feelings of anonymity, isolation, division and conflict. In many places in the course of his discussion of the division of labour and the money economy Simmel's analysis of modern experience resembles Marx's work on alienation and commodification. That is, it presents objective culture as the reification of human relations which stand above subjects and bears down upon them as an external thing. However, whereas Marx hypothesizes transcendence in the form of the recognition of class interests and class revolution, Simmel's sociology is more conservative and stoical, presenting Modernity as a formation in which many different and discordant *mentalities* emerge in culture. Frisby and Featherstone (1997: 1–25) submit that this stress on different and discordant mentalities is methodologically reconciled in Simmel's sociology in the form of a *conscious perspectivism* – a commitment to view themes from a variety of perspectives.

Within the tradition of action sociology there is a strong tendency to conflate action with interest. Acts are analyzed in terms of the intentions of actors, whether these actors are conceived in terms of individuals or collectivities. Simmel is unusual among sociologists of his day in going beyond this conflation. His concept of *sociability* endeavours to encapsulate the play form in life with others. Play for itself, without any ulterior motive, is the essence of sociability. Passing the time, day dreaming and idle chat are generally assigned low significance in action sociology. They are regarded as trivial acts of exchange and interaction. In Simmel's sociology of culture they are privileged as pivotal resources in social integration and reproduction. A parallel may be drawn with Benjamin's (1970, 1999) famous analysis of the *flaneur* and, in particular, his argument that the discarded, ordinary elements in society are the *hieroglyphics* of culture. Simmel's approach preceded Benjamin in attributing importance to the ordinary, seemingly trivial *mentalities* of everyday life.

Money

Simmel's (1900) best known work is *The Philosophy of Money*. In this massive book Simmel regards money to externalize the relations of circulation and exchange that comprise the inner life of Modernity. The accentuated consciousness of the artificial, arbitrary, transitory and contingent character of all relations is represented in monetary transactions. Money is the perfect exemplar of the tendency of objective culture to dominate subjective culture because it is frequently reified into a force which stands outside subjective life and compels us to act as if in the face of an immoveable object. Inflation, unemployment and devaluation arise from human actions and decisions but they have the quality to appear inhuman in their effects. They alienate us from subjective culture because they limit our choices and prevent us from acting as we please. From them, we learn what is objectively 'realistic' in the conduct of life and we cut the cloth of our life-choices accordingly.

Simmel's interest in the money economy derives from his reading of it as the fullest embodiment of the exchange culture that predominates in the mentalities of Modernity. For Simmel, every interaction, every look, glance and aside is an expression of the balance of reciprocal, conditional, reflexive and unstable energy that characterizes modern experience. The study of monetary exchange is therefore an effective route into the elucidation of the various and diverse exchange relationships out of which society is composed. As he (1900: 101) puts it, society, like money, is:

> a structure that transcends the individual, but that is not abstract. Historical life thus escapes the alternative of taking place either in individuals or in abstract generalities. Society is the universal, which at the same time, is concretely alive. From this arises the unique significance that exchange, as the economic-historical realisation of the relativity of things, has for society; exchange raises the specific object and its significance for the individual above its singularity, not into the sphere of abstraction, but into that of lively interaction.

Simmel regards money to be the purest form of exchange relation. There are two reasons for this. First, it is an exchange of social values. It involves two parties agreeing on a shared currency which encapsulates the social values that place upon a physical or cultural act of exchange, whether that act be based in the expenditure of labour or the accumulation of a commodity.

Second, it is predicated in trust. Without mutual trust in the money economy, the notion of a shared currency is void. This notion of mutual trust is intrinsically conditional. For it is perfectly possible for mutual judgements of value to disintegrate. On this account, economic recessions and slumps are conditions in which mutual trust relations have momentarily decomposed. However, even in these conditions social actors operate on the general assumption that trust relations will be eventually reconfigured at a new level of functionality. In every monetary transaction, the operation of reciprocal, yet contingent relations of trust, which is the foundation of the mentalities of Modernity, is revealed.

The study of money also appealed to another of Simmel's core methodological presuppositions: interconnectedness. His analysis of social relations proceeds on the basis that everything is connected to everything else. By bearing down on monetary exchange the totality of the social constellation may be captured. As Siegfried Kracauer noted (quoted in Frisby 2002: 101), from the study of money Simmel provided a comprehensive picture of the interconnectedness and entanglement of phenomena. He clearly extracts their essence in order to melt it down once more into a multitude of connections ... and reveals the many common meetings that reside within them. Amongst these phenomena belong, for instance, exchange, ownership, greed, extravagance, cynicism, individual freedom, the style of life, culture, the value of personality, etc.

This interest in elucidating the place of the concrete in the totality of relations is powerfully articulated in Simmel's view of the psychology of money. He recognizes a duality of structure in which money is commonly acknowledged to both symbolize the chain of distance between human relations and to be the embodiment of goal resolution.

To clarify the point, in the money economy an event which is remote from the immediate circumstances of subjective life can over-turn the assumptions upon which all of subjective life is conducted. The collapse of a distant market, the maintenance of an obscure credit restriction can produce inflation that decreases the value of one's assets and therefore corrodes reciprocal trust relations or unemployment, which eradicates the means of wherewithal upon which the conduct of subjective life depends. Realization of these qualities accounts for the respect and even fear in which money is held in many social circles. At the same time, money is the common object of reverie, wishes and fantasies since it is everywhere acknowledged to be a highly effective means of accomplishing desired ends. In both cases the tendency of money to produce reification in subjective culture is evident. Thus, the recognition of the interconnectedness of the money economy accentuates consciousness of the relative insignificance of subjective power. Conversely, the desire for money to act as the means of goal fulfilment logically carries the possibility of means–ends displacement in which money loses its characteristic as the intermediary of exchange and is transformed into the all-consuming end of subjective life.

Acknowledgement of the dualistic, reifying tendency of money produces a cloven psychology of money. On one hand, it breeds cynicism since to study money is to learn that value has no foundation and that it is entirely a matter of form. Simmel describes this as 'cynicism' because it dissolves a distinction between the highest and lowest social values and replaces them with a flexible attitude to form as an end in itself. On the other hand, it breeds what he calls the *blasé* attitude, a concept which, as we shall see, he develops in his analysis of the metropolis. The *blasé* attitude is indifferent to both questions of the highest and lowest social values and the flexible attitude to form. Instead it regards all exchange and interchange to be reduced to the same grey level. By way of compensation it seeks escape in the craving for excitement, the quest for extreme impressions and the passion for acceleration as an end in itself.

Does this mean that Simmel concludes that the development of the money economy reduces human freedom? His analysis of the duality of structure in the system of monetary exchange would appear to suggest as much. The division of labour produces new dependencies upon the individual and fragments experience in as much as personality is subject to the function of work. Thus, the division of labour requires the individual to subdue the whole personality in order to concentrate on the work function. Compared with feudal society, where the orientation to work was more communal and relaxed, the modern money economy requires individuals to practice calculated depersonalization. This tendency is exacerbated by the money economy, which encourages relations to be based on functional exchange and discourages the engagement of the whole personality. Yet Simmel is well aware that the condition of the free labourer is very different from the feudal serf. The free labourer has the right to withdraw labour and move from one occupation to another. Money breaks the feudal relationship between the labourer and the land and induces greater occupational, geographical and social mobility. It permits broader differentation of functions in the individual personality and, by the same token wider social differentiation. The replacement of the hierarchical ideal by the meritocratic principle means that the connections between individuals are more diverse and variable than under the feudal system. In a word money facilitates the production of *diversity*.

Money is not quite the handmaiden of diversity. The division of labour, the formation of varieties of political reflexivity and, in particular, the growth of the metropolis, are also significant. All of these factors point in the direction of greater individualism. As such they support the proposition that the development of exchange society enhances freedom. On balance, this is indeed Simmel's position. However, at the same time, he is concerned to elucidate the negative consequences of the rise of the money economy. Some have already been mentioned above, notably the tendency of calculated depersonalization, the fragmentation of the personality, isolation, reification, the domination of subjective culture by objective culture and alienation. Simmel's sociology is never unidimensional. It is in the nature of his analysis of society as a constellation of reciprocal interactions to attempt to capture not merely the diversity of these interactions but the variety of their effects. For Simmel, society is a complex totality. This imposes obligations on the interpreter of modern life. Society must be grasped not merely in terms of causal sequences but in terms of the total field of interactions and their various ramifications. This requires not only an unusual level of learning but also an extraordinary openness to interaction in all of its diverse manifestations. This is one reason why some of the most famous subjects of Simmel's essays were apprehended in his own time and arguably even today, are regarded as sociological oddities: 'The Adventurer', 'The Stranger', 'The Ruin'. These essays are an attempt to capture the diversity and esoteric qualities of exchange and interaction. They are studied not as ends in themselves, but as reflections on the interrelated character of modern experience. A passage in his (1971: 187-8) essay, 'The Adventurer' is typical, and may be cited as an example of Simmel's insistence on study society as a complex totality:

> What we call an adventure stands in contrast to that interlocking of life-links, to that feeling that those countercurrents, turnings, and knots still, after all, spin forth a continuous thread. An adventure is certainly a part of our existence, directly contiguous with other parts which precede and follow it; at the same time, however, in its deeper meaning, it occurs outside the usual continuity of this life. Never touching life's outer shell. While it falls outside the context of life, it falls, with this same movement, as it were, back into that context again ... it is a foreign body in our existence which is yet somehow connected with the centre; the outside, if only by a long and unfamiliar detour, is formally an aspect of the inside.

The Metropolis

If Simmels' analysis of the money economy represents his most complete attempt to grapple with the varieties of interaction and exchange in Modern experience, his work on the metropolis constitutes a substantial additional flank in his sociological repertoire. The Metropolis is a hive of interaction and exchange. It is the concentration of diversity and variety that the money economy in conjunction with the division of labour facilitates. It is in the metropolis that the division of labour and the weight of objective culture upon subjective culture is most evident. The concentration of quantitative relationships and their conditionality, imposes upon the psyche in specific ways. Simmel distinguishes two character types as responses to metropolitan existence.

The first is the *blasé* personality, which we have already touched upon above. The blasé personality develops such an acute consciousness of being assailed by form that it develops a defence mechanism of indifference. Nothing surprises or enchants it. It is not moved by tragedy or triumph, but maintains an even keel in the face of all new sensory data and information. The blasé personality is really a form of social retreatism, since it is predicated on disengaging with the variety and diversity of exchange and interaction. Simmel associates this retreatism with the diminution of Modern experience since it implies the forlorn ambition of dealing with Modernity on one's own terms as if others do not matter. In his (1971) essays on 'Prostitution','The Poor' and 'The Miser and the Spendthrift' he discloses many important aspects of the blasé personality, especially its delusional qualities.

The second distinctive personality type that coalesces in the Metropolis, is the *neurasthenic* personality. This is a psychology that reacts to the rapidly changing stimuli of the metropolis by developing a heightened state of excitement and nervousness. Neurasthenics are addicted to fashion, gossip and new relationships. Stability and calm is unendurable. Instead life is turned into an unquenchable quest for new sensations and stimuli. This quest is unquenchable because no new sensation or stimulus can be enduring. It is precisely the constantly changing nature of sensations and stimuli that is attractive. But this attraction is also dangerous because the neurasthenic recognizes that the anticipation of fulfilment can never be achieved through the realization of interaction. The point at which realization presents itself, is the point at which the neurasthenic loses interest and departs for fresh stimuli. The neurasthenic personality is another example of retreatism since it presupposes that interaction and exchange can never be more than fleeting and fragmentary. The achievement of the whole personality remains permanently out of the neurasthenic's grasp since it requires a degree of commitment that is beyond his capacity to make.

Both types remain recognizable features of today's cities. They reflect Simmel's thesis that objective culture dominates over subjective culture in damaging ways. Conversely he emphasizes the fecundity of relationships in the metropolis which produces unprecedented volumes of exchange and interaction. This in turn produces a fountain of rapid and unbroken internal and external stimuli. Because the metropolis is the concentration of objective culture it subjects the individual to extreme pressures of standardization and levelling down. Although the blasé and neurasthenic responses involve retreatism they are often expressed in stylized ways that emphasize eccentricity and difference. Through fashion, adornment and style of sociability the individual resists the 'levelling down' effects of objective culture. The paradox of the general blasé and neurasthenic attitudes is that they contribute to the enhancement of external diversity as the individual resorts to strategies of extreme subjectivism in order to combat standardization. These strategies lend colour to the external appearance of metropolitan exchange and interaction. However, they do not counteract the effect of objective culture. Indeed their proliferation may be read as a measure of the implosion of subjective culture as individuals resort to style and form to proclaim difference. The decisive tendencies of Modernity to replace essence with appearance and content with form are therefore reinforced.

Conclusion

As Kurt Wolff (1950: xxxiv–xxxv) observes, Simmel's sociology perpetually shades into philosophical concerns having to do with the phenomenology of Modern experience. Because the philosophy of culture is not a strong influence in either the sociology of culture or Cultural Studies, Simmel's 'philosophical sociology' has not been fully absorbed. In addition, his emphasis on Modern experience as fragmentary and incomplete results in an elliptical and impressionistic style of analysis. The difficulties in emulating this style are matched by the problems in formalizing its special qualities. No-one writes like Simmel, because Simmel's style of interpretation was a product of his unusual receptivity to Modernity. He was active in Berlin at a conjuncture when the traditional uneven habits, mores and practices of the German people were welded into the outward appearance of national unity as a result of Bismarck's economic and political revolution. Small wonder that Simmel was so obsessed with the thesis that objective culture was akin to a Minatour overwhelming subjective culture in destructive, inexorable ways.

Yet his understanding of Modernity also portrayed the wealth of new opportunities that the break with the past presented to modern men and women. Modernity evoked a particular ratio of psychological impulses and designs. These were expressed in the formation of new personality types which left their mark on objective culture. By reading Simmel, the late nineteenth century *fin de siecle* revolution in aesthetics becomes more intelligible, as does the rise of feminism, the crisis in masculinity and the antinomies of nationalism. Simmel provided an *entre* into all of these issues before they were widely debated, let alone understood.

The trajectory of development in sociology for most of the twentieth century followed a route into varieties of institutional or action sociology. Between Parsons and Marxism, Simmel fell awkwardly as an interesting, but ultimately inconsequential *curio* from a decadent age of *salon* culture and leisurely philosophizing of metropolitan experience. It was only when the defects of institutional and action sociology became transparent in the 1980s, that the value of Simmel's work on Modernity became appreciated.

The second edition of *The Philosophy of Money* published by Routledge in 1990 and edited by Tom Bottomore and David Frisby, became for a time, a best-seller on the academic Sociology list. Simmel's insistence on the fragmentary, incomplete, relativistic character of Modernity was widely interpreted as a forerunner to postmodernism. With hindsight this claim of kinship was too rash. Simmel was committed to a scientific understanding of culture and science. This was predicated in the elucidation of cultural and social life through inter-generational study. In other words it presupposed a degree of continuity which was incommensurate with the more apocalyptic views elaborated by, for example, Baudrillard and Lyotard (Rojek and Turner 1993; Rojek and Turner 1998). Yet Simmel's heritage remains under-explored in Cultural Studies and the sociology of culture. It is time to acknowledge him, not merely as the first sociologist of Modernity, but as a founding father in the sociology of culture.

Notes

1 The Birmingham School advocated the ideal of the 'organic intellectual' as the ideal intellectual labourer. The concept is borrowed from Antonio Gramsci. It refers to an intellectual who acts as a switchboard between the cutting edge ideas in society and the people. The organic intellectual is compared pointedly with the traditional intellectual. The latter is regarded as divorced from society and culture by an over-academicized perspective. In contrast the organic intellectual operates as a switch-point between the cutting edge ideas in society and the masses. The Birmingham view of intellectual labour is this deeply politicized. Work which has no overt political commitment to advance working class interests, as is the case with the labour of Simmel, is generally periphalized in the Birmingham approach.

2 Institutional sociology is concerned to delineate the key social institutions and identify their functions. The approach is most fully developed in the structural–functionalist tradition associated with Talcott Parsons and his followers. However, institutional sociology also figures in many radical approaches, notably Althusserianism, feminism and the Frankfurt School. The concepts of ideology, the repressive state/ideological state apparatus, patriarchy, the family and the culture industry, all have a negative connotation in these traditions. They are associated with functioning to increase repression and subordination. Action sociology is more concerned with the modes of interaction and their consequences. Weber's sociology and symbolic interactionism are examples of the action approach. Action sociology is janus faced. In most versions, notably Weber, Goffman and Garfinkel, it is concerned with understanding the hermeneutics and causality of social action. However, it can also address the question of transforming action through instrumental conduct (Gramsci, Hall, Gilroy).

3 Hermeneutics is a theory of interpreting human action and its consequences. Gadamer's (1960) concept of the *hermeneutic circle* holds that we can only interpret and understand a concrete act with reference to the encompassing social cosmology that produced it. The task of the intellectual labourer in the social sciences is to elucidate the parameters of the social cosmology in which agents are situated in order to elicit a more reflexive world order. *Verstehen* is the German word for understanding. The method of *verstehen* is particularly associated with the sociology of Max Weber who held that the task of action sociology is to explore human actions in terms of the subjective meaning of the act. Weber's approach urges sociologists to identify with the subjective meaning that social actors invest in behaviour.

4 A long debate exists in sociology on the question of whether sociological practice can aspire to the state of *value-freedom*. This condition envisages a direct *scientific* relation between interpretation and the elucidation of reality. It is vulnerable to attacks from cultural relativism which propose that all sociological activity is inevitably situated in a hermeneutic circle which structures agency and understanding. Weber recognized that sociology may fail to achieve the condition of value freedom. However, he urged sociologists to seek to isolate their values and articulate them. Through open, reflexive debate sociologists have the means to mitigate the influence of values on research. Weber argued that in this way sociologists can contribute to the building-up of scientific facts of society. However, they have no business in seeking to settle the ultimate values in society since these are always a matter of political and moral debate. *Value neutrality* therefore possesses a double meaning in action sociology. It refers to the methodological isolation of values in order to neutralize their influence upon research; and it also refers to the abstinence of sociology from engaging as bearers of *scientific* knowledge into the debate around ultimate values.

References

Benjamin, W. (1970) *Charles Baudelaire*, London, Verso
Benjamin, W. (1999) *The Arcades Project*, Harvard, Belknap

Frisby, D. (1981) *Sociological Impressionism,* London, Heinemann

Frisby, D. (2002) *Georg Simmel,* (Revised edition), London, Routledge

Frisby, D. and Featherstone, M. (1997)(ed) *Simmel On Culture,* London, Sage

Gadamer, H. (1960) *Truth and Method,* London, Sheed & Ward

Kracauer, S. (1995) *The Mass Ornament,* (ed Levin, T.) Cambridge, Harvard University Press

Levine, D.(1971)'Introduction', *ix–lvx,* (in) Simmel, G., *On Individuality and Social Forms,* Chicago, Chicago University Press

Simmel, G. (1900) *The Philosophy of Money,* (1978 edition) translated by Bottomore, T. and Frisby, D., London, RKP

Simmel, G. (1950) *The Sociology of Georg Simmel,* (ed Wolff, K), New York, Free Press

Simmel, G.(1971) *On Individuality and Social Forms,* (ed Levine, D.), Chicago, University of Chicago Press

Simmel, G. (1990) *The Philosophy of Money,* (revised edition, translated by Bottomore, T and Frisby, D.), London, Routledge

Stumer, M. (2000) *The German Empire,* London, Weidenfeld & Nicolson

Wolff, K.H. (1951)'Introduction', *vii–lxiii, The Sociology of Georg Simmel,* New York, Free Press

CHAPTER THREE
●●●●●●●●

The Frankfurt School

Douglas Kellner

The 'Frankfurt School' refers to a group of German-American theorists who developed powerful analyses of the changes in Western capitalist societies that have occurred since the classical theory of Marx.[1] Working at the Institut for Sozialforschung in Frankfurt, Germany, in the late 1920s and early 1930s, theorists such as Max Horkheimer, Theodor. W. Adorno, Herbert Marcuse, Leo Löwenthal, and Erich Fromm analyzed a wide variety of cultural phenomena, ranging from mass culture and communication to classical music and literature. While Adorno, Löwenthal, and Marcuse are well known as literary theorists, the Frankfurt School also produced some of the first accounts within critical social theory of the importance of mass culture and communication in social reproduction and domination. In their theory of the 'culture industry', the Frankfurt School generated one of the first models of a critical cultural studies that analyzes the processes of cultural production and political economy, the politics of cultural texts, and audience reception and use of cultural artefacts (Kellner, 1989; 1995; Steinert, 2003). I will accordingly first sketch out their ground-breaking critique of mass culture and communication and then will indicate their broad perspectives on cultural sociology, stressing both contributions and limitations.

--------------- **The Frankfurt School and the Culture Industries** ---------------

To a large extent, the Frankfurt School inaugurated critical studies of mass communication and culture, and produced the first critical theory of the cultural industries (see Kellner, 1989; 1995; 1997). Moving from Nazi Germany to the United States, the Frankfurt School experienced at first hand the rise of a media culture involving film, popular music, radio, television, and other forms of mass culture (Wiggershaus, 1994). In the United States, where they found themselves in exile, media production was by and large a form of commercial entertainment controlled by big corporations. Two of its key theorists, Max Horkheimer and Theodor. W. Adorno, developed an account of the 'culture industry' to call attention to the industrialization and commercialization of culture under capitalist relations of production (Horkheimer and Adorno, 1972). This situation was most marked in the United States where there was little state support of film or television industries, and where a highly commercial mass culture emerged that came to be a distinctive feature of capitalist societies and a focus of critical cultural studies.

During the 1930s, the Frankfurt School developed a critical and transdisciplinary approach to cultural and communications studies, combining political economy, textual analysis, and analysis of social and ideological effects of the media. They coined the term 'culture industry' to signify the process of the industrialization of mass-produced culture and the commercial imperatives that drove the system. The critical theorists analyzed all mass-mediated cultural artefacts within the context of industrial production, in which the artefacts of the culture industries exhibited the same features as other products of mass production: commodification, standardization, and massification. The culture industries had the specific function, however, of providing ideological legitimation of the existing capitalist societies and of integrating individuals into its way of life.

Adorno's analyses of popular music, television, and other phenomena ranging from astrology columns to fascist speeches (1991; 1994), Löwenthal's studies of popular literature and magazines (1961), Hertzog's studies of radio soap operas (1941), and the perspectives and critiques of mass culture developed in Horkheimer and Adorno's famous study of the culture industries (1972; Adorno, 1991) provide many examples of the Frankfurt School approach. Moreover, in their theories of the culture industries and critiques of mass culture, they were among the first social theorists to realize its importance in the reproduction of contemporary societies. In their view, mass culture and communications stand at the centre of leisure activity, are important agents of socialization, mediators of political reality, and should thus be seen as major institutions of contemporary societies with a variety of economic, political, cultural and social effects.

Furthermore, the critical theorists investigated the cultural industries in a political context as a form of the integration of the working class into capitalist societies. The Frankfurt School theorists were among the first neo-Marxian groups to examine the effects of mass culture and the rise of the consumer society on the working classes, who were to be the instrument of revolution in the classical Marxian scenario. They also analyzed the ways that the culture industries and consumer society were stabilizing contemporary capitalism and accordingly sought new strategies for political change, agencies of political transformation, and models for political emancipation that could serve as norms of social critique and goals for political struggle. This project required rethinking Marxian theory and produced many important contributions – as well as some problematical positions.

The Frankfurt School focused intently on technology and culture, indicating how technology was becoming both a major force of production and formative mode of social organization and control. In a 1941 article, 'Some social implications of modern technology', Herbert Marcuse argued that technology in the contemporary era constitutes an entire 'mode of organizing and perpetuating (or changing) social relationships, a manifestation of prevalent thought and behavior patterns, an instrument for control and domination' (ibid.: 414). In the realm of culture, technology produced mass culture that habituated individuals to conform to the dominant patterns of thought and behaviour, and thus provided powerful instruments of social control and domination.

Victims of European fascism, the Frankfurt School experienced first hand the ways that the Nazis used the instruments of mass culture to produce submission to fascist culture and society. While in exile in the United States, the members of the Frankfurt School came to believe that American 'popular culture' was also highly ideological and worked to promote the interests of American capitalism. Controlled by giant corporations, the culture industries were organized according to the strictures of mass production, churning out mass-produced products that generated a highly commercial system of culture which in turn sold the values, life-styles, and institutions of 'the American way of life'.

The work of the Frankfurt School provided what Paul Lazarsfeld (1941), one of the originators of modern communications studies, called a critical approach, which he distinguished from the 'administrative research'. The positions of Adorno, Löwenthal, and other members of the inner circle of the Institute for Social Research were contested by Walter Benjamin, an idiosyncratic theorist loosely affiliated with the Institute. Benjamin, writing in Paris during the 1930s, discerned progressive aspects in new technologies of cultural production such as photography, film, and radio. In 'The work of art in the age of mechanical reproduction' (1969), Benjamin noted how new mass media were supplanting older forms of culture whereby the mass reproduction of photography, film, recordings, and publications replaced the emphasis on the originality and 'aura' of the work of art in an earlier era. Freed from the mystification of high culture, Benjamin believed that media culture could cultivate more critical individuals able to judge and analyze their culture, just as sports fans could dissect and evaluate athletic activities. In addition, processing the rush of images of cinema created, Benjamin believed, subjectivities better able to parry and comprehend the flux and turbulence of experience in industrialized, urbanized societies.

Himself a collaborator of the prolific German artist Bertolt Brecht, Benjamin worked with Brecht on films, created radio plays, and attempted to utilize the media as organs of social progress. In the essay 'The artist as producer' ([1934] 1999), Benjamin argued that progressive cultural creators should 'refunction' the apparatus of cultural production, turning theatre and film, for instance, into a forum of political enlightenment and discussion rather than a medium of 'culinary' audience pleasure. Both Brecht and Benjamin wrote radio plays and were interested in film as an instrument of progressive social change. In an essay on radio theory, Brecht anticipated the Internet in his call for reconstructing the apparatus of broadcasting from one-way transmission to a more interactive form of two-way, or multiple, communication (in Silberman, 2000: 41ff.) – a form first realized in CB radio and then electronically-mediated computer communication.

Moreover, Benjamin wished to promote a radical cultural and media politics concerned with the creation of alternative oppositional cultures. Yet he recognized that media such as film could have conservative effects. While he thought it was progressive that mass-produced works were losing their 'aura', their magical force, and were opening cultural artefacts to more critical and political discussion, he recognized that film could create a new kind of ideological magic through the cult of celebrity and techniques such as the close-up that fetishized certain stars or images via the technology of the cinema. He also emphasized the atrophy of experience in the modern world due to the effects of media and technology, that overwhelmed the subject, created fragmentary experience, psychic shocks, and, in the case of war and other lethal technology, produced death (Benjamin, 1969: 83ff.). Benjamin was thus one of the first radical cultural critics to look carefully at the form and technology of media culture in appraising its complex nature and effects. Moreover, he developed a unique approach to cultural history that is one of his most enduring legacies, constituting a micrological history of Paris in the eighteenth century, an uncompleted project that contains a wealth of material for study and reflection (see Benjamin, 2000, and the study in Buck-Morss, 1989).

Max Horkheimer and Theodor W. Adorno answered Benjamin's optimism in a highly influential analysis of the culture industry in their book *Dialectic of Enlightenment*, which first appeared in 1948 and was translated into English in 1972. They argued that the system of cultural production dominated by film, radio broadcasting, newspapers, and magazines, was controlled by advertising and commercial imperatives, and served to create subservience to the system of consumer capitalism. While later critics pronounced their approach too manipulative, reductive, and elitist, it provides an important corrective to more populist approaches to media culture that downplay the way the media industries exert power over audiences and help produce thought and behaviour that conform to the existing society.

The Frankfurt School and Media Culture

In *Dialectic of Enlightenment*, Horkheimer and Adorno anticipate the coming of television in terms of the emergence of a new form of mass culture that would combine sight and sound, image and narrative, in an institution that would embody the types of production, texts, and reception of the culture industry. Anticipating that television would be a prototypical artefact of industrialized culture, Adorno and Horkheimer wrote:

> Television aims at a synthesis of radio and film, and is held up only because the interested parties have not yet reached agreement, but its consequences will be quite enormous and promise to intensify the impoverishment of aesthetic matter so drastically, that by tomorrow the thinly veiled identity of all industrial culture products can come triumphantly out into the open, derisively fulfilling the Wagnerian dream of the *Gesamtkunstwerk*, the fusion of all the arts in one work. The alliance of word, image, and music is all the more perfect than in Tristan because the sensuous elements which all approvingly reflect the surface of social reality are in principle embodied in the same technical process, the unity of which becomes its distinctive content ... Television points the way to a development which might easily enough force the Warner Brothers into what would certainly be the unwelcome position of serious musicians and cultural conservatives.
>
> (1972: 124, 161)

Following the model of critique of mass culture in *Dialectic of Enlightenment,* a Frankfurt School approach to the media analyzed these cultural forces within the dominant system of cultural production and reception, situating the medium within its institutional and political framework. It combined study of text and audience with ideology critique and a contextualizing analysis of how television texts and audiences are situated within specific social relations and institutions. The approach combines Marxian critique of political economy with ideology critique, textual analysis, and psychoanalytically-inspired depth-approaches to audiences and effects.

Theodor W. Adorno's article 'How to look at television' (1991) provides a striking example of a classic Frankfurt School analysis. Adorno opens by stressing the importance of undertaking an examination of the effects of television upon viewers, making using of 'depth-psychological categories'). In his words:

> The effect of television cannot be adequately expressed in terms of success or failure, likes or dislikes, approval or disapproval. Rather, an attempt should be made, with the aid of depth-psychological categories and previous knowledge of mass media, to crystallize a number of theoretical concepts by which the potential effect of television – its impact upon various layers of the spectator's personality – could be studied. It seems timely to investigate systematically socio-psychological stimuli typical of televised material both on a descriptive and psychodynamic level, to analyze their presuppositions as well as their total pattern, and to evaluate the effect they are likely to produce it ...
>
> We can change this medium of far-reaching potentialities only if we look at it in the same spirit which we hope will one day be expressed by its imagery.
>
> (Adorno 1991: 136, 151)

Adorno had previously collaborated with Paul Lazarsfeld on some of the first examinations of the impact of radio and popular music on audiences (Lazarsfeld, 1941). While working on *The Authoritarian Personality* (Adorno et al., [1950] 1969), Adorno took on a position as director of the scientific branch of the Hacker Foundation in Beverly Hills, a psychoanalytically-oriented foundation, and undertook examinations of the socio-psychological roots and impact of mass cultural phenomena, focusing on television in one study (Adorno, 1991) and the astrological column of the *Los Angeles Times* in another (Adorno, 1994).

In view of the general impression that the Frankfurt School make sharp and problematic distinctions between high and low culture, it is interesting that Adorno opens his study with a deconstruction of 'the dichotomy between autonomous art and mass media'. Stressing that their relation is 'highly complex', Adorno claims that distinctions between popular and elite art are a product of historical conditions and should not be exaggerated. After a historical examination of older and recent popular culture, Adorno analyzes the 'multilayered structure of contemporary television'. In light of the notion that the Frankfurt School reduces the texts of media culture to ideology, it is interesting that Adorno calls for analysis of the 'various layers of meaning' found in popular television, stressing 'polymorphic meanings' and distinctions between latent and manifest content.

Adorno's examples come from the early 1950s TV shows and tend to see these works as highly formulaic and reproducing conformity and adjustment. He criticizes stereotyping in television, 'pseudo-realism', and its highly conventional forms and meaning, an approach that accurately captures certain aspects of 1950s television, but which is inadequate to capture the growing complexity of contemporary television. Adorno's approach to 'hidden meanings' is highly interesting, however, and his psychoanalytic and ideological readings of television texts and speculation on their effects are pioneering, and his call to transform the institution and forms of television goes against what is sometimes presented as his elitism and lack of activism and intervention in media culture.

While Horkheimer, Adorno, Marcuse, Habermas, and other major Frankfurt School theorists never systematically engage with production, texts, or audiences of media culture, they frequently acknowledge its importance in their development of a critical theory of society, or in their comments on contemporary social phenomena. Following the Frankfurt School analysis of changes in the nature of socialization, Herbert Marcuse, for instance, noted the decline of the family as the dominant agent of socialization in *Eros and Civilization* (1955) and the rise of the mass media, like radio and television:

For Marcuse, the repressive organization of the instincts seems to be *collective*, and the ego seems to be prematurely socialized by a whole system of extra-familial agents and agencies. As early as the pre-school level, gangs, radio, and television set the pattern for conformity and rebellion; deviations from the pattern are punished not so much in the family as outside and against the family. The experts of the mass media transmit the required values; they offer the perfect training in efficiency, toughness, personality, dream and romance. With this education, the family can no longer compete (ibid.: 97).

Marcuse saw broadcasting as part of an apparatus of administration and domination in a one-dimensional society. In his words:

> with the control of information, with the absorption of individuals into mass communication, knowledge is administered and confined. The individual does not really know what is going on; the overpowering machine of entertainment and entertainment unites him with the others in a state of anaesthesia from which all detrimental ideas tend to be excluded.
>
> (ibid.: 104)

On this view, media culture is part of an apparatus of manipulation and societal domination. In *One-Dimensional Man* (1964), Marcuse claimed that the inanities of commercial radio and television confirm his analyses of the individual and the demise of authentic culture and oppositional thought, portraying broadcasting as part of an apparatus producing the thought and behaviour needed for the social and cultural reproduction of contemporary capitalist societies.

While the classical Frankfurt School members wrote little on contemporary media culture, their approach strongly influenced critical approaches to mass communication and culture within academia and the views of the media of the New Left and others in the aftermath of the 1960s. The anthology *Mass Culture* (Rosenberg and White, 1957) contained Adorno's article on television and many studies influenced by the Frankfurt School approach. Within critical communication research, there were many criticisms of network television as a capitalist institution and critics of television and the media such as Herbert Schiller, George Gerbner, Dallas Smythe, and others were influenced by the Frankfurt School approach to mass culture, as was C. Wright Mills in an earlier era (see Kellner, 1989: 134ff.).

From the perspectives of the New Left, Todd Gitlin wrote 'Thirteen theses on television' that contained a critique of broadcasting as manipulation with resonances to the Frankfurt School in 1972 and continued to do research and writing that developed in his own way a Frankfurt School approach to television, focusing on TV in the United States (1980; 1983; 2002). A 1987 collection, *Watching Television*, contained studies by Gitlin and others that exhibited a neo-Frankfurt School approach to television, and many contemporary theorists writing on television have been shaped by their engagement with the Frankfurt School, including a series of books by Douglas Kellner (1990; 1992; 2001; 2003a; 2003b) that analyze the structure of corporate media in relation to capital and the state and that interrogate specific media events such as the Gulf War, the Clinton sex scandals, the 2000 US election theft, the September 11 terror attacks and subsequent Terror War, drawing on Frankfurt School perspectives.

Habermas and the Public Sphere

The Frankfurt School also provides useful historical perspectives on the transition from traditional culture and modernism in the arts to a mass-produced media and consumer society. In his ground-breaking book *The Structural Transformation of the Public Sphere*, Jürgen Habermas further historicizes Adorno and Horkheimer's analysis of the culture industry. Providing historical background to the triumph of the culture industry, Habermas notes how bourgeois society in the late eighteenth and nineteenth centuries was distinguished by the rise of a public sphere that stood between civil society and the state and which mediated between public and private interests. For the first time in history, individuals and groups could shape public opinion, giving direct expression to their needs and interests while influencing political practice. The bourgeois public sphere made it possible to form a realm of public opinion that opposed state power and the powerful interests that were coming to shape bourgeois society.

Habermas notes a transition from the liberal public sphere which originated in the Enlightenment and the American and French Revolutions to a media-dominated public sphere in the current stage of what he calls 'welfare state capitalism and mass democracy'. This historical transformation is grounded in Horkheimer and Adorno's analysis of the culture industry, in which giant corporations have taken over the public sphere and transformed it from a site of rational debate into one of manipulative consumption and passivity. In this transformation, 'public opinion' shifts from rational consensus emerging from debate, discussion, and reflection to the manufactured opinion of polls or media experts.

For Habermas, the interconnection between the sphere of public debate and individual participation has thus been fractured and transmuted into that of a realm of political manipulation and spectacle, in which citizen-consumers ingest and passively absorb entertainment and information. 'Citizens' thus become spectators of media presentations and discourse which arbitrate public discussion and reduce its audiences to objects of news, information, and public affairs. In Habermas's words: 'Inasmuch as the mass media today strip away the literary husks from the kind of bourgeois self-interpretation and utilize them as marketable forms for the public services provided in a culture of consumers, the original meaning is reversed' (1989: 171).

The history of and initial controversy over *The Structural Transformation of the Public Sphere* are best perceived within the context of Habermas's work with the Institute for Social Research. After studying with Horkheimer and Adorno in Frankfurt, in the 1950s, Habermas investigated both the ways that a new public sphere had emerged during the time of the Enlightenment and the American and French Revolutions and how it promoted political discussion and debate. Habermas developed his study within the context of the Institute analysis of the transition from the stage of liberal market capitalism of the nineteenth century to the stage of state-and monopoly-organized capitalism of the twentieth century developed by the Frankfurt School (Kellner, 1989).

Habermas's *The Structural Transformation of the Public Sphere* is an immensely rich and influential book that has had a major impact in a variety of disciplines. It has also received detailed critique and promoted extremely productive discussions of liberal democracy, civil society, public life, and social changes in the twentieth century, among other issues. Few books of the second half of the twentieth century have been so seriously discussed in so many different fields and continue, more than fifty years after its initial publication in 1962, to generate such productive controversy and insight. While Habermas's thought took several crucial philosophical twists and turns after the publication of his first major book, he has himself provided detailed commentary on *Structural Transformation* in the 1990s and returned to issues of the public sphere and democratic theory in his monumental work *Between Facts and Norms* (1998). Hence, concern with the public sphere and the necessary conditions for a genuine democracy can be seen as a central theme of Habermas's work that deserves respect and critical scrutiny.

Habermas's critics contend that he idealizes the earlier bourgeois public sphere by presenting it as a forum of rational discussion and debate when in fact many social groups and most women were excluded. Critics also contend that Habermas neglects various oppositional working-class, plebeian, and women's public spheres developed alongside of the bourgeois public sphere to represent voices and interests excluded in this forum (see the studies in Calhoun, 1992, and Kellner, 2000). Yet Habermas is right that in the period of the democratic revolutions a public sphere emerged in which for the first time in history ordinary citizens could participate in political discussion and debate, organize, and struggle against unjust authority. Habermas's account also points to the increasingly important role of the media in politics and everyday life and the ways that corporate interests have colonized this sphere, using the media and culture to promote their own interests.

The culture industry thesis described both the production of massified cultural products and homogenized subjectivities. Mass culture for the Frankfurt School produced desires, dreams, hopes, fears, and longings, as well as unending desire for consumer products. The culture industry produced cultural consumers who would consume its products and conform to the dictates and the behaviours of the existing society. And yet, as Walter Benjamin pointed out (1969), the culture industry also produces rational and critical consumers able to dissect and discriminate among cultural texts and performances, much as sports fans learn to analyze and criticize sports events.

The Frankfurt School and British Cultural Studies

While the Frankfurt School arguably articulates cultural conditions in the stage of state monopoly capitalism or Fordism that produced a regime of mass production and consumption, British cultural studies emerged in the 1960s when, first, there was widespread global resistance to consumer capitalism and an upsurge of revolutionary movements, and then emergence of a new stage of capital, described as 'post-Fordism', postmodernity, or other terminology that attempted to describe a more variegated and contested social and cultural formation (Kellner, 1997).

Moreover, the forms of culture described by the earliest phase of British cultural studies in the 1950s and early 1960s articulated conditions in an era in which there were still significant tensions in the UK and much of Europe between an older culture based on the working class and the newer mass-produced culture whose models and exemplars were the products of American culture industries. The initial project of cultural studies developed by Richard Hoggart, Raymond Williams, and E.P. Thompson attempted to preserve working-class culture against the onslaughts of mass culture produced by the culture industries. Thompson's inquiries into the history of British working-class institutions and struggles, the defence of working-class culture by Hoggart and Williams, and their attacks on mass culture were part of a socialist and working-class-oriented project that assumed that the industrial working class was a force of progressive social change and that it could be mobilized and organized to struggle against the inequalities of the existing capitalist societies and for a more egalitarian socialist one. Williams and Hoggart were deeply involved in projects of working-class education and were oriented toward socialist working-class politics, seeing their form of cultural studies as an instrument of progressive social change.

The early critiques in the first wave of British cultural studies of Americanism and mass culture in Hoggart, Williams, and others during the late 1950s and early 1960s, thus paralleled to some extent the earlier critique of the Frankfurt School, yet valorized a working class that the Frankfurt School saw as defeated in Germany and much of Europe during the era of fascism and which they never saw as a strong resource for emancipatory social change. The 1960s work of the Birmingham School was continuous with the radicalism of the first wave of British cultural studies (the Hoggart–Thompson–Williams 'culture and society' tradition) as well as, in important ways, with the Frankfurt School. Yet the Birmingham project also eventually paved the way for a postmodern populist turn in cultural studies.

It has not been widely recognized that the second stage of the development of British cultural studies – starting with the founding of the University of Birmingham Centre for Contemporary Cultural Studies in 1963/64 by Hoggart and Stuart Hall – shared many key perspectives with the Frankfurt School. During this period, the Centre developed a variety of critical approaches for the analysis, interpretation, and criticism of cultural artefacts (see Hall, 1980b; Agger, 1992; McGuigan, 1992; Kellner, 1995). Through a set of internal debates, and responding to social struggles and movements of the 1960s and the 1970s, the Birmingham group engaged the interplay of representations and ideologies of class, gender, race, ethnicity, and nationality in cultural texts, including media culture. The Birmingham scholars were among the first to study the effects of newspapers, radio, television, film, and other popular cultural forms on audiences. They also focused on how various audiences interpreted and used media culture in varied and different ways and contexts, analyzing the factors that made audiences respond in contrasting ways to media texts.

The now classical period of British cultural studies from the early 1960s to the early 1980s continued to adopt a Marxian approach to the study of culture, one especially influenced by Althusser and Gramsci (see, especially Hall, 1980a). Yet although Hall usually omits the Frankfurt School from his narrative, some of the work done by the Birmingham group replicated certain classical positions of the Frankfurt School, in their social theory and methodological models for doing cultural studies, as well as in their political perspectives and strategies. Like the Frankfurt School, British cultural studies observed the integration of the working class and its decline of revolutionary consciousness, and studied the conditions of this catastrophe for the Marxian project of revolution. Like the Frankfurt School, British cultural studies also concluded that mass culture was playing an important role in integrating the working class into existing capitalist societies and that a new consumer and media culture was forming a new mode of capitalist hegemony.

Both traditions engaged the intersections of culture and ideology and saw ideology critique as central to a critical cultural studies. Both perceived culture as a mode of ideological reproduction and hegemony, in which cultural forms help to shape the modes of thought and behaviour that induce individuals to adapt to the social conditions of capitalist societies. Both also conceived of culture as a potential form of resistance to capitalist society and both the earlier forerunners of British cultural studies, especially Raymond Williams, and the theorists of the Frankfurt School viewed high culture as containing forces of resistance to capitalist modernity, as well as ideology. Later, British cultural studies would valorize resistant moments in media culture and audience interpretations and use of media artefacts, while the Frankfurt School tended, with some exceptions, to conceptualize mass culture as a homogeneous and potent form of ideological domination – a difference that would seriously divide the two traditions.

From the beginning, British cultural studies was highly political in nature and investigated the potentials for resistance in oppositional subcultures. After first valorizing the potential of working-class cultures, they next indicated how youth subcultures could resist the hegemonic forms of capitalist domination. Unlike the classical Frankfurt School (but similar to Herbert Marcuse), British cultural studies turned to youth cultures as providing potentially new forms of opposition and social change. Through studies of youth subcultures, British cultural studies demonstrated how culture came to constitute distinct forms of identity and group membership and appraised the oppositional potential of various youth subcultures (see Jefferson, 1976; Hebdige, 1979). Cultural studies came to focus on how subcultural groups resist dominant forms of culture and identity, creating their own style and identities. Individuals who conform to dominant dress and fashion codes, behaviour, and political ideologies thus produce their identities within mainstream groups, as members of specific social groupings (such as white, middle-class conservative Americans). Individuals who identify with subcultures, like punk culture, or black nationalist subcultures, look and act differently from those in the mainstream, and thus create oppositional identities, defining themselves against standard models.

However, British cultural studies, unlike the Frankfurt School, did not adequately engage modernist and avant-garde aesthetic movements, limiting its attentions by and large to products of media culture and 'the popular'. However, the Frankfurt School engagement with modernism and avant-garde art in many of its protean forms is arguably more productive than the ignoring of modernism and to some extent high culture as a whole by many within British cultural studies. It appears that in its anxiety to legitimate study of the popular and to engage the artefacts of media culture, British cultural studies turned away from so-called 'high' culture in favour of the popular, but such a turn sacrifices the possible insights into all forms of culture and replicates the bifurcation of the field of culture into a 'popular' and 'elite' (which merely inverts the positive/negative valorizations of the older high/low distinction). More importantly, it disconnects cultural studies from attempts to develop oppositional forms of culture of the sort associated with the 'historical avant-garde'. Avant-garde movements such as Expressionism, Surrealism, and Dada wanted to develop art that would revolutionize society, which would provide alternatives to hegemonic forms of culture.

British cultural studies – like the Frankfurt School – insists that culture must be studied within the social relations and system through which culture is produced and consumed, and that thus analysis of culture is intimately bound up with the study of society, politics, and economics. The key Gramscian concept of hegemony led British cultural studies to investigate how media culture articulates a set of dominant values, political ideologies, and cultural forms into a hegemonic project that incorporates individuals into a shared consensus, as individuals became integrated into the consumer society and political projects like Reaganism or Thatcherism (see Hall, 1988). This project is similar in many ways to that of the Frankfurt School, as are their metatheoretical perspectives that combine political economy, textual analysis, and study of audience reception within the framework of critical social theory.

British cultural studies and the Frankfurt School were both founded as fundamentally transdisciplinary enterprises that resisted established academic divisions of labour. Indeed, their boundary-crossing and critiques of the detrimental effects of abstracting culture from its socio-political context elicited hostility among those who were more disciplinary-oriented and who, for example, believed in the autonomy of culture and renounced sociological or political readings. Against such academic formalism and separatism, cultural studies insists that culture must be investigated within the social relations and system through which culture is produced and consumed, and that thus analysis of culture is intricately involved in the study of society, politics, and economics. Employing Gramsci's model of hegemony and counter-hegemony, it sought to analyze 'hegemonic', or ruling, social and cultural forces of domination and to seek 'counter-hegemonic' forces of resistance and struggle. The project was aimed at social transformation and attempted to specify forces of domination and resistance in order to aid the process of political struggle and emancipation from oppression and domination.

Some earlier authoritative presentations of British cultural studies stressed the importance of a transdisciplinary approach to the study of culture that analyzed its political economy, process of production and distribution, textual products, and reception by the audience – positions remarkably similar to the Frankfurt School. For instance, in his classical programmatic article, 'Encoding/Decoding', Stuart Hall began his analysis by using Marx's *Grundrisse* as a model to trace the articulations of 'a continuous circuit', encompassing 'production–distribution–consumption–production' (1980b: 128ff.). Hall concretizes this model with a focus on how media institutions produce meanings, how they circulate, and how audiences use or decode the texts to produce meaning.

In many versions of post-1980s cultural studies, however, there has been a turn to what might be called a postmodern problematic that emphasizes pleasure, consumption, and the individual construction of identities in terms of what McGuigan (1992) has called a 'cultural populism'. Media culture from this perspective produces material for identities, pleasures, and empowerment, and thus audiences constitute the 'popular' through their consumption of cultural products. During this phase – roughly from the mid-1980s to the present – cultural studies in Britain and North America turned from the socialist and revolutionary politics of the previous stages to postmodern forms of identity politics and less critical perspectives on media and consumer culture. Emphasis was placed more and more on the audience, consumption, and reception, and displaced engaging in production and distribution of texts and how texts were produced in media industries.

The forms of cultural studies developed from the late 1970s to the present, in contrast to the earlier stages, theorize a shift from the stage of state monopoly capitalism, or Fordism, rooted in mass production and consumption to a new regime of capital and social order, sometimes described as 'post-Fordism' (Harvey, 1989), or 'postmodernism' (Jameson, 1991), and characterizing a transnational and global capital that valorizes difference, multiplicity, eclecticism, populism, and intensified consumerism in a new information/entertainment society. From this perspective, the proliferating media culture, postmodern architecture, shopping malls, and the culture of the postmodern spectacle became the promoters and palaces of a new stage of technocapitalism, the latest stage of capital, encompassing a postmodern image and consumer culture (see Best and Kellner, 2001; Kellner, 2003).

Consequently, the turn to a postmodern cultural studies is a response to a new era of global capitalism. What is described as the 'new revisionism' (McGuigan, 1992) severs cultural studies from political economy and critical social theory. During the postmodern stage of cultural studies, there is a widespread tendency to decentre, or even ignore completely, economics, history, and politics in favour of emphasis on local pleasures, consumption, and the construction of hybrid identities from the material of the popular. This cultural populism replicates the turn in postmodern theory away from Marxism and its alleged reductionism, master narratives of liberation and domination, and historical teleology.

As argued in this chapter, there are many important anticipations of key positions of British cultural studies in cultural Marxism and a wide range of traditions and positions to draw upon for cultural studies today. Consequently, the project of cultural studies is significantly broader than that taught in some contemporary curricula that identifies cultural studies merely with the Birmingham School and their progeny. There are, however, many traditions and models of cultural studies, ranging from neo-Marxist models developed by Lukács, Gramsci, Bloch, and the Frankfurt School in the 1930s to feminist and psychoanalytic cultural studies to semiotic and post-structuralist perspectives (see Durham and Kellner, 2001; Kellner, 1995). In Britain and the United States, there is a long tradition of cultural studies that preceded the Birmingham School. And France, Germany, and other European countries have also produced rich traditions that provide resources for cultural studies throughout the world.

The major traditions of cultural studies combine – at their best – social theory, cultural critique, history, philosophical analysis, and specific political interventions, thus overcoming the standard academic division of labour by surmounting specialization arbitrarily produced by an artificial academic division of labour. Cultural studies thus operates with a transdisciplinary conception that draws on social theory, economics, politics, history, communication studies, literary and cultural theory, philosophy, and other theoretical discourses – an approach shared by the Frankfurt School, British cultural studies, and French postmodern theory. Transdisciplinary approaches to culture and society transgress borders between various academic disciplines. In regard to cultural studies, such approaches suggest that one should not stop at the border of a text, but should see how it fits into systems of textual production, and how various texts are thus part of systems of genres or types of production, and have an intertextual construction – as well as articulating discourses in a given socio-historical conjuncture.

Conclusion

To summarize, in retrospect, one can see the Frankfurt School work as articulation of a theory of the stage of state and monopoly capitalism that became dominant during the 1930s. This was an era of large organizations, theorized earlier by Austro-Marxist Rudolf Hilferding as 'organized capitalism' ([1910] 1981), in which the state and giant corporations managed the economy and in which individuals submitted to state and corporate control. This period is often described as 'Fordism' to designate the system of mass production and the homogenizing regime of capital that produced mass desires, tastes, and behaviour. It was thus an era of mass production and consumption characterized by uniformity and homogeneity of needs, thought, and behaviour producing a mass society and what the Frankfurt School described as 'the end of the individual'. No longer were individual thought and action the motor of social and cultural progress; instead giant organizations and institutions overpowered individuals. The era corresponds to the staid, conformist, and conservative world of corporate capitalism that was dominant in the 1950s with its organization men and women, its mass consumption, and its mass culture.

During this period, mass culture and communication were instrumental in generating the modes of thought and behaviour appropriate to a highly organized and massified social order. Thus, the Frankfurt School theory of the culture industry articulates a major historical shift to an era in which mass consumption and culture were indispensable to producing a consumer society based on homogeneous needs and desires for mass-produced products and a mass society based on social organization and homogeneity. It is culturally the era of highly controlled network radio and television, insipid top 40 pop music, glossy Hollywood films, national magazines, and other mass-produced cultural artefacts.

Of course, media culture was never as massified and homogeneous as in the Frankfurt School model and one could argue that the model was flawed even during its time of origin and influence and that other models were preferable, such as those of Walter Benjamin, Siegfried Kracauer (1995), Ernst Bloch (1986), and others of the Weimar generation and, later, British cultural studies. Yet the original Frankfurt School model of the culture industry did articulate the important social roles of media culture during a specific regime of capital and provided a model, still of use, of a highly commercial and technologically advanced culture that serves the needs of dominant corporate interests, plays a major role in ideological reproduction, and in enculturating individuals into the dominant system of needs, thought, and behaviour.

I have been arguing that there are many important anticipations of key positions of British cultural studies in the Frankfurt School, that they share many positions and dilemmas, and that a dialogue between these traditions is long overdue. I would also propose seeing the project of cultural studies as broader than that taught in the contemporary curricula and as encompassing a wide range of figures from various social locations and traditions. There are indeed many traditions and models of cultural studies, ranging from neo-Marxist models developed by Lukács, Gramsci, Bloch, and the Frankfurt School in the 1930s to feminist and psychoanalytic cultural studies to semiotic and poststructuralist perspectives. In Britain and the United States, there is a long tradition of cultural studies that preceded the Birmingham School.[2] And France, Germany, and other European countries have also produced rich traditions that provide resources for cultural studies throughout the world.

The major traditions of cultural studies combine – at their best – social theory, cultural critique, history, philosophical analysis, and specific political interventions, thus overcoming the standard academic division of labour by surmounting specialization arbitrarily produced by an artificial academic division of labour. Cultural studies thus operates with a transdisciplinary conception that draws on social theory, economics, politics, history, communication studies, literary and cultural theory, philosophy, and other theoretical discourses – an approach shared by the Frankfurt School, British cultural studies, and French postmodern theory. Transdisciplinary approaches to culture and society transgress borders between various academic disciplines.[3] In regard to cultural studies, such approaches suggest that one should not stop at the border of a text, but should see how it fits into systems of textual production, and how various texts are thus part of systems of genres or types of production, and have an intertextual construction – as well as articulating discourses in a given socio-historical conjuncture.

For instance, *Rambo* is a film that fits into the genre of war films and a specific cycle of return to Vietnam films, but also articulates anti-communist political discourses dominant in the Reagan era (see Kellner, 1995). It replicates the right-wing discourses concerning POWs left in Vietnam and the need to overcome the Vietnam syndrome (i.e. shame concerning the loss of the war and overcoming the reluctance to use US military power again). But it also fits into a cycle of masculinist hero films, anti-statist right-wing discourses, and the use of violence to resolve conflicts. The figure of Rambo himself became a 'global popular' which had a wide range of effects throughout the world. Interpreting the cinematic text of *Rambo* thus involves the use of film theory, textual analysis, social history, political analysis and ideology critique, effects analysis, and other modes of cultural criticism.

One should not, therefore, stop at the borders of the text or even its intertexuality, but should move from text to context, to the culture and society that constitute the text and in which it should be read and interpreted. Transdisciplinary approaches thus involve border crossings across disciplines from text to context, and thus from texts to culture and society. Raymond Williams was especially important for cultural studies because of his stress on borders and border crossings (1961; 1962; 1964). Like the Frankfurt School, he saw the interconnection between culture and communication, and their connections with the society in which they are produced, distributed, and consumed. Williams also saw how texts embodied the political conflicts and discourses within which they were embedded and reproduced.

Crossing borders inevitably pushes one to the boundaries and borders of class, gender, race, sexuality, and the other constituents that differentiate individuals from each other and through which people construct their identities. Thus, most forms of cultural studies, and most critical social theories, have engaged feminism and the various multicultural theories that focus on representations of gender, race, ethnicity, and sexuality, enriching their projects with theoretical and political substance derived from the new critical discourses that have emerged since the 1960s. Transdisciplinary cultural studies thus draw on a disparate range of discourses and fields to theorize the complexity and contradictions of the multiple effects of a vast range of cultural forms in our lives and, differentially, demonstrate how these forces serve as instruments of domination, but also offer resources for resistance and change. The Frankfurt School, I would argue, inaugurated such transdisciplinary approaches to cultural studies combining analysis of the production and political economy of culture, with textual analysis that contextualize cultural artefacts in their socio-historical milieu, with studies of audience reception and use of cultural texts.[4]

Yet there are serious flaws in the original programme of critical theory that requires a radical reconstruction of the classical model of the culture industries (Kellner, 1989; 1995). Overcoming the limitations of the classical model would include: more concrete and empirical analysis of the political economy of the media and the processes of the production of culture; more empirical and historical research into the construction of media industries and their interaction with other social institutions; more empirical studies of audience reception and media effects; more emphasis on the use of media culture as providing forces of resistance; and the incorporation of new cultural theories and methods into a reconstructed critical theory of culture and society. Cumulatively, such a reconstruction of the classical Frankfurt School project would update the critical theory of society and its activity of cultural criticism by incorporating contemporary developments in social and cultural theory into the enterprise of critical theory.

In addition, the Frankfurt School dichotomy between high culture and low culture is problematical and should be superseded by a more unified model that takes culture as a spectrum and applies similar critical methods to all cultural artefacts ranging from opera to popular music, from modernist literature to soap operas. In particular, the Frankfurt School model of a monolithic mass culture contrasted with an ideal of 'authentic art', which limits critical, subversive, and emancipatory moments to certain privileged artefacts of high culture, is highly problematic. The Frankfurt School position that all mass culture is ideological and homogenizing, having the effects of duping a passive mass of consumers, is also objectionable. Instead, one should see critical and ideological moments in the full range of culture, and not limit critical moments to high culture and identify all of low culture as ideological. One should also allow for the possibility that critical and subversive moments could be found in the artefacts of the cultural industries, as well as the canonized classics of high Modernist culture that the Frankfurt School seemed to privilege as the site of artistic opposition and emancipation.[5] One should also distinguish between the encoding and decoding of media artefacts, and recognize that an active audience often produces its own meanings and use for products of the cultural industries.

British cultural studies overcomes some of these limitations of the Frankfurt School by systematically rejecting high/low culture distinctions and taking seriously the artefacts of media culture. Likewise, they overcome the limitations of the Frankfurt School notion of a passive audience in their conceptions of an active audience that creates meanings and the popular. Yet it should be pointed out that Walter Benjamin – loosely affiliated with the Frankfurt School but not part of their inner circle – also took seriously media culture, saw its emancipatory potential, and posited the possibility of an active audience. For Benjamin (1969), the spectators of sports events were discriminating judges of athletic activity, able to criticize and analyze sports events. Benjamin postulated that the film audience can also become experts of criticism and dissect the meanings and ideologies of film. Yet I believe that we need to synthesize the concepts of the active and manipulated audience to grasp the full range of media effects, thus avoiding both cultural elitism and populism.

Indeed, it is precisely the critical focus on media culture from the perspectives of commodification, reification, technification, ideology, and domination developed by the Frankfurt School that provides a perspective useful as a corrective to more populist and uncritical approaches to media culture that surrender critical perspectives – as is evident in some current forms of British and North American cultural studies. In fact, the field of communications study was initially split into a division, described by Lazarsfeld (1941) in an issue edited by the Frankfurt School on mass communications, between the critical school associated with the Institute for Social Research and administrative research, which Lazarsfeld defined as research carried out within the parameters of established media and social institutions and that would provide material that was of use to these institutions – research with which Lazarsfeld himself would be identified. Hence, it was the Frankfurt School that inaugurated critical communications research and I am suggesting that a return to a reconstructed version of the original model would be useful for media and cultural studies today.

Although the Frankfurt School approach itself is partial and one-sided, it does provide tools to criticize the ideological forms of media culture and the ways that it provides ideologies that legitimize forms of oppression. Ideology critique is a fundamental constituent of cultural studies and the Frankfurt School is valuable for inaugurating systematic and sustained critiques of ideology within the cultural industries. It is especially useful in providing contextualizations of cultural criticism. Members of the group carried out their analysis within the framework of critical social theory, thus integrating cultural studies within the study of capitalist society and the ways that communications and culture were produced within this order and the roles and functions they assumed. Thus, the study of communication and culture became an important part of a theory of contemporary society, in which culture and communication were playing ever more significant roles, and the Frankfurt School continues to provide stimulating perspectives on the study of culture and society in the contemporary era.

Notes

1 For my general perspectives on the Frankfurt School, see Kellner (1984; 1989; 1995) and Bronner and Kellner (1989).
2 On earlier traditions of cultural studies in the USA, see Aronowitz (1993) and for Britain, see Davies (1995).
3 Articles in the 1983 *Journal of Communications* issue on *Ferment in the Field* (Vol. 33, No. 3 [Summer 1983]) noted a bifurcation of the field between a culturalist approach and more empirical approaches in the study of mass-mediated communications. The culturalist

approach was largely textual, centred on the analysis and criticism of texts as cultural artefacts, using methods primarily derived from the humanities. The methods of communications research, by contrast, employed more empirical methodologies, ranging from straight quantitative research, empirical studies of specific cases or domains, or historical research. Topics in this area included analysis of the political economy of the media, audience reception and study of media effects, media history, the interaction of media institutions with other domains of society and the like. See Kellner (1995) for analyses of how the Frankfurt School, British cultural studies, and French postmodern theory all overcome the bifurcation of the field of culture and communications into text- and humanities-based approaches opposed to empirical and social science-based enterprises. As I am arguing here, a transdisciplinary approach overcomes such bifurcation and delineates a richer and broader perspective for the study of culture and communications.

4   The contributions of the Frankfurt School to audience reception theory is often completely overlooked, but Walter Benjamin constantly undertook studies of how audiences use the materials of popular media and inaugurated a form of reception studies; see Benjamin (1969: 217ff.). Leo Löwenthal also carried out reception studies of literature, popular magazines, political demagogues, and other phenomena (1949; 1957; 1961). On Frankfurt experiments with studies of media effects, see Wiggershaus (1994: 441ff.).

5   There were, to be sure, some exceptions and qualifications to this 'classical' model: Adorno would occasionally note a critical or utopian moment within mass culture and the possibility of audience reception against the grain; see the examples in Kellner (1989). But although one can find moments that put in question the more bifurcated division between high and low culture and the model of mass culture as consisting of nothing except ideology and modes of manipulation which incorporate individuals into the existing society and culture, generally, the Frankfurt School model is overly reductive and monolithic, and thus needs radical reconstruction – which I have attempted to do in my work over the past two decades.

References

Adorno, T.W. (1941) 'On popular music', (with G. Simpson), *Studies in Philosophy and Social Science*, 9(1): 17–48.

Adorno, T.W. ([1932] 1978) 'On the social situation of music', *Telos* 35 (Spring): 129–65.

Adorno, T.W. (1982) 'On the fetish character of music and the regression of hearing', in A. Arato and E. Gebhardt (eds) *The Essential Frankfurt School Reader*. New York: Continuum, pp. 270–99.

Adorno, T.W. (1989) 'On jazz', in S. Bronner and D. Kellner (eds) *Critical Theory and Society: A Reader*. New York: Routledge, pp. 199–209.

Adorno, T.W. (1991) *The Culture Industry*. London: Routledge.

Adorno, T.W. (1994) *The Stars Down to Earth and Other Essays on the Irrational in Culture*. London: Routledge.

Adorno, T.W. et al. ([1950] 1969) *The Authoritarian Personality*. New York: Norton.

Agger, B. (1992) *Cultural Studies as Critical Theory*. London: The Falmer Press.

Arato, A. and Gebhardt. E, (eds) (1982) *The Essential Frankfurt School Reader*. New York: Continuum.

Aronowitz, S. (1993) *Roll Over Beethoven*. Hanover, New Hampshire: University Press of New England.

Benjamin, W. (1969) *Illuminations*. New York: Schocken Books.

Benjamin, W. (1999) 'The artist as producer', in W. Benjamin, *Collected Writings*, vol. 2. Cambridge, MA: Harvard University Press.

Benjamin, W. (2000) *The Arcades Project*. Cambridge, MA: Harvard University Press.

Best, S. and Kellner, D. (2001) *The Postmodern Adventure: Science Technology, and Cultural Studies at the Third Millennium*. New York and London: Guilford and Routledge.

Bloch, E. (1986) *The Principle of Hope*. Cambridge, MA: MIT Press.

Bronner, S.and Kellner, D. (eds) (1989) *Critical Theory and Society: A Reader*. New York: Routledge.

Buck-Morss, S. (1989) *The Dialectics of Seeing*. Cambridge, MA: MIT Press.

Calhoun, C. (ed.) (1992) *Habermas and the Public Sphere*. Cambridge, MA: MIT Press.

Cvetkovich, A. and Kellner, D. (1997) *Articulating the Global and the Local: Globalization and Cultural Studies*. Boulder, CO: Westview Press.

Dauks, I. (1995) *Cultural Studies, and after*. London and New York: Routledge.

Durham, M. G. and Kellner, D. (eds) (2001) *Media and Cultural Studies: Key Works*. Oxford: Blackwell.

Gitlin, T. (1972) 'Sixteen notes on television and the movement' in G. White and C. Newman, (eds) *Literature and Revolution*. New York: Holt, Rinehart and Winston.

Gitlin, T. (1980) *The Whole World Is Watching*. Berkeley, CA: University of California Press.

Gitlin, T. (1983) *Inside Prime Time*. New York: Pantheon.

Gitlin, T. (ed.) (1987) *Watching Television*. New York: Pantheon.

Gitlin, T. (2002) *Media Unlimited. How the Torrent of Images and Sounds Overwhelms Our Lives*. New York: Metropolitan Books.

Habermas, J. (1992) 'Further reflections on the public sphere', in Calhoun, C. (ed.) *Habermas and the Public Sphere*. Cambridge: The MIT Press. pp. 421–461.

Habermas, J. (1998) *Between Facts and Norms*. Cambridge, MA: MIT Press.

Hall, S. (1980a) 'Cultural studies and the Centre: some problematics and problems', in S. Hall et al. (eds) *Culture, Media, Language*. London: Hutchinson, pp. 15–47.

Hall, S. (1980b) 'Encoding/decoding', in S. Hall et al. (eds) *Culture, Media, Language*. London: Hutchinson, pp. 128–38.

Hall, S. (1988) *The Hard Road to Renewal*. London: Verso.

Hall, S. (1991) Lecture on globalization and ethnicity, University of Minnesota, videotape.

Hall, S. et al. (eds) (1980) *Culture, Media, Language*. London: Hutchinson.

Harvey, D. (1989) *The Condition of Postmodernity*. Oxford: Blackwell.

Hebdige, D. (1978) Subculture. The Meaning of Style, London: Methuen.

Hertog, H. (1941) 'On borrowed experience: an analysis of listening to daytime sketches', *Studies in Philosophy and Social Science*, 10(1): 65–95.

Hilferding, R. ([1910] 1981) *Finance Capital*. London: Routledge and Kegan Paul.

Horkheimer, M. and Adorno. T.W. (1972) *Dialectic of Enlightenment*. New York: Herder and Herder.

Jameson, F. Postmodernism, or The Cultural Logic of Late Capitalism, Durham, N.C.: Duke University Press.

Jay, M. (1973) *The Dialectical Imagination*. Boston: Little, Brown and Company.

Jefferson, T. (ed.) (1976) Resistance through Rituals, London: Hutchinson.

Kellner, D. (1989) *Critical Theory, Marxism, and Modernity*. Cambridge and Baltimore, MD: Polity and Johns Hopkins University Press.

Kellner, D. (1990) *Television and the Crisis of Democracy*. Boulder, CO: Westview Press.

Kellner, D. (1992) *The Persian Gulf TV War*. Boulder, CO: Westview Press.

Kellner, D. (1995) *Media Culture: Cultural Studies, Identity, and Politics between the Modern and the Postmodern*. London and New York: Routledge.

Kellner, D. (1997) 'Critical theory and British cultural studies: the missed articulation', in J. McGuigan (ed.) *Cultural Methodologies*. London: Sage, pp. 12–41.

Kellner, D. (2000) 'Habermas, the public sphere, and democracy: a critical intervention', in L. Hahn (ed.) *Perspectives on Habermas*. Chicago: Open Court Press.

Kellner, D. (2001) *Grand Theft 2000. Media Spectacle and a Stolen Election*. Lanham MD.: Rowman and Little field.

Kellner, D. (2003a) *Media Spectacle*. London and New York: Routledge.

Kellner, D. (2003b) *From September 11 to Terror War: The Dangers of the Bush Legacy*. Lanham, MD.: Rowman and Little field.

Kracauer, S. (1995) *The Mass Ornament*. Cambridge, MA: Harvard University Press.

Lazarsfeld, P. (1941) 'Administrative and critical communications research', *Studies in Philosophy and Social Science*, 9(1): 2–16.

Löwenthal, L. (1957) *Literature and the Image of Man*. Boston: Beacon Press.

Löwenthal, L. (1961) *Literature, Popular Culture and Society*. Englewood Cliffs, NJ: Prentice-Hall.

Löwenthal, L. (with Norbert Guttermann) (1949) *Prophets of Deceit*. New York: Harper.

Marcuse, H. (1941) 'Some social implications of modern technology', *Studies in Philosophy and Social Science*, 9(1): 414–39.

Marcuse, H. (1955) *Eros and Civilization*. Boston: Beacon Press.

Marcuse, H. (1964) *One-Dimensional Man*. Boston: Beacon Press.

McGuigan, J. (1992) *Cultural Populism*. London and New York: Routledge.

Rosenberg, B. and Manning White, D. (eds) (1957) *Mass Culture*. Glencoe, IL: The Free Press.

Silberman, M. (2000) *Bertolt Brecht on Film and Radio*. London: Metheun.

Steinert, H. (2003) *Culture Industry*. Cambridge: Polity Press.

Wiggershaus, R. (1994) *The Frankfurt School*. Cambridge: Polity Press.

Williams, R. (1961) *The Long Revolution*. London: Chatto and Windus.

Williams, R. (1962) *Communications*. London: Penguin.

Williams, R. (1974) *Television, Technology and Cultural Forum*. London: Fantana.

Stuart Hall and the Birmingham School

CHAPTER FOUR

Chris Rojek

British Cultural Studies commenced in its contemporary form in the late 1950s. Its roots were in secondary Schools, Adult Education and Extra Mural departments of Universities. The first wave of significant figures to write about working class culture seriously in the postwar period were Raymond Williams, Edward Thompson and Richard Hoggart.[1] They wrote against the grain of the core curriculum enshrined in the established Universities with its pronounced emphasis on the classical canon and 'Great Traditions' of thought. To some extent, their project consisted in validating working class culture as a subject for study in the Academy. Williams in *Culture & Society* (1958) and *The Long Revolution* (1961) and Thompson (1963) in *The Making of the English Working Class* operated in a Left wing milieu that deplored the intellectual narrowness of British academic life and sought to demonstrate the richness of working class culture. Hoggart's (1958) work was less obviously indebted to the party political traditions of the organized Left. Nonetheless, he also shared a discontent with the confined character of British academic life and a commitment to raise the profile of working class culture in the Academy. All three writers represented an approach that Hall (1980) later categorized as *culturalism*, by which he meant the attempt to understand the whole way of life of the people in terms of the experience of heritage, language and class consciousness. He contrasted this with the continental tradition of *structuralism*. The latter seeks to contextualize personal and popular experience in the framework of culture, class and historical materialism. A valid interpretation of Hall's work in the 70s, is that he sought to marry the best elements of culturalism with structuralism to produce a new synthesis.

Hoggart's role in developing Cultural Studies was, in fact, pivotal and has not been given its due in most secondary accounts (Gibson and Hartley 1998). To begin with the popular success of his book-cum-memoir of working class life in the West Riding of Yorkshire, *The Uses of Literacy* (1958), provided the archetypal case for taking working class culture seriously. Among the 'angry young man' generation of 1950s Britain it was accepted as an inspirational 'sociological' contribution. Of equal, and arguably greater cultural significance was Hoggart's achievement in persuading the University of Birmingham to accept a bequest from the publisher of Penguin books, Sir Allen Lane, to establish the Centre for Contemporary Cultural Studies on campus. Against the elitism of Oxbridge, it created a bridgehead in the Academy for the rigorous study of class and culture. Hoggart himself was the founding Director of the Centre. In 1964, among his first acts in this capacity was to recruit Stuart Hall from Chelsea College, University of London to participate in course development and teaching.

The Birmingham Centre was an unprecedented experiment in British higher education. Hall (2000) recalls it as a time of immense excitement in his intellectual career. He had the lion's share of curriculum development and the organization of pedagogy. Hoggart's (1970) original vision for the Centre was of an organisation devoted to a tripartite project of teaching and research: historical–philosophical, sociological and literary–critical, of which the most pronounced element was intended to be the latter. But under Hall's leadership from the late 1960s onwards, academic activities became more theoretical and more political.

The presiding spirit of pedagogy and research cultivated in the Centre was based in collaboration rather than hierarchy. The conventional division between lecturer and student was relaxed. Although the traditional supervisory role between academic and student was retained, the *sub-group* emerged as the nucleus of research and debate. Sub-groups were thematically organized around key subjects in theory and culture. Since cultural studies was a new area, staff and students at the Centre had the exhilarating sense of making up the curriculum as they went along. At its height, the Centre never employed more than three full-time staff. For most of Hall's time in Birmingham the staff complement was two. The mould-breaking work being done in Birmingham during the 60s and 70s and the sense of operating in an embattled environment created by the condescension and hostility of several established academics and University administrators on campus, combined to create unusually high levels of commitment to the Birmingham 'project'.

The latter is often seen as an exclusively Marxist venture, but it was in fact a coat of many colours. Intellectual labour in the Centre was obviously located on the Left. Hall and his associates adopted the orthodox New Left position in regarding Britain as a class dominated society. As the New Right emerged in the mid 70s the drift into 'the law and order society' became a defining theme of Bimingham intellectual labour. Capitalism was unquestionably the system which Hall and his associates criticized and against which they advocated a socialist political, economic and cultural alternative. In as much as this is so the Centre may be regarded as operationalizing in pedagogy and research many aspects of the broad New Left perspective embodied in the *New Left Review,* of which Hall had been editor between 1960–61. Chief among them were a disdain for the limpid insularity of British life, the espousal of the value of independent thought, sensitivity to technological change and globalism and a commitment to the socialist transformation of society.

Notwithstanding this, the Birmingham project was always more complex than a narrow identification with the traditional goals of New Left Marxism. In addition to Marxism, ideas from feminism, structuralism, post-structuralism and semiotics were thrown into the Birmingham melting pot. Hall's attitude to Marxism was anti-dogmatic. Later, in the 'New Times' thesis he was critical of those on the Left who assign a doctrinal status to Marxism. Elsewhere, he (1986) declared himself to be in favour of 'Marxism without guarantees'. By this he appears to mean a commitment to the methodology of historical materialism, an interest in the Left wing transformation of society but a retreat from the premise that class struggle is the engine of history.

Hall always emphasized the necessity of regarding intellectual labour as a political activity. He adopted Gramsci's concept of the *organic intellectual* as a role model. The organic intellectual is pointedly contrasted with 'traditional intellectuals' who align themselves with values of 'objectivity', 'detachment' and 'value freedom'. Instead the organic intellectual operates with the latest cutting edge ideas in society and engages with the oppressed. The Birmingham School approach constantly returns to the theme of demystifying ideology. The end of intellectual labour is to advance the power of the down-trodden. The organic intellectual is presented as one of the main switchboards between knowledge, power and socialist transformation.

In the high moment of the Birmingham Centre, the oppressed were theorized in terms of the working class. Working class resistance is a prominent theme in Birmingham work on schooling, youth culture and policing. However, in the final years of Hall's period in Birmingham questions of women's oppression and racism become more prominent. The concern with oppression is gradually expressed as a critique of identity in Western epistemology. The notion of centred, bounded, pure identity gradually gives way to new concepts of hybridity and hyphenated-identity (Hall 1999). These concepts became most fully elaborated in Hall's later writings on the politics of identity, 'new' ethnicity and multi-culturalism (Hall 1991a; 1991b; 1995; 1997).

With the benefit of hindsight it is evident that intellectual labour in the Centre was finally about challenging the central ideologically impregnated epistemological categories through which identity, association and practice are comprehended and practised under capitalism. This becomes appreciably more emphatic after Hall's departure to become Professor of Sociology at the Open University in 1979. His (1989a; 1993a; 1996) work on identity and post-colonialism draws on Birmingham critiques of policing, the authoritarian state and the law and order society. However, it also incorporated new themes from Foucault, Lacan, Derrida and particularly, Laclau and Mouffe (1985) to mount a comprehensive challenge to Western epistemology, especially the notion of pure, stable, integrated identity. The new emphasis on the proposition that culture is structured like a language in Hall's later writings suggests that 'the cultural turn' accomplished in the Birmingham years was succeeded, after the mid 80s, by 'the linguistic turn', in which post-structuralism rather awkwardly sits side by side with Marxism in Hall's thought.

The Birmingham Golden Age

Hall was employed in the Centre between 1964 and 1979. Arguably, this was the Golden Age of the Centre. The vitality and significance of the institution can be gauged by considering some of the students who were enrolled there and who have since gone on to achieve distinguished academic careers: Charlotte Brundson, Iain Chambers, Phil Cohen, Hazel Corby Chas Critcher, Paul Gilroy, Larry Grossberg, Dick Hebdidge, Angela MacRobbie, David Morley, Frank Mort, Paul Willis and Janice Winship. Hall favoured a ferment of intellectual exchange, drawing freely on concepts and traditions from continental Europe that had hitherto been treated as alien by the insular British establishment. He (1980) contrasted the insularity of British culturalism with *structuralism*, by which he meant a more theoretically sophisticated approach to culture. In Birmingham, the mettle of existentialism, semiotics, psychoanalysis and phenomenology was debated and tested in collective research, seminars, symposia and PhD work. But Marxism rapidly emerged as the paramount influence. In the 1970s the most important publications for which the Centre is now remembered , namely *On Ideology* (Hall *et al* 1978a), *Policing the Crisis* (Hall *et al* 1978b) and *The Empire Strikes Back* (1980), can be interpreted as operating in a theoretical framework that attempted to fuse certain aspects of Althusserian structuralism with Gramscianism. Most significantly, Althusser's theory of ideology and the functions of the state are inserted with Gramsci's analysis of 'power blocs', 'conjunctures' and of course, hegemony. Interestingly there is relatively little textual reference to Marx's work in the output of the Birmingham School. Although, Hall (1973) himself contributed an important, and oddly neglected, close textual reading of the 'Introduction' to Marx's *Grundrisse* which purported to identify a cultural basis in Marx's method of historical materialism.

It would be wrong to infer that intellectual labour in Birmingham during the golden age sought to *replace* culturalism with structuralism. Hall (1980) was critical of what he took to be the 'naïve humanism' of British culturalism. But he (1993a) was also fulsome in his praise for the work of Williams and Thompson. Although the influence of Gramsci and Althusser is pronounced in what is arguably the single most important work produced by the Centre, *Policing The Crisis* (1978b), the culturalist emphasis on class traditions and class struggle is also unmistakable.

Using Althusser's concept of 'interpellation' the Centre examined how subjects are 'hailed' or 'called into being' in capitalist society. The construction of subjectivity through schooling, the media, policing, medicine and the law is held to be crucial because they tie individuals into historically specific forms of subjectivity. Although the Frankfurt School never figured very prominently in Birmingham discussions, it is clear that Hall and his colleagues share the Frankfurt premise that the liberal consensus that the individual is free under capitalism is actually an expression of ideological domination. At the height of Althusser's influence on Birmingham, Hall (1985) claimed that there is no space 'outside' or 'beyond' ideology in capitalist society.

But one senses that Hall was always uncomfortable with the structural–functionalist strain in Althusser's thought. Instead he favoured a more flexible approach which highlighted the contradictions in the capitalist power bloc and gave due to culture as a key site of resistance. Gramsci's concept of 'hegemony' was enlisted to elucidate the idea of a cultural and economic horizon in the ordering of subjectivity.

In many ways the Centre reflects typical 60s themes of liberation and anti-authoritarianism. It sought to use knowledge to emancipate people from cultural and economic subjection by elucidating the historical roots and structures of normative coercion that order subjectivity. At the same time, it was critical of expressive, liberationist politics designed to produce a totally permissive society. Such a construct was utterly alien to Birmingham thinking on power blocs, hegemony and articulation. The agenda in Birmingham during the golden years of the Centre was to use knowledge as one instrument in liberating the working class from the shackles of domination.

While the central dynamic in this process is the accumulation of historical and cultural knowledge designed to reveal how ideology and hegemony order subjects, it would be wrong to minimize the romantic commitment to achieving a fundamental qualitative change in the character of human relations. Hall (1989b) himself emphasized the importance of the 'social imaginary' in the labour of the organic intellectual. By this he meant a space between socialism and social democracy in which issues relating to the quality and purpose of life would be examined and re-defined. However, as befits the commitment of organic intellectuals, Hall always insisted that the purpose of intellectual labour is political. The aim is to challenge the central institutions of capitalist normative coercion and elicit socialist transformation. In the 1990s Hall (1991a; 1991b) praised decentralized politics as practised, for example, by Ken Livingstone during the hay-day of the Greater London Council and acknowledged the role of social movements in challenging normative coercion. A distinctive feature of Hall's approach is the centrality it assigns to the state as the decisive institution in normative coercion. This leads to a characteristic weakness in Hall's analysis of culture, which is to read history and culture through the lens of transformations in the state and concomitant class struggles of resistance. On the whole the corporation is an underdeveloped and arguably, absent agent in Birmingham analysis. Moreover, despite the interest shown in globalization in his later writings, for most of the Birmingham years Hall's empirical interest are resolutely focused on Britain and black colonial diaspora. I shall return to take up these points in more detail later.

Encoding/Decoding

Hall resisted the tendency to revive what he regarded to be the naïve humanism of the native culturalist tradition by championing the more 'scientific' approach of Althusser and Gramsci. One early expression of this is the encoding–decoding model of media relations (Hall 1973; 1993c). Hall's application of Althusser led him to postulate ideology as permanently striving to colonize language. As he (1993c: 263–4) put it:

> I use ideology as that which cuts into the infinite semisosis of Language. Language is pure textuality, but ideology wants to make a particular meaning … it's the point where power cuts into discourse, where power overcuts knowledge and discourse; at that point you get a cut, a stoppage, you get a suture, you get an over-determination. The meaning constructed by that cut into language is never permanent, because the next sentence will take it back, will open the semiosis again. And it can't fix it, but ideology is an attempt to fix it.

This recognition of the 'suture' or the 'cut' in ideology is a product of Hall's engagement with the linguistic philosophy of Volosinov (1973) and the Marxist revisionism of Laclau and Mouffe (1985). His later work returns regularly to the argument that in 'New Times' identity is permanently 'under erasure'. This new emphasis on the contingency of identity suggests a more conditional reading of the influence of ideology. For if identity is permanently 'under erasure' the notion of the ideological determination of subjectivity cannot be tenable.

This relaxation in the concept of ideological work is not evident in the writings produced in the Birmingham golden age. For example, the encoding–decoding was a preliminary attempt to explore the colonization of ideology in the sphere of an increasingly significant feature of public information and opinion in societies based around systems of mass communication: the media message (Hall 1973). The origins of the model were partly polemical, in as much as it was intended to critique the dominant behaviourist model of mass communications research of the day, which Hall took to be enshrined in the Centre of Mass Communications Research at the University of Leicester.[2] Hall was concerned to establish the case that reception isn't a transparent and open-ended link in the communication chain. He contended that media messages are embedded with presuppositions and unreflected beliefs that pre-dispose audiences to follow 'preferred readings' of media messages. Hall sought to replace the idea that the media message is a reflection of reality and replace it with the proposition that the media message *inflects* popular consciousness in ideologi-cally approved directions. The media 'effect' is theorized as putting a particular gloss on reality that creates a virtuous circle between constructed messages and preferred readings. This is the meaning attributed to 'encoding' and it implicates broadcasters as being ideologically implicated in reproducing a particular version of social reality.

Hall is also concerned to challenge the behaviourist model of the audience as a blank subject and to replace it with the notion of 'the active audience'. The work was pub-lished at a moment when Harold Garfinkel's (1967) ethnomethodological approach was being widely debated by sociologist's. Garfinkel's contention that mainstream social sci-ence produced a model of man as a 'cultural dope' may have influenced Hall. Be that as it may, the concept of decoding is designed to highlight the capacity of the audience to actively treat media messages as alienable from their life experience and conditions of life and hence, subject them to critical or oppositional readings.

The encoding/decoding model was one of the first productions from the Birmingham Centre to create national and international interest. It was widely, and mistakenly seen as a contribution to mass communications research *per se*. In fact it expressed Hall's deeper concern with elucidating how ideology 'cuts' into language and, through this interpellates subjectivity. Hall maintained that the central agent in the process of both ordering subjectivity and achieving socialist transformation is the state. Interestingly, Birmingham analysis was almost exclusively confined to the case of the British state. Although the significance of globalization receives proper atten-tion in the 'New Times' thesis in the 80s, comparative analysis was never very promi-nent in the considerations of the Centre during its hay-day.

The Representative-Interventionist State

In an important paper (1984) Hall submits that the shift from the *laissez faire* to the representative-interventionist state in Britain started in the 1880s. Indeed the period between the 1880s and 1920s is regarded as foundational in establishing the paramount institutions of normative coercion and milieu of civil society in twentieth century Britain. The period is marked by increasing state instrumentality in ordering subjectivity through its involvement with schooling, health, the regulation of medical practice, economic policy and cultural strategy. The function of the state became to engineer a 'complex unity' of hegemony through which subjective rights and freedom are automatically and unquestionably identified with the National/Empire interest.

The rise of the representative-interventionist state derived from the emergence of a new (Liberal and later the Labour Party) 'reforming' power bloc intent on winning consent from a significant section of the working class. It was accomplished through a shifting 'war of positions' on constitutional reform, welfare rights, redistributive taxation and trade union rights. This manoeuvring itself reflected the declining profitability of the British economy in relation to the new emerging economies of Germany and the USA. However, Hall is careful to avoid any imputation that his thesis rests upon economic reductionsm. Much of his work in the 70s can be interpreted as an attack on 'vulgar Marxism', i.e., the proposition that the economic substructure finally determines the cultural and political superstructure. Gramsci's concept of hegemony appealed to Hall because it allowed for contradictions and a notion of mobile balance of power struggles in normative regulation. Indeed, the shift towards the representative-interventionist state is explained primarily in terms of a shifting war of manoeuvre between shifting cultural and political alliances, compacts and concessions.

The erosion of the lassiez-faire state is investigated with recourse to several 'fissures' arising from working class consciousness and resistance. The spread of trade unionism from the so-called 'aristocracy of labour' to unskilled and semi-skilled workers, the formation of the Labour Party and the readiness of the Liberal Party to envisage alliances with Labour weakened the hegemony of laissez-faire conservatism. By the end of the 1920s, the rudiments of a two party constitutionalism, founded upon universal suffrage, the primary institutions of corporatist bargaining and a system of public welfare provision were in place. The ideology of collectivism was ascendant over market liberalism, and the elements of the new social order and the consensus politics of social democracy were cemented.

The postwar settlement produced by the Attlee government in 1945 harnessed all of these forces into a new 'complex unity' that formed the context of hegemonic struggle from the Churchill government of the 50s to the emergence of Thatcherism and Blairism. The 1945 Labour government founded the welfare state and, through nationalization, the principle of direct state ownership and control of key industries. They elaborated a system of corporatist control involving a partnership between business, labour and the state. However, the durability of this complex unity was tested during the consumer boom of the 1950s and 60s by Britain's declining competitiveness viz-a-viz leading European economies and, of course, America and Japan. The progressive loss of Empire and wage inflation at home compounded the problems. By the late 1960s, a profound crisis in hegemony is evident in British cultural, political and economic life. Hall regards it as the beginning of the drift towards the law and order society governed by an authoritarian state which reaches fruition with Thatcherism.

In *Policing The Crisis* (1978b) the roots and history of the move from the representative interventionist state organized around consensus to the authoritarian state organized around fiat is divided into four distinct stages:

Postwar consensus (1945–61). In this period the corporatist solution is elaborated. The commitment to the welfare state, a mixed economy and identification with the American ('free') side in the Cold War is established. Concessions were made to organized labour in the form of a commitment to full employment and the welfare state. Keynesianism supported a high-wage, mass production economy that delivered economic growth but at a more modest rate than Britain's European rivals. Cultural relations became influenced by the rise of 'the affluent worker', the emergence of substantial financial power in youth culture and the growth of multi-ethnicity through positive migration policies, especially with respect to the Afro-Caribbean, India and Pakistan. In 1960 a major balance of payments crisis exposed the structural vulnerability of the British economy.

The hegemony of social democracy (1961–64). This was a transitional period in the history of the representative-interventionist state. The 'you've never had it so good' of the long 50s, consumer boom, was over. It was replaced by a social democratic variant of representative-interventionist state hegemony that appealed more to individualism and the national interest. The British were urged to look to their immemorial reserves of decency, common sense, moderation and patience. The corporatist model of management was reinforced. The state adopted the outward role of the neutral, honest broker between business and labour. Modernization, especially in the area of technology, was expounded as the key to the nation's future. At the cultural level the start of permissive society was beginning to be evident with the rise of 'pop' culture, the movement of newly affluent workers from the inner city to suburbia, conspicuous consumption and the politics of sexual liberation. However, at the economic level entrenched balance of payments problems and the run on sterling limited the state's power to modernize. When the seamen struck for higher pay, the government presented the dispute as an assault on 'the national interest'. The tactic was successful in turning the public against the seamen, but it fatally undermined the credibility of the Labour Party to present itself as an 'historic bloc' representing a qualitative transformation in the management of the nation.

The descent into dissensus (1964–70). Social democracy had produced a measure of liberalization in British life, symbolized by homosexual law reform, abortion, comprehensive education, the relaxation of drug licensing and the retreat from Sunday Observance. However, by the 1960s a moral backlash against the values of 'the permissive society' was underway. Student protests and sit-ins during the late 1960s produced a moral panic about youth and increasing worries about crime and disorder were voiced. The counter-culture reinforced this by attacking the 'permissive' order as based upon repressive desublimation and male power. Towards the end of the period the emergence of sectarian violence in Northern Ireland seemed to signal the precarious nature of national integration. Enoch Powell's predictions of racial warfare on the mainland between white and black immigrant groups contributed to the destabilization of the country. At the industrial level, wage militancy from the manual working class pointed to the re-emergence of class tensions.

The drift towards the 'law and order' society (1970–78). The surprise election of the Heath Conservative government in 1970 was based on a ticket of restoring national unity and enhancing economic competitiveness. The national interest was defined against 'extremists' and recourse was made to the law to protect 'universal' civil liberties. The Industrial Relations Act of 1971 restricted workers' rights and introduced the Industrial Relations Court to manage the 'rational' reform of labour. The commitment to interventionism was off-set by a controlled return to laissez fair principles, in which 'lame duck' companies were left to fend for themselves. Laws against civil disobedience were introduced to act as 'deterrents' to demonstrators, squatters and student activists. The police regrouped to focus intensively on 'dangerous', 'crimogenic' areas. This involved heightened policing of ethnic communities, presumed to be the main source of violent crime, including 'mugging'. The Emergency Powers Act of 1971 was hastily introduced to halt the increasing civil unrest in Ulster. What could no longer be won by *consent* was replaced by *fiat*.

1972 is 'the moment of the mugger', the point at which anti-permissive opinion recognizes an emphatic symbol of the degradation of British life. *Policing the Crisis* (1978b) demonstrates how media amplification exaggerated the severity of violent crime and further legitimated the move towards a more authoritarian state. This produced successive waves of industrial unrest between 1972 and 74, which produced an apparent U turn in government policy. Following the 1972 Budget a new Industry Bill was passed injecting huge sums of public money into industry and unprecedented powers for the state to produce a 'healthy' climate for growth.

A statutory incomes policy was introduced to control wage militancy and an attempt was made to revive the tripartite system of corporatism that had operated during the years of consensus. However, state policy was contradictory. On one side they sought to encourage public investment and 'rational' co-operation and dialogue; on the other, they created unrest by strict wage and price regulation. The state dealt with the second miner's strike in 1974, by the imposition of fuel-saving restrictions that led to the damaging three day week. Heath called a snap election in the same year on the issue of 'Who governs the country?' The defeat of the Conservatives sowed the seeds for more authoritarian solutions in the Party which culminated in the election of Margaret Thatcher. The victorious Labour government struggled to reintroduce consensus around the 'Social Contract', which promised public investment in return for agreed wage and price restraint. Despite achieving early success, the measure disintegrated ending in the fiasco of 'the winter of discontent' in which a barrage of strikes in the public sector left refuse uncollected and the dead unburied. This symbolized the failure of consensus politics organized around corporatism and seemed to legitimate a more authoritarian solution, which was duly delivered in the Thatcher adventure.

The political and cultural history of Britain in the 20th century is usually conveyed in progressive terms as the decentralization of power to the working class and, through this, the extension of civil rights. Hall's thesis stands this history on its head by holding that decentralization and the extension of civil rights produced new opportunities for co-opting 'free' citizens in the service of capitalism as well as decentralizing power 'below'. The representative-interventionist state was never interested in achieving anything greater than tokenistic integration of the working class and ethnic minorities in civil society. The analysis of this process is most elaborately presented in *Policing The Crisis* (Hall *et al* 1978b). In this book, arguably the most fully accomplished in the Birmingham *oeuvre,* the interplay between the history of British capitalism and the ordering of subjectivity is elucidated with great cogency. The book, which was published before the collapse of the Callaghan Labour government, accurately predicted a drastic swing to the authoritarian, centrist state, which used the police and the law to roll back permissive society, the welfare state and accomplish the 'modernization' of industrial relations through the massive deregulation of the market.

Hall's (1988) attacks on what he called, 'authoritarian populism' in the 80s and 90s reached a wide audience and it was at this time that he established himself unequivocally as the leading black public intellectual in Britain. His articles in *Marxism Today,* his numerous media broadcasts and his public lectures were extremely forceful, courageous and offered a massive resource of hope for the Left as they witnessed Thatcher triumph over three successive elections.

However, they were written after Hall left Birmingham to become Professor of Sociology at the Open University. Here he launched a series of course books and handbooks that disseminated the Birmingham approach to a much wider audience. This was also the period in which the internationalization of the Centre's theory and practice occurred, through the migration of a Birmingham intelligentsia outside the UK. For example, Larry Grossberg returned to American academic life where he became an influential advocate of the Birmingham project. Dick Hebdige, one of the most imaginative researchers in the Birmingham circle, followed him to California. Tony Bennett migrated to Australia where he set about conjoining the Birmingham project with certain aspects of Foucault's work.[3] Gradually, the Birmingham Centre became recognized as an important catalyst in what came to be known as 'the cultural turn' in social science, in which discursive, textual and post-identity thinking become more pronounced and economic reductionism eschewed.

By the same token, Hall achieved international recognition as a significant cultural theorist. At the same time, Birmingham influences were permeating British sociology and media and communications studies through the appointment of a number of Birmingham post-graduates to University lectureships. It would be rash to submit that the result was a new hegemony in these fields integrated around the 'complex unity' of Birmingham theory and practice. Even so, the period since the early 80s has been marked by the incorporation of Birmingham methodology and theory into the core curriculum of sociology, media and communications study and, of course, Cultural Studies. As a result Hall and his associates experienced the relatively unusual but, one imagines, deeply satisfying experience of finding their own ideas and practices moving from the margins of academic life to the core curriculum.

Critical Evaluation

The work conducted in the Birmingham Centre between the mid-1960s and 1979 was extremely productive in raising the position of working class culture in academic study. But there were important structural weaknesses with the enterprise. To begin with, despite the emphasis on widening access and stimulating the widest possible debate, the Centre typically functioned with an elusive and forbidding lexicon. Key concepts like 'hegemony', 'conjunction' and 'articulation' are often used in contradictory, not to say, incomprehensible ways. McGuigan (1992: 131) noted quite early on that Hall's analysis of the encoding and decoding process was 'flexible almost to the point of incoherence'. Wood (1998: 407) followed suit by arguing that slippage in the meaning of concepts dogs Hall's work. By way of support he lists five different meanings of the concept of articulation in Hall's writings:

> The 'ensemble of relations' which constitute 'society'. The 'discursive procedures' that transform ideology into culture or combine determinate ideologies together. The 'social force' that 'makes' subjective conceptions of the world. The 'many autonomous' parts of civil society that elicit hegemony. The 'different social practices' and 'range' of political discourses transformed into the operation of 'rule and domination'.

Anti-essentialism is perhaps the principal motif in Hall's work (Rojek 2003). He refuses to be contained by any intellectual tradition at either the levels of methodology or theory. The result is a strong tendency towards eclecticism and arguably an over-readiness to absorb new ideas. Terry Eagleton's (1996) comment that Hall frequently confuses being *'au fait'* with being *'a la mode'* is a valid critical insight, not only into Hall's work, but the entire Birmingham project.

Feminists were also highly critical of the Birmingham 'golden age'. The Women's Studies Group (1978: 11) in the Centre denounced the atmosphere of 'masculine domination of both intellectual work and the environment in which it was being carried out'. Admittedly, it is difficult to know what a known supporter of women's liberation like Hall, could have done to respond to this criticism. If he took remedial action it would tacitly admit that an atmosphere of male domination prevailed in the Centre. If he did nothing, it would confirm the feminist case. Damned if he did and damned if he didn't, Hall felt extremely discomfited. His early work is always implicitly pro-feminist and the value of feminism is explicitly acknowledged in his writings after 1979. However, the attribution of masculine domination was damaging for an anti-essentialist like Hall, whose socialism was moreover, predicated n the premise of increasing access and social inclusion.

Hall's approach came under fire from another flank within the Centre. The ethnographic work conducted by Paul Willis (1977; 1978) on 'the lads' in a West Midlands school and 'biker' and 'hippie' cultures in the same region, used notions of embodiment and emplacement which tacitly challenged Hall's stress on ideology and interpellation. Willis argued that working class actors are above all embodied and emplaced in concrete social settings which they negotiate with what he (2001: 35) later called 'sensuous knowing'. Sensuous knowing invalidates normative coercion by creating subterranean anti-structures of behaviour, Willis (1978) calls them 'profane cultures', in which normative order is challenged. Through 'the laff', 'the piss take', 'the put on' and swearing Willis's 'lads' actively created personal space and narratives of belonging in ideologically impregnated culture. This recognition is evident in Hall's collection on the use of ritual in class resistance (Hall and Jefferson 1976). However he does not assign the same level of creative opening in culture as Willis's concept of profane culture. In Hall's later writings, as we have suggested above, ideological 'closure' is relaxed, but the means through which this is accomplished is by adopting a linguistic model of culture, rather than a concrete analysis of social settings.

The intellectual labour conducted at the Centre genuinely attempted to be open and synthetic, so that connections were made between feminism, semiotics, structuralism, post-structuralism and Marxism in theoretically imaginative and productive ways. If the intense attempt to come to terms with working class culture in class dominated society sometimes resulted in obscurantist language and theoretical arguments, it also finally put paid to the elitist ideas that the only culture worth studying is high culture. The Birmingham tradition placed working class culture at the centre of Cultural Studies. Further, it demonstrated the adaptability of this culture in waging a shifting war of position and manoeuvre with the dominant class. Despite the serious problems of slippage and anti-essentialism, the accomplishments of the Centre and Hall's writings on culture are seminal in the history of Cultural Studies.

Notes

1   In some ways they were reacting to the elitist views on civilization expressed by writers like TS Eliot and FR Leavis. The emphasis on culture was partly designed to break the mould between elite power and the concept of civilization as the best or highest expressions of intellectual, artistic and scientific labour. It reflected an interest in working class cultures and the quotidian in everyday life, which was anathema to elitist views.

2   Hall can be legitimately criticized for caricaturing the position of James Halloran and his circle in Leicester. The latter were perfectly well aware of the political dimension of mass communications. But they were committed to an ideal of value neutrality that Hall had no truck with. For Hall, the labour of the 'organic intellectual' is always a matter of using knowledge in the project of emancipation. He held a politicized view of intellectual labour which queried the value of the Leicester position on *a priori* grounds.

3   Bennett's work on inter-disciplinarity at Griffith University in Queensland and his national role in widening access to higher education in Australia was important. After many years on the Gold Coast he returned in the late 90s to replace Hall as Head of Sociology in the Open University.

References

Centre for Contemporary *The Empire Strikes Back*, London: Cultural Studies (1982) Hutchinson
Eagleton, T. (1996) 'The hippest', *London Review of Books*, March pp 3–6
Garfinkel, H. (1967) *Studies in Ethnomethodology*, Englewood Cliffs, Prentice Hall

Gibson, M. and Hartley, J. (1998) 'Forty Years of Cultural Studies: and interview with Richard Hoggart,' *International Journal of Cultural Studies,* 1:1, 11–24

Hall, S. (1973) 'Encoding and decoding in the television discourse', Stencilled Occasional Paper, Birmingham Centre for Contemporary Cultural Studies

Hall, S. (1980) 'Cultural Studies: Two Paradigms', *Media, Culture & Society, 2:* 57–72

Hall, S. (1985) 'Signification, representation, ideology: Althusser and the post-structuralist debates', *Critical Studies in Mass Communication,* 2:2, 115–24

Hall,S. (1984) 'The rise of the representative/interventionist state, 18802-1920s', (in) *State and Society in Contemporary Britain,* (ed) McLennan, G., Held, D., and Hall, S., Cambridge, Polity: 7–49

Hall, S. (1985) 'Authoritarian populism: a reply to Jessop et al,' *New Left Review,* 151: 115–24

Hall, S. (1988) *The Hard Road to Renewal,* London, Verso

Hall, S. (1989a) 'Ethnicity: identities and difference', *Radical America,* 23: 9–20

Hall, S. (1989b) 'The "first" New Left: life and times' (in) *Out of Apathy* (ed) Archer, R., London: Verso, 11–38

Hall, S. (1989c) 'Authoritarian populism', (in) *Thatcherism: A Tale of Two Nations,* (ed) Jessop, B. et al, Cambridge: Polity, 99–107

Hall, S. (1991a) 'The local and the global: globalization and Ethnicity,' (in) *Culture, Globalization and the World System,* (ed) King, A., Basingstoke: Macmillan, 51–63

Hall, S. (1991b) 'Old and new identities old and new Ethnicities,' (in) *Culture, Gobalization and the World System,* (ed) King, A., Basingstoke: Macmillan, 41–68

Hall, S. (1993a) 'The Williams interviews,' (in) *The Screen Education Reader,* (ed) Alavrdo, A. et al, Basingstoke: Macmillan

Hall, S. (1993b) 'Minimal selves,' (in) *Studying Culture,* (ed) Gray, A. and McGuigan, J. (eds), London: Arnold: 134–8

Hall, S. (1993c) 'Reflections upon the encoding/decoding model', (in) *Viewing, Listening: Audiences and Cultural Reception* (ed) Cruz, J, and Lewis, J, Booulder:Westview, 253–74

Hall, S. (1995) 'Fantasy, identity, politics', (in) *Cultural Remix,* (ed) Carter, E, et al, London: Lawrence & Wishart: 63–9

Hall, S. (1996) 'Introduction: Who Needs Identity?', (in) *Questions of Cultural Identity* (eds) Hall, S. and Du Gay, P. , London: Sage

Hall, S. (ed) (1997) *Representation: Cultural Representations and And Signifying Practices,* London: Sage

Hall, S. (1999) 'Unsettling "the heritage": re-imagining the post-nation,' paper for *Whose Heritage?* Conference, North West Arts Board, Arts Council of England

Hall, S. (2000) 'Prophet at the Margins', interview with Stuart Hall, with Jaggi, M., *The Guardian,* 8 July, 8–9

Hall, S. and *Resistance Through Rituals,* London, Jefferson, T.(1975)(eds) Hutchinson

Hall, S., Lumley, B. & *On Ideology,* London: Hutchinson McLennan,G.(eds)

Hall, S., Critcher, C., *Policing the Crisis,* London: Macmillan Jefferson, T., Clarke, J.,Roberts, R. (1978)

Hoggart, R. (1958) *The Uses of Literacy,* Penguin, Harmondsworth

Hoggart, R. (1970) *Speaking To Each Other,* London: Chatto & Windus

Laclau, E. and *Hegemony and Socialist Strategy,*

Mouffe, C. (1985) London, Verso

McGuigan, J. (1992) *Cultural Populism,* London, Routledge

Rojek, C. (2003) *Stuart Hall,* Cambridge: Polity

Thompson, E.P. (1963) *The Making of the English Working Class,* Penguin, Harmondsworth

Volosinov,V. (1973) *Marxism and the Philosophy of Language,* New York: Seminar Press

Williams, R. (1958) *Culture and Society,* London: Chatto & Windus

Williams, R. (1961) *The Long Revolution,* London: Chatto & Windus

Willis, P. (1977) *Learning To Labour,* London: Saxon House

Willis, P. (1978) *Profane Culture,* London, RKP

Willis, P. (2001) *The Ethnographic Imagination,* Cambridge: Polity

Women's Studies *Women Take Issue,* London: Hutchinson Group CCCS (1978)

Wood, B. (1998) 'Stuart Hall's cultural studies and the problem of hegemony,' *British Journal of Sociology,* 49:3, 399–412.

CHAPTER FIVE

Giddens and Cultural Analysis

Absent word and central concept

John Scott

Anthony Giddens has been one of the most widely cited social theorists in English-speaking countries in the past two decades.[1] His work is widely used across the social sciences, and has been very influential among cultural analysts. Rather surprisingly, however, Giddens rarely uses the word culture in any of his many publications. Despite this apparent disregard for the *word* culture, however, the *concept* is central to his theoretical concerns. There are, in fact, two principal conceptions of culture in his work. These can be termed *culture as structure* and *culture as lifeworld*.

Culture as structure is, in fact, the central idea in Giddens' sociology. According to this view, culture consists of the underlying rules employed in social interactions and through which social systems are reproduced. These 'rules' are not the norms and values stressed by structural functionalists, they are the deeply embedded and embodied generative dispositions that organize social practices. What Giddens terms 'structure', then, is actually what structuralist and other writers have seen as the cultural codes of social life.

Culture as lifeworld also figures centrally in Giddens' work. In describing the organization of actual social systems, he uses the term 'lifeworld' to designate the whole way of life in a society. This comprises the everyday, mutual knowledge and consciousness of social groups and their more systematic 'intellectual' formations and cultural products (Giddens, 1986).[2] He traces the demise of cultural tradition in the face of rationalization and reflexivity, and he places particular emphasis on the part played by the media of mass communication.

In this chapter, I will explore these two ideas as they have developed in Giddens' work. Despite his lack of attention to the word culture, I will show, the idea of culture has been a central concern.

Giddens' Intellectual Project

Anthony Giddens was born into a lower middle-class family in suburban North London in 1938. He escaped what he has described as this 'enclosed wasteland' through grammar school and university. It was at university – the University of Hull – that he discovered sociology, studying this in a department that combined social anthropology with sociology. His undergraduate studies were followed by an MA in Sociology at the London School of Economics, and he wrote his dissertation on the sociology of sport under the supervision of David Lockwood. He has candidly admitted that this had more to do with an interest in sport than in sociology, and, following a pattern that he has described as one of drift rather than choice (Giddens and Pierson, 1998: 38), he obtained a job teaching social psychology in the Department of Sociology at Leicester University in 1961. The department, at that time, had the largest concentration of sociologists in Britain. Its dominant influences were Ilya Neustadt and Norbert Elias, and it was through the influence of Elias – a former student of Alfred Weber and teaching assistant to Karl Mannheim – that Giddens became committed to an academic life. In Elias he discovered a way in which his interest in sport could be used to enlarge his sociological understanding and to open up new areas of enquiry.

During brief sabbatical periods in 1968 and 1969 at Simon Fraser University and the University of California at Los Angeles, Giddens began to read and write for his first major work, on the classical sociological tradition (Giddens, 1971). He moved to Cambridge University in 1969, and it was at Cambridge that he produced all his most important works in social theory, publishing more than ten sole-authored monographs in the 21 years between 1971 and 1992. In his final years at Cambridge, Giddens worked on the political implications of his social theory (Giddens, 1994), and he began to regard his theoretical framework as complete, so far as his own contributions to it were concerned. He moved to a new post as Director of the London School of Economics in 1997, where he concentrated on the task of integrating this work with the political project of Tony Blair and the 'New Labour' government that had been elected in that year (Giddens, 1998; 2000). He has been widely described as Blair's 'favourite intellectual', and after leaving the LSE, he became a member of the House of Lords in 2004.

Giddens' earliest explorations in social theory were undertaken as a critical response to Parsons' (1937) interpretation of the history of sociology. Parsons had been the key figure in the mainstream of sociology from the 1940s through to the 1970s, and even those who were critical of his structural functionalism had largely accepted his account of the history of sociology. This disciplinary history legitimated sociology in an often hostile intellectual climate and was a crucial element in the identity of the professional sociologist. In tackling Parsons' view of history, then, Giddens was forging a radically new direction and self-identity for sociology.

Parsons had depicted Durkheim and Weber – and, to a lesser extent, Pareto – as the towering figures of classical sociology. He saw them as having constructed an approach to sociology that broke with the pre-scientific and ideological approaches that preceded them. The period between 1890 and 1920, when they and their contemporaries produced their works, marked a 'great divide' in social theory. Scientific sociology was firmly entrenched on the 'modern' side of this divide and was uniquely placed to understand the key institutions of the modern society that had given it birth. Parsons saw himself as the heir to this classical tradition, building on its foundations to establish a comprehensive framework of scientific sociological analysis (Giddens, 1976a; 1972b).

Giddens attacked this view root and branch. He recognized the importance of Durkheim and Weber, though he interpreted their ideas very differently (Giddens, 1971), and he saw greater continuities between them and their predecessors. There was no single, sharp division between 'ideology' and 'science', and all social thought had to be seen as inextricably tied to its social and political context (Giddens, 1972a; 1972c). Most significant, however, was his rehabilitation of Marx. While Parsons had virtually ignored Marx – assigning him to the ideological side of the great divide – Giddens sought to incorporate Marx and the wider currents of Marxism into the mainstream of sociology's history.

Although Durkheim remains an important figure in Giddens' work, the key thinkers in his reconstruction of sociology were Weber and Marx. He initially used their ideas to build a powerful synthesis of work on social stratification (Giddens, 1973) that can be seen as carrying forward many of the arguments of Lockwood (Lockwood, 1956; 1958; 1960). The latter was seen, at the time, as a broadening and enlarging of what was then known as 'conflict theory' (Dahrendorf, 1957; Rex, 1961), the main counter-current to Parsonian 'consensus theory'. Lockwood, however, was ambivalent about the label 'conflict theory' and preferred to emphasize the contribution of his work to a larger systemic study of social life (Lockwood, 1964; see also Scott, 1995: Ch. 5). Giddens, too, saw that a broader conspectus was necessary, and he began an extensive programme of reading into emerging ideas in ethnomethodology, linguistic philosophy, and hermeneutics, and these soon led him to a consideration of structuralism. This reading bore its first fruit in his *New Rules of Sociological Method* (Giddens, 1976b), where he set out what he has described as the 'overall project' that was to guide his work for the next 20 years (Giddens and Pierson, 1998: 44).

This intellectual project was to understand the form of modernity that had motivated the works of the classical sociological theorists and to explore the distinctive features and continuing transformation of contemporary modernity. Giddens brought together a critical reading of French and German theory (Giddens, 1979) with a comprehensive reassessment of Marx's social theory (Giddens, 1981), and from the middle of the 1980s he moved from critical exposition to a presentation of his own views on the origins and future of modernity (Giddens, 1984; 1985; 1990). He built a definitive theoretical framework, which he came to call 'structuration theory', and he applied this to the emergence and transformation of modernity. During the early 1990s, he returned to some of the social psychological issues with which he had been concerned in his earliest teaching job, tracing the relationships between the large-scale features of modern societies and the issues of intimacy and self-identity that arise in contemporary modernity (Giddens, 1991; 1992).

Culture as Structure

Giddens' social theory is an explicit attempt to address a contradiction that has, he feels, bedevilled serious discussion of the direction that should be taken by sociological analysis. Throughout its history, and especially since the ending of the structural functionalist monopoly, theorists in sociology have tended to divide between those who accord analytical priority to the actions of individuals and those who gave this priority to systems and social wholes (O'Neill, 1973).

Those who argue that the focus of attention must be on individuals and their social actions have seen these as the building blocks for larger social processes. Weber and the symbolic interactionists of the Chicago School have been the main inspiration, though rational choice theorists in mainstream economics and the social exchange theorists who have followed them in sociology have advocated the same position. These 'methodological individualists' and 'action theorists' have argued that social organization and social institutions must be seen as the direct and knowledgeable creations of acting subjects. Individual actors are free agents, creatively producing the variety of social forms through which they live. All 'macro' phenomena are reducible to these micro-level processes.

The opposing position emphasizes the autonomous properties of 'society' and 'social facts'. Central advocates of this view have been Durkheim and such structural sociologists as Radcliffe-Brown, Parsons, and the structural functionalists, though it is found also in many strands of Marxism. These 'methodological collectivists' and 'system theorists' have emphasized the objectivity of social institutions and the external and constraining powers that they exercise over individuals and their actions. Social systems are deterministic forces, moulding individuals to their needs, and they cannot be reduced to the actions of individuals.

Giddens holds that this theoretical dualism between individual actions and social systems, between agency and determination, is misconceived. Sociologists do not have to choose one side or the other in this theoretical dispute. Actions and systems, he argues, are interdependent, and satisfactory theories of them must be complementary. Reconstructed and recast, the two bodies of theory will fit together seamlessly. Sociology should be working towards the integration of these two strands of theory into a single explanatory framework.

While action and system theories can be seen as two aspects of a larger theory, it is not necessary for each and every sociologist to work at this larger theory. Much sociological work can be undertaken on the basis of a methodological 'bracketing'. This is a means of analytical isolation in which questions that occur in one area are temporarily put to one side in order to study issues relating to the other. Actions can often be analysed without taking any direct account of the complexities that arise at the system level. A researcher can, for example, study individual action and interaction by placing methodological 'brackets' around the institutions and collectivities that comprise the systemic features of social life. These system processes figure simply as the 'conditions' under which actions take place. Similarly, individual action can be bracketed in order to allow an institutional analysis of systems and their integration to be undertaken, without the need for any explicit analysis of the complexities involved in individual action.

For many purposes, however, this bracketing is inadequate, and it is necessary to explore the relationships between action and system. A full account of individual action has to be grounded in an account of the systemic features of social life that both constrain it and make it possible. Similarly, a full account of a social system can make sense only if grounded in an account of the individual actions that produce and reproduce it. It does not follow, however, that one can be reduced to the other. Integration is not the same as conflation.[3] Social theory must operate at both levels to understand the complex articulation between them. Giddens argues that the apparent opposition or 'dualism' between action and system can be overcome only if it is seen as reflecting a *duality* in the social structure that mediates them. Individual actions are shaped by a social structure, and the patterned features of social systems are the outcome of socially structured human actions. Patterns in social actions and social systems are the results of a process of structuring, which Giddens refers to as 'structuration'. Social structures are the means or medium through which actions are shaped and organized. At the same time, however, structures are produced and reproduced by the very actions that they organize. They are a consequence or outcome of structured actions within structured social systems. These two aspects of structure – as medium and as outcome – are what Giddens refers to as the 'duality of structure'.

In making this point, Giddens gives the idea of social structure a central place in his work. The concept of social structure is, of course, used very widely in sociology (López and Scott, 2000), but Giddens' concept is most unusual and quite distinctive. Giddens notes, in fact, that his concept of structure is what many would refer to as 'culture', and he specifically mentions the parallel between his own ideas and the work of Bauman on culture (Bauman, 1973; see Giddens, 1979: 268, n. 30). For most sociologists, social structures are the institutional and relational patterns of social systems. Examples would include kinship structures, class structures, and political structures. Thus, social structure, as the patterning of social phenomena, is often seen through an analogy with 'the skeleton or morphology of an organism or ... the girders of a building' (Giddens, 1984: 16). Giddens recognizes this as a legitimate usage for descriptive purposes, but he argues that a more fundamental concept of social structure is needed.

For Giddens, a social structure consists of the rules that individual actors draw upon in the actions that reproduce social systems. Giddens' usual phrasing is that structure consists of 'rules and resources'. The addition of 'resources', however, is never properly theorized. The part played by resources in social life is, nevertheless, consistently emphasized by Giddens, and I will show that this is better seen separately from the cultural structure of 'rules'. Rules are the cultural mechanisms through which actions and social systems are organized. While the patterns found in social actions and social systems reflect these 'structures', patterns and structures are not the same things. Structures are quite distinct from the properties of the action processes and social systems themselves, though they are 'instantiated' in them.

Such structures are not directly observable or amenable to conscious experience: they exist 'virtually' in the observable patterns, but they are not reducible to these (Giddens, 1976b: 127; 1981: 26). They exist only in the traces that their use leaves behind in the properties of social systems and the memories of individuals. Patterned flows of action, codified norms and laws, measurable rates of activity, recurrent sets of relationships, and so on, must be recognized as the observable, external manifestations that serve simply as indicators of the structures that actually organize social life. The rules that comprise social structures are the key objects of sociological investigation. They are the means through which social actions and social systems are able to exist; they make social life possible.

This distinction between unobservable structures and the observable patterns they produce is something that Giddens developed from his reading of structuralist theory. With the structuralists, he turned to Saussure's account of language (De Saussure, 1916) as a basis for understanding all other social phenomena. According to Saussure, the speech patterns found in everyday talk and conversation result from the application of definite rules of grammar (rules of syntax, semantics, phonology, etc.). These rules do not exist anywhere separately from the speech, but they can be identified and formulated by linguists as ways of explaining that speech. Competent speakers of English, for example, are able to form plural expressions in real time by adding appropriate endings to root words and making certain other regular changes to them. Linguists, for their part, can formulate the rules that govern this: when to add 's', when to add 'en', and so on. These linguistic rules, however, are not present in the consciousness of the individual speakers as they speak, and individual speakers may be completely unaware of the rules that they follow unreflectively. Nevertheless, it is because the members of a linguistic community share these rules that it is possible for them to speak and to understand the speech of others.

Giddens follows the structuralists in extending this account of speech to all forms of social action. The flow of actions is governed by definite rules, of which the actors may be unaware, and the task of sociological analysis is to uncover the non-linguistic rules that make action possible. The sociologist, like the linguist, produces a theoretical model with explicitly formulated rules, and this must be seen as an intellectual formulation of the actual rules that operate, generally without any conscious awareness, in and through the actions of individuals. Actual rules, Giddens holds, are generalizable procedures of action. They are akin to formulas in that they allow actors to show 'the methodological continuation of an established sequence' (Giddens, 1984: 21), but they exist as capacities, abilities, and dispositions rather than as conscious and explicit statements.

Giddens argues that actors may not consciously know the rules that inform their actions, but that they always know them tacitly in the same way that individuals know the rules of grammar: they know *how* to continue speaking and acting, even if they are rarely able to state the rules that they are following. When people successfully learn how to speak Japanese, how to drive a car, how to cook a meal, how to vote in an election, how to work in an office, and so on, the rules that comprise these skills are embedded in their minds and bodies as specific skills, capacities, and dispositions that are likely to be available for conscious recall and codification only in partial and distorted forms.

Giddens develops this view through a social psychology that he derives from the ideas of the symbolic interactionists and from Weber's account of subjectivity, to which he adds insights from psychoanalysis and from Foucault's explorations into subjectivity and discourse. Central to this is the relationship between what he calls practical consciousness and discursive consciousness. Practical consciousness operates unreflectively through trial and error to build up routine patterns of action. It is the means through which motivating forces are organized into routines and habits of action that allow people to pursue their wants and desires in unproblematic ways without the need to constantly make decisions over action alternatives. Habits of action rest on persisting dispositions or tendencies that embody the structural rules that make the action possible. They are the product of those socialized dispositions that Bourdieu (1972) has analysed through his concept of the habitus. Indeed, much confusion would have been avoided if Giddens had used the word habitus, rather than the word structure.

Actors do, however, reflect on their actions in order to evaluate their success. This allows their actions to become matters for the discursive consciousness through which they 'account' for their actions by invoking the 'reasons' that led to them. Through this reflexive rationalization of action, actors attempt to formulate discursive interpretations of the rules that have shaped their actions. In doing so, they may be able to make their actions the objects of rational investigation and control. It is rarely the case, however, that they will attain a full and accurate discursive knowledge of the actual rules that inform their actions. The legal statutes, books of grammar, written rules for games, guides to etiquette, and so on that are produced discursively do not contain true rules: they are interpretations and codifications of the procedural rules that inhere in the skills, capacities, and dispositions exercised by the actors. They are, in this sense, analogous to the theoretical models produced by sociological investigators in their sociological discourse.

Giddens' formulation of this position is strikingly close to that of Garfinkel (1967), whose 'ethnomethodology' is explicitly concerned with the rule-like 'methods' used by people in generating and accounting for actions. Culture, in the sense of 'structure', comprises the tacit, taken-for-granted stock of knowledge that Schütz and Luckmann (1973) saw as providing the typifications and definitions that underpin the expectations through which routine everyday actions are organized.

This view of culture leads Giddens to understand social change differently from many other sociologists. Observable changes in the patterns of social actions and social systems have to be seen as resulting from rule change. By speaking grammatically, the speakers of a language contribute to the reproduction of its rules of grammar, and by speaking in innovative 'non-grammatical' ways, they contribute to the transformation of the existing rules. Similarly, social change more broadly results from actions that, whether consciously or not, disregard existing rules or introduce new ones. Social change, then, rests upon a cultural change. This is not to imply that Giddens holds to an idealist view of social change, as he also invokes – but does not properly theorize – the part played by resources. It is the interplay between cultural rules and material resources that determines the direction of social change.

Culture as Lifeworld

On the basis of his first concept of culture – culture as structure – Giddens builds an account of larger systems of action. His theory of 'structuration' is the means through which encultured, rule-following, agents are able to produce and reproduce the cultural and other systems that figure in more conventional 'structural' sociologies. Through their socialization into their culture, people acquire those dispositions that form the structure, or habitus; through the routinized actions generated by these dispositions, they reproduce their whole way of life.

There are, according to Giddens, three types of disposition and these underpin the three 'structural dimensions' along which social actions and social systems vary. These dispositions comprise the semantic, the regulative, and the transformative capacities of human agency.[4] While these operate closely together in all real situations, they are analytically distinguishable because of the different types of rules that inhere in them.

The semantic capacity in human agency operates through processes of communication and signification to establish shared meanings and definitions in social interaction and to build, at the system level, symbolic orders, interpretative schemes, and modes of discourse. It involves rules that have a 'constitutive' or semantic significance – rules that make it possible for people to understand one another and to constitute social reality as meaningful. Through this capacity, signs are established for use in the communication of meaning and for the production of mutual knowledge. The regulative capacity of human agency operates through processes of sanction and legitimation to establish expectations and obligations in social interaction and to build, at the system level, various forms of normative regulation, such as custom and law. It involves rules that have a 'regulative' or moral significance – rules that make it possible for people to control one another and ensure the continuity of established social patterns. Through this capacity, conceptions of validity are established for use in the normative sanctioning of actions through moral judgements (Giddens, 1976b: 104–13; 1979: 81–111). These semantic and regulative capacities are, of course, closely related to each other, and rules cannot be sharply divided into two completely distinct categories. Indeed, they combine together to form what Giddens has called a 'common culture' or 'form of life'. They are central to culture in that narrower sense that Habermas (Habermas, 1981a; 1981b) has referred to as the socio-cultural lifeworld.

Giddens says little to elaborate on this point of view at the general level. The way of life, it may be surmised, comprises the communal relations of intimacy, family, and neighbourhood and the normative rules – the customs and 'folkways' – through which they are organized. It is a codified and crystallized culture embodied in the social institutions that constrain their actions. It does, however, co-exist with economic and political systems produced through similar rule-following actions. He explores this through the idea of the transformative capacity.

The transformative capacity of human agency operates through processes of power and domination to establish interpersonal power and constraint and to build, at the system level, the economic and political institutions through which allocation and coordination can take place (Giddens, 1981: 28). This capacity depends on the resources that are available to actors, but Giddens has focused most of his attention on the rules that govern access to and control over these resources. It is these rules that define the transformative capacity. Through rules of possession and mobilization – which may be codified as property and authority – resources can be made available as means or facilities for action and can be built into forms of domination. It is here that is found the true significance of 'resources' in Giddens' work. Contrary to what he actually says, resources are not an aspect of structure as he uses that term. Structure consists of the rule-bound capacities through which resources play their part in social life. The material objects that function as resources, however, do exist separately and independently of the rules that constitute and regulate them and that allow them to play a part in the exercise of power and domination. Resources exist as what Lockwood (1956) referred to as the 'substratum' of the cultural and normative patterns of a society, and Giddens seems to assume a similar point of view. They comprise the political economy in a form of social life and, as such, establish patterns of inequality and, therefore, of autonomy and dependence among actors (1981: 50). Having said this, it must be recognized that the linkage between rules and resources is remarkably untheorized in Giddens' work and that he does not, therefore, set out a fully satisfactory account of the non-cultural aspects of social life.

Giddens uses these ideas to produce a classification of social institutions, summarized in Figure 5.1. Signification through semantic mechanisms is of primary importance in the formation of the symbolic orders and modes of discourse that form the world-views of societies and collectivities. Signification cannot, however, operate alone. Secondary processes of domination and legitimation are always involved in the reproduction of these social institutions. A world-view must also involve a pattern of domination and moral sanctioning if an effective pattern of social control is to be established over the actors who are socialized into it (1981: 47). It is in this way that patterns of signification may come to have an ideological function: 'ideology consists of structures of signification which are harnessed to the legitimation of the sectional interests of dominant groups' (ibid.: 61). All signification involves some degree of domination, but ideological forms exist when structures of signification serve the interests of dominant classes or other dominant social groups. Thus, the conjunction of signification, domination, and legitimacy in a context of class division establishes an effective class hegemony.

Habitus	Primary structural dimension	Secondary structural dimension	Institutional forms
Semantic capacity	Signification	Domination Legitimation	Symbolic orders, modes of discourse
Transformative capacity	Authoritative domination	Legitimation Signification	Political institutions
	Allocative domination	Legitimation Signification	Economic institutions
Regulative capacity	Legitimation	Domination Signification	Law, modes of regulation

Figure 5.1   Structural dimensions of social systems
Source: Modified from (Giddens, 1979: 107; 1981: 47).

Legitimation through regulative mechanisms is of primary importance in the formation of legal institutions and other modes of normative regulation. It is through processes of legitimation that legal and customary orders are established and come to be regarded as valid and, therefore, obligatory. Such normative orders can be very complex, and Giddens shows that secondary processes of domination and signification are always involved. The building of a legal order requires the establishment of a degree of mutual understanding with respect to the application of particular laws, and the enforcement of institutionalized normative expectations depends upon the availability of resources that enforcing agents can use to make the moral sanctions effective.

Signification and legitimation are particularly closely linked together in the formation of the socio-cultural lifeworlds through which people acquire a sense of meaning and of personal and collective identity. It is through these means that people come to live in a world that is meaningful to them and that provides a framework of expectations and obligations that help to ensure that they do not experience the egoism and anomie that Durkheim (1897) saw as resulting from the weakening or failure of collective representations and a *conscience collective*.

Domination through the transformative use of resources comprises the 'system' or political economy that underpins the socio-cultural lifeworld, though Giddens does not consistently use this Habermasian terminology. This mechanism of domination, in its most systematic form, operates through two distinct types of social institutions. The authoritative use of resources is expressed through political institutions such as states, political parties, and other formal organizations. The allocative use of resources, on the other hand, is expressed through economic institutions such as property, markets, and technologies of production. In each case, however, secondary processes of legitimation and signification must sustain institutions of domination. Authority in the political institutions that comprise nation–states and international agencies, for example, is sustained through the communicative understanding of their commands and decisions and through the legitimation of these by a framework of validity and obligation. Similarly, systems of property and market exchange rest on the legal frameworks and symbolic codes that Durkheim (1893) described as the 'non-contractual element' in contractual relations of negotiation and exchange.

Social systems in their most general sense, then, are seen by Giddens as comprising clusters of social institutions that are organized around the structural dimensions associated with the various structured dispositions that constitute human agency. The economic and political institutions of domination are fundamental features of all societies, but they co-exist with the symbolic and regulatory institutions that form their socio-cultural lifeworlds. Social systems differ according to the extent to which these institutions are distinguished from each other and are differentiated into specialized and identifiable clusters. A central feature of modernity, Giddens argues, is the high level of institutional differentiation that it brought into being, and he uses his institutional concepts to explore the emergence and development of this modernity.

Culture and Modernity

Giddens has consistently argued that sociology has to be seen as a product of modernity and that it must take modernity as its specific object of investigation. The major substantive task of his work, then, is to use his general theoretical concepts to construct a model of the key elements in modernity. It is important to explore modern culture, in both senses identified, and to see how culture is involved in the reproduction of specifically modern systems of action. This task cannot, however, be undertaken in isolation, and Giddens sees it as necessary to explore the pre-modern forms of society from which modernity emerged and that still survive in many parts of the modern world. Equally, it is important to speculate about the future forms of society that might follow modernity. While eschewing the evolutionary concerns of many of the nineteenth-century sociologists, Giddens constructs a classification of societal types and of the patterns of development from one to another.

This typology begins with the simplest tribal societies, such as wandering bands of hunters and gatherers and more settled agricultural communities (Giddens, 1981: 92–4). Giddens traces the ways in which many such societies have been incorporated into various types of historical empire. These empires are large-scale agrarian societies in which there are marked class divisions and a differentiation of political and economic institutions from the socio-cultural lifeworld (Giddens, 1981: 105–8; 1985: Ch. 2). Political and economic institutions – states and markets – are focused in the cities, which become the 'power containers' from which central control is exercised by a dominant social class. In imperial world systems, such as the Roman Empire, states developed as political forms that were institutionally quite separate from their environing cities and were the principal means through which resources could be authoritatively used to control their extensive territories.

As well as collecting tax revenues, such states collected, retained, and controlled information and knowledge, on an unprecedented scale, through record-keeping, archiving, and surveillance. Writing was the principal means of communication and information storage. Codified cultural knowledge is stored in texts and documents of all kinds. This allowed mediated interactions to occur across large expanses of time and space, and it encouraged the building of the institutional supports of state domination. The cultures of imperial systems comprised elaborate religious ideas and institutions, and their religious orders were central to the legitimation of state power. In the most developed imperial systems, these were 'rationalized' world religions such as Christianity, Buddhism, Confucianism, and Islam, seen by Weber as the seedbeds of systematic rational thought.

All pre-modern societies are organized through their 'traditional' culture. Signification and legitimation build institutions that are sustained by custom, religion, and traditional authority. People conform to social expectations unreflectively, largely without any rational consideration, simply on the basis of their emotional commitment to traditional ways of acting and their corresponding habits of action. By contrast, modern societies are built around a systematic rationalization of social life that ushers in a reflexive culture. The socio-cultural lifeworld loses its traditional character and becomes more supportive of rational, reflexive actions. Tradition is challenged and undermined by rational forms of thought that transform social institutions into the radically new forms of modernity.

The break with the culture of traditionalism occurred first in Western Europe, where feudal institutions gave way to rationalized forms of economic and political domination and religious culture was subject to a process of secularization. The Enlightenment thinkers ignited the spark of modernity. Disregarding the cultural rules that underpinned traditionalism, they adopted new rules that required the reflexive and calculative consideration of alternatives. Their ideas introduced rational considerations to all areas of social life. The spread of these new rules lay behind the observable transformation in social institutions. This institutional rationalization occurred first in the economic sphere, as a result of the specific conjunction of circumstances highlighted by Weber in his account of the relationship between the Protestant ethic and the spirit of capitalism (Weber, 1904–5; 1919–20). It rapidly spread to other spheres of social life and it acquired a momentum that was all but irresistible. As rational organization transformed one area after another, tendencies towards traditionalism were continually undermined. Pre-modern societies with their 'traditional' characteristics survived in ever-diminishing enclaves as modernity spread across the globe. These societies were, increasingly, drawn into the modern world and found it more difficult to sustain their archaic characteristics. In the western heartland of modernity, the traditional elements persisted only in vestigial form, as the world became ever more rationalized.

What, then, are the institutional characteristics of modernity, according to Giddens? In describing these, he focuses on the characteristic patterns of domination found in modern societies. These he sees as involving highly differentiated economic and political institutions and their formation into capitalist economies and nation–states. These are the basis on which all the other institutional features of modernity are organized. These other institutional features are those of the socio-cultural lifeworld that result from the signifying and legitimating processes that underpin capitalist and nation–state forms. Giddens particularly highlights the legal institutions and modes of regulation that define citizenship, sovereignty, and property and commercial law, together with the media of communication and forms of community that are involved in the establishment of common languages and common symbols of collective identity within national societies. These various factors of modernity are summarized in Figure 5.2.

The key institutions of a capitalist economy are capitalist commodification (which Giddens calls simply 'capitalism') and industrialism. A system of capitalist commodity production operates through competitive markets for goods and labour power and rests on a class division between owners of capital and propertyless wage labourers. Capitalist businesses employ labour that is itself a commodity, and they are the means through which the private ownership of the means of production leads to the accumulation of wealth in commodity form. This commodification of resources is made possible by the existence of money. This is, Giddens argues, a 'symbolic token', a particular type of abstract system, that makes it possible to 'disembed' the exchange of goods and services from particular local contexts and so to transform interpersonal relations into relations among commodities. Capitalist commodification, then, results in the reification of social relations (Giddens, 1990: 22–6, drawing on Simmel, 1900). Industrialism is a system of institutions in which the production of goods is undertaken through the intensive use of machine technology, a complex division of labour, and inanimate sources of energy. The means of production are organized into rationalized systems of factory, office, and machine technology that enlarge human productive powers beyond the levels possible in pre-modern societies that depended simply on human and animal power.

It was the consolidation of capitalist commodification in Western Europe that made possible the later expansion of industrial technology that is conventionally described as the 'Industrial Revolution'. Capitalist commodification, then, was a precondition for the dynamic expansion of industrialism and it is the specific conjunction of capitalist commodification with industrialism that defines the principal economic characteristics of modernity.

The key political institutions of modernity are those of the nation–state, though Giddens sees similar processes occurring in certain other types of formal organization, such as large business enterprises. The nation–state is organized around the institutions of surveillance and militarism. Modern systems of surveillance allow state authority to operate with much greater intensity than was possible in city–states and imperial states. Following Foucault and Weber, Giddens highlights the building of sophisticated systems of information gathering and bureaucratic forms of administration through which subject populations can be supervised and their deviance controlled. Militarism, on the other hand, is the means through which modern states have achieved a monopoly over the means of violence and, in consequence, a high level of internal pacification. Force and violence are centralized within the state and

Structural dimension	Institutional clusterings	Institutional axes of modernity	Actual institutions	Globalized form
Signification *semantics dimension*	Symbolic orders, semiotic codes, and modes of discourse		Media of communication; conceptual community	Gobal information systems
Domination–Authority	Political	Surveillance	Nation-state	International system of states and world military order;
		Militarism		Inter-governmental agencies; military alliances and treaties
transformative dimensions				
Domination–Allocation	Economic	Industrialism	Capitalist economy	International division of labour and ecological problems of one world
		Capitalism		
Legitimation *regulative dimension*	Legal and repressive		Citizenship, rule of law, sovereignty	Human rights

Figure 5.2 Institutional clusters of modernity

its agencies and are no longer matters of routine resort for private or public bodies. Armies, police forces, and prisons are mechanisms of social control that operate through the enhanced capacities for coercion that are made possible by the formal and rational organization of violence that Giddens refers to as the 'industrialization' of force and warfare. Surveillance and militarism, therefore, operate closely together, and it is their specific combination, as nation–states, that defines the political characteristics of modernity.

The building of an autonomous capitalist economy through commodification and industrialism was not possible without the parallel separation of an autonomous nation–state through which populations could be pacified and administered. Modern 'societies' are largely co-existent with the boundaries of nation–states. It is within the boundaries of nation–state societies that economic relations, legal institutions, and forms of communication and community are concentrated. Modern societies have been organized around class politics, whereby the ideological hegemony of a dominant class is countered by politically organized labour movements that attempt to defend and protect the position of workers at their place of work and, through the formation of socialist and leftist political parties, to influence the exercise of state power and build 'social democratic' reforms. Central to this is the demand for civil rights and democracy that Marshall saw as a central feature of modern citizenship (Marshall, 1949).

Although there is a tendency for 'national' societies and economies to coincide with the boundaries of nation–states, 'international' linkages have always been important. Nation–states have more tightly defined and more strongly defended boundaries than pre-modern states, and they are elements in inter-state systems that are marked by endemic international conflict and warfare. Similarly, capitalist economies are involved in international chains of trade and investment that embed them in a 'world system' of the kind described by Wallerstein (1974; 1980; 1989). From the middle of the nineteenth century until well into the twentieth century, this network of international economic relations centred on the City of London and its myriad banking and merchant enterprises (Giddens, 1984: 319–24, citing Ingham, 1984).

Rationalization also makes itself felt in the cultural lifeworld. Communal relations are disembedded from local contexts and cast in more universal, abstract forms. Localities are no longer experienced as bounded and self-contained contexts for action, and people's interactions are no longer limited to direct face-to-face relations. People associate with one another not through the *gemeinschaftslich* bonds of the traditional community, but in more abstract societal forms. Individuals can now engage in 'action at a distance', thanks to the techniques of transportation and communication that are made possible by modern science and technology and that are organized by capitalist enterprises and nation–states. The first breaks with the all-pervasiveness of direct face-to-face encounters had occurred with the invention of writing and printing, and the gradual spread of literacy. The introduction of postal services and then telegraphs and telephones transformed the material basis of these systems of communication and made it possible for communication to take place over ever-greater distances. The electronic media of communication are the latest forms through which this disembedded interaction takes place.

The particular significance of the modern mass media, Giddens argues, lies in the specific ways that they pattern and transmit knowledge. He argues, first, that the mass media construct reality through what he calls a 'collage effect'. Events are dis-embedded from their context for reporting alongside a whole series of otherwise unconnected events in a newspaper or television news bulletin. At the same time, the news is presented alongside other articles and programmes (sport, entertainment, advertising, etc.) in a similar collage of events and images. The second feature of the mass media that he emphasizes is the intrusion of distant events into everyday con-sciousness that they make possible. More and more of the experiences that people have depend not on their own local and personal knowledge, but on mass media rep-resentations of distant events. They experience the world in mediated form, and this form of mediation involves the collage effect. Giddens here echoes the arguments of Baudrillard (1981) concerning the mediated character of contemporary culture. Mass media images are central to the social imagination, and the social reality in which people live becomes a hyperreal cultural formation.

Giddens' view of the mass media has been spelled out by John Thompson (1995), though his views should certainly not be identified with those of Giddens. According to Thompson, interaction takes the form of 'mediated quasi-interaction' whenever it depends on mass communications. That is, communications are not oriented towards specific others but are broadcast to an indefinite audience and in a predom-inantly monological (one-way) form. The mass media offer little possibility for dia-logical interaction with their audiences. In mediated quasi-interaction, there can be no reflexive monitoring of the actions of others.

Culture and Reflexivity in Late Modernity

Giddens' explorations into modernity have raised questions about the forms of social life that may develop out of modernity. It is in his consideration of late modernity that Giddens gives the greatest attention to the cultural systems of the lifeworld. His conception of culture as 'structure' underpins everything that he has written on modernity, but his account of modern culture is less well developed than his account of capitalism and the nation–state. In turning to those trends that he sees as mark-ing the new stage of late modernity, however, he examines in great depth the forms of reflexivity that characterize the late modern lifeworld.

These questions have often been discussed in terms of a contemporary stage of postmodernity, but Giddens is sceptical about such claims. He recognizes, however, that there have been far-reaching changes in the structure of modernity in the contemporary world, and he conceptualizes these changes as aspects of a period of late modernity. In late modernity, all the principal institutional elements of moder-nity have been 'radicalized', eliminating virtually all the remaining features of pre-modernity and traditionalism and starkly exposing modernity in all its formally 'rational' characteristics. Giddens alludes to the prospect that late modern features may, indeed, point beyond modernity to a radically transformed form of society, though not to the kind of postmodernity conventionally depicted.

Central to the period of late modernity, according to Giddens, is globalization. The growth and intensification of inter-state and inter-economy transactions in the modern world system link distant events together and produce a shifting system of political alliances and geo-political blocs. This has also led to the declining autonomy of specifically 'national' societies (Giddens, 1985: 166; 1990: 65–9). Global capitalist commodification and the growing internationalization of state politics have been extended through a parallel globalization of both industrialism and militarism. An international division of labour and system of production extends across the world, and militarism develops into a world military order that is organized around a balance of power and the coordinated action of core states against peripheral ones.

Giddens recognizes a corresponding tendency towards the globalization of the symbolic orders and systems of mediated communication that comprise the principal elements in the lifeworld. There is now, he argues, a world-wide sharing of knowledge and cultural representations. The globalization of the mass media, partly a result of the globalization of communications technology and of communications businesses, has a significant cultural impact. Giddens gives particular attention to the global 'pooling' of information through news broadcasts, which ensure that information is no longer bound to particular localities but is broadcast immediately across the globe. This global pooling of knowledge is central to the world financial system, where the prices of stocks and shares, currencies, interest rates, and information about other economic variables can be transmitted, almost instantaneously, across the world, from one financial centre to another. Similarly, international political responses to localized political events and natural disasters are shaped by the ways in which they are presented and communicated through news broadcasts. Broadcast forms of entertainment are, increasingly, global products transmitted and syndicated in societies far removed from those where they are produced.

The key implications of this globalization have been drawn out in what Giddens, following Beck (1986), sees as a 'risk society'. The Enlightenment emphasis on the cultural application of science and technology promised an increase in human control over nature and the dangers that it posed for human beings. Giddens argues that the global spread of capitalist industrialism has meant that the reality in late modernity is that technology has itself become a source of danger and hazard. Technologically induced risks – 'manufactured risks' – are themselves globalized, as each locality faces the further risk that it will experience hazards generated elsewhere in the world. Acid rain produced by the industries of Western Europe, for example, falls disproportionately on the forests of Northern Europe. Such manufactured risks as pollution, environmental devastation, and global warming increasingly overshadow any natural or 'external risks' that are unmediated by human actions and technology. In late modernity the very idea of an unmediated source of risk become meaningless.

Global risks make themselves felt in all the key institutional clusters of modernity. Global capitalism runs the risk that its economic growth mechanisms will collapse;

the global, technologically created environment of 'one world' faces ecological disaster; the global intensification of surveillance mechanisms generates risks of totalitarian political repression (Bauman, 1989); and global militarism threatens nuclear or other forms of large-scale warfare.

The central cultural implication of this globalization of risk is that risk monitoring becomes a central element in the reflexivity of action. As the 'dangers' that are generated by modern technologies grow, so the calculation of the risks that they involve becomes an ever more central feature of modern culture. Systems of rational discourse and social practice aimed at controlling these risks – insurance, social welfare, and political intervention – become far more important. Such risk consciousness also becomes a part of people's everyday lives and of their immediate personal experiences. Thinking in terms of risk becomes more or less inevitable, even when people may choose to ignore these risks (Giddens, 1991: 125–6).

Giddens has traced the implications of this growth of risk and risk culture for the formation of self-identity in the socio-cultural lifeworlds of late modernity. In everyday life, he argues, people try to build a taken-for-granted world, a sense of stability and order, that allows them to get on with everyday activity by 'bracketing off' their uncertainties and anxieties. So long as their actions are successful, their picture of the world is reinforced and their anxieties can remain at bay. They live within a protective cocoon that provides them with an ontological security and is the basis from which they can calculate risks and cope with dangers.

Tradition provided a framework of predictability and certainty for pre-modern cultures, making the future predictable and minimizing anxiety (ibid.: 48). Under these circumstances, people's lives – their trajectories of self – followed prescribed and pre-ordained transitions, and it is in this sense, as Durkheim (1893) showed, that the 'individual' and individual choice did not exist in a traditional society.

In modern societies, people can no longer rely on pre-established precepts and practices, and their actions must be constantly subject to revision in the light of new information and knowledge. Individual choice becomes a necessity, and rational, scientific knowledge becomes a central element in the exercise of this choice. People no longer have the kind of local, contextual knowledge that allowed their pre-modern counterparts to cope with life. They must resort to experts and the technical knowledge that they have developed into 'expert systems'. As knowledge becomes more technical, individuals cannot judge the knowledge of those that they consult and they must take their expertise on trust. Choice and deliberation are informed by expert information.

Modernity, however, has always depended on reformulated and reconstructed traditions, such as patriarchal views of gender and sexuality, the authority of science, the national and religious ideologies that legitimate social movements, and so on. Late modernity involves a 'de-traditionalization' as these reformulated traditions are themselves subjected to critical examination (Giddens, 1994). Reflexive thought challenges science itself: all forms of knowledge are now open to question, critique, and revision. People can no longer have any faith in either the judgements of the experts or their own assessment of these judgements. This situation of 'radical doubt', Giddens argues, is 'existentially troubling' for people, and their experience of risk is shaped by this radical doubt. People can neither trust the knowledge of experts, nor make satisfying decisions for themselves. Each individual must come to his or her own assessment of the risks that they face in their lives and the available solutions to these risks.

As a result of this, each person is forced to regard their sense of self and identity as a 'reflexive project' (Giddens, 1991: 32, 75). The differentiation of the modern life-world into a plurality of competing and alternative cultural lifeworlds (Berger and Luckmann, 1966), each with its own specific lifestyles, means that individuals constantly move between lifeworlds and must negotiate the transitions and choices that they make among these 'lifestyle sectors' (Giddens, 1991: 83). Leaving home, getting a job, becoming unemployed, forming a new relationship, facing illness, and so on, all pose risks and choices that must be reflexively negotiated. For this reason, argues Giddens, strategic life planning becomes a major source of anxiety. Only in relations of intimacy and close friendship – 'the pure relationship' – do people feel that they can escape from this (Giddens, 1992).

This chronic anxiety about the self is bound up with the rise of the academic disciplines of psychology and sociology, which allow the development of expert systems available to advise, instruct, and discipline individuals. Alongside the growing number of economic and political experts is an expansion of those who claim expertise in relation to social relations and self-identities. At one level, psychotherapies are a response to the egoism and anomie of modern culture, but they are also a means through which reflexivity can be organized: 'Therapy is not simply a means of coping with novel anxieties, but an expression of the reflexivity of the self' (Giddens, 1991: 34). There has been a massive growth in the number of counsellors, therapists, and consultants who specialize in managing the reflexive self (ibid.: 33; see also Rose, 1998). Radical doubt about expert systems, however, means that individuals must choose their own experts. They must choose, for example, from among the range of cognitive, behavioural, and psychoanalytical therapies with no real guidance from the character of the expert knowledge itself.

Globalization and the changes in self-identity in late modernity are the principal elements in Giddens' view of contemporary politics and they are the basis for his own engagement in practical politics. Earlier stages of modernity were organized around class-based politics, but in late modernity this has given way to a cultural politics centred around new forms of social movement. One important dimension of contemporary politics relates to the institutional features of late modernity and is organized around the characteristic risks that they generate. This is what Giddens calls the politics of inequality. The other dimension of contemporary politics – the politics of identity – concerns the shaping of the self and identity. The politics of inequality centre on the emancipation of people from the systems of domination that shape their lives and the risks that these systems generate. The labour movement remains an important element in emancipatory political struggles, but it now operates alongside other social movements. Ecological movements such as the European Greens emerged and grew around the risks of the created environment;

Modernity	Late modernity		Postmodernity
	Risks and political tendencies	Political movements	
Politics of inequality: systems of domination			
Surveillance	Totalitarian repression	Democratic movements	Democratic participation
Militarism	Global warfare	Peace movements	Demilitarization
Industrialism	Ecological disaster	Ecological movements	Humanized technology
Capitalism	Economic collapse	Labour movements	Post-scarcity
Politics of identity: socio-cultural lifeworld			
Damaged solidarities	Radical doubt and ontological insecurity	Lifestyle movements	Autonomy, dialogic democracy

Figure 5.3   Late modernity and postmodernity compared

peace movements developed around the risks inherent in global militarism; and the free speech and democratic rights movements crystallized around concerns over the extension of surveillance.

However, Giddens gives particular emphasis to the politics of identity within the socio-cultural lifeworld. He sees this politics as a broadening of concerns first raised by feminists in the women's movement. The broadened concern for lifestyle issues that is opened up by contemporary reflexivity aims to support the construction of selves that are able to live autonomously and to deal with the characteristic anxieties of late modernity (Giddens, 1991: Ch. 7).

Giddens sees his own 'third way' in politics as a means of building on these emerging concerns and helping to build a framework of politics that goes beyond the opposition of capitalism and socialism that characterized early modernity (see Figure 5.3). The third way and the emancipatory social movements with which it is associated, Giddens argues, are possible means through which late modernity might, indeed, give way to some kind of postmodernity. The form of postmodern society that inheres in the emancipatory politics of inequality and identity is one that is organized around a transformation in each of the four principal institutional dimensions of modernity. Capitalism will become a post-scarcity system of distribution; industrial technology will be 'humanized'; democratic participation at all levels will transcend the totalitarian and centralizing tendencies of state surveillance; and the global structure of alliances will be demilitarized. Equally, the cultural lifeworld would organize its plurality and diversity around the conditions necessary for autonomy in the choice of lifestyles. The damaged solidarities of the spocio-cultural lifeworld would be rebuilt and a framework of 'dialogic democracy' established. This is a democracy that operates through effective and autonomous dialogue in all spheres of life and that involves, in particular, a 'democracy of the emotions' (Giddens, 1994). There is, of course, nothing inevitable in this, and the achievement of political emancipation is a contingent outcome of political debate and political conflict.

Thus, Giddens sees any claim that contemporary societies are already postmodern as premature. The cultural and other changes apparent in contemporary societies are those already characteristic of post-traditional societies, but developed in a radical form as the 'reflexive modernity' of the late modern epoch. Although he feels it is possible to chart the contours of a post-modern social order and to see this as a potential inherent in the emancipatory movements of the late modern period, actual postmodern structures are still a long way from being established.

Conclusion

Giddens' cultural analysis, then, is central to his sociology and his politics, despite his reluctance to use the word culture. I have shown that he holds to two conceptions of culture. His concept of structure points to the cultural rules that, I have argued, should be seen as the socialized capacities and dispositions that constitute the habitus and that Giddens explores by drawing on Garfinkel's ethnomethodology. This conception of *culture as structure* underpins all the key ideas in his structuration theory. His analysis of signification and legitimation points to the socio-cultural lifeworld within which people live their everyday lives and construct the narratives of self that are the basis of their sense of self-identity. This conception of *culture as lifeworld* is central to his substantive theory, where he explores the relationship between systems of political and economic domination, on the one hand, and the cultural lifeworld, on the other. He traces the contrast between traditional and modern cultural lifeworlds and explores the way in which the modern lifeworld has been radicalized in a late modern, but not yet postmodern direction. In pursuing this, Giddens examines the interplay between material resources and cultural rules, though I have argued that he fails to adequately theorize this problematic relationship. This issue underpins the relations between domination and the cultural lifeworld and between the politics of inequality and the politics of identity. While culture may be a missing word in Giddens' sociology, it is, arguably, his central and most important concept.

Notes

1 Some aspects of this chapter draw on the earlier account in Scott (1995: Ch. 9). I am grateful to José Lópe, Rob Stones, and Tim Edwards for their comments on an earlier draft.

2 Thus, Thompson, a writer close to Giddens, holds that 'culture is the pattern of meanings embodied in symbolic forms, including actions, utterances and meaningful objects of various kinds, by virtue of which individuals communicate with one another and share their experiences, conceptions and beliefs' (Thompson, 1990: 132, emphasis removed).

3 This is the argument of Margaret Archer (1988; 1995) who, nevertheless, argues that Giddens' work is marked by conflationist tendencies.
4 Only the term 'transformative capacity' is used by Giddens, who does not explicitly label the other capacities. I have labelled them according to the kinds of rules that he sees as embodied in them.

References

Archer, M.S. (1988) *Culture and Agency.*
Archer, M.S. (1995) *Realist Social Theory: The Morphogenetic Approach.* Cambridge: Cambridge University Press.
Baudrillard, J. ([1981] 1983) *Simulations.* New York: Semiotext(e).
Bauman, Z. (1973) *Culture as Praxis.* London: Routledge and Kegan Paul.
Bauman, Z. (1989) *Modernity and the Holocaust.* Cambridge: Polity Press.
Beck, U. ([1986] 1992) *Risk Society: Towards a New Modernity.* London: Sage.
Berger, P.L. and Luckmann, T. ([1966] 1971) *The Social Construction of Reality.* Harmondsworth: Allen Lane.
Bourdieu, P. ([1972] 1977) *Outline of a Theory of Practice.* Cambridge: Cambridge University Press.
Dahrendorf, R. ([1957] 1959) *Class and Class Conflict in an Industrial Society.* London: Routledge and Kegan Paul.
de Saussure, F. ([1916] 1966) *Course in General Linguistics.* New York: McGraw-Hill.
Durkheim, E. ([1893] 1984) *The Division of Labour in Society.* London: Macmillan.
Garfinkel, H. (1967) *Studies in Ethnomethodology.* Englewood Cliffs, NJ: Prentice-Hall.
Giddens, A. (1971) *Capitalism and Modern Social Theory.* Cambridge: Cambridge University Press.
Giddens, A. (1972a) 'Durkheim's political sociology', in A. Giddens (ed.) *Studies in Social and Political Theory.* London: Hutchinson.
Giddens, A. (1972b) 'Four myths in the history of social thought', in A. Giddens (ed.) *Studies in Social and Political Theory.* London: Hutchinson.
Giddens, A. (1972c) *Politics and Sociology in the Thought of Max Weber.* London: Macmillan.
Giddens, A. (1973) *The Class Structure of the Advanced Societies.* London: Hutchinson.
Giddens, A. (1976a) 'Classical social theory and the origins of modern sociology', *American Journal of Sociology* 81: 703–29.
Giddens, A. (1976b) *New Rules of Sociological Method.* London: Hutchinson.
Giddens, A. (1979) *Central Problems in Social Theory.* London: Macmillan.
Giddens, A. (1981) *A Contemporary Critique of Historical Materialism,* vol. 1: *Power, Property and the State.* London: Macmillan.
Giddens, A. (1984) *The Constitution of Society.* Cambridge: Polity Press.
Giddens, A. (1985) *A Contemporary Critique of Historical Materialism,* vol. 2: *The Nation State and Violence.* Cambridge: Polity Press.
Giddens, A. ([1986] 1987) 'Structuralism, post-structuralism and the production of culture' in A. Giddens (ed.) *Social Theory and Modern Sociology.* Cambridge: Polity Press.
Giddens, A. (1990) *The Consequences of Modernity.* Cambridge: Polity Press.
Giddens, A. (1991) *Modernity and Self-Identity.* Cambridge: Polity Press.
Giddens, A. (1992) *The Transformation of Intimacy.* Cambridge: Polity Press.
Giddens, A. (1994) *Beyond Left and Right.* Cambridge: Polity Press.
Giddens, A. (1998) *The Third Way.* Cambridge: Polity Press.
Giddens, A. (2000) *The Third Way and Its Critics.*
Giddens, A. and Pierson, C. (1998) *Conversations with Anthony Giddens.* Cambridge: Polity Press.
Habermas, J. ([1981a] 1984) *The Theory of Communicative Action,* vol. 1: *Reason and the Rationalisation of Society.* London: Heinemann.
Habermas, J. ([1981b] 1987) *The Theory of Communicative Action,* vol. 2: *The Critique of Functionalist Reason.* London: Heinemann.

Ingham, G.K. (1984) *Capitalism Divided?* London: Macmillan.

Lockwood, D. (1956) 'Some remarks on the social system'. *British Journal of Sociology, 7.*

Lockwood, D. ([1958] 1993) *The Black-Coated Worker.* Oxford: Oxford University Press.

Lockwood, D. (1960) 'The new working class', *European Journal of* Sociology, 1: 248–59.

Lockwood, D. (1964) 'Social integration and system integration', in Zollschan, G. and Hirsch, W. (eds) *Explorations in Social Change.* New York: Houghton Mifflin.

López, J. and Scott, J. (2000) *Social Structure.* Buckingham: Open University Press.

Marshall, T.H. ([1949] 1963) 'Citizenship and social class' in T.H. Marshall (ed.) *Sociology at the Crossroads.* London: Heinemann.

O'Neill, J. (ed.) (1973) *Modes of Individualism and Collectivism.* London Heinemann.

Parsons, T. (1937) *The Structure of Social Action.* New York: McGraw-Hill.

Rex, J.A. (1961) *Key Problems of Sociological Theory.* London: Routledge and Kegan Paul.

Rose, N. (1998) *Inventing Our Selves: Psychology, Power and Personhood.* Cambridge: Cambridge University Press.

Schütz, A. and Luckmann, T. ([1973] 1974) *Structures of the Life-World*, vol. 1. Evanston, IL: Northwestern University Press.

Scott, J. (1995) *Sociological Theory: Contemporary Debates.* Cheltenham: Edward Elgar.

Simmel, G. ([1900] 1978) *The Philosophy of Money.* London: Routledge and Kegan Paul.

Thompson, J.B (1990) *Ideology and Modern Culture.* Cambridge: Polity Press.

Thompson, J.B. (1995) *The Media and Modernity.* Cambridge: Polity Press.

Wallerstein, I. (1974) *The Modern World System I: Capitalist Agriculture and the Origins of the European World-Economy in the Sixteenth Century.* New York: Academic Press.

Wallerstein, I. (1980) *The Modern World System II: Mercantilism and the Consolidation of the European World-Economy, 1600–1750.* New York: Academic Press.

Wallerstein, I. (1989) *The Modern World System III: The Second Era of Great Expansion of the Capitalist World-Economy, 1730–1840s.* New York: Academic Press.

Weber, M. ([1904–5] 2002) 'The Protestant ethic and the spirit of capitalism', in P. Baehr, and G.C. Wells (eds) *Max Weber: The Protestant Ethic and the 'Spirit' of Capitalism, and Other Writings.* Harmondsworth: Penguin.

Weber, M. ([1919–20] 1927) *General Economic History.* New York: Greenberg.

PART II

CONTEMPORARY CULTURAL THEORY

CHAPTER SIX
●●●●●●●●

Zygmunt Bauman, Culture and Sociology

Peter Beilharz

Culture is ubiquitous, and so, it sometimes seems, is cultural studies. The visual turn now replaces the cultural or linguistic turn of the post-war period in Western intellectual life. Ours is a visual age, an age, apparently, of image, sign, symbol. The emergence of popular culture as an intellectual concern, posited by Antonio Gramsci, and developed through the work of the Birmingham School has led to a process where textuality rules, whether in written or especially in visual form. Whether or not film or video replaces the book, or essay, these are nevertheless cultural forms which have material frameworks and constraints. Modes of information are still, in some senses, modes of production or creation. Culture needs to be interpreted within and against the framework of social relations which makes it possible, and frames its availability.

If in this context cultural studies is transfixed with representation, ordinary sociology is often so tired as to seem useful without being interesting. There are exceptions; the work of Zygmunt Bauman is one of them. His work is exceptional because it responds to the signs of the times, but mediates this practical level of culture with the theoretical culture we inherit from the classics, not least here Marx, Weber and Freud. Bauman develops some of leading claims and critiques of classical sociology to formulate a critique of modernism, and then to anticipate the postmodern, even as he insists that a sociology of the postmodern may be more powerful or less immanent than a postmodern sociology.

In this chapter I offer a reading of Bauman's views on culture back through the work of his classical interlocutors, especially Marx, Weber, and Freud. Returning to his early work, especially *Culture as Praxis* (1973b) and *Towards a Critical Sociology* (1976), my argument is that these initial sensibilities are worked through with passing reference to Foucault and especial reference to Lévi-Strauss and the idea of structuring as an activity. Culture is a structuring activity, sometimes successful and sometimes happy, sometimes significant as creative or ordinary or tragic destruction, sometimes more anthropologically indicative of the incremental repetition and innovation of everyday life. Bauman makes sense of culture by manoeuvring its immediate contents against the larger signs and waves of our times, from capitalism to rationalization. Bauman follows the classical tradition in discerning patterns or trends of culture, mediated by power or domination. Like the process he seeks to interpret, Bauman innovates by mediating between the cultural signs of the times and the sense that there are larger social dynamics or logics behind them. To innovate is to work within and out of tradition. Culture emerges out of traditions, however invented. Bauman's traditions are many, strong and varied, as are his innovations (Beilharz, 2000).

Marx's Shadow

Critical theory takes its stand against traditional theory: both of these traditions had first to be invented. Critical theory begins with Marx. Bauman is always in Marx's shadow. This is apparent not only in the heavier contours of capitalism, alienation and verification, but also in more suggestive moments or clues, as in the case of the idea of second nature. Marx's lifelong project in the critique of political economy is itself a critique of a culture of production. The great power of capital lies in its protean capacity of creative destruction, and in its ability to naturalize this form of production and the forms of life that correspond with it. Marx's curiosity about ideology persists across his life's work, even if it were an exaggeration to say that he develops a robust theory of ideology or culture. Instead we encounter a series of hints from the *German Ideology* through to the image of commodity fetishism in *Capital*. Culture becomes more fully central for Marxism with the emergence of Western Marxism, in response to the cultural specificity of the Russian Revolution, and the critical theory of the Frankfurt School, which can be seen as a response to fascism. If the Bolsheviks seek, among other things, to generate a modernist, or Taylorist industrial culture, the Nazi hope of a Thousand Year Reich is also a pre-eminently cultural project. Social engineering is also a cultural project. The signal figure in Western Marxism here becomes Gramsci, whose critical purposes are stretched across these utopias and their specifically Italian variants.

The greater thinker of culture, connecting Marx's critique of political economy to the work of the Frankfurt School, is the Hungarian Georg Lukács. Lukács' *History and Class Consciousness* (1971) goes further than any other period text in the direction of problematizing the themes of reification, alienation and objectification. Lukács is also the pivotal connection between Marx's critique of culture and Weber's: the idea of the rationalization of the world from this point is equally enmeshed with the problems of commodification and rational calculation. As Karl Löwith was to explain the parallel in his remarkable 1932 study, *Max Weber and Karl Marx*, (1982) the two greats of German sociology could best be aligned as philosophers of history with an eye to the diagnosis of the situation of the times, characterized in the logic of alienation for Marx and the logic of rationalization for Weber. What Lukács had accomplished in *History and Class Consciousness* was to fuse the two perspectives. Lukács's emphasis on the more Marxian theme, of commodification, nevertheless located this process within the horizon of world rationalization. Lukács reinforced the centrality of capitalism to modernity at the same time as he expanded the optic of modernity to include capitalism, rather than the other way around. Culture hence rests on reification, or the re-enchantment as well as disenchantment of the world. The magic of commodities, for Marx, works like the magic of religion for Feuerbach, with the difference that the god of the commodity is unrelenting; we have no alternative but to work, consume and die.

Yet there are alternatives, and this is one persistent motif across Bauman's work; if we did this, we could still do other. And if we cannot find fulfilment in the public life of capitalism or bureaucracy, we can seek out objectification, or non-alienated relationships at home, or in the private sphere. This is the context in which Bauman picks up the idea of second nature, in *Towards a Critical Sociology* (1976). Hegel suggests the idea, which Marx plays with and implies is a core theme for sociology. To say that we naturalize a commodified world is also to say that we make second nature of it. Capitalism becomes imprinted within our culture and internalized within the psyche, to the extent that we cannot imagine (or we believe we cannot imagine) that there was ever any other way to live. For Bauman, then, both 'nature' and 'culture' are by-products of human practice. Culture is the level of reality between us and nature. The problem in sociology, for Bauman, arrives at the point at which 'culture' or 'society' is turned into a god no less demanding than the magic of commodity fetishism. Durkheim, in turn, for his part deifies society, confirming the status of sociology as the science of this dubious object. Bauman's scepticism at Durkheim's achievement goes right through to *Society Under Siege* (2002b), where society is viewed as an hypostatization of a kind which culture can never be. Where the idea of society fetishises, that of culture pluralizes. Into the twentieth century, for Bauman, we witness a bifurcation between two streams of scientific and critical sociology. The stream of critical sociology parallels that of critical theory and Western Marxism.

From Freud to Weber

If Lukács posited the necessary synthesis of Marx and Weber, it was critical theory that turned to Freud. Freud is a significant presence in Bauman's sociology, along with all these others, but at the level of culture rather than subject. This is not only because of the centrality of the psyche, or the unconscious, matters themselves which Bauman does not dwell upon until later, when he turns to the face of the other and the problem of ethics in *Postmodern Ethics* (1992). Bauman's use of Freud takes on the broader, civilizational horizons rather than the more closely psychoanalytical dimensions of his project. Freud's famous book, known to us as *Civilization and its Discontents* originally used the word *Kultur* as its subject, and while there is a long controversy, itself cultural, over the relationship between the idea of civilization and that of culture, the elision here is significant. Civilization, in Freud's English-language title, could be read as referring to a surplus of culture. Progress rests on the suppression of instincts; human civilization needs a second nature, a new condition which denies animal nature. We are bound to our misery, as moderns. The background images of the Greeks never leave us. In Marx, it may be the figure of Prometheus, in Weber, Sisyphus, in Freud, Oedipus who stalks us.

More generally, our misery will with good fortune be less that of material deprivation, and more that of self-incurred tutelage. Human creatures are equally capable of self-constitution and self-destruction, even if the manifestations of this process or condition vary. Bauman chases this theme into the essays gathered in *Postmodernity and its Discontents*, where the sense is that today we reverse or modify the deal which Freud observed in 1930 (Bauman, 1997). Bauman's fear is that, where we in the West perhaps traded freedom against security in the years of the post-war welfare state, today's citizens happily trade security (often that of others) against the illusory hope of individual freedom. Ours is the age of the new individualism, which means that ours is a new cultural moment, or else that of the return of an older personal liberalism in newly technologized and valorized forms.

Bauman's twist on Freud, here on the themes of changing forms of humanly-created discontents, is less imposing than his dialogue with the ghost of Freud in *Mortality, Immortality and Other Life Strategies* (1993a). Now culture figures, as in Freud, as a prosthetic against death. Death is the vital, absent presence in sociology; it is the very reason for being of culture. We create in the face of death; it is the prospect of death which motivates us to seek immortality, to build, to create and pro-create, to preserve and extend the traditions which we inherit. Culture begins as survival, and becomes a process of constitution. As Bauman puts it:

> Human culture is, on the one hand, a gigantic (and spectacularly successful) ongoing effort to give meaning to human life; on the other hand, it is an obsti-nate (and somewhat less successful) effort to suppress the awareness of the irreparably surrogate, and brittle character of such meaning.
>
> (ibid.: 8)

If our image of classical culture is shadowed by the figures of Sisyphus, Prometheus and Oedipus, modern Western culture's striking figures are the images of Faust and Frankenstein. Humanism's desperate attempt to make gods of men stumbles at the very point of mortality; gods do not die. Nationalism becomes the ersatz solution, offering group immortality where there is no immortality for individuals.

Some nationalisms may be less poisonous than others; radicals for long have liked to think that the nationalism of the oppressed is more legitimate than the nation-alisms of the victors. In Bauman's way of thinking, this kind of distinction is difficult to sustain, for the first turns too easily into the second. The revolutionary mentality seeks to reverse the dialectic of master and slave rather than to transcend it. All forms of nationalism, progressive or not, rest on the postulation of an other, an enemy to be destroyed. History here is less immediately the history of class struggles, and more directly the ongoing overthrow and renewal of masters and slaves. Certainly this is the image of history we associate with Max Weber: domination will never end; poli-tics, ethics and aesthetics increasingly become marginal to the instrumental rational-ities of markets and states. Bauman shares Weber's diagnosis, but not necessarily his prognosis. Bauman retains an anthropological optimism within a historical pes-simism regarding the human condition in modern times. Second nature never seeps entirely into the fibres of our souls. What we know about modernity seems even more acutely evident in postmodern times. Things, people, relationships and institutions change, contingency rules, all that is solid melts into air. Yet Bauman's elective affinity with Weber is clear, especially in the project of *Modernity and the Holocaust* (1989). This is, essentially, a Weberian argument or an argument of Weberian sympathy. For here, to extend Lukács, capitalism may be one formal precondition of fascism, but it is the logic of rational calculation rather than commodification that holds up the operations of Auschwitz.

Bauman's analysis of the Holocaust is necessarily multicausal. The general controversy around *Modernity and the Holocaust* concerns Bauman's insistence that the Holocaust was only possible as a modern phenomenon (see Beilharz, 2002). Industrial killing on a mass scale was dependent on modern technology and bureaucracy, though Bauman nowhere identifies modernity and fascism. The point, rather, is that modernity is a necessary if insufficient context for the Holocaust. Modern bureaucracy itself did not cause the Holocaust, either; yet alongside the murderous ideology of the Final Solution, the bureaucratic mentality was vital to its application. Bauman's sociology still travels with the spirit of Weberian sociology, for its curiosity here is in character, or personality structure. Weber's famous interest in Puritanism in *The Protestant Ethic and the Spirit of Capitalism* is primarily in its culture, only secondarily in its institutional forms. Weber's sociology here again coincides with Marx's, for their combined curiosity is in what Bauman follows under the category second nature. The curiosity we have in capitalism or bureaucracy is in what kinds of creatures these make us – specialists without spirit, hedonists without heart, individual consumers rather than collective producers, or in extreme circumstances followers of rules who are oblivious to the face of the other.

Bauman's interest in personality-types reflects his enthusiasm for Simmel as well as his connection to Weber. Simmel most famously suggested the stranger as a modern character-type – she who comes and goes and stays, who may be offered the provisional or probationary belonging of assimilation, as were the Jews in Germany before 1933, that kind of belonging at the behest of the host which is always tentative, always open to suspension at the will of the host. Bauman's response to the image of the stranger is indeed to continue the period identification of the stranger and the Jew, not least in his masterwork, *Modernity and Ambivalence* (1993b). Bauman's gift lies in his capacity to connect the diagnosis of the present with the heritage of critical sociology, so that he proceeds to invent names for new character-types, most notably the dyad of tourist and vagabond, a new type of relationship in the image of master and slave, now with mobility rather than capital or even cultural capital as the source of domination's divide.

Enter Foucault

The broad sympathy of Bauman's sociology is German, but with this twist: his is a specific, East European critical theory. It is Germanic, but it is neither parochial nor nationalist. It crosses borders, as does world history. Its broad orientation is European, this more than British or American. And it is open to the French, not least in sociology and anthropology. Here there are two striking presences – those of Michel Foucault and Claude Lévi-Strauss, the latter even more powerful than the former. Foucault's significance in recent intellectual history remains open to debate. Foucault's project is both brilliant and fascinating, yet its reception is often acontextual, minimizing the significance of other key French thinkers from the Annales School to Canguilhem who were crucial to his cultural formation and to that of modern French critique. Its reception also avoids Foucault's debt to the Frankfurt School and to Weber, the logic of whose work his own project follows and extends. In its Anglo reception, especially, and given the extraordinary influence of Althusserian Structuralist Marxism into the 1980s, Foucault often became viewed as the new Marx. Whether this enthusiastic reception reflects the precise nature of Foucault's contribution remains to be established. What is clear is the extent to which, having spurned Weber and Lukács, those parts of the Left intelligentsia who became Foucault's champions often responded to the kindred themes of power and rationality in his work. Foucault was available to those moving out of Althusser in ways that Weber, Gramsci and Lukács were not. Bauman was not part of this Anglo trend; the ethics of his Marxism were humanist, rather than structuralist or scientific in their claims. The Renaissance Marxism of Czech, Hungarian and Polish intellectuals in the 1960s connected to the early Marx, to the *Paris Manuscripts* rather than to the claims of *Capital*. Bauman's use of Foucault, then, is more selective, even if powerful. The key text here is *Memories of Class*, its title as evocative of Freud, again, as of Marx.

Memories of Class marks the beginning of Bauman's adieu to Marx, at least in the formal sense, for otherwise the broader motif for radical intellectuals would be once a Marxist, always a postMarxist (Bauman, 1982). The use of the idea of memory to distance the concept of class cuts both ways. The centrality of class, not least for culture, is something Bauman wants to distance himself from. In the British tradition, especially, class has always been caught up with status; thus the centrality of T.H. Marshall's conjunction of citizenship and class. *Memories of Class* indicates both their pertinence or presence, and the sense that these are memories that weigh on us, like the past. Bauman remains much taken by this sense, which we associate with Marx's historical writing, that we are haunted by the ghosts of the past. Indeed, these ghosts also hold up our culture, whether they call us back to the foundational class struggles of the nineteenth century or the life of the Holocaust as a ghost. The more general issue is the anthropological sense that we are creatures who work out of memory, out of culture, out of the invention of tradition. This means that we engage in different patterns of recognition and misrecognition. The particular connection with Foucault here is in Bauman's use of *Discipline and Punish* as a way to think not about institutions of incarceration but the factory, which is indeed from one perspective an institution of confinement and discipline itself. The result, in Bauman's hands, is, so to speak, a Foucauldian curiosity with a Marxian inflection, for this approach takes us back to Marx's *Capital* as a sociology of the factory and its discipline of the proletarian subject, body and soul. The object of capitalist culture is to generate output, results, by the routinization of labour, the body and its skills and the internalization of this process as second nature.

This is why the most intriguing of interim categories in this field remains the idea not of capital, on the most abstract level, or labour process, on the most concrete, but of Fordism, which connects us back to Gramsci. Fordism is the culture of modernizing capitalism, *par excellence*, precisely because it combines a culture of production with a culture of capacity to consume, both of which depend on the naturalization of this way of being in the world. The limit of Fordism is its national frame, in its presupposition that the local producers are also the consumers of the goods that they produce, though Fordism of course also always had a global reach, not least through South America. In the period of post-war boom, however, the point is that class struggle becomes internalized by the distributive logic of capitalism itself. Labour is integrated into the capitalist system, and becomes legitimate as a systemic actor. This does not, however, make a proletariat of happy robots, as C. Wright Mills sarcastically suggested. In Bauman's view, we could neither be happy – for we are bound by our discontents – nor robotic, as we could at most mimic the motions of obedience, while our minds wander off elsewhere. Nevertheless, the point remains that the modernist factory, like the institutions of schooling or incarceration, relied on strategies like those anticipated in Bentham's imaginary Panopticon, and while post-Fordist production might rely more on flexibility and the cultivation of some working autonomy, the possibilities of electronic surveillance, say, in telephone call centres are expanding. While there may be an apparent shift of the dominant form of culture from the Voice to the Eye, older patterns of domination persist, not least across the global system. Bauman connects these images back again to the dialectics of master and slave and to the centrality of movement; his most powerful critique of the process we call globalization is less to do with the fear of cultural homogenization than with the ethics of asymmetrical distribution of life-chances. As Bauman puts it, glocalization involves globalization for some people, localization for some others. The participants in this dyad, still, are held together not only by difference but more directly by dependence and exploitation.

The Structuralist Promise

Structuralism was, and remains, an extraordinary phenomenon in recent intellectual history. Its influence was compulsive for 20 years; and now its presence is an absence. Louis Althusser, the most famous of Marxist structuralists, insisted that he was never a structuralist. The three kings of structuralism were thought to be Foucault in history of the sciences, Jacques Lacan in psychoanalysis and Claude Lévi-Strauss in anthropology. Althusser's credentials, in comparison to these thinkers, were always Marxist. Bauman's opening to structuralism, however, was cultural rather than political. Where Althusser and his followers claimed that capitalism was maintained by a determinate mode of production and its cultural, ideological and political superstructure, Lévi-Strauss sought otherwise to ponder the possibility that all humans were combined by a universal mental structure which meant that they all told similar stories in different ways. Culture-making was universal, but the creation of cultures was relative.

The idea of structure was a familiar one, back through Freud to Marx. If for the followers of Freud the unconscious was structured like a language, *langue* behind *parole*, for the followers of Marx, the capitalist structure of wage – labour relations held up the phenomenal world of commodities which presented itself to us in everyday life as prior. Bauman's attraction, here, was more to the idea of structuring as an activity. Structuralism, for Bauman, was an interesting if unconvincing project. For meaning was contextual, rather than semantic; think only of a word like 'fuck', whose meaning might vary from ecstatic to insulting, depending entirely on context. Humans have great potential, for Bauman, even when they create sameness, conformism, boredom or cruelty. But meaning is ambivalent; ambivalence becomes a motif of our times, and is characteristic of our meaning-giving capacities. The issue, for Bauman even in 1973, is that the empirical reality of each culture can be said to be full of 'floating' signs (Bauman, (1973b) 1999: 75). The idea of communication presumes stability or order, which is one thing we do not find here. The purpose of culture, therefore, is less communication than 'ordering'; only ordering is highly variable and fraught. Just as the pursuit of recognition generates misrecognition, so does the ordering activity fail, generate disorder, even chaos.

There is no such thing as order, only orders, resulting from different kinds of will-to-order. Order is a graded notion; the level of orderliness is measured by the degree of predictability. Ordering reduces chaos, but does not dispel it (ibid.: 79). Here it is system, not language (as the structuralist followers of Saussure would insist) which is conceptually prior, with the proviso that 'system' represents the will-to-system. Language, in any case, cannot be the master metaphor for social sciences. Social structure, contingent in turn, needs then to be understood as activity, as the result of human praxis. Bauman retains the animating interest of the young Marx in the idea that humans are sensual, suffering creatures whose understanding is best to be located in the pattern of their activities, whether good, evil or just pedestrian. Bauman's interest here is persistently anthropological, and it is this which in turn connects him to Lévi-Strauss. For he maintains the Marxian focus on anthropology in its dual sense – in the cultural anthropology of how humans manifest their spirit through creation and destruction (and in modernity, in creative destruction), as well as in the philosophical anthropology which seeks to puzzle over human capacity, character, autonomy and dependence.

This old word, praxis, is now as rarely encountered as its Marxian mate, dialectic. If the second was misused as a kind of interpretative magic, the first, praxis, had its own halo in the 1960s, and it was this which the scientific socialism of Althusser sought to dispel. For Althusserians it was structure, or the level of truth behind practical experience, which offered real insight. Bauman's historic connection to humanist Marxism suggested otherwise; at least, it insisted that one important purpose of a critical sociology is to observe and interpret the manifest contents of common behaviour, in ritual, routine or in innovative form. This brings us to Bauman's major work in the field, *Culture as Praxis*.

Bauman begins from the premise that while there have been endless attempts either to catalogue definitions of culture, or else to bring down new and final definitions, what is really necessary here is typology. Bauman indicates three main fields of discourse on culture. Bauman's first field of discourse concerning culture is the hierarchical: some people have more culture than others. Culture in this sense is aligned to its oldest meaning, of cultivation, as in agriculture. The value conferred upon cultivation, here, itself introduces the idea of value; some cultures are worth more than others. This is the idea of culture as civilization, where as in *Civilization and its Discontents* culture can also cut both ways. But this realm of culture can also be viewed as a matter of personal development, self-cultivation or *Bildung*, developing endowments into talents, so that it also has a more democratic, or distinct note; we cannot develop endowments that we do not have. The second field is anthropological, or historical – it pluralizes cultures, as travel or movement indicates is necessary. The travelling idea of culture is classical: it opens with Herodotus, and the observation of human difference. This field of usage may still be hierarchical, in the way that it values, for here the silent ground of judging difference is the sense of 'different to us'. Bauman's third proposed field of culture is generic. Rather than observing difference, as in the second approach, the generic way of thinking presents the reality of culture as its unity. We all do the same things – we are born, love, procreate, eat, shit and die – only the way we carry out these cultural practices is different. One way of thinking this difference in unity is via the work of Clifford Geertz, though Bauman's stronger attraction here is to the work of Lévi-Strauss. Culture, however, is for Bauman a process, rather than a result. As he puts it here, 'Structure … is a less probable state than disorder' (Bauman, 1973a: 54). Culture is what Bauman calls the structuring activity; it represents the tension or struggle between freedom and dependence.

The Structuring Activity

Culture as Praxis ([1973] 1999) is an interesting book to return to, three decades after its first appearance. It is the only one of Bauman's early English-language books to be republished, in which Bauman revisits the field he himself tilled earlier. Bauman's Introduction to the Second Edition (1999) dusts off its references and authorities; some cultural markers lose their significance over time. The nature of Bauman's self-reflexivity, however, is such as to make him wonder what is living and what is dead in these pages. For culture is also defined by the fact that it recycles. *Culture as Praxis* is itself part of our intellectual culture. Culture relies also on habit, or habitus; so that what is innovative in one moment looks repetitive or merely habitual later. Yet culture, as Bauman argues here, is often associated with the realm of freedom, as is nature with the realm of necessity. The ambivalence of creativity is apparent. It is a prejudice of the Enlightenment that the world is an essentially human creation; modernity is by definition future-oriented, henceforth it is no longer good enough to be creatures of habit (ibid.: xi). Henceforth, culture, or consciousness, must be consciously formed. The central distinction in thinking about culture here, in Bauman's 30-year revisitation, is twofold. We use culture to refer to creativity or innovation, but also to normative regulation, or social reproduction. Rather than the sense that culture is threefold, hierarchical/differential/generic as in the earlier typology of *Culture as Praxis*, this dual distinction evokes rather the logic of *Towards a Critical Sociology*, where the significant distinction is that between system-maintenance (and conformism) and critique (or creativity). Parsons' view of structure is as system, not tradition, habitus or muddling through. Systems are based on boundaries; their purpose is to assimilate difference, even if they ultimately cannot do so.

At this point in his revisitation Bauman turns directly to Lévi-Strauss, for his own sense in retrospect is that it is the work of Lévi-Strauss which made *Culture as Praxis* possible, or called it into being. Thus, Bauman, in 1999:

> The first insight into the futility of the 'systemic' conception of culture was the formidable work of Claude Lévi-Strauss, whose work inspired most of this book's arguments. Rather than as an inventory of a finite number of values overseeing the whole field of interaction or a stable code of closely related and complementary behavioural precepts, Lévi-Strauss portrayed culture as a structure of choices – a matrix of possible, finite in number yet practically unaccountable permutations.
>
> (ibid.: xxvii)

Lévi-Strauss's sense of culture crosses all three of the broader fields indicated by Bauman, if especially the second, differential and third, generic, for the diversity of permutations goes together with a comparability of purpose; and the sense of choice, or a repertoire of choices remains central. It is because Lévi-Strauss sees structuring as an activity that he can push the image of structure from a cage to a catapult; from a trimming/truncating/cramping/fettering device to a determinant of freedom; from a weapon of uniformity into the tool of variety; from a protective shield of stability into the engine of never-ending and forever incomplete change (ibid.: xxvii).

Notwithstanding Lévi-Strauss's elevation of the value of synchrony over diachrony or history, his effect on Bauman was liberatory. Thus Bauman chooses, from his own later intellectual repertoire, to align Lévi-Strauss and Castoriadis. The parallel is already suggested in the cage to catapult story, for catapults also destroy, and as Castoriadis insisted, there is nothing irredeemably good or positive about creativity; the Holocaust and the Gulag were also the results of creativity. Culture is creation, as well as reproduction; but this claim of itself tells us nothing of the content or value of culture. Cultures are open to criticism, but in the plural. Cultures travel, or are constituted in the movement or traffic which is so central to the present.

So distinct a figure is Lévi-Strauss in Bauman's repertoire that he is the only thinker about whom Bauman writes a vignette, in the form of an entry in a social theory text. In his entry on 'Claude Lévi-Strauss' Bauman presents Lévi-Strauss's work as an essential step away from the ethnographic obsession with the idea that the anthropologist can become immersed in the culture of the other. From here it is but a short step to the idea articulated by Joel Kahn, that the project before us is an anthropology of modernity: in the dual sense, that our others are also modern, and that we stand to learn a great deal from seeking to take an anthropological distance from our own modernities, to treat them as though they were, are, also exotic (Bauman, 2002a; Kahn, 2001). The foreign becomes familiar at the same time as the familiar is made foreign; or that, at least, is the orienting purpose of our activity. All cultures are mythological; myths are good to think with, or at least some myths are enabling while others are disabling.

In a tellingly cultural confession, Lévi-Strauss informs us that he had 'Three Mistresses' – Marxism, psychoanalysis and geology. These are not each irredeemably structuralist, but they are all structural, indicating the difficult yet apparently unavoidable spatial images of critique: 'surface' and 'depth' (Bauman, 2002a: 201). Bauman's point of insistence is to maintain the duality of focus, to succumb neither to surface image or representation, nor only to summon up the hidden depths behind them. The practice of sociology, in this way of thinking, is to mediate between the two levels of reality, analysis and activity. The strength of a cultural sociology, unlike some work in cultural studies, is to insist on the reality beyond the text as well as the reality in the text.

A Little Glass of Rum

The point of cultural sociology, to put it differently, is to seek to hold together culture and power, image or symbol and relationship. Bauman's attraction to Marx, Weber, Freud and Foucault can best be seen in this light. Bauman takes his distance from the redemptive, or Faustian stream in Marx; he is more highly animated by the problems of the time than by the obsession of Freud's followers with the unconscious or with language. With Weber, and later Foucault, both under the sign of Nietzsche, Bauman worries the dark side of modernity. With Lévi-Strauss, he negotiates the ambivalence of our worlds. This is nowhere more apparent than in the way in which Bauman connects the figure of the stranger, from Simmel, to the hints offered by Lévi-Strauss on assimilation and expulsion in *Tristes Tropiques*, veritably a desert-island book, arguably for us, certainly for Bauman. Here Lévi-Strauss speculates, in closing his book over a little glass of rum, that if we studied societies from the outside, it would be tempting to distinguish two contrasting types: those which practise cannibalism – that is, which regard the absorption of certain individuals possessing dangerous powers as the only means of neutralizing those powers and even of turning them to advantage – and those which, like our own society, adopt what might be called the practice of *anthropemy* (from the Greek, *emein*, to vomit); faced with the same problem, the latter type of society has chosen the opposite solution, which consists in ejecting dangerous individuals from the social body and keeping them temporarily or permanently in isolation away from all contact with their fellows, in establishments specially intended for this purpose. Most of the societies which we call primitive would regard this custom with profound horror; it would make us in their eyes, guilty of that same barbarity of which we are inclined to accuse them because of their symmetrically opposite behaviour (Lévi-Strauss, 1955: 508). Such institutions of separation might be called concentration camps, more specifically death camps (in Nazi Germany) or detention centres (in contemporary Australia).

Bauman's variation on this critical theme is to view order-building as a war of attrition against strangers and the strange. As he elaborates:

> In this war (to borrow Lévi-Strauss's concepts) two alternative, but also comple-mentary strategies were intermittently deployed. One was *anthropophagic*, annihilating the strangers by *devouring* them and then metabolically transform-ing into a tissue indistinguishable from one's own. This was the strategy of *assimilation*: making the different similar; smothering of cultural or linguistic dis-tinctions; forbidding all traditions and loyalties except those meant to feed the conformity to the new and all-embracing order; promoting and enforcing one and only one measure of conformity. The other strategy was *anthropoemic*, *vomiting* the strangers, banishing them from the limits of the orderly world and barring them from all communication with those inside. This was the strategy of *exclusion* – confining the strangers within the visible walls of the ghettos or behind the invisible, yet no less tangible, prohibitions of *commensality, connu-bium* and *commercium*, 'cleansing' – expelling the strangers beyond the fron-tiers of the managed and manageable territory; or, when neither of the two measures was feasible – destroying the strangers physically.
>
> (Bauman 1997: 16)

Anthropophagic strategies follow the logic of assimilation, always a superior strategy to exclusion, except within its own limits: assimilation is an attack on difference or ambivalence, and its tolerance is volatile, depends on political and nationalist senses of limits. Liberal tolerance is always preferable to exclusion, but its availability is depen-dent on the will of the host. Anthropoemic strategies follow the logic of expulsion, dis-cipline and punish along ethnic or racial lines. The modernist state strategy is precisely, for Bauman, one which acts out the dynamic of creative destruction. Except that the logic even of totalitarian power is never complete, and the residual humanity left both in matters and slaves never subsides. Culture persists, even in the face of power.

Conclusion

Bauman's encounter with Lévi-Strauss is suggestive, though it is by no means singu-lar; his interlocutors are many and various, and this is one reason why his work is interesting. Bauman's more recent elucidation of this especial enthusiasm within his repertoire is by no means novel, however; culture recycles as well as innovates, redis-covers as well as inventing.

If it is intellectually fruitful here to cast an eye back over Bauman's earlier English-language work, it is also culturally advantageous, in order to contemplate his own means of creation and repetition or revisiting. For Bauman flags the significance of these ideas as far back as his Leeds Inaugural Lecture of 1972. There Bauman indicated project, rather than prospectus:

> Lévi-Strauss himself acknowledged his intellectual debt to Marx: 'The famous statement by Marx, "men make their own history, but they do not know how they are making it" justifies, first, history and, second, anthropology.' Structuralism is designed to provide precisely the 'how' answer. There are limits to both human freedom of manoeuvre and society's freedom to choose the patterns it imposes on its members.

> Being determined and being creative are not two diametrically opposed modes of existence; they are, in fact, two in one, the double face of the same human condition. Science and art finally meet again after many decades of schism. If they did not meet so far, it was because no relevant meeting ground had been found. Now it can be provided by the study of the universal structure of human culture, in which two capacities of humans – objective and subjective – fuse into one.

> (Bauman, 1972: 197–8)

This is not the language that Bauman would employ today, but the ideas are roughly continuous. Neither sign nor language, but repertoire rules.

Zygmunt Bauman's work begins with culture, travels through socialism and ends with the critique of modernity as order, which generates excess. We suffer our excess of material life or things – we in the West inhabit a world infinitely more reified than Lukács's Budapest – but we also suffer moral excess, the inability to know limits, to know when to desist. The excess results in waste, in human waste, wasted lives, in a culture of extremes. Ordering can be as benign and contingent or conditional as it can be triumphalist, progressive or destructive. In *Legislators and Interpreters*, Bauman juxtaposes what he calls the gardening strategy of modernism with the gamekeeping ethic which precedes it. Bauman had his turn at gardening, or at least at attempting to help rebuild, reorder a local, Polish world in ruins after the Second World War. Today Bauman is a gamekeeper; this is his personal ethic, a way of thinking where nature and culture are not too far separated, where creative destruction might also be distanced, as in an anthropology of modernity.

References

Bauman, Z. (1972) 'Culture, values and science of society', *University of Leeds Review*, 15(2): 185–203.

Bauman, Z. (1973a) 'The structuralist promise', *British Journal of Sociology*, 24: 67–83.

Bauman, Z. ([1973b] 1999) *Culture as Praxis*, 2nd edn. London: Sage.

Bauman, Z. (1976) *Toward a Critical Sociology*. London: Routledge.

Bauman, Z. (1982) *Memories of Class*. London: Routledge.

Bauman, Z. (1989) *Modernity and the Holocaust*. Cambridge: Polity.

Bauman, Z. (1992) *Postmodern Ethics*. Cambridge: Polity.

Bauman, Z. (1993a) *Mortality, Immortality and Other Life Strategies*. Cambridge: Polity.

Bauman, Z. (1993b) *Modernity and Ambivalence*. Cambridge: Polity.

Bauman, Z. (1997) *Postmodernity and Its Discontents*. Cambridge: Polity.

Bauman, Z. (2002a) 'Claude Lévi-Strauss', in A. Elliott and L. Ray (eds) *Key Contemporary Social Theorists*. Oxford: Blackwell, pp. 197–203.

Bauman, Z. (2002b) *Society Under Siege*. Cambridge: Polity.

Beilharz, P. (2000) *Zygmunt Bauman: Dialectic of Modernity*. London: Sage.

Beilharz, P. (ed.) (2002) *Zygmunt Bauman*. London: Sage, 4 vols.

Kahn, J. (2001) 'Anthropology and modernity', *Current Anthropology*, 42, (5): 651–80.

Lukács, G. (1971) *History and Class Consciousness*. London: Merlin.

Lévi-Strauss, C. (1955) *Tristes Tropiques*. Harmondsworth: Penguin.

Löwith, K. (1982) *Max Weber and Karl Marx*. London: Allen and Unwin.

Foucault

CHAPTER SEVEN

Interpretive analytics and the constitution of the social

Tim May and Jason Powell

Introduction

My objective has been to create a history of the different modes by which, in our culture, human beings are made subjects.

(Foucault, 1983: 208)

Michel Foucault's work covered an enormous range of topics and has been influential across a variety of disciplines. At the same time it can be puzzling for those wishing to understand its implications for analysing cultural relations. Foucault was a 'masked philosopher' who deliberately sought to avoid being aligned with any particular school of thought: 'It is true that I prefer not to identify myself, and that I'm amused by the diversity of the ways I've been judged and classified' (1997: 113).

Despite this preference, writers have identified affiliations, influences and the productivity of encounters with the work of other scholars and traditions: Nietzsche and Weber (Braidotti, 1991; Owen, 1997); Marx (Smart, 1983); Kuhn (Dreyfus and Rabinow, 1982); Gramsci (Kenway, 1990) feminisms (Sawicki, 1991; McNay, 1994) and Habermas (Ashenden and Owen, 1999). Commentators have also suggested new terminologies to capture the essence of his approach: 'interpretative analytics' (Dreyfus and Rabinow, 1982), 'modes of information' (Poster, 1984), 'governmentality studies' (Burchell et al., 1991; Dean, 2004), and the analysis of 'dispositifs' (Deleuze, 1992). In addition, his ideas have become influential in a variety of fields of investigation aside from cultural studies: criminology (Garland, 1985), management and organization (Knights and McCabe, 2003), social research (Kendall and Wickham, 1999), philosophy (Armstrong, 1992) and sociology and politics (Burchell et al., 1991).

Foucault's refusal to be characterized in particular ways may be interpreted as a designed socio-political strategy central to his overall philosophy (Raulet, 1983). He rejects any allusion to certainty in social and political life and holds that there is no universal understanding beyond history – placing him at odds with currents in Marxism, as well as rationalist thought in general. That being noted, we can find imperatives that receive differing degree of emphasis throughout his work, one of which is 'to discover the relations of specific scientific disciplines and particular social practices' (Rabinow, 1984: 4). He has raised an awareness that disciplines, institutions and social practices operate according to logics that are at variance with the humanist visions that are assumed to be culturally embedded (Powell and Biggs, 1999; 2000). In other words, the overt meanings given to activities do not correspond to their overall consequences. Whether these outcomes are intended or accidental was less important to Foucault than the analysis of power. As Barry Smart (1983: 77) points out, Foucauldian analysis asks of power: 'How is it exercised; by what means?', and second, 'What are the effects of the exercise of power?' Within those strategies and tactics, investigation would need to be centred on the mechanisms, the 'technologies' employed and the consequences of change.

One example of this disjuncture between humanist vision and cultural practices and its effects on the direction of modernity derives from Foucault's (1977) analysis of 'utilitarianism'. A pervasive theme of Foucault's work is the way in which the panopticon technique 'would make it possible for a single gaze to see everything perfectly' (ibid.: 173). Foucault describes how panopticism (based on the design of the utilitarian philosopher and social reformer Jeremy Bentham) becomes a process whereby certain mechanisms permeate social systems beyond actual, physical institutions. Techniques are thus 'broken down into flexible methods of control, which may be transferred and adapted ... [as] ... centres of observation disseminated throughout society' (ibid.: 211–12).

The mechanisms used to extend the reach of centres of power through the social body will vary depending upon the grounds upon which they are required to operate. Their function is to rouse and sustain moral interpretations of particular social behaviours throughout intermittent observation such that their objects come to internalize their own surveillance around given norms of conduct. One important facet of Foucault's analysis of these processes is his preoccupation with historical periods in which conventional values are in flux as in the case of 'madness', 'discipline' and 'sexuality' (Foucault, 1967; 1977; 1978) and how the emergence of cultural discourses then inform commonsensical understandings of 'normality' (McNay, 1993). There are, in other words, periods in which particular sites and forms of conduct are subject to novel mechanisms and technologies in order to facilitate the transition from one state of affairs to another (Butler, 2000). These technologies may be overtly applied during periods of flux until moral relations have been accepted, while during the process of their application they both modify and are modified by the individuals or groupings charged with their implementation. Although Foucault does not impose any sense of causality on the development of such discourses, it is possible to discern the need for both an explicit moral reason and a method of operation, shaped to whatever new contexts are appropriate.

As Rouse (1994) has pointed out, an examination of the relationship between power and knowledge is central to interpreting and understanding social phenomena via a Foucauldian framework. One of the consequences of power and knowledge is that rather than the focus on the explicit use of a particular technique of knowledge by someone in power to cause a certain effect, attention is drawn to the reflexive relationship between both elements. This leads to a concern with:

> the epistemic context within which those bodies of knowledge become intelligible and authoritative. How statements were organised thematically, which of those statements counted as serious, who was empowered to speak seriously, and what questions and procedures were relevant to assess the credibility of those statements that were taken seriously ... The types of objects in their domains were not already demarcated, but came into existence only contemporaneous with the discursive formations that made it possible to talk about them.
>
> (ibid.: 93)

So, just as knowledge shapes what action is possible and what power is exercised, those actions also shape the creation of new knowledge and what is thereby given credence. Over time, legitimate *'domains'* are established which both define what is real and what can be done about it. Other possible interpretations are simultaneously discounted and delegitimized. The result is a view and mode of practice in which power and knowledge support each other. These domains not only sustain, for example, certain professional discourses, they mould what those professions might become. This analysis of power and knowledge emphasizes their entwinement and the processes that occur as a particular domain takes shape. It also marks a distinction between what a method for both understanding and obtaining knowledge produces and the relationship between the shaping of that product and the distribution of power.

How did Foucault proceed to 'uncovering' discourses and practices? To address this, the chapter examines a series of analytical tools for social inquiry. First, these relate to archaeology and genealogy as essential backdrops for understanding subjectivity. The chapter then moves its focus to the construction of the modern subject in terms of classification practices, dividing practices and self-subjectification practices. From this it examines three categories for understanding the constitution of social relations: the body, the individual and population. Finally, we reflect on the legacy of Foucault for social inquiry.

Analytical Tools for Thinking

Archaeological analysis

It is through 'historical investigation' that scholars can understand the present. However, when utilising historical inquiry, scholars should 'use it, to deform it, to make it groan and protest' (Foucault, 1980: 54). Foucault (1972; 1977) uses his methodological 'tools' to disrupt history at the same time as giving history a 'power/ knowledge' re-configuration and that makes his approach so distinctive and relevant to social theory and cultural analysis. In *The Archaeology of Knowledge* (1972), Foucault discusses 'archaeology' as the analysis of a statement as it occurs in the historical archive. Further, archaeology 'describes discourses as practices specified in the element of the archive' (ibid.: 131), the archive being 'the general system of the formation and transformation of statements' (ibid.: 130). While an understanding of language would ask what rules have been provided for a particular statement, the analysis of discourse asks a different question: 'How is it that one particular statement appeared rather than another?' (ibid.: 27).

The use of an archaeological method explores the networks of what is *said* and what can be *seen* in a set of social arrangements: in the conduct of an archaeology there is a visibility in 'opening up' statements. For example, the work of Brooke-Ross (1986) illustrates how the rise of 'residential care' in Western culture produces statements about the 'residents' old age' while statements about 'their ageing' produces forms of visibility which reinforce the power of residential care. Such visibility is consolidated by resource allocation; the cost of residential care stands at £8 billion per year (Powell, 2001) – hence the consolidation of statements pertaining to ageing reinforces institutions such as residential care and the revenue they generate. In this context archaeology charts the relationship between statements and the visible and those 'institutions' which acquire authority and provide limits within which discursive objects may exist.

In this approach we can see that the attempt to understand the relations between statements and visibility focuses on those set of statements that make up institutions such as prisons – instructions to prison officers, statements about time-tabling of activities for inmates and the structure and space of the carceral institution itself. This leads to the production of:

> a whole micro-penality of time (lateness, absences, interruptions of tasks), of activity (inattention, negligence, lack of zeal), of behaviour (impoliteness, disobedience), of speech (idle chatter, insolence), of the body (incorrect attitudes, irregular gestures, lack of cleanliness), of sexuality (impurity, indecency).

> (Foucault, 1977: 178)

The crucial point is that this approach draws our attention to the dynamic inter-relationship between statements and institutions. Second, the attempt to describe 'institutions' which acquire authority and provide limits within which discursive objects may act, focuses again on the institution which delimits the range of activities of discursive objects (Powell and Biggs, 2000) – it is at this point that an exploration of the architectural features of the institution would be used to understand spatial arrangements. In a similar context, Goffman (1968) wrote about how spatial arrangements of 'total institutions' operate to provide care and rehabilitation at an official level and capacity, underneath the surface. Such institutions curtail the rights of those within them:

> Many total institutions, most of the time, seem to function merely as storage dumps for inmates ... but they usually present themselves to the public as rational organizations designed consciously, through and through, as effective machines for producing a few officially avowed and officially approved ends.

> (Goffman, 1968: 73)

One fundamental difference between Goffman and Foucault's interpretations of institutions would be, however, that whereas Goffman claims that total institutions are untypical of society as a whole, Foucault's critique stresses that the carceral elements of institutional life encapsulates a core feature of social life. One reason for wanting to study prisons, aside from its prior neglect, was:

> the idea of reactivating the project of a 'genealogy of morals', one which worked by tracing the lines of what one might call 'moral technologies'. In order to get a better understanding of what is punished and why, I wanted to ask the question: how does one punish?

> (Foucault, 1989: 276)

Foucault never felt totally comfortable with archaeological analysis and felt that discourses did not reveal the irregularities ongoing within social practices (Biggs and Powell, 2001). As a result he developed his methodology during the course of his investigations.

Genealogical analysis

Foucault acquired the concept of 'genealogy' from the writings of F. Nietzsche. Genealogy still maintains elements of archaeology including the analysis of statements in the 'archive' (Foucault, 1977; 1980; 1982). With genealogy, Foucault (1977) added a concern with the analysis of power/knowledge which manifests itself in the 'history of the present'. As Rose (1984) points out, genealogy concerns itself with disreputable origins and 'unpalatable functions'. This can, for example, be seen in relation to psycho-casework, care management and probation practice (Biggs and Powell, 1999; 2001; May, 1991; 1994). As Foucault found in his exploration of psychiatric power: 'Couldn't the interweaving effects of power and knowledge be grasped with greater certainty in the case of a science as "dubious" as psychiatry?' (1980: 109).

Genealogy also establishes itself from archaeology in it approach to discourse. Whereas archaeology provides a snapshot, a 'slice' through the discursive nexus, genealogy focuses on the processual aspects of the web of discourse – its ongoing character (ibid). Foucault did attempt to make the difference between them explicit:

> If we were to characterise it in two terms, then 'archaeology' would be the appropriate methodology of this analysis of local discursiveness, and 'genealogy' would be the tactics whereby, on the basis of the descriptions of these local

discursivities, the subjected knowledge's which were thus released would be brought into play.

(ibid.: 85)

Foucault is claiming that archaeology is a systematic method of investigating official statements such as dispostifs (McNay, 1994). Genealogy is a way of putting archaeology to *practical* effect, a way of linking it to cultural concerns:

A genealogy of values, morality, asceticism, and knowledge will never confuse itself with a question for their 'origins' , will never neglect as inaccessible the vicissitudes of history. On the contrary, it will cultivate the details and accidents that accompany every beginning; it will be scrupulously attentive to their petty malice; it will await their emergence, once unmasked, as the face of the other. Wherever it is made to go, it will not be reticent – in 'excavating the depths', in allowing time for these elements to escape from a labyrinth where no truth had ever detained them. The genealogist needs history to dispel the chimeras of the origin, somewhat in the manner of the pious philosopher who needs a doctor to exorcise the shadow of his soul.

(Foucault, 1984: 80)

The Making of the Modern Subject

Foucault's use of genealogy cannot be divorced from an understanding of power, nor can the constitution of the subject. With this in mind, our approach will be to consider his analytical ingenuity via an examination of different modes through which 'subjectivity' is constituted. Foucault (1982; 1983) grounded this as a pivotal mode of analysis that has been deployed in reflections on his own life (Miller, 1993). Subjectivity appears as both an experiential and discursive strategy that 'goes beyond theory' (Dreyfus and Rabinow, 1982) and provides us with a way to problematize the explanatory value and relevance of his analyses.

We will discuss Foucault's approach to subjectivity in terms of classification, dividing and self-subjectification practices. These operate in ways to structure subjectivity under the auspices of the 'rise of modernity' where, commencing in the seventeenth century, the social sciences, early capitalism and institutions began to co-ordinate new ways of objectifying 'populations' in western societies. In Foucault's analysis, the realm of the 'social' becomes the object of enquiry. Here, the term 'social' means: 'The entire range of methods which make the members of a society relatively safe from the effects of economic fluctuation by providing a certain security' (Donzelot, 1980 p: xxvi). Thus, in *Discipline and Punish* (1977), Foucault

traces the historical emergence of the social as a domain or field of inquiry and intervention, a space structured by a multiplicity of discourses emanating from the human sciences which, in their turn, are derived from, yet provide, a range of methods and techniques for regulating and ordering the social domain.

(Smart, 1983)

Classification practices

Foucault's (1980) main concern was to show that the 'truth' status of a knowledge derives from the field in which it, as a discourse, is employed and not from the interpretation of a subject's thoughts or intentions. Discourses are powerful in that they operate as a set of rules informing thought and practice and the operation of these decides who or what is constituted as an object of knowledge. The relationship between the subject and truth should be viewed as an effect of knowledge itself. Quite simply, the subject is not the source of truth. As Foucault put it: 'what if understanding the relation of the subject to the truth, were just an effect of knowledge? What if understanding were a complex, multiple, non-individual formation, not "subjected to the subject", which produced effects of truth?' (Foucault, in Elders, 1974: 149).

Knowledge is not separate from the realm of 'practice'. Knowledge is a practice that constitutes particular objects – non-theoretical elements – that are part of practice itself. Knowledge and the subject of knowledge are fused as part of the relationship between knowledge and power that is socially constructed:

> The important thing here, I believe, is that truth isn't outside power, or lacking in power: contrary to a myth whose history and functions would repay further study, truth isn't the reward of free spirits, the child of protracted solitude, nor the privilege of those who have succeeded in liberating themselves. Truth is a thing of this world: it is produced only by virtue of multiple forms of constraint. And it induces regular effects of power. Each society has its regime of truth, its `general politics' of truth.

(Foucault, 1980: 131)

Foucault is deliberately questioning the individual subject's will to construct as he sets about exploring the relationship between 'discourse' and 'subjectivity'. What emerges is a grounded understanding of power/knowledge construction and reconstruction as discourses transform people into types of subjects – as classifying practices. Through these techniques of knowing, human attributes are studied, defined, organized and codified in accordance with the meta-categories of what is 'normal'. Classifying practices and techniques of normalization designate both the objects to be known and the subjects who have the power to speak about them. Discourses thus encompass both the objective and subjective conditions of human relations (1973: 232) and these emerging forms of social regulation, characterized by notions of discipline, surveillance and normalization, are core to his theoretical studies (Foucault, 1977).

The knowledge and practices are also referred to as 'epistemes' which are 'the total set of relations that unite at a given period, the discursive practices that give rise to epistemological figures, sciences and formalised systems' (Foucault, 1972: 191). Social science disciplines, in different ways, order the status of those who can validate knowledge through inquiry. Foucault designates a discourse's function of dispersing subjects and objects as its 'enunciative modality' (ibid.: 50). This modality encompasses roles and statuses and circumscribed subject positions. Together they act to structure the space of surveillance where the institutionalization of knowledge is formed.

Dividing practices

Dividing practices are deployed in order to maintain social order – to separate, categorize, normalize and institutionalize populations. In *Madness and Civilization* (1967), *The Birth of the Clinic* (1973) and *Discipline and Punish* (1977), Foucault illustrates how 'unproductive' people were identified as political problems with the 'rise of modernity'. The state divided these people into 'the mad', 'the poor' and 'the delinquent' and subsequently disciplined them in institutions: asylums, hospitals, prisons and schools (Foucault 1977). These exercises of 'disciplinary power' were targeted at the subject and constituted techniques in these institutions. For instance, as we noted earlier, in *Discipline and Punish* Foucault argues that since the eighteenth century, prison authorities increasingly employed subtle regulatory methods of examination, training, timetabling and surveillance of conduct on offenders in which we find a whole 'micro-penality'. Overall, dividing practices are seen as integral to the rationalism of the Enlightenment narratives of liberty, individuality and rights and as coalesced with governmental forms of audit and calculation.

Self-subjectification practices

The previous modes of classification and dividing practices co-exist. Professions examine, calculate and classify the groups that governments and institutions regulate, discipline and divide. The third mode of self-subjectification is more intangible. These practices designate the ways in which people turn themselves into social subjects. Foucault claims that self-subjectification entails the deployment of technologies of the self: 'Techniques that permit individuals to affect, by their own means, a certain number of operations on their own bodies, their own souls, their own selves, modify themselves, and attain a certain state of perfection, happiness, purity, supernatural power' (Foucault, 1982: 10). In Foucault's work, self-subjectification practices proliferate in the domain of sexuality because the occupying sciences of medicine, psychology and psychoanalysis obligate subjects to speak about their sexuality. In turn, these scientific domains characterize sexual identity as pathologically 'dangerous' (Foucault, 1980). Thus, the association of sexual truth with self-subjectification gives 'experts' their power.

Self-subjectification practices inter-relate with classification and dividing practices to construct modern subjects. For instance, subjects are created by human sciences that classify problems, identities and experiences; the systems of power that divide, stratify and institutionalize types of 'elderly' subjects and the technologies of the self provide individuals with the reflexive means to problematize themselves. What Foucault seems to be confronting us with is a disturbing vision that our ideas about the depth of human experience are simply cultural veneers that exist in an interplay between power and knowledge. Shumway calls this a 'strategy of exteriority': a strategy that 'does not stem from a claim that the true being plain and visible, but from a rejection of the claim that the true is systematically disguised' (1989: 26). Foucault's analysis of subjectification practices highlights techniques used by administrative powers to problematize subjects and the games of truth employed by those who seek to know them through classification techniques.

Subjectivity: Three Domains

Foucault juxtaposes his axis of classifying, dividing and self-subjectification practices with one that delineates three domains of subjectivity: the body, the individual and population. These domains detail how modes of subjectivity impinge on modern social relations.

The body

The 'body' is a subject of discursive and political identification. In *Discipline and Punish* (1977), Foucault claims that penal practices produce the 'soul' of the offender by disciplining the body and corporealizing prison spaces. In prisons, the body's most 'essentialist needs' – food, space, exercise, sleep, privacy, light and heat – become the materials upon which schedules, timetables and micro-punishments are enacted. The body discipline developed in prisons has parallels throughout the broader disciplinary society. Indeed, the success of modernity's domination over efficient bodies in industry, docile bodies in prisons, patient bodies in clinical research and regimented bodies in schools and residential centres attests to Foucault's thesis that the human body is a highly adaptable terminus for the circulation of power relations (McNay, 1993). It would be a mistake to believe Foucault is alone in arguing that the rule of the body is fundamental to modern politico-economical and professional regimes of power. Critiques of the domination of the body were the mainstay of Frankfurt theorists such as Adorno and Horkheimer (1944) long before Foucault's work. As he noted of their work:

> As far as I'm concerned, I think that the Frankfurt School set problems that are
> still being worked on. Among others, the effects of power that are connected
> to a rationality that has been historically and geographically defined in the

West, starting from the sixteenth century on. The West could never have attained the economic and cultural effects that are unique to it without the exercise of that specific form of rationality.

(Foucault, 1991: 117)

Foucault's contribution, however, is to locate the ways in which 'bio-power' and disciplinary techniques construe the body as an object of knowledge. For example, *The History of Sexuality* depicts the dominion with which nineteenth-century experts constructed a hierarchy of sexualized bodies and divided the population into groups of 'normal', 'deviant' and 'perverted'.

While Foucault's definition of the body has inspired numerous debates, the task of refinement and problematization has largely been the province of feminist scholars. Foucault has been criticized for his lack of sensitivity and attention to gender inequality and women's history, thereby requiring theoretical revision in order to overcome such limitations (Powell and Biggs, 2000). Feminists have stressed that the body is both a site of regulation, where gendered identities are maintained and a site of resistance, where they are undone and challenged. McNay agrees with Foucault that 'sexuality is produced in the body in such a manner as to facilitate the regulation of social relations' (1993: 32). However, contra Foucault, she notes that not all aspects of sexuality, corporeality and desire are products of power relations. Passionate social relationships do not necessarily facilitate introspective forms of surveillance. 'Relationships' can transform disciplinary spaces and engage in disrupting practices. Coupled with this, Butler (1990: 141) claims that body performances that connect women to fictional feminine identities can be disrupted to expose the discretionary contingency of identities.

The individual

If disciplinary gaze is a first step, then 'interiorization' of that gaze is the second. Foucault's social contructivism, consisting of classification and dividing practices, technologies of the self and political grids of bodies and populations has fuelled his critics' claims that he deprives human subjectivity of agency (Smart, 1983). Minson claims that Foucault burdens the body with being the true subject of history and 'the flickering counterpart to the dull individual of sociology' (1985: 93). Foucault emphasizes two important aspects of individual agency that counteract his critics. First, the victims of modernity's disciplinary matrix – the prisoners, patients, and children – can subvert the regulatory forms of knowledge and subjectivity imposed upon them. Second, while power/knowledge relations construct governable individual subjects, such subjects are not fixed in their conditions of ruling and do become agents of resistance to them (Foucault, 1977; 1991a). To investigate the 'how' of power then requires:

taking the forms of resistance against different forms of power as a starting point … it consists of using this resistance as a chemical catalyst so as to bring to light power relations, locate their position, find out their point of application and the methods used. Rather than analyzing power relations from the point of view of its internal rationality, it consists of analyzing power relations through the antagonism of strategies.

(1982: 211)

Power is exercised on free subjects and guides, but does not necessarily determine, conduct.

In this formulation the individual is not the traditional subject caught in a war between domination and liberation. Rather, the individual is the personal space where both active and passive aspects of human agency and identity surface in the context of material practices. The production of identity is implicated in the production of power which is both positive and negative. Identity may be imposed through the surveillance of a subject population. This surveillance produces both discipline (that is, conformity to the norm), and the disciplines (regulated fields of knowledge and expertise). Disciplinary surveillance involves first individualizing each member of the population to facilitate the collation of observations across the population.

From these observations, statistical norms are produced relating to a multitude of characteristics. These norms are then applied back to the subjected individuals who are categorized, evaluated and acted upon according to their relation to the produced norm. Foucault's work focused on the 'history of the present' and 'power/knowledge' synthesis and how the subject was formed (Foucault, 1977; 1978). Here Foucault's work is on the 'microphysics of power' and the interplay of power relations, dividing practices and tactics in particular contexts (Foucault, 1977): the 'doctor' and 'patient'; 'prison officer' and 'prisoner'; 'teacher' and 'student' and 'social worker' and 'older consumer' (Biggs and Powell, 2001).

The population

Foucault outlines how the modern state enhanced its power by intervening in the very life of the 'bio-politics of the population' (1980: 139). Biopolitics leads to his perspective of politics or 'governmentality' (1991a: 90). In this process, power has two poles. First, a pole of transformation and, second, the human body as an object of control and manipulation. The first revolves around the notion of 'scientific categorization', for example, 'species' and 'population'. It is these categories that become objects of systematic and sustained political intervention. The other pole is not 'human species' but the human body: not in its biological sense, but as an object of control and manipulation. Collectively, Foucault calls these procedures 'technologies' which centre around the 'objectification' of the body. The overall aim is to forge: 'a docile body that may be subjected, used, transformed and improved' (1977: 198).

As modernity unfolded, Western administrators rationalized their management of social problems with technically efficient means of population control: statistics, police, health regulations and centralized welfare. Such means constituted governmentality: an assemblage of ruling practices, knowledge authorities and moral imperatives that converged on the population in order to extend the reach of the state. The controversial point is that governmentality is more complex than state power. Custodial institutions and health programmes configured individuals into sub-strata of the population. For example, pension policies define 'the elderly' as a particular group of people, while statistics elaborate their status as a demographic entity (an 'ageing population'). Thus, the disciplinary formation of subjects as a population makes possible the government of subjectification.

Discussion: The Legacy and its Implications

> It may be that the problem about the self does not have to do with discovering what it is, but maybe has to do with discovering that the self is nothing more than a correlate of technology built into our history.
>
> (Foucault, 1993: 222)

Foucault's formulation presumes the notion that individual lives are never quite complete and finished – that in order to function socially, individuals must somehow work on themselves to *turn* themselves into subjects. The notion of 'technologies' offers the opportunity for a particular analysis of the sites and methods whereby certain effects on the subject are brought about. We spoke earlier of how objectifying technologies of control are, for example, those invented in conformity with the facets of discourses provided by criminality, sexuality, medicine and psychiatry. These are deployed within concrete institutional settings whose architecture testifies to the 'truth' of the objects they contain. Thus, the possibilities of self-experience on the part of the subject are, in themselves, affected by the presence of someone who has the authority to decide that they are 'truly' ill such as a 'doctor' of medicine (Powell and Biggs, 2000). However, 'subjectifying' technologies of self-control are those through which individuals:

> effect by their own means or with the help of others a certain number of operations on their own bodies and souls, thoughts, conduct and way of being, so as to transform themselves in order to attain a certain state of happiness, purity, wisdom, perfection or immortality.
>
> (Foucault, 1988: 18)

The important issues that Foucault raises via a questioning of the centrality of the subject are associated with 'truthful' formulations of the task or the problem that certain domains of experience and activity pose for individuals themselves. The boundaries of self-experience change with every acquisition, on the part of individuals, of a possibility, or a right, or an obligation, to state a certain 'truth' about themselves. For example, biotechnology in popular culture can tell a 'truth' of selling a dream of unspoken desire of 'not growing old' to people. However, it is the self-experience of subjects that can refute, deny and accept the 'truth' claims of biotechnology. In the case of lifestyles in popular culture, the active adoption of particular consumer practices, such as uses of biotechnology contributes to a narrative that is compensatory in its construction of self (Biggs and Powell, 2001). Thus, the recourse to the notion of technologies of self is capable of accommodating the complexity of the 'subject'.

Although Foucault maintained the distinction between the technologies of power/domination and the technologies of self, these should not be regarded as acting in opposition to or in isolation to one another. Indeed, Foucault frequently spoke of the importance of considering the contingency of both in their interaction and interdependence, by identifying specific examples: 'the point where the technologies of domination of individuals over one another have recourse to processes by which the individual acts upon himself and, conversely, the points where the technologies of the self are integrated into structures of coercion' (Foucault, 1993: 203). The distinction should therefore be considered as a heuristic device and not the portrayal of two conflicting sets of interests. Overall, we should see Foucault's entire works as providing ways of understanding social relations that require on our part active interpretation, not passive regurgitation.

To take one modern example of how we might think with, alongside (and against perhaps?) Foucault. Consider the question: how is modern bio-ethics rooted in a specific configuration of subjectivity? The body culturally represents the best hiding place, a hiding place of internal illnesses that remains inconspicuous until the advent of 'expert' intervention. In other words, what are the effects of this problematization, given its conditions of possibility? Subjective relations to the self will be affected to the extent that social life confronts individuals with the proposition that this subjective truth – the truth of their relation to themselves and to others – may be revealed by 'bodies', which are also object of manipulation, transformation, desire and hope. In this way we might anticipate through 'culture' (Morris, 1998) the relations between illnesses, new technologies, power, the body and desire. When facing an illness, this involves a deliberate practice of self-transformation and such tranformativity must pass through learning about the self from the truth told by personal narratives within popular culture. How are this culture and the body itself, however, interacting with and being changed by advances in bio-medical technology and the power of huge pharmaceutical companies?

Foucault is often seen as a structuralist, along with those such as Barthes, Althusser and Lévi-Strauss. In reply to questions which sought to make such parallels, he was consistent: 'I am obliged to repeat it continually. I have never used any of the concept which can be considered characteristic of structuralism' (1989, 99). Perhaps the best way to view this is by examining his idea of historical 'events'. He refuses to see events as symptomatic of deeper social structures and focuses upon what seems to be marginal as indicative of relations of power. Events thereby differ in their capacity to produce effects. The following quote helps us see how this can be applied to cultural analysis:

> The problem is at once to distinguish among events, to differentiate the networks and levels to which they belong, and to reconstitute the lines along

which they are connected and engender one another. From this follows a refusal of analyses couched in terms of the symbolic field or the domain of signifying structures, and a recourse to analyses in terms of the genealogy of relations of force, strategic development, and tactics. Here I believe one's point of reference should not be to the great model of language (*langue*) and signs, but to that of war and battle.

(Foucault, 1980: 114)

What about those questions concerned with whose culture, whose identity and how is this produced? These are the questions that preoccupied Foucault. His refusal to see power as a property of, say, a particular class, immediately leaves a question over his politics in terms of the idea of struggle. As he said: 'I label political everything that has to do with class struggle, and social everything that derives from and is a consequence of the class struggle, expressed in human relationships and in institutions' (1989: 104).

This leaves us with a question: against whom do we struggle if not those who hold and exercise power without legitimacy? Who creates cultures and how might alternative forms find public expression and does this change anything? These questions immediately bring forth issues concerning the relationship between Foucault and Marxist theory. Class structure, race and gender are key determinants of the position of individuals in capitalist society. It is difficult for 'techniques of resistance' to be mobilized when particular groups are de-commodified and marginalized and lose their social worth and voice (Biggs and Powell, 2001). At the same time Foucault sees subjectivity not as a fabricated part of a deeper reality waiting to be uncovered, but as an aspect of the reality systematically formulated by resistances and discourses. He sidesteps the binary relationship set up by Marxist theory between true and false realities, ways of knowing and political consciousness (Foucault, 1980) and seeks to loosen knowledge, ideas and subject positions from categories of social totality, for example, social formation, mode of production, economy and society.

Culture is rearticulated in Foucault's thought to historical and societal features ignored in those models of social reality that 'read off' culture according to deeper structures . Foucault looks to areas such as medicine, sexuality, welfare, selfhood and the law, and to marginalized social groups, local politics and the micro-levels of culture. In these studies he found social, discursive and historical substrata in which relations of domination were apparent that were not simply reducible to modes of economic exploitation. The idea of 'governing' then captures the ways in which the 'possible field of action of others' (Foucault, 1982a: 221) are structured. Yet, in inheriting this approach, authors have produced panoptic visions in which resistance is subsumed within impersonal forces. This results from overlooking two main aspects in Foucault's work. First, in terms of his own question, what are the 'limits of appropriation' of discourse? Without this in place, all does appear quiet on the battleground. Second, and relatedly, the agonism that exists between power and freedom (May,1999). This suggests that where there is power, there is also resistance; power thus presupposes a free subject. If there is no choice in actions, there is no power.

A slave, therefore, is not in a power relationship, but one of physical constraint (Foucault, 1982).

Foucault notes three types of struggle: (1) those against domination; (2) those against exploitation; and (3) those against subjection and submission. The latter, while rising in importance in the contemporary era, do not do so to the exclusion of domination and exploitation as many of his followers have appeared to suggest. To understand why particular actors enjoy more power than others, as opposed to seeing power as a 'machine in which everyone is caught' (Foucault, 1980: 156), an account of resistance is needed. Because Foucault views freedom as part of the exercise of power, he does not provide for such an account. Yet, in answer to a question concerning 'power as evil', he spoke of the need to resist domination in everyday life: 'The problem is rather to know how you are to avoid these practices – where power cannot play and where it is not evil in itself' (Foucault, 1991b: 18).

What makes Foucault's overall theoretical work inspiring is how he animates and locates problems of knowledge as 'pieces' of the larger contest between modernity and its subjects. By downplaying the individual subject, Foucault shows how 'bodies' and 'populations' are sites were 'human beings are made subjects' by 'power/knowledge' practices (Smart, 1983: 44). To look for a possible form of trangression in order to change social relation, we must examine within contemporary arrangements the possibility for it to be 'otherwise'. We thus find, in Foucault's later work, an insistence upon the reversibility of discourses through 'resistance'. Subjects of power are also 'agents' who can strategically mobilize disjunctures in discourses and in so doing, open up the world of possibility in a world that seeks order through discipline and surveillance. Now we begin to see how a situation of one-sided domination can give way to a two-way dialogue without assuming an 'essence' to the other that relieves us of the need to understand their world-view. At a time where dominance through military power and money is such a routinized feature of global politics, what greater urgency is there?

Conclusion

In his essay on Kant's 'What is Enlightenment?' (*Was ist Aufklärung?*), Foucault writes of his work as being an 'historical ontology of ourselves' through a critique of what we do, say and think. He makes clear throughout the essay what this form of critique is not: not a theory, doctrine, or body of knowledge that accumulates over time. Instead, it is an attitude, 'an ethos, a philosophical life in which the critique of what we are is at one and the same time the historical analysis of the limits that are imposed on us and an experiment with the possibility of going beyond them' (Foucault, 1984: 50). What is the motivation for this work? 'How can the growth of capabilities be disconnected from the intensification of power relations?' (ibid.: 48). There is no 'gesture of rejection' in this ethos. It moves beyond the 'Outside-inside alternative' in the name of a critique that 'consists of analyzing and reflecting upon limits' (ibid.: 45). The purpose being 'to transform the critique conducted in the form of necessary limitation into a practical critique that takes the form of a possible trans-gression' (ibid.: 45). Overall, it is genealogical in form: 'it will not deduce from the form of what we are what it is impossible for us to do and to know; but it will sepa-rate out, from the contingency that has made us what we are, the possibility of no longer being, doing, or thinking what we are, do, or think' (ibid.: 46). The ideal lies in the possibility of setting oneself free. To examine the internal modes of the order-ing of truth, but not in the name of a truth that lies beyond it, is seen to open up possibilities for its transgression.

Despite criticisms that his work lacked a normative dimension (Fraser, 1989), the orientation of Foucault's approach is clear. The issue translates into one of how one-sided states of domination can be avoided in order to promote a two-sided relation of dialogue. Foucault's interventions were practically motivated. The journey for these investigations being from how we are constituted as objects of knowledge to how we are constituted as subjects of power/knowledge. What we can take from Foucault is the insight that critical approaches to cultural analysis cannot practise on the presupposition that there is an essence to humanity. The idea of coming to know ourselves differently and viewing the possibilities for transformation, is about interpreting ourselves differently. Between self-definition and social situation lies the potential to render the 'cultural unconscious apparent' (Foucault, 1989: 73).

References

Adorno, T. and Horkheimer, M. (1997) Dialectic of Enlightenment, originally published 1994. Translated by Cumming, J. London: Verso

Armstrong, T.J. (ed.) (1992) Michel Foucault: Philosopher. London: Harvester Wheatsheaf.

Ashenden, S. and Owen, D. (eds) (1999) Foucault Contra Habermas: Recasting the Dialogue between Genealogy and Critical Theory. London: Sage.

Biggs, S. and Powell, J.L. (2000) 'surveillance and elder abuse: the rationalities and technologies of community care' Journal of Contemporary Health, 4(1): 43–a.

Biggs, S. and Powell, J.L. (2001) 'A Foucauldian analysis of old age and the power of social wel-fare', Journal of Aging and Social Policy, 12(2): 93–111.

Braidotti, R. (1991) Patterns of Dissonance, New York: Routledge.

Brooke-Ross, R. (1986) quoted in Langan, M. and Lee, P. (eds.)(1988) Radical Social Work Today, London, Unwin Hyman.

Burchell, G., Gordon, C. and Miller, P. (eds) (1991) The Foucault Effect: Studies in Governmentality. London: Harvester Wheatsheaf.

Butler, J. (2000) 'Merely Cultural', New Left Review, 227: 33–34.

Davidson, A. (1986) 'Archaeology, genealogy, ethics,' in D. Hoy, (ed.) Foucault: A Critical Reader. Oxford: Basil Blackwell.

Dean, M. (2004) Governing Societies. Maidenhead: Open University Press/McGraw-Hill.

Deleuze, G. (1992) 'What is a dispositif?', in T.J. Armstrong, (ed).

Donzelot, J. (1980) The Policing of Families. Michel Foucault: Philosopher. London: Harvester Wheatsheaf. London: Random House.

Dreyfus, H. and Rabinow, P. (1982) Michel Foucault: Beyond Structuralism and Hermeneutics. Chicago: University of Chicago Press.

Elders, F. (ed.) (1974) Reflexive Waters: The Basic Concerns of Mankind. London: Souvenir Press.

Foucault, M. (1967) *Madness and Civilisation*. London: Tavistock.

Foucault, M. (1972) *The Archaeology of Knowledge*. London: Tavistock.

Foucault, M. (1973) *The Birth of the Clinic*. London: Routledge.

Foucault, M. (1976) *The History of Sexuality*. Harmondsworth: Penguin.

Foucault, M. (1977) *Discipline and Punish*. London: Tavistock.

Foucault, M. (1978) 'Governmentality', in G. Burchell, (ed.). (1991). *The Foucault Effect: Studies in Governmentality*. London: Harvester Wheatsheaf.

Foucault, M. (1980) *Power/Knowledge: Selected Interviews and Other Writings, 1972–1977*. Edi. C. Gordon, New York: Pantheon.

Foucault, M. (1982) 'The Subject and Power'. In Dreyfuss, H. and Rainbow, P. Michel Foucas: Beyond Structuralism and Hermeneutics, Chicago: University of Chicago press

Foucault, M. (1983) 'The subject of power', in H. Dreyfus, and P. Rabinow, (eds) *Michel Foucault: Beyond Structuralism and Hermeneutics*. Brighton: Harvester.

Foucault, M. (1984) *The Foucault Reader*. Edi. P. Rabinow, Harmondsworth: Penguin.

Foucault, M. (1988) 'Technologies of the self', in L.H. Martin, et al. (eds) *Technologies of the Self*. London: Tavistock.

Foucault, M. (1989) *Foucault Live: Collected Interviews 1961–1984*. Edi. E. Lotringer, Trans. J. Johnston. New York: Semiotext(e).

Foucault, M. (1991a) *Remarks on Marx: Conversations with Duccio Trombadori*. Trans. R.J. Goldstein, and J. Cascaito. New York: Semiotext(e).

Foucault, M. (1991b) 'The ethic of care for the self as a practice of freedom: an interview with Fornet-Betancourt, R., Becker, H. and Gomez-Müller, A., Trans. J.D. Gauthier Snr, in J. Bernauer, and D. Rasmussen, (eds) *The Final Foucault*. Cambridge, MA: MIT Press.

Foucault, M. (1993) 'About the beginning of the hermeneutics of the self', Political Theory, 21: 198–227.

Foucault, M. (1997) *Ethics: Subjectivity and Truth. The Essential Works, Vol. 1*. Edi. P. Rabinow, Trans. R. Hurley. et al. London: Allen Lane.

Garland, D. (1985) *Punishment and Welfare*. Aldershot: Gower.

Goffman, E. (1968) Asylums: Essays on the Social Situation of Mental Patients and other Inmates. Originally published in 1961, Harmondsworth: Penguin.

Kendall, G. and Wickham, G. (1999) *Using Foucault's Methods*. London: Sage.

Kenway, J. (1990) *Education and the Right's Discursive Politics: Private versus State Schooling'* in Ball, S. (ed.) Foucault and Education: Disciplines and Knowledge, London: Routledge.

Knights, D. and McCabe, C. (2003) *Innovation and Organisation: Guru Schemes and American Dreams*. Maidenhead: Open University Press/McGraw-Hill.

May, T. (1991) *Probation: Politics, Policy and Practice*. Milton Keynes: Open University Press.

May, T. (1994) 'Transformative power: a study in a human service organisation', *Sociological Review*, 42 (4): 618–38.

May, T. (1999) 'From banana time to just-in-time: power and resistance at work', *Sociology*, 33(4): 767–83.

McNay, L. (1994) *Foucault*. Cambridge: Polity.

Miller, J. (1993), The Passion of Michel Foucault, New York: Simon and Schuster.

Minson, J. (1985) Genealogies of Morals: Nietzsche; Focault, Donzelot and the Eccentricity of Ethics_, New York: St. Martins's Press.

Morris, D.B. (1998) Illness and Culture in the Postmodern Age, London: University of California Press.

Owen, D. (1997) *Maturity and Modernity: Nietzsche, Weber, Foucault and the Ambivalence of Reason*. London: Routledge.

Paster, M. (1984) *Foucalt, Marxism and History*. Cambridge: Polity.

Powell, J. and Biggs, S. (1999) 'Surveillance and Elder Abuse: The Rationalities and Technologies of Community Care' in *Journal of Contemporary Health*, 4, (3), 43–44.

Powell, J.L. and Biggs, S. (2000) 'Managing old age: the disciplinary web of

Powell, J.L (2001) 'The NHS and Community Care Act (1990) in the UK: a critical review', *Sincronia: Journal of Social Sciences and Humanities*, 5(3): 1–10 .

Power surveillance and normalization', *Journal of Aging and Identity*, 5(1): 3–13.

Rabinow, P. (ed.) (1984) The Foucault Reader, Harmondsworth: Penguin.

Raulet, G. (1993) 'Structuralism and Post-Structuralism: An Interview with Michel Foucault', *Telos* 55 (Spring 1983).

Rose, N. (1984) The Psychological Complex, London: Routledge.

Rouse, J. (1994) 'Power/Knowledge' in Gutting, G. (ed.) The Cambridge Companion to Foucault, Cambridge: Cambridge University Press.

Sawicki, J. (1991) Disciplining Foucault: Feminism, Power and the Body, London: Routledge.

Shumway, D. (1989) Michel Foucault, Charlottesville: University Press.

Smart, B. (1983) *Foucault, Marxism and Critique*. London: Routledge and Kegan Paul.

Framing Bourdieu's Work on Culture

CHAPTER EIGHT
●●●●●●●●

Derek Robbins

Bourdieu's 'Bind'

In one of his late articles, co-authored with Loïc Wacquant, entitled 'Sur les ruses de la raison impérialiste' (Bourdieu and Wacquant, 1998) and translated as 'On the cunning of Imperialist Reason' (Bourdieu and Wacquant, 1999), Bourdieu presented indicative analyses which sought to demonstrate the contention stated in the first sentence, that: 'Cultural imperialism rests on the power to universalize particularisms linked to a singular historical tradition by causing them to be misrecognized as such' (Bourdieu and Wacquant, 1999: 41). The statement drew upon the notion of *méconnaissance* which Bourdieu had elaborated in *La reproduction* (Bourdieu and Passeron, 1970) to argue that school curricula were presented as universally valid so as to conceal the extent to which they were in reality the means by which the arbitrary power of socially and culturally dominant classes was arbitrarily sustained under the guise of absolute legitimacy. There was, therefore, continuity in Bourdieu's resistance to attempts to deploy culture to euphemize power relations. At bottom, this continuity arose from Bourdieu's distrust of any cultural form that might become the reified instrument of social control, as opposed to cultural forms which are the expressions of the habitus of social agents who become the instruments for constructing their own systems of cultural exchange. It was politically important for Bourdieu that cultural products should not acquire spurious autonomy but should remain in a non-deterministic relationship to the social trajectories of their producers and their consumers, both of whom colluded reciprocally in the construction of specific cultural fields in which specific cultural products acquired meaning and were assigned value.

Among the cultural products now being diffused universally and insidiously as universally pertinent was, for Bourdieu, the very notion of 'culture' itself. What was being internationally diffused was a view of culture which was the construct of a small, essentially Western, international intellectual elite. At two points in 'Sur les ruses de la raison impérialiste', 'Cultural Studies' were the specific object of Bourdieu's attack. In the first case, the argument is combined with an attack on the role of publishing houses in promoting spurious universalization – an attack which relates to Bourdieu's critique in the 1990s of the role of the mass media in subverting the autonomy of the intellectual field as institutionalized in universities. After commenting adversely on some practices of the Basil Blackwell publishing house, Bourdieu continued:

> Thus it is that decisions of pure book marketing orient research and university teaching in the direction of homogenization and submission to fashions coming from America, when they do not fabricate wholesale 'disciplines' such as Cultural Studies, this mongrel domain, born in England in the 1970s, which owes its international dissemination (which is the whole of its existence) to a successful publishing policy. Thus the fact, for instance, that this 'discipline' does not exist in the French university and intellectual fields did not prevent Routledge from publishing a compendium entitled *French Cultural Studies*, on the model of *British Cultural Studies* (there are also volumes of *German Cultural Studies* and *Italian Cultural Studies*). And one may forecast that, by virtue of the principle of ethnico-editorial parthogenesis in fashion today, we shall soon find in bookstores a handbook of *French-Arab Cultural Studies* to match its cross-channel cousin, *Black British Cultural Studies* which appeared in 1997 (but bets remain open as to whether Routledge will dare *German-Turkish Cultural Studies*).
>
> (Bourdieu and Wacquant, 1998: 47)

Bourdieu proceeded to argue that the effects of publishing policies were among the factors which explain the hegemony that US production exercises over the intellectual world market. Institutionalized or commercialized effects such as these could not, however, 'completely explain' that hegemony. Bourdieu was lamenting that what, by analogy with economic discourse, he had called in 1971 the 'market of symbolic goods' in which cultural producers traded their own products in a collectively consolidated cultural market, had become an actual economic market which is in the hands of cultural entrepreneurs. The dominant cause of the degradation of cultural exchange, therefore, was the role played by dealers in the cultural import–export business. Bourdieu sought to subject their activities to sociological analysis, challenging the supposed autonomy of the economic field as he was to do shortly after in his *Les structures sociales de l'économie* (2000). Here, again, Bourdieu mentions cultural studies critically. He claims that it is one of several disciplines which have claimed to represent the interests of the dominated while, in fact, reinforcing a culturally rootless domination of 'cultural' conceptualization. As Bourdieu puts it:

> As for those in the USA who, often without realizing it, are engaged in this huge international cultural import–export business, they occupy for the most part dominated positions in the American field of power and even in the intellectual field. Just as the products of America's big cultural industry like jazz or rap, or the commonest food and clothing fashions, like jeans, owe part of the quasi-universal seduction they wield over youth to the fact that they are produced and worn by subordinate minorities (see Fantasia, 1994), so the topics of the new world

vulgate no doubt derive a good measure of their symbolic efficacy from the fact that, supported by specialists from disciplines perceived to be marginal or subversive, such as Cultural Studies, Minority Studies, Gay Studies or Women's Studies, they take on, in the eyes of writers from the former European colonies for example, the allure of messages of liberation. Indeed, cultural imperialism ... never imposes itself better than when it is served by progressive intellectuals ... who would appear to be above suspicion of promoting the hegemonic interests of a country against which they wield the weapons of social criticism.

(Bourdieu and Wacquant, 1998: 50–1)

It should now be clear that Bourdieu found himself in a bind in respect of 'cultural theory' which was indicative of an ambivalence in his general stance. I want now to explore that ambivalence in more detail. I shall suggest that the ambivalence was made seriously problematic for Bourdieu at the point when he began to lose control over his own cultural production, when, in other words, his products ceased to be exclusively given meaning within an intellectual field of his own creation (substantially through the efficacy of the publication after 1975 of the *Actes de la recherche en sciences sociales* under his direction) and fell, instead, into the hands of multinational publishing houses and international cultural dealers. Finally, I shall give some specific attention to *La distinction,* published in French in 1979 as the culmination of empirical research first published as 'anatomie du goût' in 1976 in *Actes de la recherche,* and then subsequently published in English translation in paperback by Routledge in 1986, by which date Polity Press had commenced the task of publishing Bourdieu's work which it has continued, almost monopolistically, ever since.

Briefly, we can say that Bourdieu's 'bind' was that his personal project from the beginning had been to adopt social scientific method to analyse cultural behaviour and cultural forms. This remained possible within the French tradition, but, increasingly, Anglo-US discourse which autonomized 'culture', detaching it from its social roots and divorcing it from its social function, came to dominate the international field of cultural conceptualization. Bourdieu wanted both to resist and to deploy the power of the international field within which his works began to circulate after the end of the 1970s. Hence the ambivalence of Bourdieu's general stance: he wanted to mobilize the field which was surreptitiously neutralizing his message.

—— The Ambivalent Function of the Intellectual Field in Bourdieu's Theory ——

Bourdieu always argued that we have to guard against the extent to which our personal perceptions are controlled by the dominant ways of seeing the world advanced by those possessing dominant power. He liked to quote Thomas Bernhard, particularly, for instance, at the beginning of a lecture which he gave in Amsterdam in June, 1991, which was subsequently included in *Practical Reason* (1998) as an article entitled: 'Rethinking the state: genesis and structure of the bureaucratic field'. Bourdieu quoted from Bernhard's *Alte Meister Komodie*:

> School is the state school where young people are turned into state persons and thus turned into nothing other than henchmen of the state. Walking to school, I was walking into the state and, since the state destroys people, into the institution for the destruction of people.
>
> (Bourdieu, 1998: 35)

He suggested that the passage from the novel suited his intention well since his purpose in the lecture would be to 'subject the state and the thought of the state to a sort of *hyperbolic doubt*' (ibid.: 36). The lecture was delivered not long after the publication of *La noblesse d'état* (1989) – translated into English as *The State Nobility* in 1996 – in which Bourdieu had analysed the ways in which French private educational institutions – *grandes écoles* – were instrumental in perpetuating the political power held by a privileged minority in French society, but a similar point had been made much earlier in 'Systèmes d'enseignement et systèmes de pensée' (1967) – translated into English as 'Systems of education and systems of thought' in M.F.D. Young, *Knowledge and Control* (1971). At that date, Bourdieu was trying to define his position in relation to structuralism. He had recently completed his translation of Panofsky's *Gothic Architecture and Scholastic Thought* (published in French in 1967) and was recognizing – as he was to make explicit in 'On Symbolic Power' (given as a lecture at Harvard in 1973 and published in English translation in J.B. Thompson (ed.) *Language and Symbolic Power*, 1991b) – that Panofsky had taken neo-Kantianism beyond Cassirer's analysis of transcendental symbolic forms towards a sociological analysis of the mechanisms of domination involved in imposing homologies between educational practices and social tastes. Panofsky had shown that the structural affinity between Gothic architecture and scholastic thought had been socially constructed through the agency of the curriculum of cathedral schools. The structured mindset was not a function of universal human characteristics but the consequence of particular social conditions. The dominant architectural taste of the period was a function of the dominant schooling. This revelation showed Bourdieu that he needed to develop an understanding of potential strategies which might enable individual agents to challenge the mechanisms by which minds are controlled.

Alongside Bourdieu's conviction that social control insidiously exercised by 'neutral' state apparatuses had to be opposed, was an equally strong conviction that dominant institutions and dominant modes of thought can only be modified or subverted from within – that oppressive structures can only be changed by a process of reconstruction which does not deny the phenomenal reality of what prevailed before. The kind of poststructuralist position that Bourdieu was beginning to articulate during the 1960s did not seek to negate the benefits of structuralist analysis. On the contrary, the accumulated systems of thought of previous generations are inscribed in human agents by a process of inter-generational transmission. New generations are the 'inheritors' of the old and their dispositions to act – their *habitus*, to use Bourdieu's term – are circumscribed by early upbringing. These inherited and circumscribed dispositions engage with objectivated structures which are themselves institutionalized forms of dominant *habitus*. Human agency involves the exercise of limited freedom so as to modify those social structures which have historically succeeded in achieving some trans-historical objective status. It was this positive side of the agency/structure dualism rather than the oppressed, mind-controlled dimension emphasized by the Thomas Bernhard quote, that Bourdieu explored in 'Intellectual field and creative project' which he first published in 1966 in an issue of *Les Temps Modernes* devoted to the 'problems of structuralism'. Individual artists or thinkers do not produce in a vacuum, but the contexts of their productivity are explicable sociologically. However, Bourdieu was not interested in constructing retrospectively sociologies of knowledge, art or literature which would explain productivity *ex post facto*. The problem of this kind of structuralism was that it superimposed a model of structural explanation on the actual agency/structure struggles of past producers. For Bourdieu, 'creative projects' are not autonomous projects but, instead, projects which necessarily are located within 'intellectual fields' of reception which, in part, are constitutive of the creativity. In other words, any writer or thinker operates with a set of inscribed impulses to write and think which are the products of early upbringing or formative education. Equally, however, the act of writing is not one of free expression of this intrinsic inheritance. Intellectual production is a constant negotiation or compromise between the impulse to be 'self'-expressive and the need to communicate meaningfully within a common discourse that has acquired some objective standing. The relationship between intellectual field and creative project is reciprocal while, also, the two elements are infinitely variable or contingent.

The Ambivalent Function of the Intellectual Field in Bourdieu's Practice: Algerian Analyses and the Discourse of Acculturation

Bourdieu's position was fundamentally ambivalent because he wanted to insist that our thoughts are partly conditioned by those of our predecessors or teachers while also wanting to insist that in recognizing this situation we are empowered to exercise some limited freedom to 'play the field' which constrains us. This was the basis for Bourdieu's ambiguity in relation to Cultural Theory. From his very first published work, *Sociologie de l'Algérie* (1958), Bourdieu was interested in culture and cultural adaptation. It could be said that it was always his personal creative project to understand acculturation processes. This project derived initially from his philosophical training at the Ecole Normale Supérieure. Clearly influenced by his reading of Husserl, Heidegger, Sartre and Merleau-Ponty, Bourdieu's interest was related to Sartre's *Sketch for a Theory of the Emotions* (1962 [1936]) and was an attempt, following Heidegger, to introduce a temporal dimension into descriptive phenomenology. The problem of acculturation was an extension of the problem of inter-subjectivity for existential phenomenology. In an interview of 1985, Bourdieu said of his early fieldwork in Algeria that it arose out of his research 'into the "phenomenology of emotional life", or more exactly into the temporal structures of emotional experience' (Bourdieu, 1990: 6–7). Bourdieu's early difficulty, however, was to locate his project within an established intellectual field.

There was nothing in Bourdieu's philosophical training which would have made him conceptualize situations in terms of 'culture'. He showed no interest in the elements of *Kulturgeschichte* transmitted to France by Raymond Aron in his *La philosophie allemande* (1938). Bourdieu always remained hostile to the attempts of Dilthey, Rickert and others to find a hermeneutic mode of analysis of culture and society that might be different in kind from the scientific mode which was the legacy of positivism. He confronted raw phenomena in Algeria and his disposition was to understand inter-subjective relations in the context of social change extraneously imposed by colonial intervention. To acquire this understanding, he needed a conceptual apparatus and the bibliography of *Sociologie de l'Algérie* provides evidence of Bourdieu's intellectual apprenticeship. The Bibliography lists two main kinds of texts. First, Bourdieu read accounts of the social history of North Africa and of North African Islam. Second, he read books which gave him methodological guidance. He cited Weber's *Gesammelte Aufsätze zur Religionssoziologie*, but, mainly, it appears that he was largely self-taught by reference to American books on acculturation. In particular, for instance, the Bibliography lists the following: Herskovits, *Acculturation*, 1938; Keesing, *Culture Change* (Stanford University Press, 1953); Mead, *Cultural Patterns and Technical Change* (Mentor Book, 1955); Siegel, *Acculturation* (Stanford University Press, 1955); and Spicer, *Human Problems in Technological Change* (1955).

The books which Bourdieu cites fall into two categories. There are those which are specifically about acculturation understood in terms of culture contact and racial contact while there are others which are concerned with the relationship between cultural and technological change. The first is essentially the product of the work of the 1920s and 1930s whereas the second is the product of the post-World War II American interest in global modernization through technical advance. I want to focus on the influence of Herskovits.

In 1935, the American Social Science Research Council's Committee on Personality and Culture established a sub-committee on acculturation composed of Redfield, Linton and Herskovits. The committee observed that acculturation was an indistinct concept. They believed that 'a series of studies prepared in accordance with a single plan or outline would be extremely useful for the testing of certain hypotheses.' (Linton, 1940). They produced a report which endeavoured to define terms so as to stimulate future enquiries to be conducted within a common conceptual framework. There was, in other words, an attempt to scientize the analysis of acculturation.

Herskovits's book of 1938 appends the 1936 report of the sub-committee, but Herskovits wrote a long introduction in which he continued to clarify definitions and in which he expressed some of his personal reservations about the report which had been jointly authored. Herskovits insisted that the analysis of acculturation involves the study of culture carriers. He wrote: 'For the moment, it can however be assumed that culture does not exist apart from human beings, and that where contact between cultures is mentioned a certain human contact must be taken for granted as the only means by which culture can spread from people to people or from generation to generation' (Herskovits, 1938: 11). This view had methodological implications which connected with Herskovits' original training as an historian. He continued: 'This use of real history thus characterizes studies of acculturation, rather than assumptions of historical contact based on reconstructions made by working out distributional analyses' (ibid.: 15).

Herskovits spends a great deal of time differentiating between assimilation, diffusion, and acculturation. His assumption is that acculturation is a reciprocal contact whereas assimilation involves enforcement. He approvingly quotes the comment that 'The problem of acculturation, when we are considering the American Indians in relation to their adjustment to European culture, is a problem of assimilation' (ibid.: 7).

He also clarifies a distinction between diffusion and tradition. He writes:

> Diffusion, this process by means of which culture spreads in space, is contrasted ... with tradition, which represents the means by which a given culture persists in time; that is, the means by which the content of a culture is handed down from one generation to another within the same society. (ibid.: 13)

Herskovits emphasized the need to exploit known history in describing acculturation processes. He argued that the study of acculturation mainly involved normal anthropological research procedures but he thought that there was one special point to be considered. He expressed it in the following way:

> For where European and native cultures under contact are being studied, the elements from the student's own culture tend to be taken more or less for granted by him. Hence this must be carefully guarded against lest the resulting ethnographic description be thrown badly out of focus.
>
> (ibid.: 18)

Finally, Herskovits gave detailed attention to the methodology of adopting an historical approach to the analysis of cultural change. He insisted that it was possible to 'reconstruct the life of the people as it was lived before the acculturative process set in' (ibid.: 23) and that this reconstruction constituted a kind of 'base-line' for measuring the acculturation process.

The book by Herskovits clearly informed Bourdieu's practice. It constituted a kind of handbook or textbook for his work. First of all, Bourdieu accepted the heavy orientation towards supposing that there is no biological, racial factor in acculturation. Bourdieu paid no attention to ethnic differences in his account of Algerian cultural change. Second, Bourdieu adopted Herskovits's historical approach. The essence of the *Sociologie de l'Algérie* is that it offers a reconstruction of the Algerian status quo ante, precisely the sort of base-line account which Herskovits recommended. Importantly, Bourdieu shared Herskovits's view that the definition of the 'culture' of a geographical region was problematic. The opening paragraph of *Sociologie de l'Algérie* is significant here:

> It is obvious that Algeria, when considered in isolation from the rest of the Maghreb, does not constitute a true cultural unit. However, I have limited my

investigation to Algeria for a definite reason. Algeria is specifically the object of this study because the clash between the indigenous and the European civilizations has made itself felt here with the greatest force.

(Bourdieu, 1958: 5; Bourdieu, 1962: xi)

Bourdieu was insisting, in other words, that the motor for his analysis was not a desire to understand a pre-given cultural identity but, rather, a desire to understand the cultural processes whereby that phenomenal entity constituted itself. The notion of Algeria as a cultural unit was an uneasy artifice, a mirage situated somewhere in the middle between the constructivism of indigenous people and the conceptualization of observers.

From Acculturation Analysis to Sociology of Education and on to the Sociology of Social Action

In spite of his historical training, Herskovits was still locked within a frame of thinking that required him to try to find scientific explanations of acculturation phenomena. Hence it was important for him to isolate acculturation from assimilation and diffusion from tradition in order to establish a discrete category of phenomenon that could be called acculturation and could be scrutinized as such. By contrast, Bourdieu brought his phenomenological orientation to bear on the same set of problems. This meant that he was not interested in analysing the process of adaptation between cultures in abstract but, instead, in analysing the readjustments of values of people who were forcibly moved from one cultural situation to another. Bourdieu was interested both in the ways in which traditional values were sustained intergenerationally within Algerian tribes and in the ways in which individuals adjusted those values when they encountered new situations.

The English translation of *Sociologie de l'Algérie – The Algerians* – appeared in 1962 with a Preface by Raymond Aron. An established sociologist, Aron was Bourdieu's mentor for the first few years of the 1960s but, in those same years, he attended the seminars of Lévi-Strauss and it is evident from the second edition of *Sociologie de l'Algérie* (1961) that Bourdieu had made presentational changes which were seeking to secure his credentials as an anthropologist. Meanwhile, *Travail et travailleurs en Algérie* (1963) and *Le déracinement, la crise de l'agriculture traditionnelle en Algérie* (1964) were the slightly delayed publication of sociological research carried out in 1960–61 immediately before Algeria's achievement of independence. Bourdieu intended that his publications should contribute to political debate about the condition of Algeria and its future. Some of Bourdieu's earliest articles were published in *Les Temps Modernes* which is indicative of his inclination to offer reports of his researches which would be politically engaged rather than contributions to academic discourses. Even though Aron was a political sociologist, there was no sense in which Bourdieu was seeking to communicate his findings in the field of political science. Back in France in 1962 – working at the University of Lille and in Aron's research group in the Ecole des Hautes Etudes en Sciences Sociales – Bourdieu pursued his interest in acculturation in his analyses of the experiences of students. The uncertainty continued about the 'field' within which his work should be located. The research report published as a working paper of the Centre de Sociologie Européenne in 1964 was entitled 'Les étudiants et leurs études', while the influential publication that adapted this research report was entitled *Les héritiers, les étudiants et la culture* (1964).

The anthropological orientation of the book, expressed in the title, was confirmed by an opening quotation from Margaret Mead, but it rapidly was regarded as a contribution to the sociology of education. One strand of Bourdieu's work in the 1960s did increasingly seem to be located within the field of the sociology of education, culminating in the publication of *La reproduction* in 1970 which, significantly, was sub-titled: *Eléments pour une théorie du système d'enseignement*. This text was a turning-point, both in respect of Bourdieu's own approach to the analysis of educational and cultural phenomena and, relatedly, in respect of the emergence of competing fields of reception across national sub-fields. I have argued elsewhere (Robbins, 2000) that Bourdieu's analyses of cultural phenomena in the 1960s (in relation to museums/art galleries and in relation to photography, published, respectively, as *L'amour de l'art*, 1966, and *Un art moyen*, 1965) were not liberated from the controlling conceptual framework of the sociology of education. During the 1960s, Bourdieu's interest in the accessibility of various cultural forms was linked with his interest in access to education and to the problem of the dominance within the educational system of exclusive cultural assumptions. *La reproduction* opened the way to the study of cultural forms in themselves. It is important that Bourdieu consolidated this breakthrough by launching his own journal – *Actes de la recherche en sciences sociales* – in 1975, introducing the first number with an article – 'Méthode scientifique et hiérarchie sociale des objets' (Bourdieu, 1975) – which insisted that the common feature of his practice was that all phenomena should be subjected to social scientific scrutiny regardless of whether the phenomena as such might prenotionally be given 'topic' labels. Bourdieu sought to counteract the proliferation of 'sociologies of' – of education, of culture, of religion, or whatever – and to counteract the tacit league tables of sociological practice and practitioners whereby, for instance, the sociology of religion might still retain dominant status by comparison with the sociology of sport. The establishment of the *Actes*, specifically emphasizing the performativity of research, was a deliberate attempt to subvert topic-specific journals and to institutionalize research practice founded on methodology rather than phenomenal objects.

It was during the same period when Bourdieu was constructing his own 'intellectual field' by means of the *Actes de la recherche*, that he also came to recognize the distorting effects of communication between differently constituted national intellectual fields. The years in which *Homo academicus* germinated spanned the period in which Bourdieu moved from simply practising sociology of knowledge towards recognizing that this sociology could become a form of international cross-cultural action. Much of the information for that book was gathered at about 1968 when Bourdieu undertook a 'sociology of knowledge' analysis of Parisian higher education. This was the period of *Le métier de sociologue* (1968), 'Champ intellectuel et projet créateur' (1966), 'Sociology and Philosophy in France since 1945' (1967) and the work on Panofsky, in which Bourdieu was advocating a 'sociology of sociology' as a form of Bachelardian 'rupture épistémologique' and also beginning to articulate the poststructuralist emphasis on agency which was presented in *Esquisse d'une théorie de la pratique* (1972). *Homo Academicus* re-visited the early data in the light of the work of the 1970s, particularly the project on 'Le Patronat' which was subsequently published in *La noblesse d'état* (1989) and, of course, the work on taste which led from the article on 'L'anatomie du goût' to *La distinction* (1979). In other words, the text of *Homo Academicus* was able to superimpose the sociological analysis articulated in his 'Les stratégies de reconversion' (1973) on the primary sociology of knowledge. This meant that the text was no longer a sociology of ideas but instead a sociology of the deployment of ideas in the position-taking of social agents – situating agents and ideas in the competing fields of power and economics.

By the time of the publication of *Homo Academicus* (1984b), however, the text was not simply an analysis which now recognized the relationship between agency and structure within Parisian higher education (including Bourdieu's reflexive recognition of his own position and agency). It was much more. The text was an instrument of Bourdieu's agency. Around the time of his appointment to the Chair of Sociology at the Collège de France in 1981, Bourdieu had been aware that he was about to be associated with an institution which already possessed recognized 'institutional capital' and that this association could affect him ambivalently. On the one hand, the institution strengthened his formal authority and his capacity to hold influential power but, on the other, the institution might symbolize an educational tradition which would seem to be at odds with the view of education that Bourdieu had developed in his empirical research of the 1960s. The issue which Bourdieu explored in an article of 1975 on fashion – 'Le couturier et sa griffe' (Bourdieu and Delsaut, 1975) – was relevant to his own intellectual situation. He wanted to be able to harness the power of the institution without forfeiting the convictions which arose from his personal *habitus*. From the mid-1980s, Bourdieu was acutely conscious of the same tension in the relationship between his international label (*griffe*) and the specific social conditions which generated his research, his conceptual framework, and his published findings. 'The genesis of the concepts of habitus and field' (1985) was an attempt to apply reflexively to his own concepts the approach which he had accepted in earlier articles such as 'Genèse et structure du champ religieux' (1971). If, as Bourdieu argued in *Le métier de sociologue* (1968), concepts are tools, elements of an *ars inveniendi*, what happens to them when they become severed from the conditions in which they were instrumentally effective? What is the appropriate reaction to their being used pragmatically for different purposes in different contexts?

Cultural Analyses within an Internationalizing 'Field'

Bourdieu worried about this fundamental issue and his anxiety lay behind much of his work between 1985 and 1995 by which time, it seemed, he almost decided that his *griffe* was beyond his personal control and that he could only still exercise the kind of influence he wanted by direct social action and by adopting communicative devices which would by-pass the global market of theoretical texts – the management of the publishing venture, *Liber: Raisons d'agir*; participation in the production of the film, *La sociologie est un sport de combat*; and active encouragement of European social movements. Bourdieu's concern manifested itself forcibly in the Preface to the English Edition of *Homo Academicus* (1988) and in articles which discussed the misrepresentation of his work: 'Concluding remarks: for a sociogenetic understanding of intellectual works' (1993), which outlined a framework for analyzing international intellectual transmission: 'Les conditions sociales de la circulation internationale des idées' (1990) and 'Les ruses de la raison impérialiste' (2000), which directly considered conceptual transfer such as most of the essays collected in *Practical Reason* (1998b), and which reflected more generally on the international function or potential function of intellectuals: 'Epilogue: on the possibility of a field of world sociology' (1991a) and 'The corporatism of the universal: the role of intellectuals in the modern world' (1989).

Although *La Distinction* was manifestly about culture, therefore, Bourdieu did not see himself as making a contribution to Cultural Studies or to the development of Cultural Theory. Throughout the 1970s, Bourdieu was regarded in England as a sociologist of education, as the French counterpart to Basil Bernstein. The New Left English theorists who were responsible for the development of Cultural Studies had all come from intellectual backgrounds in the Arts and Humanities and History. They had little to do with the 'new directions for the sociology of education' which were launched by the book edited in 1971 by M.F.D. Young entitled *Knowledge and Control*. It contained two articles by Basil Bernstein and two articles by Bourdieu – 'Intellectual field and creative project' and 'Systems of education and systems of thought'. These articles by Bourdieu were reproduced several times in England during the 1970s within the field of the sociology of education which flourished as a result of the establishment of the Open University. It was the influence of Richard Nice that effected the transition of the reception of Bourdieu's work from the field of education to the emerging field of Cultural Studies. Nice translated two short articles by Bourdieu in 1977 when he was working at the Centre for Contemporary Cultural Studies, in the same year as the publication of his translation of Bourdieu's *La reproduction*. Stuart Hall discussed Bourdieu's work in his *On Ideology* (1978) while the new journal *Media, Culture and Society* carried the first translated extracts from *La distinction* in its second number (1980) with an introductory article on Bourdieu written by Nick Garnham and Raymond Williams entitled 'Pierre Bourdieu and the sociology of culture'. Bourdieu had become a theoretical reference point for those English radical literary critics and historians who colluded in a *méconnaissance* of their institutional position by transferring the capital associated with the Humanities to the new field of Cultural Studies. The adoption of Cultural Studies was a strategy of reconversion which sustained their institutional power. Bourdieu's work was received 'theoretically' in order to legitimize cultural analysis, and this occurred without any reference to Bourdieu's educational analyses or to the epistemology outlined in *Esquisse d'une théorie de la pratique*.

There was a reverse appropriation occurring at the same time. Bourdieu quoted Williams's *Culture and Society* several times in 'Champ intellectuel et projet créateur' – although it is clear that Bourdieu would have regarded Williams's position in advocating the recognition of 'structures of feeling' in history as a form of soft structuralism. Williams's work provided Bourdieu with some analysis on which to base his post-structuralist critique. Bourdieu ran a seminar at the Ecole Normale Supérieure in the late 1960s out of which emerged his analyses of Flaubert and Manet. Bourdieu was developing a sociology of culture rather than an analysis of the relations between hypostatized 'culture' and 'society'. At the same time, Passeron translated Hoggart's *The Uses of Literacy* as *La Culture du Pauvre* in 1970. Passeron's introduction shifted Hoggart's work out of the English context of literary and cultural study into the French field of social anthropology. Equally, this was the period in the early 1970s when the French reception of the work of Basil Bernstein reinforced the association between language codes, linguistic capital and educational achievement. Those aspects of English thinking which were linking the sociologies of language, education, and culture were absorbed within the Centre de sociologie européenne. When, therefore, Bourdieu launched the *Actes de la recherche en sciences sociales* in 1975, he was able to appropriate the theorizing of the English New Left intellectuals on his own terms before they began to appropriate him for their purposes. Close attention to the publication of extracts from the work of Williams, Thompson, Hobsbawm and Klingender in the *Actes de la recherche* of 1976, 1977, and 1978 would show that the contextualization had the effect of situating the received texts in their socio-historical contexts. Bourdieu's endeavour had the effect of de-theorizing the texts of those intellectuals who were beginning to look to Bourdieu to provide theoretical legitimacy for their unreflexive theorizing.

The Production and Reception of *La Distinction* as a Case Study of Anglo-French Conceptual Exchange

The French production of *La distinction: Critique sociale du jugement* (1979) and its reception in the UK provides one case study of the tension in framing Bourdieu's work on culture. It is a tension which throws light on the trans-national and social conditions of the struggle for dominance between the sociology of culture and Cultural Studies.

Bourdieu's text of 1979 consolidated an account which he had offered, with Monique de Saint Martin, of an 'anatomy of taste', published in *Actes de la recherche* in 1976. That text was based on empirical research originally undertaken in 1963 at the same time as both the work which was separately used for articulating the notion of 'cultural capital' in relation to the prior knowledge and tastes of students (published in *Les Héritiers*, Bourdieu and Passeron, 1964) and the work deployed for the analysis of the social uses of photography (published in *Un Art moyen*, Bourdieu et al., 1965). The 1976 article also drew on further researches which had been carried out in 1967–68. The thinking which led to the writing of *La Distinction* stood in relation to previous empirical research in rather the same way as did *Homo Academicus* (1984b) to the sociological analysis of structures of knowledge in Paris on the eve of the events of May 1968. In both cases, the later texts transformed the structuralism which had influenced the earlier enquiries and sought to offer, instead, an account of the dynamics of social position-taking. Whereas the earlier empirical research had assumed that knowledge and tastes were reflections of class conditions, the later, summative texts argued that the choices of acquired learning and taste are strategies adopted by social agents in finding their ways through a constantly changing social system. Between 1963 and 1976 Bourdieu had, in other words, rejected the kind of analysis of culture offered in a Marxist tradition represented at the time in the work of Lucien Goldmann, but he had equally resisted the alternative temptation to regard cultural artefacts as somehow transcendent or beyond sociological scrutiny. Referring deliberately to his article of 1972 entitled 'Le marché des biens symboliques', Bourdieu began his Introduction to *La distinction* with the following sentence:

> Il y a une économie des biens culturels, mais cette économie a une logique spécifique qu'il faut dégager pour échapper à l'économisme. Cela en travaillant d'abord à établir les conditions dans lesquelles sont produits les consommateurs de biens culturels et leur goût, ... [There is an economy of cultural goods, but this economy has a specific logic which we must disentangle so as to avoid economism. That needs to be done by first working to establish the conditions in which the consumers of cultural goods and their taste are produced, ...]

> (Bourdieu, 1979: i; my translation)

This, tacitly, was Bourdieu's dismissal of Marxism while, at the same time, it anticipates his later rejection of neo-liberal economism. Equally, however, Bourdieu began the first chapter in the following way:

> Il est peu de cas où la sociologie ressemble autant à une psychanalyse sociale que lorsqu'elle s'affronte à un objet comme le goût, ... La sociologie est là sur le terrain par excellence de la dénégation du social.

> (Bourdieu, 1979: 9)

> 'Sociology is rarely more akin to social psychoanalysis than when it confronts an object like taste, ... Here the sociologist finds himself in the area par excellence of the denial of the social.'

> (Bourdieu, 1984, 9: 11)

It was precisely this balance in Bourdieu's work that appealed to the English New Left which was seeking to secure an institutionalized academic identity through the establishment of Cultural Studies. Volume 2, Number 3 of *Media, Culture and Society*, July, 1980, edited by Nicholas Garnham, focused on the work of Bourdieu. The number contained an article by Garnham and Williams entitled: 'Pierre Bourdieu and the sociology of culture: an introduction' as well as two extracts from *La distinction* published in advance of the translation of the full text, and a translation of Bourdieu's

'La production de la croyance: contribution à une économie des biens symboliques' (1977). All the translations were made by Richard Nice who was a member of staff at the time at the Centre for Contemporary Cultural Studies at the University of Birmingham. Garnham wrote a short Editorial to the number which was headed by a quotation from the last few sentences of Nice's translation of Bourdieu's *Esquisse d'une théorie de la pratique* (1972), published as *Outline of a Theory of Practice* in 1977. These sentences read:

> The denial of economy and of economic interest, which in pre-capitalist societies at first took place on a ground from which it had to be expelled in order for economy to be constituted as such, thus finds its favourite refuge in the domain of art and culture, the site of pure consumption – of money, of course, but also of time convertible into money. The world of art, a sacred island systematically and ostentatiously opposed to the profane, everyday world of production, a sanctuary for gratuitous distinterested activity in a universe given over to money and self-interest, offers, like theology in a past epoch, an imaginary anthropology obtained by denial of all the negations really brought about by the economy.
>
> (Bourdieu, 1977: 197, in Garnham, 1980: 207)

Garnham began his Editorial by seeking to relate Bourdieu's work to the agenda for Cultural Studies suggested by Stuart Hall in his 'Cultural studies: two paradigms', published in Issue 1, Volume 2 of the new journal. Hall had contended that neither 'structuralism' nor 'culturalism' would do 'as self-sufficient paradigms of study' but that they did have 'a centrality to the field which all other contenders lack because between them they address what must be the core problem of Cultural Studies'. Garnham continued to quote Hall's account of this 'core problem', saying of Hall that: 'On the solution to this 'core problem' will turn the capacity of Cultural Studies to supersede the endless oscillations between idealism and reductionism ... They continue to hold out the promise of a properly materialist theory of culture' (Garnham, 1980: 207). Certainly Bourdieu was seeking to avoid both idealism and reductionism but, as we have seen, this meant, for Bourdieu, recognizing the 'economy' of cultural goods without accepting economistic reductionsim. Bourdieu was not seeking to 'hold out the promise of a properly materialist theory of culture' but, rather, the promise of a properly sociological theory of culture which would have the capacity to subject the economy of cultural production and consumption to sociological analysis. It is perhaps significant that the opening sentence of *La distinction* quoted above was curtailed in Richard Nice's translation. Bourdieu's bald: 'Il y a une économie des biens culturels, mais cette économie a une logique spécifique qu'il faut dégager pour échapper à l'économisme.' (Bourdieu, 1979: i) and the following half-sentence are rendered by Nice in the following way: 'There is an economy of cultural goods, but it has a specific logic. Sociology endeavours to establish the conditions in which the consumers of cultural goods, and their taste for them, are produced, ...' (Bourdieu, 1984a: 1). The explicitly adverse remark about economism is suppressed just as, in using the quotation from *Outline of a Theory of Practice*, Garnham made no specific reference to the fact that Bourdieu was clearly stating that the denial of economic interest takes different forms in different social circumstances. In short, the early response to Bourdieu's *La distinction* indicates that there was an attempt to ignore Bourdieu's rejection of Marxist, materialist economism. The attempt to appropriate Bourdieu's work was an attempt precisely to accommodate him to the economism which he was at pains to avoid.

Conclusion

Space does not allow for a detailed examination of the progress of Cultural Studies in the period from 1980 to the present. I would simply suggest that as the Marxist influence declined, so the assumptions about the autonomy of culture revived. It became explicable, therefore, that Bourdieu should regard the existence of 'Cultural Studies' and 'cultural theory' as manifestations of exactly the kinds of ideologically motivated and 'aristocratic' rejections of the social sphere that he had sought to expose in analysing the variations of taste in *La distinction*. Bourdieu did not seek to articulate any cultural theory. He sought to subject the totality of cultural phenomena to sociological analysis. A natural extension in the 1990s of the ways in which Bourdieu earlier had jointly undertaken sociological analyses of knowledge and education and art, photography, and taste would have been for him to analyse sociologically the phenomenon of Cultural Studies as a subject within Higher Education institutions. This is a task, after his death, still to be undertaken. We still need vigilantly to analyse sociologically the processes of social distinction which are underwritten by the concepts of culture presupposed by Cultural Studies and their associated theories.

References

Bourdieu, P. (1958) *Sociologie de l'Algérie*. Paris: Presses Universitaires de France.
Bourdieu, P. (1962) *The Algerians*. Boston: Beacon Press.
Bourdieu, P., Darbel, A, Rivet, J.-P, and Seibel, C. (1963) *Travail et travailleurs en Algérie*, Paris-La Haye, Mouton.
Bourdieu, P., and Sayad, A. (1964) *Le déracinement, la crise de l'agriculture traditionnelle en Álgérie*, Paris, Ed. de Minuit.
Bourdieu, P. and Passeron, J.-C. (1964) *Les héritiers*. Paris: Editions de Minuit.
Bourdieu, P., Boltanski, L., Castel, R., and Chamboredon, J.-C. (1965) *Un art moyen*. Paris: Editions de Minuit.
Bourdieu, P. (1966) 'Champ intellectuel et projet créateur', *Les Temps Modernes*, 246. Translated as Bourdieu, 1971b.
Bourdieu, P., Darbel, A. and Schnapper, D. (1966a) *L'amour de l'art*. Paris: Editions de Minuit.
Bourdieu, P. and Reynaud, J.D. (1966b) 'Une sociologie de l'action, est-elle possible)', *Revue française de sociologie*, VII, 4.
Bourdieu, P. and Passeron, J.-C. (1967) 'Sociology and philosophy in France since 1945', *Social Research*, XXXIV, 1.

Bourdieu, P. (1967a) Postface to and translation of E. Panofsky, *Architecture gothique et pensée scolastique*, Paris: Editions de Minuit.

Bourdieu, P. (1967b) 'Systèmes d'enseignement et systèmes de pensée', *Revue internationale des sciences sociales*, XIX, 3.

Bourdieu, P. (1967c). 'Condition de classe et position de classe', *Archives européennes de sociologie*, VII(2): 201–23.

Bourdieu, P. (1968) 'Structuralism and theory of sociological knowledge', *Social Research*, XXXV, 4.

Bourdieu, P., Chamboredon, J.-C. and Passeron, J.-C. (1968) *Le métier de sociologue*. Paris: Mouton-Bordas.

Bourdieu, P. (1970) 'The Berber house or the world reversed', *Social Science Information*, IX, 2.

Bourdieu, P. and Passeron, J.-C. (1970) *La reproduction*, Paris: Editions de Minuit.

Bourdieu, P. (1971a) 'L'opinion publique n'existe pas', *Noroit*, 155.

Bourdieu, P. (1971b) 'Intellectual field and creative project', in M.F.D. Young (ed.) *Knowledge and Control*. London: Collier-Macmillan.

Bourdieu, P. (1971c) 'Genèse et structure du champ religieux', *Revue française de sociologie*, XII, 3, 295–334.

Bourdieu, P. (1972) *Esquisse d'une théorie de la pratique*. Geneva: Droz.

Bourdieu, P. (1973) 'The three forms of theoretical knowledge', *Social Science Information*, XII, 1.

Bourdieu, P., Boltanski, L. and de Saint Martin, M. (1973) 'Les stratégies de reconversion. Les classes sociales et le système d'enseignement', *Information sur les sciences sociales*, XII, 5, 61–113 – translated as Bourdieu, P., with Boltanski, L., and de Saint Martin, M., 1977.

Bourdieu, P., and Delsaut, Y. (1975) 'Le couturier et sa griffe. Contribution à une théorie de la magie', *Actes de la recherche en sciences sociales*, 1, 7–36.

Bourdieu, P. (1975) 'Méthode scientifique et hiérarchie sociale des objets', *Actes de la recherche en sciences sociales*, 1, 4–6.

Bourdieu, P. and Saint Martin, M. de (1976) 'Anatomie du goût', *Actes de la recherche en sciences sociales*, 5, 2–112.

Bourdieu, P., Boltanski, L., and de Saint Martin, M. (1977) 'Change in social structure and changes in the demand for education', in Giner, S., and Scotford-Archer, M., *Contemporary Europe. Social structures and Cultural Patterns*, London, Routledge and Kegan Paul.

Bourdieu, P. (1979) *La distinction: Critique sociale du jugement*. Paris: Editions de Minuit.

Bourdieu, P. (1984a) *Distinction: A Social Critique of the Judgement of Taste*. Cambridge, MA: Harvard University Press.

Bourdieu, P. (1984b) *Homo academicus*. Paris: Editions de Minuit.

Bourdieu, P. (1985) 'The Genesis of the Concepts of Habitus and Field', *Sociocriticism*, Pittsburgh–Pa-, Montpellier, 2, 11–24.

Bourdieu, P. (1988) *Homo Academicus*, Oxford, Polity Press.

Bourdieu, P. (1989) 'The Corporatism of the Universal: the Role of Intellectuals in the Modern World' (*Telos*) 81, Fall, 99–110.

Bourdieu, P. (1989) *La noblesse d'état: Grandes écoles et esprit de corps*. Paris: Editions de Minuit.

Bourdieu, P. (1990a) *In Other Words: Essays Towards a Reflexive Sociology*. Oxford: Polity Press.

Bourdieu, P. (1990b) 'Les conditions sociales de la circulation des idées', *Cahiers d'histoire des littératures romanes*, 14(1–2): 1–10.

Bourdieu, P. (1991a), 'Epilogue: on the possibility of a field of world sociology', in P. Bourdieu and J.S. Coleman (eds) *Social Theory for a Changing Society*. Boulder, CO: Westview Press.

Bourdieu, P. (1991b) *Language and Symbolic Power*. ed. J.B. Thompson. Oxford: Polity Press.

Bourdieu, P., Chamboredon, J.-C. and Passeron, J.-C. (1991) *The Craft of Sociology*. Berlin: de Gruyter.

Bourdieu, P. (1993) 'Concluding remarks: for a sociogenetic understanding of intellectual works', in C. Calhoun, E. Lipuma, M. Postone (eds) *Bourdieu: Critical Perspectives*. Oxford: Polity Press, pp. 263–75.

Bourdieu, P. (1996) *The State Nobility. Elite Schools in the Field of Power*, Oxford, Polity Press.

Bourdieu, P. and Wacquant, L. (1998) 'Sur les ruses de la raison impérialiste', *Actes de la recherche en sciences sociales*, 121–2, 109–18.

Bourdieu, P. (1998a) *La domination masculine*. Paris: Editions du Seuil.

Bourdieu, P. (1998b) *Practical Reason: On the Theory of Action*. Oxford: Polity Press.

Bourdieu, P. and Wacquant, L. (1999) 'On the cunning of imperialist reason', *Theory, Culture and Society*, 16(1): 41–58.

Bourdieu, P. (2000) *Les structures sociales de l'économie*. Paris: Editions du Seuil.

Fantasia, R. (1994) 'Everything and Nothing: the Meaning of Fast-Food and other American Cultural Goods in France', *The Tocqueville Review*, 15(7).

Garnham, N. (1980), editorial introduction to *Media, Culture and Society*, 2.

Herskovits, M.J. (1938) *Acculturation: The Study of Culture Contact*. New York: J.J. Augustin.

Robbins, D. (2000) *Bourdieu and Culture*. London: Sage.

Sartre, J-P. (1962 [1936]) *Sketch for a Theory of the Emotions*. London: Methuen.

Young, M.D. (1971) *Knowledge and Control*. London: Collier-Macmillan.

CHAPTER NINE

'Speculation to the Death'

Jean Baudrillard's theoretical violence

William Merrin

I have dreamt of a force five conceptual storm blowing over the devastated real.

(1997: 42)

The Jean Genie

Jean Baudrillard is increasingly being recognized as one of the most important cultural theorists, with his original and perceptive analyses becoming standard reference points for any understanding of contemporary cultural processes and experience. He is also, however, one of the most controversial theorists, his work arousing surprisingly passionate responses, ranging from the hostility of academics, many of whom retain a deep suspicion towards the 'postmodern' excesses of his work and thought, to his elevation for a wider public and media to übercool icon: a media and pop-cult sign name-dropped by journalists taking the temperature of the cultural *Zeitgeist* to signal their own clued-up cachet; required reading for the aspirant avant-garde and intellectual cognoscenti who liberally misquote and misinterpret his work; essential sign of good taste for the Ikea pine-effect coffee tables of the culturally literate; ready-made quotation or reference point for any knowing cultural production, article or argument and, in the metaphorical epitome of semiotic commodification, with 'Philosophy Football''s 1990s range of intellectually inspired football shirts – *Baudrillard as T-Shirt*. His public lectures sell out, his photographic exhibitions attract widespread attention; his visits to this country are reported in the broadsheet press, accompanied by interviews and articles – one even labelling him 'the David Bowie of philosophy' (*The Guardian*, G2, 14.3.2000: 14–15), while conferences, personal appearances and book-signings draw minor crowds. And when Neo opened up his copy of *Simulacra and Simulation* in *The Matrix* (1999), Baudrillard became probably the only cultural thinker ever to inspire a big-budget Hollywood blockbuster. For his critics, however, this popularity only confirms his unholy spell. Baudrillard retains his hint of sulphur as an evil *genie* of postmodern appearances.

For the English-speaking world at least, the origins of these fault lines lie in the reception of 'postmodernism' in the early 1980s, an emerging movement which began to stir debate among left-leaning scholars in Australia, Canada, America, and later Britain. With little regard for the complexities of his position or his own disinterest in the concept, Baudrillard was quickly identified as one of its key theorists by both its supporters and detractors, and, as 'the High Priest of Postmodernism' (Baudrillard, 1989), he became a target for the vocal critique being developed by the Left. Arthur Kroker's sympathetic Marxist reading of his work (Kroker, 1985; Kroker and Cook, 1988) was the spur for Douglas Kellner's critical response, developed across a series of articles, introductions and the first book on his work (Kellner, 1987; 1988; 1989; Best and Kellner, 1991; Kellner, 1994: 1–23), and for the related critiques offered by Callinicos (1989) and Norris (1990; 1992). Their interpretation of Baudrillard's work as reactionary in its movement away from Marxism; as nihilistic in its celebration of postmodern life and rejection of truth and reality, and as charlatanistic in its style and method, though at best weak and, at its worst, seriously flawed, has nevertheless had a lasting effect upon his reputation, with its more simplistic claims still being commonly repeated. In contrast to this, a more sophisticated line of interpretation began to be developed by Mike Gane (1991a; 1991b; 1995; 2000a), and a different picture of Baudrillard emerged through the 1990s with the waning of the controversy over postmodernism (with its *de facto*, but ultimately pyrrhic, victory as it faded from debate); with a growing list of books (Stearns and Chaloupka, 1992; Rojek and Turner, 1993; Kellner, 1994, Genosko, 1994; 1999; Levin, 1996; Zurbrugg, 1997; Butler, 1999; Grace, 2000) and articles (Gane, 2000b) developing an informed critical literature and appreciation of his work, and with the availability in translation of his major writings; and the gradual penetration of his ideas across a range of disciplines and subject areas such as sociology, cultural studies, media and communication studies, visual culture, photography, art theory and history, social and cultural history, philosophy, geography and architecture. Regardless of one's personal antipathies, Baudrillard had become intellectually unavoidable.

It is the aim of this chapter to consider why this should be so; to offer an introduction to some of the central themes of Baudrillard's work in order to highlight his contribution towards our understanding of contemporary society and culture, as well as his challenge to established disciplines, paradigms, and methodologies such as those of cultural theory itself. The chapter begins by looking at Baudrillard's critique of consumption, together with his semiotic–symbolic distinction, his critique of the political economy of the sign and its later development with the foregrounding of the concept of simulation, turning then to consider how these ideas are deployed in his critique of technology and contemporary media and in his critical depiction of our western civilization and its processes. Finally, it considers possible critical responses to Baudrillard's work and offers a defence of it in the light of his theoretical methodology.

'Everything is Sign, Pure Sign ...'

Jean Baudrillard was born – appropriately, he later claimed – 'in 1929, just after Black Thursday ... at the time of the first great crisis of modernity' (1990b: 144). For him, the Great Depression and the crisis of overproduction were solved by the system's recognition that the population needed to be mobilized as consumers not merely as labourers and producers, thus, he argues, consumption ensured the system's survival and reproduction, providing a new model of socialization and illusory participation in society (1975: 144). While it was the maturation of this 'consumer society' in the post-war period that Baudrillard took as the subject of his earliest work, in retrospect, his entire career can be seen to be concerned with tracing both its development and the outline within it of its own possible crisis and 'catastrophic turn' (1990b: 144).[1]

France's post-war consumer society was the product of a series of modernizing socio-economic and technological changes foregrounding consumer goods, the media, advertising and fashion. As the structures of society and 'everyday life' itself were being transformed these became important new areas to be theorized, and a vibrant intellectual milieu developed that would prove to be highly influential upon Baudrillard's project. From early sympathies with the existentialist and humanist Marxist project – with Sartre's post-war exploration of concrete 'situated' life, Lefebvre's discussion of alienated everyday life and of the 'bureaucratic society of controlled consumption', and the later critique of the new alienations of 'one dimensional society' by Marcuse, and of the 'society of the spectacle' by Debord and the Situationists – Baudrillard also became interested in the opposing structuralist movement, associated with Barthes' semiological analysis of consumer society, and the work of Lévi-Strauss, Althusser, and Lacan, and the emerging poststructuralism of Derrida and the *Tel Quel* group. In addition, a growing interest in technology and media can be seen in his reading of Ellul and Simonden's 1950s work on the dominance of 'technique', and McLuhan and Boorstin's 1960s work on the electronic media and their effects. Perhaps one explanation for these competing influences is Baudrillard being drawn to both the Marxist critique of the consumer societies, as representing not an increase in personal freedom and fulfilment but the penetration of control, constraint and alienation into every aspect of private life, and to structural and technical analyses of the operation of this society and of its production of individual behaviour, thought and experience; all themes which would figure strongly in his own early work.

Baudrillard came late to this scene, completing a thesis in sociology with Lefebvre at Nanterre in 1966 where he lectured in sociology until retiring in 1987 to concentrate on his writing and public lecturing. His earliest publications on literary theory and in the pro-Situationist journal *Utopie* (see 2001a), were followed by a series of books and essays developing an original critique of consumer society – *The System of Objects* (1968 [1996a]), *The Consumer Society* (1970 [1998a]), and *For a Critique of the Political Economy of the Sign* (1971 [1981]). His 1973 book *The Mirror of Production* (1975) developed his critical position and analysis of the sign, which were taken up in his major work *Symbolic Exchange and Death* ([1976] 1993b). It is this trajectory, therefore, that we need to first consider, as the critique of consumption and of political economy and its model offered in these texts represents one of Baudrillard's most important contributions to cultural theory. It can be seen to comprise five related elements: (1) the semiological analysis of consumption; (2) the theory of the symbolic; (3) the critique of political economy; (4) the social logic of consumption as a mode of social integration and control; and (5) the positioning of the symbolic as an external and oppositional force.

Baudrillard's semiological analysis of consumer society, developed first in *The System of Objects*, drew upon Barthes' semiology which had taken up Saussure's claim that his own linguistic theories could be used to study the wider life of signs in society (Saussure, 1986). Barthes applied them accordingly to the post-war world of goods, objects and messages to understand these as signs within a system of meaning generated in their collective, structural inter-relationships and individual, internal structural relationships, including their second-order cultural connotation, or 'myth' (Barthes, 1973a). Following Barthes, Baudrillard sees the system of objects of consumer society as organized as a semiotic system but his analysis is less systematic than Barthes' (in 1973b; 1990), placing more emphasis upon the human relationship with the object world (Baudrillard, 1996a: 40).

For Baudrillard, consumption is a contemporary phenomenon, its modernity arising not from its increased volume but from its organization as a system of signs governed by a code of signification (ibid.: 200). Consumption, therefore, is not a physical process – the act of buying an object – but rather an idealistic one, in which it is the *idea* and the meaning of the object, message, image, or product that is desired, taken and employed for one's own benefit. It is '*an activity consisting of the systematic manipulation of signs*' (ibid.: 200), of the manipulation and appropriation of their 'signified' (ibid.: 203). If this consumption has come to represent 'a defining mode of our industrial civilisation' (ibid.: 199), then our western societies are founded on a prior and on-going process of semioticization – on the transformation of the object and all relations, history, culture, communication, and meaning into an organized system of signs to be combined and consumed in their difference. Against the contemporary sign Baudrillard contrasts 'traditional symbolic objects', which, as 'the mediators of a real relationship or a directly experienced situation' bear the 'clear imprint' of that relationship, remaining 'living objects' in being bound to human activity (ibid.: 200). Signs originate with the end of this symbolic relationship, reducing it to simple semiotic elements which, combined in the sign, derive their social meaning now from their 'abstract and systematic relationship to all other sign objects' (ibid.: 200). For Baudrillard, therefore, the defining historical characteristic of western society is its semiotic elimination and transformation of symbolic relationships, a process affecting the entire mode of human experience, meaning and activity as all relations become relations of consumption – relations with and ultimately, between, signs.

One of the strengths of Baudrillard's work is the number and depth of the examples employed to illustrate these semiotic processes. In *The System of Objects*, for example, he traces the development of interior design from the 'traditional environment' of the 'Bourgeois interior', which personifies its complex affective, familial and social relationships in its 'presence' and 'symbolic dignity', to the modern designed interior. The latter liberates the object as a mobile, weightless sign to be manipulated by their user (ibid.: 15–19), an 'active engineer of atmosphere' (ibid.: 26), who, in the process, though freed from the weight of the symbolic, is enslaved to the semiotic system and its code. This passage from the symbolic to the semiotic and the resulting increase in social control are also seen in his discussion in *The Consumer Society* of the body, fashion and sexuality (1998a: 129–50; see also 1993b: 87–100, 101–24; 1990a), which are all divested of symbolic meaning, with the body, for example, being abstracted as an object requiring a constant investment and semiotic labour 'to smooth it into a smoother, more perfect, more functional object for the outside world' (1998a: 131). In its management for personalization, distinction and prestige, today the body is integrated into consumption as 'the finest consumer object' (ibid.: 131), immeasurably deepening the processes of social control (ibid.: 136) with an alienation more profound than any found in industrial exploitation (ibid.: 132). The fashion model epitomizes this transformation of the body, as, in its erasure of the symbolic and calculated, stylized, functional, atmospheric signification, it is no different, Baudrillard argues, from the other mute objects of consumer culture (ibid.: 133–4).

From Baudrillard's earliest works, therefore, we already find a clear statement of the organizing principle of his career in the distinction of the semiotic and symbolic, the origins of the semiotic in the abolition of the symbolic, the characterization of our society as defined by this transformation, and a critical sympathy with the symbolic and its power against the semiotic processes of the West. The importance of this critical sympathy for the symbolic for Baudrillard's work cannot be overstated, although the concept has often been neglected in the critical literature due to the common assumption that he lacks a critical position, merely celebrating postmodernity; the relative unfamiliarity of the English-speaking world with the concept and the specific tradition of French, Durkheimian social anthropology from which he derives it, and the complex and sometimes contradictory path by which he arrives at its full articulation. To understand the development and role of the concept of the symbolic and of 'symbolic exchange' in his work, we first need, therefore, to understand its Durkheimian derivation.

This Durkheimian tradition, developed from the *Année Sociologique's* study of 'primitive' societies and from Mauss's works in this field, especially his *Sacrifice: Its Nature and Function* in 1899 (Hubert and Mauss, 1964), and *A General Theory of Magic* in 1904 (Mauss and Hubert, 1972), received its classic statement in 1912 in Durkheim's own study of tribal religion, *The Elementary Forms of the Religious Life* (Durkheim, 1915). Mauss's popularization of Durkheim and 1925 study *The Gift: Forms and Functions of Exchange in Primitive Societies* (Mauss and Hubert, 1966) were themselves influential in the tradition, inspiring in particular, the short-lived 'College of Sociology' from 1937–39 (see Hollier, 1988), whose members, including Roger Caillois and Georges Bataille, radically developed this sociological-philosophical anthropology, Caillois especially in his 1939 book *Man and the Sacred* (Caillois, 1980), and Bataille in a series of early essays (Bataille, 1985) and later books such as *The Accursed Share* (Bataille, [1949] 1985), *Eroticism* [1957] (1962) and *Theory of Religion* [1973] (1992). What unifies this tradition, and what Baudrillard takes as the basis for the 'symbolic', is the emphasis upon a mode of collective experience or social relationship and its immediate moment of meaning and communication. Durkheim's description of the 'sacred' is the exemplar here – not as a truly religious condition but instead as a real transformation of the individual and a higher experience in tribal festivities caused by the excited, violent, active experience with others of a collective 'state of effervescence'. In such religious festivals, raised beyond the profane world of everyday labour and survival, the individual feels themselves 'transported into a special world … filled with exceptionally intense forces that take hold of him and metamorphose him' (Durkheim, 1915: 218). The communion of the group transforms the individual in the moment.

Another example of these social relationships and mode of communion is found in Mauss's theory of the 'gift' (*don*), based on his study of the primitive exchange system founded on the divestment, not accumulation, of wealth, itself closely tied to tribal festivities and the sacred. The *scene* of the gift is important here as it both creates positive social relations, as the gift communicates the giver and cements ties, while also prompting an agonistic cyclical competition in which individuals or groups attempt to accrue social power and rank by humbling the other with the generosity of their gift, creating an indebtedness only effaced with a greater counter-gift. Mauss drew implicitly anti-economistic implications from this, seeing the gift relationship as producing a social scene and meaning since lost in the reduction of humanity to the 'calculating machine', *homo oeconomicus* (Mauss and Hubert, 1966: 74), and the College of Sociology developed this critique of the contemporary world as one defined by the loss of a mode of collective experience (with Bataille identifying the victory of Christianity, the Protestant Reformation, industrial capitalism and the rational-scientific world-view as key contributors to this process), and by an impoverished, individualistic 'restricted' economy in which the energies and resources of life itself are reduced and hoarded not squandered for pleasure (see Bataille, 1991).

Baudrillard is the leading heir of this tradition (see Merrin, 1999a), unifying its conception of this mode of relations as 'symbolic exchange', extending both its analysis of the destruction of this mode in contemporary Western societies, in his critique of semiotic consumption, and its anti-economism, in his related critique of the system of 'general political economy' in *The Consumer Society* (1998a) and essays of that period (1981). The critique of political economy begins with the rejection of the still popularly dominant model of consumption which sees it as a natural and inevitable process, based on hypothesizing an individual 'subject' alone in nature with fundamental 'needs' which must be satisfied for survival and happiness, for example, by a system of production to serve these primary needs (1998a: 69). Resisting the Marcusian option of criticizing 'false' needs created by capitalism (Marcuse, 1986: 4–5), Baudrillard opts instead for the more radical line of rejecting *the very concept of needs*, based on their relative, social nature and determination (1981: 81; 1998a: 73) and the Durkheimian argument that such survivalist economies do not exist, as the production of social relationships and distinctions or an excess for feasts and rites takes precedence over individual need in tribal societies (1981: 74, 76, 81). The flawed survivalist anthropology was, therefore, only the creation of political economy, enabling it to establish a 'human essence grounded in nature', naturalizing, supporting and ideologically legitimizing the existence and organization of its economic system (1981: 72; 80).

Thus, for Baudrillard, the concept of 'needs' is created by political economy itself to mobilize us to consume and thus to reproduce the system (1998a: 74–5). This consumption, for Baudrillard, therefore, *has no relationship to physical or psychological satisfaction or happiness*, instead, following Barthes, Veblen and Marcuse respectively, he sees it as a system of communication, of social hierarchy and distinction, and of social integration and control (ibid.: 60–1, 94). It does not represent freedom, sovereignty, or individuality, but, as we are socialized and trained into the code (ibid.: 81), only the process of our semiotic 'personalization' and production (ibid.: 87–98) as part of the 'total organisation of everyday life' (ibid.: 29). This, for Baudrillard, is the 'social logic' and operation of consumption.

Baudrillard develops these ideas in *For a Critique of the Political Economy of the Sign*, describing an expanded 'general political economy' whose 'object' (the commodity and sign) is dominated equally by the logics of use-value, exchange-value, and sign-value (1981: 123–9). Baudrillard now applies his critique of political economy, his claim that it produces and employs a secondary content, use-value, to ground and support, via 'needs', the operations of the entire system and its dominant form, exchange-value, to the operation of the sign. The semiotic system similarly rests, therefore, on producing and employing a secondary content, the signified and referent, which apparently refer to 'an autonomous concrete reality' (ibid.: 155), to ground, naturalize and legitimate the abstractions and operation of the dominant form, the sign-value of the signifier. The 'reality principle' and 'reality effect' of the sign, which appear to us as undeniable and self-evident as the existence of human needs for survival, are revealed again by Baudrillard to be the process of and cover for the reduction and transformation of the symbolic and the establishment of an entire semiotic system producing reality itself for our consumption (ibid.: 143–63). Only the processes of the symbolic are truly outside of this expanded political economy and its unifying and dominant system of value and its formalized exchange, Baudrillard argues, representing a 'radical rupture' of value (ibid.: 125), transgressing and destroying its operation (ibid.: 123–9). Here, therefore, Baudrillard clearly arrives at the symbolic as the only 'beyond' of semiology (ibid.: 159), being expelled in its very institution (ibid.: 160) and unnameable within it (ibid.: 162), but remaining his radical hope for an active force against the sign and its totalitarian processes – its process of the production of reality itself. Today, he says, 'signs must burn' (ibid.: 163).

Baudrillard completes this critique of the political economy of the sign in his next book, *The Mirror of Production* (1975: 50) through a critique of Marxism and its historical materialism. His argument here is simple and effective: in adopting the categories of political economy, he says, Marxism cannot illuminate the very different, symbolic processes of 'pre-industrial' societies (ibid.: 21–51, 69–91), projecting instead this economistic model onto all earlier societies, historically universalizing and naturalizing its economic rationality, thus serving as its ideological support (ibid.: 33) in seeing all history through 'the spectral light of political economy' (ibid.: 66). By this token, Baudrillard also argues, Marxism could not even illuminate its own age, in adopting a model of the working class imposed by the Bourgeoisie (ibid.: 152–9), and cannot reflect ours either as capitalism has matured since his death into our expanded political economy, into the 'monopoly' phase of the code and its semiotic processes (ibid.: 124–9). But these semiotic processes are radicalized here by Baudrillard as he describes now the sign's absorption of its signified-referent 'to the sole profit of the play of signifiers' (ibid.: 127), a 'structural revolution in value' which would also open his next book (1993b: 6–9), in which signs no longer refer to any objective reality, but exchange among themselves such that 'all of reality then becomes the place of a semiurgical manipulation, of a structural simulation' (1975: 128). This extension of the symbolic, however, is matched by the irruption within it of the 'symbolic demand', the problem of the demand for 'symbolic integration' and meaning to which the system can only respond with simulation, to create 'the illusion of symbolic participation' though its consumer and media culture (ibid.: 143–7). Again, however, the demand cannot be definitively expelled and it remains an active, oppositional force against the semiotic.

We can see in Baudrillard, therefore, the dual development of a radical Durkheimian analysis of the symbolic and its role as a site of opposition and transformation, and a semiotic analysis of the processes of contemporary society allied to a critique of its wider code of value. Semiotic and symbolic, therefore, are always entwined and spiral together in Baudrillard's work, both in their development and in their radicalization, and this is seen again in *Symbolic Exchange and Death* [1976] (1993b) which continues to develop their form and relationship. It is here that we find Baudrillard's essay 'The Orders of Simulacra' (1993b: 50–86), which, together with the 1978 essay, 'Precession of the Simulacra' (1994b: 1–42), represents his most famous work on semiotic 'simulation', a concept introduced in and developed from his earlier work on the sign and its processes but here foregrounded as a dominant process in contemporary society. Baudrillard's three orders of simulacra – tracing the referential transformations of the sign since its emancipation from the medieval symbolic world in the Renaissance, through the industrial, to our own 'code-governed' era and its generation of forms from their model, '*conceived according to their very reproducibility*' (1993b: 56–7) – have received much critical attention. Its value lies, however, not in charting a succession of socio-economic formations from the Renaissance, through modernity to postmodernity (his later addition of a fourth order invalidates this (1992a: 15–16; 1993c: 5–6)), but in its Foucault-inspired (Foucault, 1970) genealogy of the dominant sign forms of each era, and their simulacral production of the real.

To understand this, we need to understand first of all that Baudrillard is not simply claiming a loss of reality today, rather, he is pointing to referential reality itself as a historical product (see 1993b: 60–1), and, second, that he sees this reality as the product of simulacra, of the signs produced in each era and their epistemological effects. The simulacrum, therefore, is not a postmodern phenomena; indeed, it is instead an ancient theological and philosophical concept, used to describe the efficacy and power of an image to simulate and thus to assume for us the force of reality, and appear as what it represents, thereby abolishing the very distinction of 'real' and 'image', of 'truth' and 'falsity'. The simulacrum, therefore, has no relationship to 'pretending' (1994b: 3) as it does not produce an 'unreality' but precisely an efficacious reality that destabilizes this distinction and the simplistic materialist–idealist dichotomy it rests upon. Although the West has repeatedly tried to demonize and domesticate this simulacral process (Merrin, 2001), it returns today, as Baudrillard recognizes, in the development of our reproductive technologies and their production of our experience of the real.

For Baudrillard, our contemporary simulacra are semiotic productions, generated from and operating according to their precessionary models, 'substituting signs of the real for the real' (1994b: 2), to produce our reality from their circulation and commutation. He sees the process of simulation as having four main effects. First, it leads to 'indeterminacy', as the simulacrum erases the possibility of distinguishing truth and falsity, and moves beyond any grounding or objective external reference or value as its own effective reality (1993b: 57). Second, and paradoxically simultaneously, it leads to an increased determination, in its production and programming of the real, as the simulacrum has no finality, destination or possibilities other than those 'there in advance, inscribed in the code' (ibid.: 59), its reality being produced from the playing out and materialization of this model. Third, in this programming of experience and expectation, it functions as a means of integration and 'social control' (ibid.: 60), Baudrillard argues, as the 'diffraction of models' and their realization play a 'regulative role' today (ibid.: 70). Fourth, the result of this simulation is both 'hyperrealism' and 'indifference' as experience is both heightened by the passage of the real into the hyperreal – the semiotic 'aesthetic' hallucination of reality' (ibid.: 74) but also fundamentally dissuaded by its 'neutralization' of symbolic relations, meaning, passions and possibilities (ibid.: 9).

If Baudrillard's description of the simulacrum has a clear lineage in his earlier description of the sign and its processes and of the social logic of consumption, these ideas are extended here as Baudrillard now sees all of social life as dominated by this 'operational simulation' (ibid.: 57). 'Today reality itself is hyperrealist', he writes: 'reality is immediately contaminated by its simulacrum' (ibid.: 74). Of the many examples he gives of this, from political economy, fashion, the body and sexuality (1993b), to ethnology, Disneyland, Watergate, reality TV, cinema, advertising, and hypermarkets, etc. (1994b), one of the best is his discussion of polls and referenda (1993b: 61–70). Here, from a critique of opinion polls and the 'simulacrum of public opinion' they produce whose only effect is within the equally simulacral party system (ibid.: 65–6), Baudrillard develops a critique of the 'referendum mode' operating throughout our consumer and communicational culture, and its continuous testing and prompting of audience responses along pre-programmed 'stimulus/response' lines whose anticipated, designated and pre-coded replies function not to discover our reality but to produce and contain us within the system. Simulation operates again, therefore, as a means of social integration and control, in its production of reality and neutralization of all real response, speech or critical expression and action (ibid.: 67–9), acting as a 'leukaemia infecting all social substance, replacing blood with the white lymph of the media' (ibid.: 67). Baudrillard's theory of simulation clearly does not represent a nihilistic abrogation of political and ethical responsibility (see Best and Kellner, 1991), but, on the contrary, an intensification of his concern at the totalitarian programming and control of our entire reality.

Although Baudrillard escalates here his picture of the semiotic and its control, he does not abandon us to joyless nihilism as Kellner suggests (Best and Kellner, 1991: 127), as he also escalates his description of the symbolic and its resistant processes to counter this. The symbolic – and its 'reversibility' – are 'inevitable' he argues (1993b: 2), and it remains to 'haunt' the society which has attempted to expel it with the possibility of its own death and reversion (ibid.: 1). It irrupts not simply in resistant, symbolic phenomena, but at the heart of the system's own operation, as the result of its own linear accumulation and development, as 'the fatality of every system committed by its own logic to total perfection and therefore to a total defectiveness, to absolute infallibility and therefore irrevocable breakdown' (ibid.: 4). Such a fatality produces a new symbolic strategy of resistance, not of opposition, but of exacerbation, wherein, Baudrillard says, 'things must be pushed to the limit where, quite naturally, they collapse and are inverted' (ibid.: 4).

Thus, far from Baudrillard's escalating theory of simulation providing proof, as his critics assert, of his complicity with the postmodern system, his theoretical strategy and methodology itself represent a mode of resistance: a mode of theorizing aiming precisely at pushing both our critical awareness of the system's extremes and thus also the system itself to its hoped for collapse. His critique, in *Forget Foucault* ([1977] 1987), of Foucault's theory of power and defence of a Maussian 'symbolic challenge' as a force of reversal against all accumulated power (ibid.: 53–4), reinforces his critical position and confirms his career-long attempt to discover and promote positive modes and forms of resistance and reversal and a defensible critical position against the dominant system. Baudrillard, however, becomes increasingly sensitive to the problems of articulating this position leading to a succession of reformulations of the symbolic. The first of these, introduced in *Forget Foucault*, reframes the symbolic-semiotic distinction around 'seduction' and 'production' (ibid.: 21). His defence of 'seduction' as a mastery of appearances and reversal of the semiotic project in its withdrawal 'from the visible order' that creates a symbolic relationship is an important development in his critical position (ibid.: 21), but it also allows him, through the concept of 'production', to step up his picture of the semiotic and its processes and this is clearly seen in his developing critique of technology and media.

Are Friends Electric?

Baudrillard's increasing interest in contemporary media and technology represents an extension of both his early interest in semiotic 'communication' (1998a: 60) and 'the network of signs and messages' it creates (1981: 200), and of his symbolic critique of this simulacral mode of relations. For Baudrillard, the electronic media represent one of the main sources of the sign's production and dissemination, reinforcing its abolition of the symbolic and its simulacral and unilateral mode of communication. Thus his critique of media and technology closely follows his critique of the sign and of consumer culture.

This critique is made explicit in the 1971 essay, 'Requiem for the Media' (1981: 165–84) where, defining communication as 'a reciprocal space of speech and response' creating immediate symbolic relations, rather than 'the simple transmission-reception of a message', Baudrillard argues, contrary to all our intuition, that our mass media are characterized by their 'non-communication' (1981: 169). This is because they abolish those symbolic relations to replace them with a simulacral form whose only reciprocity is in pre-programmed, controlled feedback systems such as letters, phone-ins, or, today, emails (1981: 181). Thus, for him, radio and television are a poor substitute for the collective communion of the symbolic, but Baudrillard also offers here a critique of communication theory and its *simulation model* of communication', which, in its formalization of its elements reduces and excludes all 'the reciprocity and antagonism' of interpersonal communication (1981: 179). Despite his own reservations about the concept's formal connotations (1993a: 57), Baudrillard's project, therefore, revolves around the symbolic as a mode of communication, abolished and simulated in our contemporary media culture, in its own competing mode of 'communication'.

Baudrillard's first discussion of media comes in a 1967 review (2001a: 39–44) of McLuhan's newly translated *Understanding Media* (McLuhan, 1994) where he adopts McLuhan's emphasis on the form of media, but turns this towards his own project to argue that the media's primary effect is to replace the symbolic with the semiotic, transforming 'the lived, unique, eventual character of that which it transmits' into 'a sign which is juxtaposed among others in the abstract dimension of TV coverage' (2001a: 42). Expanding on this in *The Consumer Society*, he argues, contrary to McLuhan, that the media do not produce a direct 'participation' in the world, but instead offer a 'filtered, fragmented world' 'industrially processed' by the media 'into sign material' (1998a: 124). 'So we live', Baudrillard says, 'sheltered by signs, in the denial of the real', safe in the absence from a world with the alibi of participation in its simulacrum (ibid.: 34). Here, therefore, Baudrillard draws more upon Boorstin's (1961) book *The Image* (Boorstin, 1992) than on McLuhan, employing his idea of the 'pseudo-event' to describe 'a world of events, history, culture, and ideas not produced from shifting contradictory, real experience, but *produced as artefacts from elements of the code and the technical manipulation of the medium*' (Bandrillard, 1998a: 125). Thus the media are central to the 'vast *process of simulation*' taking place 'over the whole span of daily life', producing the event and all experience from its semiotic model, with this simulation assuming the '*force of reality*', abolishing the latter 'in favour of this *neo-reality of the model* which is given material force by the medium itself' (ibid.: 126).

Baudrillard, therefore, accepts McLuhan's approach to media, but believes it must be extended and envisaged 'at its limit' (1983a: 102), where its critical conclusions are systematically reversed (see Merrin, 2002). This is seen in his use of the concept of 'implosion', which, for McLuhan, referred to the geographical, temporal and, most importantly, affective contraction of the globe under the speed of electronic technologies. For Baudrillard, in contrast, it is the semiotic process 'where simulation begins' (1994b: 31), with the implosion of the poles of the symbolic relationship which institutes the sign (1981: 65) and of the sign's absorption of its referent to produce reality from its own play of signifiers (1975: 127). The media operate as a 'macroscopic' extension of these processes as they do not dissolve away to give us perfect access to the real, rather their simulacra implode with the real 'in a sort of nebulous hyperreality' (1983a: 100) in which 'even the definition and distinct action of the medium are no longer distinguishable' (ibid.: 101), resulting in a mutual dissolution of reality and medium (1994b: 30).

All attempts to get closer to this real technologically only perfect this simulacrum, Baudrillard argues, as 'the more closely the real is pursued ... the greater does the real absence from the world grow' (1998a: 122). The increasing perfection of the real only results in a 'hyperreality', a concept incorporating two processes for Baudrillard, being first of all the inevitable result of all attempts to realize the real *as the real* and to set it above the real as its exemplar, and, second, the result of the technical perfection of the image from its model which produces an excessive hyper-fidelity eclipsing and coming to define for us our own experience. This semiotic hyperrealization again abolishes any symbolic relationship as, Baudrillard says, faced with such an image, 'we have nothing to add ... nothing to give in exchange' (1990a: 30), being reduced to staring 'fascinated and dumb-founded' at the empty banality of the real, 'approaching and sniffing this cadaver-like hyper-similitude' and 'hallucinating on platitude' (1983b: 42–3).

It is in his work, *In the Shadow of the Silent Majorities* ([1978] 1983a), however, that Baudrillard presents his most systematic picture of the media's destruction of relations and meaning, tracing the emergence of Western society 'on the ruins of the symbolic' in the Renaissance (ibid.: 65), and the fate of the forms of simulated sociality ('the social') it produced to replace it. Baudrillard sees our societies as desperately trying to produce and stage this social – a scene of communication, response, activity, and meaning – but all their electronic technologies which they employ only hasten the collapse and 'implosion' of this already simulacral sociality, he argues. The effort of the staging and the over-production of meaning, information and communication, together with the masses, own non-response and disinterest is 'directly destructive of meaning and signification', Baudrillard argues (ibid.: 95). No-one can understand, hold, or use all that is produced, thus 'we live in a universe where there is more and more information and less and less meaning' (ibid.: 95). Simulation, therefore, again has a neutralizing effect, a 'dissolving and dissuasive action', upon those very realities it attempts to produce (ibid.: 96), though, as 'the alpha and omega of our modernity', the 'immense energies' we expend on this production cannot be halted by us (ibid.: 97–8).

Baudrillard's concept of 'the masses' here has proven controversial but it is derived from a McLuhanist rather than a Marxist or sociological framework, as a product of the medium and its reception, though, against McLuhan, this mass is a also a resistant force of inertia against the media (ibid.: 4), cancelling 'the electricity of the social' it attempts to produce (ibid.: 1–2). Thus, for Baudrillard, the media produce not a unified, conscious and empathetically aware global citizenry but a force refusing and coalescing with the circuit of communication (ibid.: 90), a force comprised, as a 1992 lecture makes clear, of blind particles, passing like commuters on individual trajectories, avoiding all contact with others and 'all the potential violence' of exchange (1992b).

This reversal of McLuhan is seen again in Baudrillard's use of his concepts of 'hot' and 'cold' (McLuhan, 1994: 22–32). Though Baudrillard retains them as a metaphor for user participation in the media form, and agrees that our electronic media are 'cold', for him this represents not a high participation but their abolition of a 'hot' symbolic mode of relations and participation. Compare, for example, he says, the 'hot' live event with its 'emotional charge' and symbolic meaning and participation, with the 'cool', processed, semiotic 'television event' (1990a: 160), and its cold simulacra and relations. The 'cold media', therefore, cannot produce the heat of symbolic meaning and participation to rescue the cold social, as their very form, Baudrillard argues, leads to 'the freezing of every message' and 'the glaciation of meaning' (1983a: 35). Hence his critique of an attempt by German TV to dramatize the Holocaust, to rekindle a cold historical event through cold media (1994b: 49–51). Not only can the 'cold light' of television never illuminate such an event, but, in replacing the memories and lives of the survivors for us, television actually functions as an extension of the gas chambers, as 'a cold monster of extermination' (ibid.: 50), producing the same process of 'forgetting' and of 'liquidation' (ibid.: 49). So, for Baudrillard, 'cold' comes to stand as a stark metaphor for the entropic heat-death of all symbolic relations and meaning through our electronic media, which, contrary to all their promises and apparent production, extend not life, but death.

Baudrillard's reformulation of the semiotic in *Forget Foucault* as the order of 'production' allows him to radicalize his critical picture of Western society and to emphasize the production and materialization of the real as its defining characteristic. This is '*pro-duction* in the literal sense', Baudrillard says, meaning 'to render visible, to cause to appear and to be made to appear: *pro-ducere*' (1987: 21), hence he again subsumes industrial production as part of a wider historical process marking the West. Today, he argues, our informational and communicational technologies become the primary site of this drive for the real, their 'orgy of *production*' and of '*realism*', representing the 'rage to summon everything before the jurisdiction of signs' (1990a: 32): to make everything real, visible, produced, and marked; to transcribe, record, gather, prove, index and register every aspect and form, and to perfectly realise and make instantly available all reality (1987: 21–2). His example of this is pornography whose fantasy is not sexuality but reality, as 'a forcing of signs, a baroque enterprise of signification' (1990a: 28), that assumes the reality of sexuality can be manifested in its gynaecological, hypervisible, 'instantaneous, exacerbated representation' (ibid.: 29). This is our modern form of unreality, Baudrillard says, created by *adding to the real*, and engaging, 'more reference, more truth, more exactitude … having everything pass over into the absolute evidence of the real' (ibid.: 29). If, in pornography, this process leads, as Baudrillard says, to 'the devastation of the real' (ibid.: 31), then its consequences for a 'pornographic culture *par excellence*' are clear (ibid.: 34).

In *Fatal Strategies* ([1983] 1990c), Baudrillard escalates again this picture of the production of the real to chart the exponential growth of our communicational systems, and their 'metastatic' processes – their growth, like cancer cells, beyond their own meaning, limit, form and finality, into a superfluous production and useless excrescence, as a form of 'death' haunting the living, he says (ibid.: 32). The potentialization of all processes results, Baudrillard argues, in the 'obscene' – the end of the symbolic 'scene' and its meaning in the obviousness, visibility, and transparency of the world (ibid.: 50–70), and in a schizophrenic subject unable now to define the limits of their own being against this 'absolute proximity' of all things, absorbed now within the circuit of communication (ibid.: 69–70). Baudrillard calls this order the 'transpolitical' (ibid.: 25), a state representing the generalization of categories to their 'ecstatic', 'pure and empty form' (ibid.: 9), their disappearance as determinant forms, and their pure simulation in the commutation and circulation of value. In *The Transparency of Evil* ([1990] 1993c) this 'orbital' circulation becomes the basis of a fourth order of simulacra – the '*epidemic of value*', a 'fractal mode of dispersal' in which value 'radiates in al directions' (ibid.: 4–6). Modernity's 'liberation', therefore, is again (see 1996a: 18) exposed not as a real emancipation, progress, or realization of transcendence, but as a productive materialization and unleashing that leads only to simulation, indeterminacy, and our own 'inescapable indifference' (1993c: 4).

This escalation allows Baudrillard to develop both his analysis and examples of these processes, but it is also an important strategy in opening the space for the discovery of new forms of the symbolic and its internal and external resistance to this system. Thus a society devoted to the productive materialization of the world in all its 'positivity' – in its self-evidence, technical, operational perfection, and 'aseptic whiteness' – a society expunging all negativity, expelling all symbolic violence, otherness and evil in 'a vast campaign of plastic surgery' (ibid.: 45) in favour of a 'vacuum-sealed existence' (ibid.: 61), becomes vulnerable, at the point of its sterile, overprotection, to its own 'internal virulence' and 'malignant reversibility' (ibid.: 62). Anomalous, viral pathologies, such as AIDS, cancer, terrorism, drug addiction, and computer viruses (ibid.: 67), are produced within and by this system itself, as forces of 'evil', that is as symbolic forces of 'reversibility' (ibid.: 65), that homoeopathically save us at least, Baudrillard claims, from the greater threat of perfection (ibid.: 68). For total positivity and 'prohylaxis' are 'lethal' he says, as 'anything that purges the accursed share in itself signs its own death warrant' – that of its own, unlimited, catastrophic development (ibid.: 106). Thus, having expelled evil we cannot respond to its adoption, by Iran, for example, as 'the absolute weapon' against 'all western values', as a means of 'symbolic violence' we are now defenceless against (ibid.: 81–8).

Thus, it is in non-Western societies that Baudrillard finds an external symbolic force challenging the West: a force of 'radical otherness' or 'alterity' that the West has historically tried to exterminate by its reduction to 'difference', an Enlightenment,

Humanist discourse that, as in semiology, abolishes the symbolic to incorporate it into a system of values and their exchange that, in their hierarchical ordering, also leads to racism (ibid.: 128–9). Under the universalist, harmonious guise of humanism, and through its global reach, the West has successfully pursued 'the total homogenisation of the world' (ibid.: 130); a critique of Western modernity Baudrillard develops in detail in *The Illusion of the End* ([1992] 1994a). Our society is marked by this reduction of otherness, for example, in its communication systems and in its cloning (1993c: 121; see 1993c: 114–17; 2000: 3–30), but, Baudrillard says, this 'radical exoticism' survives as an irreducible force outside it in tribal societies and other cultures, such as Brazil, Australia, Japan and the Islamic world, wherever possible resisting and reversing its processes (1993c: 124–55).

The latest phase of Baudrillard's critique of the West and its technologies begins with *The Perfect Crime* ([1995] 1996b), continuing to the present (Zurbrugg, 1997; Baudrillard, 1998b; 2000; 2001c). his description there of 'the perfect crime' of the extermination of the real is an extension of his claim that, in the world of simulation, the real has passed beyond its own meaning and finality ('ex-terminus') into indeterminacy (2000: 61–2), while developing his argument that it was itself only ever a simulation – a 'principle' imposed upon the prior 'radical illusion' of the world (1996b: 16): its non-identicality to and inexchangability for itself; for the subject's consciousness and representation. This 'unbearable' state was exorcised by the realization of the world, 'to make it exist and to signify at all costs' for the subject by the simulation of its 'reality', through a 'gigantic enterprise of disillusionment' leaving 'an absolutely real world in its stead' (ibid.: 16). Today, therefore, we do not lack reality as 'reality is at its height' (ibid.: 64), 'the unconditional realisation of the world' (ibid.: 25) having brought a 'saturation by absolute reality' (ibid.: 62). At its extreme this simulation results, Baudrillard argues, in a 'virtualization', understood here not as an unreality not yet passed into actuality but rather as that which now dissuades and proscribes reality (2000: 50). Hence Baudrillard's critique of our contemporary electronic 'virtual' technologies and their 'high definition', 'real-time' operation and effects, a critique already gaining momentum through the 1990s in his discussion of the 'non-event'.

Here Baudrillard returns to and radicalizes again his earlier Boorstinian analysis of the semiotic production of events (1998a: 125–6), now seeing *all events* as simulations, as 'non-events' in their instant passage into the media. 'Things no longer really take place', he says, 'while nonetheless seeming to' (1994b: 16): whereas once the event was something that happened, something *produced*, now, as in Benjamin's work of art, it is something *reproduced* (ibid.: 21), 'it is something designed to happen. It occurs, therefore, as a virtual artefact, a reflection of pre-existing media defined forms' (1993c: 41). The event as a symbolic scene – as lived and experienced, with its own 'aura', 'glory', time, rhythm, unfolding, and historical impact – gives way to its semiotic realization from its model. Such events have 'no more significance than their anticipated meaning, their programming and their broadcasting' (1994b: 21), being instantly transferred 'into the artificial womb of the news media' (ibid.: 20), a combination of 'artificial insemination and premature ejaculation' producing forced and hurried events, spectacular in their explosion onto the screens, yet ultimately unsatisfying and unconvincing (ibid.: 31). Predictable and empty, they occur, Baudrillard says, with 'the strange aftertaste of something that has happened before, something unfolding retrospectively' (ibid.: 19), their pre-processed meaning removing all personal relationship to and investment in them, and their programming and real-time realization and dissemination preventing them from even 'happening'. Having a 'maximal' diffusion but 'zero' historical resonance (ibid.: 58), they are immediately replaced by other 'events', superseding each other in spectacular procession, each aiming to be definitive yet each having 'less and less meaning' (ibid.: 58), hollowing out before them 'the void into which they plunge' (1994b: 19), blazing momentarily upon the screen of the media to barely leave a retinal afterglow.

In this real-time transmission the medium and message and reality and image implode in a simulation, the scene of the event becoming 'a virtual space', the site of a 'definitive confusion', with the source and its information 'interfering drastically' to create a feedback effect casting 'a radical doubt on the event' (ibid.: 5–6; 57). Thus, Baudrillard says, 'the real event is wiped out by news ... All that remains of it are traces on a monitoring screen' (ibid.: 56). McLuhan's globally extended, shared electronic reality becomes, for Baudrillard, a world of processed and programmed experience, in which all media productions merge as 'events' whose reality, value, meaning and significance all become exchangeable and undecidable, all consumed at home for pleasure in the comfort and distance of the sign. Although the contemporary procession of celebrity, soap, sports, and television and popular culture 'events' could provide ample evidence of these 'non-events', Baudrillard instead turns to the most heavily mediated and important news events as the paradoxical proof of his theory.

Hence his controversial claims in *The Gulf War Did Not Take Place* ([1991] 1995a) which, far from denying the military operation and casualties, develops rather a critique of both the military production and mediated reception of this event. Militarily, this was a technologically realized simulation of war – a production of war from its model that, in its success, excluded all reciprocity, conflict or Iraqi resistance, resulting not in a 'war' but in a massacre of Iraqi forces. 'Won in advance', Baudrillard says, 'we will never know what an Iraqi taking part with a chance of fighting would have been like' (ibid.: 61). Meanwhile the Western audience consumed this 'war' in the comfort of their homes, without any personal experience, risk or danger. From this perspective even September 11th remains a non-event, in its instant passage into live breaking news for its audience who consumed the rolling coverage, speculation, and edited montages of the explosions and collapsing towers without any experience of the actual scene. However, the symbolic may still irrupt at the heart of the system's non-events, hence, Baudrillard says, the pure spectacle of September 11th was also 'the absolute event', representing 'the purest symbolic form of challenge' by Islamic terrorism against the Western 'historical and political order' (2001b: 8).

Even the 'perfect crime' of the extermination of the real may not be perfect (2000: 63), therefore, as the symbolic again breaks through to disrupt the processes of virtuality. Similarly, radical illusion 'cannot be dispelled' (1996b: 19), Baudrillard argues, and, he adds, may even be using technology today as the scene of its appearance. Moving from a pessimistic, Heideggerian critique of the fate of the real under technology Baudrillard now asks, therefore, whether the world might not be using technology as a means of preserving or even of showing its radical illusion (1995b: 85; Zurbrugg, 1997: 38). Alongside radical physics and cosmology, therefore (1996b), and building on his earlier analyses of the object (1990c; 1993c: 172–4), Baudrillard increasingly emphasizes in both his personal practice and Barthes-inspired (Barthes, 1993) reflections on photography (Zurbrugg, 1997; Baudrillard, 1996b: 85–9; 1998b: 89–101; 1999; 2001c: 139–47) its possibilities as a technological medium as a route to the symbolic. Against the contemporary 'automatic proliferation', and 'forced signification' and 'prostitution' of images (1999: 151, 148, 139; see Barthes, 1993: 117–19), comes the possibility of photography 'wresting a few exceptional images' (1999: 145) which, in their surprise, stillness and suspense, both capture the light of the object and are 'seized' by it (ibid.: 145–6), offering an experience of the world in its otherness and 'non-objectivity' (2001c: 139). Oddly, therefore, it is in the objective lens of human technology that Baudrillard discovers the hope of moving beyond the subject and its entire representational metaphysics and resulting production and extermination of the real, for another mode of experience, another – symbolic-relationship to the world.

'To Think Extreme Phenomena ...'

To think extreme phenomena, thought must itself become an extreme phenomenon.

(1996b: 66)

As Mike Gane has said, 'no-one as yet, really knows how to read Baudrillard' (Critchley, 1999). If, therefore, most of his critics have yet to hit him, as most 'launch their derision too soon, and miss the target' (Gane, 1995: 120), it must equally be recognized that he has also so far eluded most of his more sympathetic commentators: Baudrillard is never quite where you believe him to be and always more than you think. Baudrillard himself has commented on the 'reductive' criticism he has often received (Zurbrugg, 1997: 45), but even positive attempts to explain his work to a wider audience risk a reductive selection and interpretation, in merely producing another simulacrum of his work. If an introduction such as this cannot, therefore, offer *the* Baudrillard, it aims at least to offer a way to *approach* Baudrillard, a framework within which to begin to read him, and, hopefully, a basis upon which to surpass it, to move closer to what he himself might be.

There is much to be gained from this: even taking his work, as I have, as a critical analysis of contemporary society, its relevance is obvious. Baudrillard provides many brilliant examples and, although space prevents the use of others here, clearly many of his ideas remain instantly recognizable to us and can easily be applied to our consumer and media culture. Thus this chapter has been written on my own assumption that there are many important aspects of Baudrillard's work that can help illuminate our cultural experience: especially his critique of consumption, his critique of political economy and its postulates, his Durkheimian theory of the symbolic, his theory of simulation, his analysis of electronic media and their processes, his characterization of the Western production of the real and its resulting hyperrealism, his theory of the 'non-event', his concern with this system's social control, and his search for resistant, symbolic forces within a system so perfect that, 'you only have to be deprived of breakfast to become unpredictable' (1996c: 19). All of these offer valuable, critical conceptual resources for the cultural theorist, and many popular 'events' such as the death of Princess Diana repay a Baudrillardian analysis (see Merrin, 1999b).

But Baudrillard's critics are right in one respect: the question of our response to his work is a vital one. To date, most responses have chosen the negative refusal of his ideas and rejection of his work, to reduce his claims back to established positions assumed as superior. The Left's critique of Baudrillard, advanced by Kellner, Norris and Callinicos, is paradigmatic here, being notable for its ideological aversion to his non-Marxist analysis, its extreme hostility (see Best and Kellner, 1991; Norris, 1992), and its success in establishing the terms of his academic reception. Its picture, however, of Baudrillard's personal nihilism, his denial of the existence of reality, his uncritical celebration of postmodernity, lack of any critical, transformative project, and lack of any coherent philosophical project and foundation or expression, is one whose limitations and errors become obvious with any more detailed reading of his work. In addition, the critical literature has responded to more specific criticisms, countering Kellner's (1989; 1994) claims of Baudrillard's 'postmodernism' (Gane, 1991a; 1991b), correcting Norris's assertion (1992) that Baudrillard denied the physical existence of the Gulf War (Merrin, 1994; Patton, in Zurbrugg, 1997: 121–35); responding to Sokal and Bricmont's attack (1998) on his use of scientific terminology (Gane, 2000a: 46–56); defending his concept of the masses (Butler, 1999), and offering a sympathetic reading of his possible relationship to and use for feminism (Grace, 2000; Gane, 1991b; 2000), in response both to vocal feminist critics such as Gallop (1987), Plant (in Rojek and Turner, 1993), and Moore (1988) and, it must be said, Baudrillard's own negative view of feminism.

As Gane suggests, such critiques are notable for missing their target. So, while the simulacrum faces an opposition and derision, failing to recognize the long-standing theological and philosophical pedigree of this concept in the West (Merrin, 1999a), the symbolic, by contrast, is rarely challenged, other than for misplaced claims of its idealism or nostalgia (Baudrillard is clear, it is an agonistic, not a utopian, form which is not relegated to a golden age but always radically possible now). Actually, as Gane admits (1995:120), it is in the symbolic that Baudrillard becomes open to criticism, as it remains a Western image of tribal societies (Merrin, 2001: 103), an image of a 'good savage' (Lyotard, 1993: 106), derived by Baudrillard from secondary sources (Gane, 1995: 120), to serve as an experiential reality and critical foundation against the processes of the simulacrum which, apparently, proscribe such a foundation (Merrin, 2001: 103–4). In his defence, however, Baudrillard has been concerned throughout his career both with the necessity of discovering such a critical position and with the problems of its articulation. His reformulations of the symbolic, from 'symbolic exchange' to 'seduction', the 'fatal', 'evil', 'radical alterity', and 'radical illusion' to 'singularity' (see 1998b), and his search for those forces of reversal against the system, all strengthen his work, though, ultimately, they do not escape the limitations of such a position.

But all such negative critiques are based on a de-escalation, returning us to a prior state and its accepted reality and morality and as such are poor responses to the gift and challenge of Baudrillard's work. Instead, if we want to move beyond him, we should accept his own invitation – 'please follow me' (1983c: 86) – which enters us into a different critical game entirely. To understand why we need first to understand his methodology which is derived from the impossibility of developing an empirical theory to reflect reality in a society dominated by simulation. Just as McLuhan responded to our 'rear-view mirror' perception (Benedetti and Dehart, 1997: 186–7), with his anticipatory 'probes', which aimed to push reality, to make our environment visible at its limits (McLuhan and Zingrone, 1995: 236), so Baudrillard develops 'one strategy' (1993a: 82): that of 'theoretical violence', a 'speculation to the death whose only method is the radicalisation of hypotheses' (1993b: 5). Theory must itself become an 'extreme phenomenon' in order to steal a march on the extreme phenomena of this world (1996b: 66) and push them towards their collapse (1993b: 4–5). Theory, therefore, is 'both simulation and challenge' (1993a: 126) – a Situationist, paraphysical, and McLuhanist-inspired simulation and provocation and a Maussian gift and symbolic challenge to the real (1994c; see also 1996b: 94–105). The result is to advance ideas without believing in them, as a 'conceptual weapon against reality'; one that, if realized by the world, to become true, loses any critical force it once had (1994c: 4).

The simulacrum was one such weapon, and, as a Japanese interviewer told Baudrillard, now it is realized everywhere, 'we no longer have any need of you' (1996d: 7). Ultimately the world escalates to disarm theory, reducing it to a passive reflection of reality: everything 'falls back unfailingly into truth', Baudrillard says (1997: 8), negating all challenge. This is a reduction we collude in as all questioning of this reality attracts either laughter (1994c: 1) or hostility, for, he says, 'the fact is that attacks on the reality principle itself constitute a graver offence than real life violence' (1993c: 42). Baudrillard, however, still believes a 'radical thought' can operate against this, using a theoretical violence, a strategic conceptual strike (1990b: 46; 1997: 34), to remodel reality in its symbolic challenge (1998b: 69). Thought has to be 'exceptional, anticipatory, and at the margin' to outpace 'the hell of the real' (1996b: 102). The escalation and reversion which mark Baudrillard's work, therefore, have to be understood as both analytic tools to reflect the real and strategic weapons devoted to pushing this real, to imagining and contributing towards the end of the system he describes (1998b: 23).

This is Baudrillard's radical methodology and it introduces a paradox for our reading of his work. In refusing to empirically mirror the real, Baudrillard rejects and radically critiques the naïvety of all other cultural theories and the possibility of cultural theory and sociology itself. He also, however, derives his own critique from an established Durkheimian sociological tradition and so, at some level, remains caught within its processes (Gane, 1995: 120–1), while advancing a theory that, as I have argued, has considerable relevance for understanding our contemporary culture. While this may merely show how far the real has advanced in realizing his ideas and thus may yet be a barometer of the seriousness of our condition, it also opens up the space for a more interesting response to him. For, if to 'follow' another is, as Baudrillard says, a 'murderous' game (1983c: 78), stealing the other's goal from him (1993c: 156), then following Baudrillard, discovering his ideas in the world and realizing his work for him, brings, with its success, Baudrillard's disappearance, his reduction to truth. Only a violent opposition to his work, therefore, can keep him alive as a theorist. But there is another option too: of following Baudrillard and moving beyond him. If Baudrillard's ideas are challenges to the real, and challenges to theory and the process of theorizing, they are also a challenge to us. The only acceptable response to the gift, is not to refuse, which only lowers oneself, but to accept and to give back more. This is what we must now attempt: this speculation to the death is our challenge; this escalation and reversal are what Baudrillard himself wants (Zurbrugg, 1997: 42, 45). Please follow him.

Note

1   Except, of course, for Baudrillard, the passage to a 'transeconomics' takes us beyond such an event: 'the 1929 crisis could not recur today. It has been replaced by perpetual crisis simulation' (1990b: 217).

References

Barthes, R. (1973a) *Mythologies*. London: Paladin Books.
Barthes, R. (1973b) *Elements of Semiology*. New York: Hill and Wang.
Barthes, R. (1990) *The Fashion System*. Berkeley, CA: University of California Press.
Barthes, R. (1993) *Camera Lucida*. London: Vintage Books.
Bataille, G. (1962) *Eroticism*. London: Marion Boyars Publishers Ltd.
Bataille, G. (1985) *Visions of Excess. Selected Writings, 1927–1939*. New York: Zone Books.
Bataille, G. (1991) *The Accursed Share, Vol. 1*. New York: Zone Books.
Bataille, G. (1992) *Theory of Religion*. New York: Zone Books.
Baudrillard, J. (1975) *The Mirror of Production*. St Louis, M: Telos.
Baudrillard, J. (1981) *For a Critique of the Political Economy of the Sign*. St Louis, M.: Telos.
Baudrillard, J. (1983a) *In the Shadow of the Silent Majorities*. Semiotext(e): New York.
Baudrillard, J. (1983b) 'What are you doing after the orgy?' *Artforum* Oct., pp. 42–6.
Baudrillard, J. (1983c) *Please Follow Me* (with Sophie Calle, *Suite venitienne*). Seattle: Bay Press.
Baudrillard, J. (1987) *Forget Foucault*. New York: Semiotext(e).
Baudrillard, J. (1989) 'Politics of seduction', *Marxism Today* January, pp. 54–5.
Baudrillard, J. (1990a) *Seduction*. London: Macmillan.
Baudrillard, J. (1990b) *Cool Memories*. London: Verso.

Baudrillard, J. (1990c) *Fatal Strategies*. London: Pluto Press.

Baudrillard, J. (1992a) 'Transpolitics, transsexuality, transaesthetics', in W. Stearns and W. Chaloupka (eds) *Jean Baudrillard. The Disappearance of Art and Politics*. London: Macmillan, pp. 9–26.

Baudrillard, J. (1992b) 'The vanishing point of communication', lecture, 18 November, Loughborough University of Technology (text unpublished).

Baudrillard, J. (1993a) *Baudrillard Live: Selected Interviews*, ed. M. Gane. London: Routledge.

Baudrillard, J. (1993b) *Symbolic Exchange and Death*. London: Sage Publications.

Baudrillard, J. (1993c) *The Transparency of Evil*. London: Verso.

Baudrillard, J. (1994a) *The Illusion of the End*. Cambridge: Polity Press.

Baudrillard, J. (1994b) *Simulacra and Simulation*. Michigan: University of Michigan Press.

Baudrillard, J. (1994c) 'Radical thought' (translation of *La Pensée Radicale*) http://www.ctheory.com/a25–radical_thought.html (contacted June 1997; page numbers refer to print-out copy).

Baudrillard, J. (1995a) *The Gulf War Did Not Take Place*. Sydney: Power Publications.

Baudrillard, J. (1995b) 'Symbolic exchange: taking theory seriously: an interview with Jean Baudrillard, (with R. Boyne and S. Lash), *Theory, Culture and Society* 12(4): 74–45.

Baudrillard, J. (1996a) *The System of Objects*. London: Verso.

Baudrillard, J. (1996b) *The Perfect Crime*. London: Verso.

Baudrillard, J. (1996c) *Cool Memories 2*. Cambridge: Polity Press.

Baudrillard, J. (1996d) 'Vivisecting the 90's: an interview with Jean Baudrillard', interview with Caroline Bayard and Graham Knight, http://www.ctheory.com/a24–vivesecting_90's.html (interview for *Research in Semiotic Inquiry/Recherches semiotiques* Vol. 16, No. 1–2, Spring 1996. Contacted June 1997; page numbers refer to print-out copy).

Baudrillard, J. (1997) *Fragments; Cool Memories 3*. London: Verso.

Baudrillard, J. (1998a) *The Consumer Society*. London: Sage Publications.

Baudrillard, J. (1998b) *Paroxysm*. London: Verso.

Baudrillard, J. (1999) *Within the Horizon of the Object: Objects in This Mirror Are Closer Than They Appear. Photographs 1985–1998*. ed. P. Weibel. Graz: Hatje Cantz Publishers.

Baudrillard, J. (2000) *The Vital Illusion*. New York: Columbia University Press.

Baudrillard, J. (2001a) *The Uncollected Baudrillard*. ed. G. Genosko. London: Sage.

Baudrillard, J. (2001b) 'The spirit of terrorism', *Cyber-Society List*, Archive, http://www.jicsmail.ac.uk/cgi-bin/wa.exe?A2=ind0111andL=cybersociety-liveandF=andS=andP=6436 (contacted December 2001; page numbers refer to print-out copy).

Baudrillard, J. (2001c) *The Impossible Exchange*. London: Verso.

Baudrillard, J. (2002) *Screened Out*. London: Verso.

Benedetti, P. and Dehart, N. (1997) *Forward Through the Rear View Mirror, Reflections On and By Marshall McLuhan*. London: MIT Press.

Best, S. and Kellner, D. (1991) *Postmodern Theory*. London: The Macmillan Press Ltd.

Boorstin, D.J. (1992) *The Image*. New York: Vintage Books.

Butler, R. (1999) *Jean Baudrillard: The Defence of the Real*. London: Sage.

Caillois, R. (1980) *Man and the Sacred*. Connecticut: Greenwood Press.

Callinicos, A. (1989) *Against Postmodernism: A Marxist Critique*. Cambridge: Polity Press.

Critchley, S. (1999) *A Companion to Continental Philosophy*. Oxford: Blackwell Publishers.

De Saussure, F. (1986) *Course in General Linguistics*. Chicago: Open Court.

Durkheim, E. (1915) *The Elementary Forms of the Religious Life*. London: Allen and Unwin.

Foucault, M. (1970) *The Order of Things*. London: Routledge.

Gallop, J. (1987) 'French theory and the seduction of the feminine', in A. Jardine and P. Smith (eds) *Men in Feminism*. New York: Methuen.

Gane, M. (1991a) *Baudrillard's Bestiary: Baudrillard and Culture*. London: Routledge.

Gane, M. (1991b) *Baudrillard: Critical and Fatal Theory*. London; Routledge.

Gane, M. (1995) 'Radical theory: Baudrillard and vulnerability'. *Theory, Culture and Society*, 12(4): 109–23.

Gane, M. (2000a) *Jean Baudrillard: In Radical Uncertainty*. London: Pluto Press.

Gane, M. (ed.) (2000b) *Jean Baudrillard: Masters of Social Theory* (4 vols.) London: Sage.

Genosko, G. (1994) *Baudrillard and Signs; Signification Ablaze*. London: Routledge.

Genosko, G. (1999) *McLuhan and Baudrillard: The Masters of Implosion*. London: Routledge.

Grace, V. (2000) *Baudrillard's Challenge: A Feminist Reading*. London: Routledge.

Hollier, D. (ed.) (1988) *The College of Sociology. 1937–39*. Minneapolis: University of Minnesota Press.

Hubert, H. and Mauss, M. (1964) *Sacrifice: Its Nature and Function*. Chicago: University of Chicago Press.

Kellner, D. (1987) 'Baudrillard, semiurgy and death', *Theory, Culture and Society* 4: 125–46.

Kellner, D. (1988) 'Postmodernism as Social Theory', *Theory, Culture and Society* 5: 239–69.

Kellner, D. (1989) *Jean Baudrillard: From Marxism to Postmodernism and Beyond*. Cambridge: Polity Press.

Kellner, D. (ed.) (1994) *Baudrillard: A Critical Reader*. Oxford: Basil Blackwell Ltd.

Kroker, A. (1985) 'Baudrillard's Marx' in *Theory, Culture and Society* 2/3, pp. 69–83.

Kroker, A. and Cook, D. (eds) (1988) *The Postmodern Scene: Excremental Culture and Hyper-aesthetics*. London: Macmillan.

Levin, C. (1996) *Jean Baudrillard: A Study in Cultural Metaphysics*. London: Prentice Hall.

Lyotard, J-F. (1993) *Libidinal Economy*. London: The Athlone Press.

Marcuse, H (1986) *One-Dimensional Man*. London: Routledge and Kegan Paul.

Mauss, M. and Hubert, H. (1966) *The Gift: Forms and Functions of Exchange in Primitive Societies*. London: Cohen and West Ltd.

Mauss, M. and Hubert, H. (1972) *A General Theory of Magic*. London: Routledge and Kegan Paul.

McLuhan, E. and Zingrone, F (1995) *Essential McLuhan*. London: Routledge.

McLuhan, M. (1994) *Understanding Media*. London: MIT Press.

Merrin, W. (1994) 'Uncritical criticism? Norris, Baudrillard and the Gulf War', *Economy and Society,* 23(4): 433–58.

Merrin, W. (1999a) 'Television is killing the art of symbolic exchange: Baudrillard's theory of communication', *Theory, Culture and Society,* 16(3): 119–40.

Merrin, W. (1999b) 'Crash, bang, whallop, what a picture! The death of Diana and the media', *Mortality,* 4(1): 41–62.

Merrin, W. (2001) 'To play with *phantoms*: Jean Baudrillard and the evil demon of the simulacrum', *Economy and Society,* 30(1): 85–111.

Merrin, W. (2002) 'Implosion, simulation, and the pseudo-event: a critique of McLuhan', *Economy and Society,* 31(3): 369–90.

Moore, S. (1988) 'Getting a bit of the other – the pimps of postmodernism', in R. Chapman, and J. Rutherford, (eds) *Male order: Unwrapping Masculinity*. London: Lawrence and Wishart.

Norris, C. (1990) *What's Wrong with Postmodernism?* London: Harvester Wheatsheaf.

Norris, C. (1992) *Uncritical Theory: Postmodernism, Intellectuals and the Gulf War*. London: Lawrence and Wishart.

Rojek, C. and Turner, B.S. (eds) (1993) *Forget Baudrillard?* London: Routledge.

Sokal, A. and Bricmont, J. (1998) *Intellectual Impostures*. London: Profile.

Stearns, W. and Chaloupka, W. (eds) (1992) *Jean Baudrillard: The Disappearance of Art and Politics*. London: Macmillan.

Zurbrugg, N. (ed.) (1997) *Jean Baudrillard: Art and Artefact*. London: Sage.

PART III

CONTEMPORARY CULTURAL ANALYSIS

Reconceptualizing Representation and Identity

CHAPTER TEN
●●●●● ●●●

Issues of transculturalism and transnationalism in the intersection of feminism and cultural sociology

Ann Brooks

Introduction

Issues of representation and the construction of identity can be seen as organizing principles for exploring intersecting debates in the area of feminism, sociology and cultural studies. Many feminists have made an intellectual shift from the disciplinary constraints of sociology to the unapologetically interdisciplinary terrain of cultural studies. The interdisciplinary matrix of cultural studies has provided a framework within which feminist, postmodernist and postcolonial theoretical debates have coalesced. The trandisciplinary context of cultural studies incorporating sociology, critical ethnography, film, literature and cultural politics has provided a dynamic, intellectual nexus for those working at the interface of feminism, postmodernism and postcolonialism. It is maintained in this chapter that whereas the interdisciplinary nexus of cultural studies has always been characterized by a 'desire to transgress established boundaries' (Stratton and Ang, 1996), the intersection of feminism and cultural studies has become increasingly significant for the transcultural and transnational conceptualization of debates on representation and identity. This chapter examines intersecting debates in the area of feminism and cultural studies and highlights the emergence of new conceptions of subjecthood and identity framed by the discourses of transculturalism and transnationalism. New cultural and ethnic identities have emerged, carrying with them new conceptions of subjectivity and offering a number of possibilities for feminists working in the area to open up spaces for the emergence of new subject positions and new places from which to speak. This chapter examines how discourses on transculturalism and transnationalism have made debates on subjectivity, representation and identity much more contested.

Transculturalism and transnationalism have produced new conceptions of subject-hood, subjectivity and identity as new cultural and ethnic boundaries have emerged. These new cultural and ethnic identities carry with them the need for new concep-tions of subjectivity and require the opening-up of new subject positions and new spaces and places from which to speak. This emphasis requires a transdisciplinary approach to the analysis of representation and identity. Thus, for many theorists of the transcultural and transnational, including feminists, postcolonial theorists, post-modernists, anthropologists and theorists of globalization, there has been a need for an intellectual shift from the disciplinary constraints of sociology, geography and his-tory to the unapologetically interdisciplinary terrain of cultural studies. The transdis-ciplinary context of cultural studies has provided a framework for the incorporation of a number of disciplinary areas, all of which lend themselves to an analysis of rep-resentation, subjectivity and identity, including cultural sociology, critical ethnogra-phy, film, literature and cultural politics. The first part of the chapter examines the interdisciplinary nexus of cultural studies, and shows how it has provided a frame-work for intersecting discourses on feminism, postcolonialism and postmodernism to coalesce. The second part of the chapter focuses on an understanding of transcultur-alism and transnationalism in the development of new conceptions of subjectivity and identity and in demanding new discourses within which subjectivity, representa-tion and identity can be reflected. The final section of the chapter suggests new ways to conceptualize issues of representation, subjectivity and identity.

The Transdisciplinary Context of Cultural Studies: New Discursive Frameworks for Understanding Representation and Identity

The interdisciplinary nexus of cultural studies has always been characterized by a 'desire to transgress established boundaries and to create new forms of knowledge and understanding not bound by such boundaries' (Stratton and Ang, 1996: 362), cultural studies has increasingly become a vehicle for transnational and transcultural conceptualizations and framing of debates on representation and identity. Stratton and Ang claim that:

> as cultural studies is rapidly becoming an internationally recognized label for a particular type of intellectual work, it is crossing not just disciplinary boundaries, but also cultural-geographical boundaries. Cultural studies is now being

practiced in many different parts of the world ... and is rapidly becoming a central site for critical intellectualism in the postmodern, postcolonial, post-communist new world (dis)order.

(ibid.)

Cultural studies has now become recognized as a global interdisciplinary forum for a range of intellectual and political debates and has been significant for advancing the transcultural and transnational framing of debates on conceptualizations of representation and identity. The focus of the second part of the chapter is on the concepts of representation and identity as organizing principles for examining debates in the area of cultural studies, film and media. It examines how feminist and postcolonial theorists have interrogated cultural and filmic discourses in the process of reconceptualizing colonial representation, subjectivity and identity.

The politics of representation and the construction of identity: cultural studies – 'transborder cultural flows'

Cultural studies has been the interdisciplinary matrix where contested debates on representation and identity, the global (international) and the local (national), the hegemonic 'centre' (Britain, America) and the 'margins' (Australia, Canada, New Zealand) have occupied centre stage. As McKenzie Wark observes:

The growth of cultural studies, seen from the point of view of the effects of the development of new media technologies, is part of the phenomenal increase in the volume and velocity of transborder cultural flows[1] that are increasingly marking all of us into 'cruising grammarians', to borrow a phrase from Morris (1988: 195).

(Wark, 1992: 435)

Wark's argument has significant implications for those concerned with issues of cultural hegemony. Writers and theorists such as Simon During claim that cultural studies has now developed into 'a genuine global movement' reminding us, (1993: 13), however, that the 'Australian cultural studies critic Meaghan Morris's critical observation that "the word international" comes to work in cultural studies as it does in the film and record industries as a euphemism for a process of streamlining work to be "interesting" to American and European audiences' (Morris, 1992a: 456).

The response of those involved in cultural studies 'at the margins' is, as Stratton and Ang note, 'the appropriation of the specifying category of the "post-colonial" by Australian, Canadian and New Zealand practitioners of cultural studies' (1996: 367). They claim that this can be seen as 'the strategic invocation of an alternative frame of meaning of "international", one that counters the hegemonic "world" order led by American and British cultural studies' (ibid.). While wary of those who uncritically take 'the national as the privileged site of the particular' because of the inherent risks of exclusivity, Stratton and Ang argue for a reconsideration of the 'concrete, process of particularization itself, and for the interrogation of its politics. Adopting the category of the postcolonial is one such strategy for articulating a notion of 'politics' based on particularization, which they claim 'has the possibility of problematizing both the universal and the national' (ibid.). Stratton and Ang outline three models of cultural studies: the postcolonial, the diasporic and the subaltern.

The cultural studies debate has been vigorous in Australia and has been, in part at least, framed by the decline of both Britain and the United States, in terms of any notion of global cultural hegemony. The process of interrogation of cultural studies within Britain and America by diasporic, feminist and postcolonial discourses has led to a pluralized conception of cultural studies and a process of self-reflection on issues of representation and identity. In commenting on the position of cultural studies in the United States, Stratton and Ang comment: 'cultural studies has become an intellectual home for the unprecedented eruption of non-dominant race, gender and ethnic voices in the American public arena' (ibid.: 377).

Cultural studies – 'empowering validation of the marginal'

The framing of an Australian cultural studies emanating from a 'postcolonial speaking position' does not imply a univocality in that position or even agreement that the category of the postcolonial is the most appropriate one. As Stratton and Ang observe: '[t]he very applicability of the category of the postcolonial to contemporary Australia is, understandably rejected by Aboriginal people, for whom living in "Australia" means living in a permanently colonial condition, never post-colonial' (ibid.: 139). The postcolonial speaking position is one characterized by contradiction and contestation in terms of some of the advocates. Graeme Turner 'has been one of the most vocal resenters of the Anglo-American hegemony in "international" cultural studies and the centrality of British cultural studies in it' (ibid.: 379). Despite his hostility towards British cultural studies, much of Turner's work understands cultural studies as framed within the 'notion of a "history from below", which he has borrowed from British cultural studies' (ibid.). By contrast, Meaghan Morris and John Frow 'have rejected such an account of Australian cultural studies, favoring a more independent locally oriented account instead' (ibid.: 380).

Turner develops his arguments for an Australian cultural studies in opposition to elements of British cultural studies. He recognizes that 'the point of connection between British and Australian cultural studies ... is the empowering validation of the marginal,[2] although the naming of the marginal differs greatly from one context to another' (ibid.: 378). In adopting this oppositional position of centre and margins as regards Australian cultural studies, Turner claims that: 'Cultural studies has a lot to gain from the margins, and it should do its best to investigate the ways in which their specific conditions demand the modification of explanations generated elsewhere' (1992b: 650).

Turner, while stating 'I am not a postcolonial theorist' (1992a: 426), self-consciously positions himself in a postcolonial speaking position and positions Australia and

Australian cultural studies 'at the margins' confronted by the Anglocentric, neo-colonialist 'universalism' characterized by British cultural studies. Stratton and Ang comment that '[t]he politics of the position is to assert "Australia" in the face of a powerful ... "Britain". But this Australian postcolonial position is also, profoundly informed by the former settler colony's residual preoccupation, if not obsession, with what used to be the mother country' (1996: 380).

The relationship between representation and identity in relation to conceptualizing an Australian cultural studies and indeed 'Australianism' is a complicated one and Turner recognizes the difficulties:

> On the one hand a defence must be mounted of the nation that there is a national culture which may not be 'organic' or 'authentic' but which nonetheless systematically produces differences and interests which should be respected, maintained and, at times protected. On the other hand, those who have reservations about the idea of the nation have to insist that it is, after all, imaginary, and that its momentum towards unity is to be resisted and interrogated.
>
> (Turner, 1992: 428)

While Turner recognizes the dangers of attempting to 'fix' a conception of national identity, his model of an Australian cultural studies falls dangerously close to being caricatured by Meaghan Morris's conception of the relationship between 'settler subjectivity – primarily but not exclusively articulated in Australia by Anglo-Celtic people ... and cultural studies'. As Morris observes: 'To use an Australianism, dominion subjects are the "whinging whites" of international cultural studies. Dubiously postcolonial, prematurely postmodern, constitutively multi-cultural but still predominantly white, we oscillate historically between identities of colonizer and colonized' (1992a: 471).

Morris shares with Angela McRobbie (1994) (see also Brooks 1997a; 1997b) an interest in the 'micropolitics of everyday life'. In Morris's essay 'Afterthoughts on "Australianism"'(1992a), she puts the Australian conception of 'mateship' on the cultural studies agenda. As she observes: '[s]ince mateship is an everyday medium of micro political pressure ... it also thrives in those oppositional milieux (feminist, anti-racist, multiculturalism, gay and lesbian activist) which most affect to despise it from its exclusionary determinants and its current complicities of power' (ibid.: 469). In framing 'mateship' within a cultural studies context, Morris 'dismantles' its overt masculinist and nationalist rhetoric and draws on it as a metaphor with which to explore conceptions of 'Australianism'. In doing so, she addresses aspects of Australia's postcolonial identity, both as colonized and coloniser.

Morris, like McRobbie operates at a number of different levels of analysis. She shares with McRobbie two dimensions in her critical cultural studies repertoire, first, her desire to '"create a place from which to speak" that allows a feminist voice to do more than "answer back" to hegemonic modes of discourse' (Wark, 1992: 434). Second, her objection to cultural studies is conceived in terms of an opposition between academic and popular discourse. As McKenzie Wark observes: '[h]er work is a process of creating spaces in which feminist voices can be heard ... somewhere between the popular and the academic' (ibid.: 440).

Morris has rebuked Turner for overstating the significance of the binary of British high culture as against Australian popular culture (see Morris, 1991). Whereas Turner's response to the hegemonic tendencies of British cultural studies is to fret about the rules of the game, Wark comments that '[i]n the essays of Meaghan Morris, there is a playful, self-conscious version of this dilemma of authority as it appears from the antipodean end of the line ... Morris writes in a manner which is self-consciously antipodean but which does not necessarily have anything to do with being Australian' (Wark, 1992: 443).

The difference between Turner and Morris is ultimately one of 'vulnerability' of positioning. Turner attempts to assert a 'postcolonial identity' for cultural studies but does not attempt to conceptualize postcolonial feminist discourse within this formulation. Morris discusses the problem of 'identity' in both feminist and antipodean discourse. As Wark comments:

> she takes *all* this on board – colonial antipodality *and* feminism as minor and difficult speaking positions – and gets away with it. In multiplying the difficulties of finding a place and a rhetorical means to speak, Morris has improvised solutions. For example she treats the question of defining the feminist content of an enquiry into everyday life as 'an invitation to make up answers as I go along'.
>
> (1998b: 188)

A critical postcolonial perspective can be seen to be highly productive for cultural studies, as Stratton and Ang note, through its ability to shift the focus of cultural studies to a 'transnational dimension', so that the conceptualization of cultural struggle and cultural power 'is now located as enacted *between* "societies" as well as *within* "societies"' (Stratton and Ang, 1996: 381). However, this is not the only model which can interrogate a hegemonic cultural studies framework. The work of Stuart Hall provides the basis of a second model suggested by Stratton and Ang, which is the diasporic model. The particular inflection given to British cultural studies by the 'representational politics' advocated by Stuart Hall and the interjection of his own intellectual and personal biography frame a speaking position which is identified by Hall himself as 'diasporic'. This model is one trajectory which accommodates Bennett's articulated need for mobilization of an international cultural studies *'rendez-vous* among the marginals themselves, bypassing the presence of the hegemonic center' (ibid.).

Hall's personal history in relation to cultural studies has been formative in terms of the development of British cultural studies, and Hall's increasingly autobiographical contribution has led to a greater reflexivity within British cultural studies around the 'peculiarities of "Britishness"'. As Stratton and Ang observe, 'what the diasporic position opens up is the possibility of developing a post-imperial British identity, one based explicitly on an acknowledgement and vindication of the "coming home" of the colonized Other' (ibid.: 383). The impact of the work of Hall (1992: 1993) and

Gilroy (1987, 1992, 1993) has done much to interrogate a conception of national identity around which British cultural studies has coalesced.

These two models: the diasporic and the postcolonial, while raising a range of important issues for cultural studies in terms of 'global' and 'national' discourses, are not without limitations. There are still speaking positions which remain marginalized by these models. 'One such position ... would be the indigenous (whose voice has been scarcely heard in cultural studies anywhere)' (Stratton and Ang, 1996: 385). The contribution of Aboriginal writers in Australia and Maori writers in New Zealand still leaves the intellectual high ground of cultural studies unmarked. Stratton and Ang suggest a third model – the subaltern – which they describe as 'a position to be distinguished from both the diasporic and the postcolonial as it tends to be spoken from a very different geo-political and geo-cultural space, namely the Third World' (ibid.: 385). Rey Chow (1993) raises the implications of the use of 'subaltern', which , as Chow, points out, 'when construed in terms of *foreignness* of race, land and language, can blind us to political exploitation as easily as it can alert us to it' (1993: 9). Chow points up the implications of this type of binary construction, because 'the representation of "the other" as such ignores ... the class and intellectual hierarchies within these other cultures' (ibid.: 13). The intersection of feminism with the postcolonial is a significant intervention into these debates and has implications for the increasingly transcultural and transnational framing of debates on representation and identity.

Transnationalism and transculturalism and the postcolonial

The intersection of transculturalism and transnationalism with discourses on the postcolonial has provided fertile territory for reconceptualizing debates on subjectivity and identity. The relationship between postcolonialism, transculturalism and transnationalism has both epistemological and historical dimensions as Hall (1996) shows. The concept of the postcolonial provides a conceptual repertoire to facilitate an understanding of a process of global transformation or transculturation. Hall provides a critical overview of the concept of the postcolonial in terms of its wider theoretical framework on the 'politics of representation'. Hall deals elegantly with the epistemological and chronological dimensions of the postcolonial concept, particularly with regard to its potential as a mechanism for deconstructing binaries. As Hall observes, while the concept of the postcolonial is by its very nature 'universalizing' (Hall, 1996: 246), because of its high level of abstraction, it need not get trapped by uniformity in its application. As Frankenberg and Mani observe:

> The 'postcolonial' as an axis of subject formation is constructed not simply in dialogue with dominant white society, but is an effect of engagement between particular subjects, white society, region of origin and region of religious and/or political affiliation, what Paul Gilroy (1990/91) describes as 'the dialectics of diasporic identification'.
>
> (1993: 302)

In reframing the discourses on 'colonization', the narrative framework established by the postcolonial positions 'colonization' as something more than the exercise of colonial power in different parts of the world. Hall understands the significance of the 'postcolonial' in terms of a global, hegemonic process, central in the development of capitalist modernity. As he comments: 'I think it is signifying the whole process of expansion, elaboration, conquest, colonization and imperial hegemonization which constituted the 'outer face', the constitutive outside, of European and then Western capitalist modernity after 1492' (Hall, 1996: 249). This has strong parallels with Ong's (1999) conception of 'flexible citizenship' in the growth of Chinese transnational capitalism.

The concept of the postcolonial is not about describing a particular state of historical or contemporary relations as they apply to one society rather than another. It is about 're-reading' and rethinking 'colonization' as part of what Hall describes as 'an essentially trans-national and transcultural "global" process' (1996: 247). It is about the deconstruction of the binary structures within which relationships are framed and represented. Hall describes the process as a move from one conception of difference to another (Hall 1992a) and he draws on the distinction elaborated by Derrida (1978) between difference and '*différence*'. This shift from difference to '*différence*' is, as Hall notes: 'It obliges us to re-read the binaries as forms of transculturation, of cultural translation destined to trouble the here/there cultural binaries forever' (Hall, 1996: 247). In its move to a position of 'transculturalism', previously established relationships captured by the binary framing of relations have to be rethought. Postcolonial analysis 'produces a decentred, diasporic or "global" rewriting of earlier, nation-centred imperial grand narratives' (ibid.). The concept of what Gilroy (1993) identifies as the 'diasporic' is central here in understanding the shift in relations. The notion of the diasporic supplements and displaces the centre/periphery binary so fundamental in the met narratives around 'colonization' and reorganizes and reshapes global relationships.

Hall shows that '[i]t is in the reconstitution of the epistemic and power knowledge fields around the relations of globalization through its various historical forms' (1996: 50) that gives the postcolonial its transcultural and transnational potential, and that defines the 'postcolonial' moment. The postcolonial is thus sensitive to a number of dimensions including the 'question of hybridity ... the complexities of diasporic identification which interrupt any "return" to ethnically closed and "centred" original histories' (ibid.). When colonization is thus situated within the revised postcolonial narrative framework, and '[u]nderstood in its global and transcultural context', colonization can be seen to have made 'ethnic absolutism an increasingly untenable cultural strategy'(ibid.).

The central issue for Hall is the process of 'transculturation' which characterizes the nexus of colonial relations. Through this process

> colonization so refigured the terrain that, ever since, the very idea of a world of separate identities, of isolated or separable and self-sufficient cultures and economies, has been obliged to yield to a variety of paradigms designed to capture these different but related forms of relationship.
>
> (1996: 253)

Those who are critical of this model of the postcolonial make an epistemological distinction between a rational logic and a deconstructive one, one such critic is Dirlik (1992) whose criticisms of the postcolonial are twofold. The first point that he makes is that it is:

> A post-structuralist, post-foundationalist discourse, deployed mainly by displaced Third World intellectuals making good in prestige 'Ivy League' American universities and deploying the fashionable language of the linguistic and cultural 'turn' to 'rephrase' Marxism, returning it 'to another First World language with universalistic epistemological pretentions,
>
> (Dirlik, 1992: 346)

Linked to this, is Dirlik's second point which is that poststructuralist, anti-foundationalist underpinnings of the postcolonial make it incapable of dealing with 'capitalism's structuring of the modern world' (Dirlik, 1992: 346). In addition, Dirlik claims that poststructuralism is preoccupied with questions of identity and not able to give 'an account of the world outside the subject' (ibid.). The parallels between poststructuralism and the postcolonial in the writings of postcolonial intellectuals is taken up by Bulbeck (1998) who claims that for this group postmodernism and postcolonialism are coterminous:

> In the hands of postcolonial writers like Edward Said, Homi Bhaba, Abdul JanMohammed, Gayatri Spivak (most of whom are academics in European or North American universities), postmodernism becomes post-colonialism, a discourse which attempts to heal the 'epistemic violence (to borrow Spivak's phrase) of imperialism' (Emberley 1993: 5). The contradictory experiences of those located between a 'homeland' and western academic privilege, or as fourth world peoples in a first world nation, is particularly explored by the postcolonial writers.
>
> (Bulbeck, 1998: 14)

While Bulbeck's conclusions are over-simple, there is little doubt that the postcolonial intellectual, both feminist and non-feminist, provides an interesting case study of a site for the transculturalism and transnationalism conceptualizations of debates on representation and identity.

The feminist postcolonial intellectual – a case study of transculturalism and transnationalism in redefining subjectivity and identity

Key to the development of a range of conceptualizations which draw on a cultural studies frame of reference has been the work of both feminist and non-feminist postcolonial intellectuals. This group encompasses the ideas of feminism, postcolonial theory, postmodernism combined with the experiences of transcultural and transnational analysis. Feminist and non-feminist postcolonial intellectuals have led to an interdisciplinary fusion of ideas and concepts drawing on feminist theory, literary criticism, critical ethnography and film theory. Feminist (and non-feminist) post-colonial intellectuals provide a site for the intersection of debates on feminism, post-colonialism, transculturalism and transnationalism. Many have and are operating within cultural studies discourses. The interdisciplinary matrix of cultural studies has provided a framework within which feminist, postmodernist and postcolonial theo-retical debates have coalesced. The intersection of feminism and cultural studies has become increasingly significant for the transnational and transcultural conceptualiza-tion of debates around representation and identity. One such feminist postcolonial intellectual is Trinh T. Minh-ha (1988a; 1988b; 1989; 1991; 1995a; 1995b). Trinh (1989) raises concerns about the framing and language of postcolonial theory in terms of using 'the "master's" tools to dismantle his house' (ibid.), in addition, Trinh 'refuses to be "ghettoized" through the separate and/or combined essentialisms of gender, race or ethnicity, seeing these consolidating positions – politically strategic as they may at first appear – as new houses or rather out-houses of the "master(s)"' (ibid.).

Trinh's main treatise *Woman, Native, Other* (1989), subtitled *Writing, Postcoloniality and Feminism* addresses the question 'how can feminist discourse represent the cate-gories of "woman" and "race" at the same time?' (Suleri, 1995: 275). This is the sub-text of many of the contested debates on feminist and postcolonial discourses, for Trinh, the answer lies in relocating 'her gendering of ethnic realities on the inevitable territory of post feminism' (ibid.). Trinh's work is characterized by the intersection of postcolonial, feminist and poststructuralist discourses and she is criticized by writers such as Suleri for having a 'free-floating understanding of "postcolonial"' (Suleri, 1995: 276).

Gayatri Chakrovorty Spivak (1985a; 1985b), like Trinh T. Minh-ha, combines fem-inist poststructuralist and postcolonial discourses in her work. Both are diasporic intellectuals operating in theoretical terms at the 'high end of deconstruction' and both are fundamentally concerned with the recognition of 'difference'. However, when it comes to the question of the recovery of the subaltern voice, there are sig-nificant points of difference. The question of 'who is permitted to speak on behalf of whom?' can often become an issue of 'appropriation'. This can result in what Trinh has called 'the nativist line of teaching the "natives" how to be bona-fide anti or decolonized others' (Trinh, 1989: 59). The use of appropriation is analyzed by Trinh in her essay 'All Owning Spectatorship'. She describes in detail how white liberal fem-inists intervene in the work of a Third World woman film-maker to 'remind' her of the significance of 'class'. Trinh's point is that expectations held by Western feminists of Third World women in relation to issues around representation illustrate how 'the mandatory concern for class in the exclusive context of films on and by Third World members is itself a class issue' (ibid.). Speaking on behalf of a minority, in the form of an 'appropriating' voice, is closely linked to what has been identified 'as a more insidious version of appropriation' that is the projection of the burden of authentic-ity onto the minority' (Gunew and Yeatman, 1993: xvii). The framing of authentic-ity for Trinh is an aspect of the way 'that differences are caught up in the oppositional binary categories of oppressor and oppressed' (Trinh, 1989: 59).

Spivak's work, while having parallels with Trinh's, comes to quite different conclusions regarding the articulation of oppression by colonized women (see Brooks, 1997a). Spivak in her now famous dictum, 'The subaltern cannot speak', raises questions concerning 'whether or not the possibility exists for any recovery of a subaltern voice that is not a kind of essentialist fiction' (Ashcroft et al., 1995: 8). Spivak (1985a: 122, 129) claims that, 'There is no space from where the subaltern (sexed) subject can speak', 'The subject as female cannot be heard or read'. Spivak derives her theoretical position from studying the 'discourse of *sati* [widow sacrifice], in which the Hindu patriarchal code converged with colonialism's narrativization of Indian culture to efface all traces of woman's voice' (Parry, 1995: 36).

Spivak, in taking this position, aligns her thinking with the work of Stuart Hall and others in their recognition of the problem of attempting to define an 'uncontaminated authenticity' for the colonized subject. As Ashcroft shows: 'Although she expresses considerable sympathy for the project undertaken in contemporary historiography to give voice to 'the subaltern' who has been written out of the record by conventional historical accounts, Spivak raises grave doubts about its theoretical legitimacy (Ashcroft et al., 1995: 8).

Spivak looks to 'the postcolonial woman intellectual' to 'give the subaltern a voice in history' using a deconstructive approach. However, in examining the application of Spivak's model to a reading of Jean Rhys's (1968) novel *Wide Sargasso Sea*, her analysis does not appear to extend to the 'native woman'. As Parry observes, while 'Spivak does acknowledge that *Wide Sargossa Sea* is "a novel which rewrites a canonical English text within the European novelistic tradition in the interests of the white Creole rather than the native" (Spivak, 1985c: 253)' (Parry, 1995: 36), she fails to conceptualize Creole culture in terms of a cultural politics of location, as situated between the discourses of English imperialism and black Jamaican culture. As Parry notes: 'her discussion does not pursue the text's representations of a Creole culture that is dependent on both yet singular, or its enunciations of a specific settler discourse, distinct from the texts of imperialism' (ibid.).

Even when opportunities are available for the reframing of the subaltern in colonial history: 'Spivak's deliberated deafness to the native voice' results in her own writings severely restricting 'the space in which the colonized can be written back into history' (ibid.). This is the case even when interventions are possible 'through the deconstructive strategies devised by the post-colonial intellectual'. One of the reasons for this is the problematic nature of the concept of 'post-colonial intellectual' which Spivak recognizes as 'implicated in the Europeanisation/hybridisation of all culture in the aftermath of imperialism' (Ashcroft, 1995: 10). This creates the same conceptual and theoretical difficulties for Spivak as the use of the term 'subaltern'.

The work of the postcolonial Indian theorist and writer Homi Bhabha, also writing in the context of the United States, while sharing with Spivak, a desire to deconstruct the unidirectional and univocality inherent in the work of postcolonial theorists such as Franz Fanon, differs significantly from Spivak on the issue of the recouperation of the native voice. Parry (1995: 41) summarises Bhabha's position as follows. Bhabha maintains that whereas Said's position as articulated in *Orientalism* (1978) 'unifies the subject of colonial enunciation in a fixed position as the passive object of discursive domination', he [Bhabha] highlights the multiple and contested nature of colonialism's discursive regime. In the process, Parry maintains that Bhabha 'by showing the wider range of stereotypes and the shifting subject positions assigned to the colonized in the colonialist text, ... sets out to liberate the colonial from its debased inscriptions as Europe's monolithic and shackled Other, and into an autonomous native "difference"' (Parry 1995: 41). While Bhabha recognizes the role of the postcolonial intellectual in deconstructing the colonial metanarrative, it is the subaltern voice which effects the change. As Parry observes: '[f]or Bhabha, the subaltern has spoken, and his reading of the colonialist text recover a native voice ...' (ibid.) (Parry 1995: 41).

Thus, whereas for Spivak the subaltern has no voice that can answer back 'after the planned epistemic violence of the imperialist project' (ibid.), for Bhabha, colonial discourse is subjected to 'recurrent instances of transgression performed by the native' which are captured in Bhabha's concepts of 'mimicry', 'sly civility' and 'hybridity'. As Bulbeck notes: 'mimicry, mockery and ironic reversals challenge the West's discourse without adopting fully the discourse of the subordinate colonised groups (Bhabha, 1994: 81)' (cited in Bulbeck, 1998: 53). Hybridity, for Bhabha, is possibly the most common and effective form of subversive opposition since it shows, as Bhabha observes, the 'necessary deformation and displacement of all sites of discrimination and domination'. Hybridity is a term that Bhabha uses to describe the notion of mixed or hybrid identities which encompass the contradictory history of colonization, in contradistinction to the concept of a pure identity. Bulbeck claims that Bhabha describes this process as 'contramodernity rather than postmodernity' (Bhabha, 1991: 59), a process which Stuart Hall notes 'comes between well established identities and breaks them up' (Hall, in Terry, 1995: 60). One of the main criticisms of Bhabha's work has been his failure to address gender in his analysis, as McClintock observes '[e]xcept for a cursory appearance in one paragraph, women haunt Bhabha's analysis as an elided shadow – deferred, displaced and disremembered' (McClintock, 1995: 362–3).

The concept of gender mimicry is significant in the work of the French feminist Luce Irigarary (1985) who 'suggests that in certain social contexts women perform femininity as a necessary masquerade' (McClintock, 1995: 62). Bhabha transposes the idea of mimicry in the colonial context and explores mimicry as 'one of the most elusive and effective strategies of colonial power and knowledge' (Bhabha, 1984: 126). It is Bhabha's transposition of 'aesthetic categories' (irony, mimesis, parody) framed within psychoanalytic discourse and deployed 'in the context of empire' that is so original in Bhabha's work. While recognizing the centrality of the concept of mimicry in Bhabha's analysis, McClintock notes that 'for Bhabha here, colonial authority appears to be displaced less by shifting social contradictions or the militant strategies of the colonized than by the formal ambivalence of colonial representation itself' (McClintock, 1995: 63). She raises the important question of whether ambivalence, while crucial in Bhabha's work, 'is sufficient to locate agency in the internal fissures of discourse' (ibid.). McClintock shows how Bhabha, in his essay 'Signs Taken for Wonders', (1985), develops further the idea of mimicry, in this case less 'as a self-defeating colonial strategy than as a form of anti-colonial refusal'. As Bhabha claims, mimicry now 'marks those moments of civil disobedience within the discipline of civility: signs of spectacular resistance' (Bhabha, 1985: 162). As McClintock notes, this brings Bhabha's strategic positioning of mimicry closer to that of Irigaray's where mimicry is established 'as a strategy of the disempowered' (McClintock, 1995: 64).

Mimicry – a gendered discourse?

The essentialism of Irigaray's psychoanalytic position is well established in that she 'argues for mimicry as a specifically female strategy' (ibid.). In so doing, she fails to acknowledge the issues of race and class. Bhabha's theorizing of mimicry elevates race and in the process elides the concepts of gender and class. This elision creates a model of gendered mimicry in Bhabha's work, as McClintock notes, 'Bhabha effectively reinscribes mimicry as a male strategy without acknowledging its gendered specificity' (ibid.). Thus the ironic title of Bhabha's work 'Of Mimicry and Man' is literally just that, a postcolonial discourse with men at its center. In the process, McClintock observes 'masculinity becomes the invisible norm of postcolonial discourse' (McClintock, 1995: 64). One of the issues raised by McClintock in her analysis of Bhabha's conception of colonial mimicry and ambivalence is to what extent the potential for subversion can be equated with historical agency. McClintock claims: 'Ambivalence may well be a critical aspect of subversion, but it is not a sufficient agent of colonial failure' (McClintock, 1995: 67).

The role of feminist and non-feminist postcolonial intellectuals has contributed to a vigorous debate on issues of subjectivity and identity. The transcultural and transnational dimensions of the debates are shown in both the character of the diasporic intellectual and in their transdisciplinary focus. Both feminist and non-feminist diasporic intellectuals have made important contributions to debates on subjectivity and representation, drawing on a range of interdisciplinary discourses including cultural theory, feminism, postmodernism, poststructuralism and critical ethnography.

Transculturalism and Transnationalism in the Development of New Conceptions of Subjectivity and Identity

Globalization has led to the transnationalization of genders, classes, ethnicities and 'publics' (Gole, 2002), however, as Dirlik (1999) notes, this has not occurred equally among all groups and he concludes that while it may 'be more valid to speak of transnational classes or a transnational feminism', attention to the concept of place is important to understand the contradictory developments. Dirlik maintains that it is essential in understanding any conceptualization of culture, in any anti-hegemonic or critical sense, to understand the concept of place and indeed 'regionalization'. While recognizing the significance of Dirlik's and others (Olds et al., 1999) contribution to the theorization of place and regionalization, it has become increasingly difficult to speak of national cultures and identities, given the transformative character of transnationalism and transculturalism. This chapter seeks to follow Ong and Nonini's (1997) theorization of globalization and transnationalism in moving beyond 'place-bound' theories in understanding diasporic cultures, identities and subjectivities and in their representations.

Drawing on the model developed by Nonini and Ong (1997), two case studies will be considered, the first used by Nonini and Ong in the development of their model, that of diasporic Chinese transnationalism. The second, the growth of contemporary Islam and the 'politics of veiling' in issues around gender representation, subjectivity and identity. Acknowledging the limitations of place-bound theories of identity, implied in terms such as 'territory, region, nationality and ethnicity' (Nonini and Ong, 1997: 5), these authors' point to the development of a new theoretical language for understanding new identities and subjectivities. This theoretical language, they argue, emerging from cultural studies and anthropology approaches, is combined with an interpretive political economy approach. It is this approach, I argue here, which offers a more dynamic understanding of the relationship between transnationalism and transculturalism and the politics of representation and identity.

In her analysis of diasporic Chinese transnationalism, Ong studies the 'flexible citizenship of Chinese global capitalists' and suggests that we consider the 'transnational practices and imaginings of the nomadic subject and the social conditions that allow his flexibility' (1999: 3). As Ong states, the Chinese global capitalists she describes are not simply 'adroitly navigating the disjuncture between political landscapes and the shifting opportunities of global trade'. Rather, 'their very flexibility in geographical and social positioning is itself an effect of novel articulations between regimes of the family, the state and capital' (ibid.). Ong, in her work, is concerned with 'human agency and its production and negotiations of cultural meanings within the normative milieus of late capitalism' (ibid.). So what is the significance of this theoretical approach and how can it be located alongside other 'theoretical languages'. As Nonini and Ong (1997: 9) explain:

> Flexible accumulation, according to David Harvey (1989: 147), rests on flexibility with respect to labor processes, labor markets, products, and patterns of consumption. It is characterized by the emergence of entirely new sectors of production, new ways of providing financial services, new markets, and above all, greatly intensified rates of commercial, technological and organizational innovation.

Fundamentally, these changes are associated with the enhanced and increased mobility of people, commodities, ideas and capital on a global scale.

The strength of this position is the ability to synthesize an analysis of markets, production, consumption, and transnational labour patterns, and to combine 'all aspects of economic (and hence cultural) life, in this latest episode of what Harvey

(1989) refers to as "time – space compression"'. This can be combined with an analysis of new distinctive lifestyles (see also Brooks, 2006) 'grounded in high mobility (both spatial and in terms of careers), new patterns of urban residence, and new kinds of social integration defined by a consumerist ethic' (ibid.: 11). Featherstone (1990) has described these new social arrangements as 'third cultures', which he defines as emerging from 'global cultural flows' which transcend control of nation – states. Nonini and Ong (1997) maintain that Chinese transnationalism forms one such 'third culture' which provides 'alternative visions' to Western modernity and 'generates new and distinctive social arrangements, cultural discourses, practices and subjectivities'. Perhaps most crucial, new identities are thereby constituted – 'new types of flexible personal controls, dispositions, and means of orientation, in effect a new kind of habitus' (Featherstone, 1990: 8).

  In adopting this position Nonini and Ong take a postmodern approach to the geopolitical roots of Chinese transnationalism. As they themselves acknowledge, their perspective seeks to go beyond 'a post-Orientalist' approach (see Dirlik, 1993; Wilson and Dirlik, 1994) by focusing on ethnographical detail of social and cultural practices related to Chinese transnationalism. Nonini and Ong claim that their approach combines an understanding of economic, political and cultural reconfigurations which define Chinese transnationalism. So what are the implications for Chinese identities and subjectivities of an analysis of transnationalism and transculturalism? Nonini and Ong claim:

> In recasting the analysis of identities and subjectivities, we reject the conventional assumption that a person simply 'has' or 'possesses' an identity ... In contrast, critical anthropology, feminism, and cultural studies have come to view identities and bodies, through variously marked, possessed, and experienced, as unstable formations constituted within webs of power relations ... Different identities – gender, race, nationality, subculture, dominant culture-intersect in and constitute an individual ... The different subject positions of diaspora Chinese, formed by their allegiances to various places, as well as by a propensity to sojourning as a way of life, engender contradictory subjectivities that are at once fluid, fragmentary but also enabling of an agency to circumvent certain modalities of control, while taking advantage of others.
>
> (1997: 24–5)

The implications of these new types of subjectivities is that the nation – state and its accompanying ideology are now a highly contested domain when it comes to remaking identity. Thus both nation – state and national identities are increasingly eroded by the constituent elements that go to make up globalization (Hall, 1991). Stuart Hall has long indicated how aspects of globalization have redefined modernist concepts of nationhood and national identity. As Nonini and Ong (1999: 26) show: 'Transnational publics are framing new Chinese subjectivities that are increasingly independent of place, self-consciously postmodern and subversive of national regimes of truth.'

Transnationalism and transculturalism in transforming contemporary Islamic publics and representations

Globalization and the formation of different classes, ethnicities and genders have not only impacted on diasporic Chinese, they have also had a significant impact on the Islamic world, with the growth of Islamism and of Islamization. The migration of Muslim groups, the emergence of a Muslim middle class, and the significance of gender in the emergence of such publics have led to Islamic cultural formations becoming popular subjects of cultural criticism. As Gole observes:

> In the 'second wave' of Islamism, actors of Islam blend into modern urban spaces, use global communication networks, engage in public debates, follow consumption patterns, learn market rules, enter into secular time, get acquainted with values of individuation, professionalism and consumerism, and reflect upon new practices. But a more cultural orientation [e.g. the end of Islamism] does not mean a less political one ... Islam penetrates even more into the social fiber and imaginary, thereby raising new political questions.

> (2002: 174)

Gole (1996), previously writing about contemporary 'veiling practices' of Muslim women, highlights the significance of gender in the public visibility of Islam, and shows how women become important religious and political agents through the emergence of the veil as a symbol of politicized Islam. Gole shows that:

> The Islamic headscarf is deliberately appropriated, not passively carried and handed down from generation to generation. It is claimed by a new generation of women who have had access to higher education ... Instead of assimilating to the secular regime of women's emancipation, they press for their embodied difference (e.g. Islamic dress) and their public visibility (e.g. in schools, in Parliament) and create disturbances in modern social imaginaries. Islamic women hurt the feelings of modern women and upset the status quo; they are playing with ambivalence, being both Muslim and modern without wanting to give up one for the other. They are outside a regime of imitation, critical of both subservient traditions and assimilative modernity.

> (2002: 181)

Thus, as Gole points out, Muslim women find themselves a visible representation of 'difference', from both a sometimes hostile West, and a confused and divided Islam. Gole maintains that the practice of veiling reflects not a subjugation of Muslim women to traditional religious practices:

> On the contrary, it bears a new form, the outcome of a selective and reflexive attitude that amplifies and dramatizes the performative signs of 'difference' ... the new covering suggests a more rather than less potent Islam, which accounts

for secular counter-attacks against the headscarf for being not an 'innocent' religious convention but a powerful 'political symbol'.

(ibid.: 183)

Traditionally denied any visible presence in the public sphere, Muslim women's representation of contemporary Islam has redefined both gender roles and representations of women, as Gole (ibid.: 189) observes:

> Women are the principal actors in this process as they display the boundaries between private and public ... Islamism reinforces the boundaries in social relations through regulating bodily practices in public spaces; this regulation in turn serves as a public display of Islamic subjectivity.

Gole is writing about contemporary Islam and the practice of veiling, drawing on the example of the secular state of Turkey and from a European perspective. However, similar issues have emerged in South-east Asia, and feminist writers have highlighted similar tendencies in Malaysia. Malaysia, like Turkey, is not an Islamic state, however, unlike Turkey, which is a secular state, in Malaysia, Islam is the official religion of the country and the constitution assumes all Malays are Muslim (Nagata, 1994). There has been an intense Islamization in the country in the past two decades. Lelia Ahmed (1992: 236) suggests that 'the reimagined revivalist Islam' is an Islam redefining itself against Western values. While there has been a crackdown against radical Islamist groups since the emergence of anti-state terrorist cells in Malaysia and Singapore, it is unlikely that the broader movement of 'revivalist Islam' will change. The positioning of women and the family within these debates has always been central. Ong (1990) argues that controlling the definition of Malay womanhood and the family was crucial in the struggle between state power and revivalist Islam over the changing body politic in Malaysia. Ong saw the bodily covering of Malay university student supporters of revivalism as a 'subversive bricolage' registering 'protest over cultural dislocations linked to colonial and post-colonial domination' (Ong, 1990: 269) (see also Stivens, 2000: 7).

The practice of 'veiling' in this context can be seen to have both religious and ethnic expression. It has been argued that working-class women have found in Islamic practice a sense of social worth denied by the social order, whereas middle-class women are essentially victims of a governance by Islam (Ong, 1987; 1990). Stivens argues that for urban middle-class Malay women, there are a number of dimensions to the veiling process. The first is 'a neonationalist symbol of a specifically Malay modernity that has deep ethnic and class repercussions' (cf. Ong. 1990) (Stivens, 1998: 114); second, a commitment to a particular form of Islamic modernity and an escape from the sexualizations of modernity by the West. The transformative character of contemporary Islam is still developing and its outcome remains to be seen.

What is clear from the analysis of both case studies, Chinese transnationalism and contemporary Islamic publics, is the vibrancy that a combined cultural studies, critical ethnography, feminist and anthropology approach can bring to an understanding of the differentiated nature of diasporic groupings represented in different genders, classes and ethnicities. This approach enriches the monovocalism of sociology's traditional modernist metanarratives around class, gender and ethnicity. In addition to the intersection of feminism and postcolonialism which has already subverted sociology's traditional boundaries, there has been an extension of these debates into the area of filmic and media discourse, in particular, links between theorizing 'travel' and its implications for deconstructing colonial representations and the 'imperial gaze' within cinematographic discourse.

The politics of representation and the construction of identity – cultural studies as a site for reconceptualizing colonial representation, subjectivity and identity

Feminist and postcolonial theorists have interrogated historiographical and cultural discourses in the process of reconceptualizing colonial representation, subjectivity and identity. An important body of work has emerged around theorizing 'travel' as developed in the work of James Clifford (1992). An important additional and related area is that of critical ethnography. An example of a critical ethnographic approach to Chinese transnationalism is expounded in the work of Ong and Nonini. They are critical of 'the American cultural studies approach that treats transnationalism as a set of abstracted, dematerialized cultural flows, giving scant attention either to the concrete, everyday changes in people's lives or to the structural reconfigurations that accompany global capitalism' (Nonini and Ong, 1997: 13).

While they recognize the valuable work contained in the journal *Public Culture* in the area of transnational mass media, publics, and cultural politics (see Gole, 2002), in carving out a new idea for anthropological investigation, they express concern about what is left out of this analysis in terms of describing the ways in which people's everyday lives are transformed by the effects of global capitalism. As Nonini and Ong (1997: 13) observe: 'While we have learned much from and value the focus on social imaginaries, new globalized literary and aesthetic genres, and abstracted culture flows, we are apprehensive about the limitations of what might be called *lite* anthropology.' They highlight the work of Clifford in considering 'travel' as an alternative to 'the village' for contemporary ethnography.

Travel, the 'imperial gaze' and colonial representation

There are a number of dimensions to the conceptualization of 'travel' and its implications for the constitutive role of culture in the formation of 'imperial relations'. This has been captured in literary and filmic discourse.

Benedict Anderson has persuasively argued in his analysis of the development of vernacular print culture, visual and literary culture played a crucial role in the construction of the 'imagined' national communities in Europe that underpinned the imperial ideologies and administrations of the eighteenth, nineteenth and twentieth centuries (Lewis, 1996: 13).

Kaplan develops this idea in relation to filmic discourses and illustrates 'Hollywood's modernist fascination with white male and female explorers and entrepreneurs as well as with British colonialism' (Kaplan, 1997: 15). What is clear from the writings of white women colonial travellers, in their cinematographic representation, and in the construction of the 'imperial gaze' in film, is that western women were complicitous in the 'Orientalist vision'. In *Gendering Orientalism: Race, Femininity and Representation* (1996), Reina Lewis explores the position of European women as active agents in cultural production within imperial discourses. She examines a number of historical studies which have explored 'Western (mainly middle-class) women's experience of, and involvement in, imperialism'. Lewis maintains that:

> This was for the white scholar a painful but necessary journey, allowing us to grapple with the multiple contradictions of a female imperial subjectivity. For black and other scholars of colour, it marked the entry or re-entry, of the colonial and postcolonial repressed – speaking of the iniquities of the colonial past and the continued epistemological violences of ideologies of racial and sexual difference.
>
> (1996: 2)

Kaplan explores another dimension of theorizing travel, captured in the work of diasporic women film-makers, particularly in the 1980s and 1990s, conveying very different conceptions of 'the imperial gaze' and 'looking relations'. Kaplan draws parallels in her work between the 'imperial' and 'patriarchal' gaze although many feminist writers, theorists and practitioners are critical of the continuing usage of conceptual frames of reference such as 'patriarchy'. A further dimension of 'travel' theory outlined by Kaplan is the area of growth of new digital technologies and the implications of this for issues of subjectivity and representation. As Kaplan notes: '[i]n the new cyber age, problems relating to modernist inter-racial and inter-gender looking in relations and power imbalances may be subordinated to larger changes in cultural organization (or disorganization) brought about by new technologies' (1997: 22).

Deconstructing colonial representations and theorizing travel and its links with the 'imperial gaze' is one way to interrogate the nature of inter-racial and intergender looking relations. bell hooks draws out some powerful connections between travel and imperialism, establishing links between this and conceptions of 'whiteness' in the black imagination. As hooks notes: 'Searching the critical work of postcolonial critics, I found much writing that bespeaks the continued fascination with the way white minds, particularly the colonial imperialist traveler, perceive blackness, and very little expressed interest in representations of whiteness in the black imagination' (1992: 339).

In the process of theorizing black experience, hooks 'seek[s] to uncover, restore, as well as to deconstruct, so that new paths, different journeys are possible' (ibid.: 342). hooks explores Said's (1983) and Clifford's (1992) work on theorizing travel and notes that both offer stable, fixed conceptions of theory. Said claims that theory can 'threaten reification, as well as the entire bourgeois system on which reification depends with destruction'. Clifford, as hooks notes, attempts to expand: 'the travel/theoretical frontiers so that it might be more inclusive, ... and put alongside it or in its place a theory on the journey that would expose the extent to which holding onto the concept of "travel" as we know it is also a way to hold onto imperialism' (hooks, 1992: 343).

Travel theory provides an interesting conceptual framework for exploring different sets of relationships and different representations. For some, as hooks notes, conventional conceptualizations of travel maintain a fascination with imperialism and convey what Rosaldo (1988) refers to as 'imperialist nostalgia'. However, theorizing travel outside these 'conventional borders' offers possibilities for using: 'travel as a starting point for discourse ... associated with different headings – rites of passage, immigration, enforced migration, relocation, enslavement, homelessness ... Theorizing diverse journeying is crucial to our understanding of any politics of location' (hooks, 1992: 343).

Clifford shows in his work that theory is not conceptualized in a vacuum and is always written from a specific location where place often marks 'different concrete histories of dwelling, immigration, exile, migration'. As hooks goes on to note, it is imperative to understand the hegemonic implications of one experience of travel which can make another experience impossible to be heard. 'From certain standpoints, to travel is to encounter the terrorizing force of white supremacy' (ibid.: 344).

The relationship between inter-racial looking and representing whiteness is a complex one and is conveyed in literary and cinematographic discourses. There is a significant history of film, conveying different aspects of 'inter-racial looking relations'. Kaplan explores: 'structures of the gaze in film images of white males traveling to expatriate foreign lands in the nineteenth and ealy twentieth centuries, through complex gaze and looking structures in the travels of white women, traveling in men's wake with a variety of motives, (1997: 14). Kaplan highlights the contradictory position of white colonial women travelers whose subjectivities are 'caught between objectification in white patriarchy and white privilege in colonialism' (ibid.: 15). She contextualizes the position of this group of women within the hegemonic structure of the 'male (patriarchal) gaze' and the 'imperial gaze'.

Lidia Curti (1996) provides an interesting analysis of one such woman and her representation in film. Curti focuses on the intersection of imperialist and subaltern discourses in the traveller Jane Bowles's writing and in her subsequent representation in films drawn from a number of books written by male authors. Curti describes Bowles, who was born in 1917 and spent much of her life in Tangier and died in a psychiatric institution in Malaga in 1973, as 'a nomadic writer, in some ways a typical American intellectual, like – and at the same time unlike – other occidental women writers, who in the first half of this century went to Europe, particularly Paris, in search of their art and themselves' (Curti, 1996: 124). Like many other women travellers, in her travelling she 'was observed', travelling as Curti notes 'by the male gaze'. A number of male writers observed Jane Bowles's travelling, including her husband and fellow traveller Paul Bowles, as well as other writers including William Burroughs, Truman Capote, Tennessee Williams, Gore Vidal and others. Curti shows how the 'male gaze' and the 'observing eye' have been given cinematographic form in a number of contemporary films, including Bernado Bertolucci's *The Sheltering Sky*, based on Paul Bowles's novel (1949), and ... David Cronenberg's *Naked Lunch* after the novel by William Burroughs (1959)' (ibid.). The focus of the following summary is on Bertolucci's film *The Sheltering Sky*. My choice here is partly related to my great empathy with Curti's intelligent analysis but also to a personal fascination with Jane Bowles's work and to Bertolucci's cinematographic representation.

The inflection of the male gaze in both Paul Bowles's novel and Bertolucci's film is apparent in the 'distorted vision of Jane's sexual promiscuity ... where the encounters taking her away from her partner are heterosexual from the outset' (ibid.: 125). However, the signifiers in novel and film are of an even more defining order. As Curti notes in Paul Bowles's novel, the 'heroine's' main motivation is to escape the Western world and in both the novel and the film, there is the sense of this being 'her final flight'. She (the heroine) decides to 'lose herself in nothingness, the nothingness that is the Western signifier of losing yourself: "going native"' (ibid.). The 'going native' process of 'annihilation' begins with her absorption in 'her sexual enthralment with her Arab lover' (ibid.). The signifiers of death and personal destruction are frequently represented as female, as Said points out, this association is one of the common traits of 'orientalism'. Said notes that '[t]he Oriental was linked thus to elements in western society (delinquents, the insane, women, the poor) having in common an identity best described as lamentably alien' (Said, 1978: 270).

This indecipherability of female behaviour is in the traditions of representations of the 'female hysteric' and, as Yegenoglu notes, 'the typography of femininity as enigmatic, mysterious, concealing a secret behind its veil, is projected onto the iconography of the Orient' (Yegenoglu, 1992: 49). Curti makes an interesting point about Yegenoglu's work, in that while her observations are interesting, she fails to raise the notion of the 'ambivalence' of the veil and its contestation of the 'Orientalist vision' (see Trinh, 1988b). Yengenoglu 'sees Western women as complicitous in the Orientalist vision' (Curti, 1996: 137).

Jane Bowles's only finished novel *Two Serious Ladies* and her short stories reveal a different emphasis to those aspects of her life emphasized through the 'male gaze' of her husband Paul Bowles and Bertolucci's film. Curti notes that '[i]t is the spiral dialectic on travelling rather than the linearity of narrative that is fundamental to Jane Bowles's writing' (ibid.: 130). The emphasis in her work is on the conflict between the safety and stability of what is familiar and 'leaving the safe shelter of their culture and home' for what is seen as 'a moral imperative' – travelling. Curti points out that while Jane Bowles's writing is related to her life, it is not autobiographical. Bowles's novels deal with the ambivalent relationship between sexual ambiguity and ethnic difference. Curti points out that ethnic diversity and racial hybridity give an 'interzone character' to Bowles's work:

> It could be said that Jane Bowles embodies the Westerner's gaze on the other
> culture, to exercise her power and impress her presence on the subaltern
> woman, ultimately to possess or try to possess her. She could be described as

the accomplice of imperialist discourse, a discourse that, according to Homi Bhabha [1994], does nothing but search, in the analysis of the other, for the construction ... of a 'regime of truth'.

(Curti, 1996: 137)

Curti's analysis of Jane Bowles's work and her representations in literary and filmic discourses highlights the difficulties of establishing a 'fixed' speaking position that 'ignores the multiple and shifting sites occupied by the speaking subject' (ibid.). It also highlights the inescapable interrelationship of the imperial and the 'male gaze'.

Travelling, inter-racial looking relations and women film-makers

Diasporic groups and movements have established patterns of transculturalism and transnationalism in relation to a range of discourses and have made debates on subjectivity, representation and identity, a much more contested one. Kaplan notes that in the hands of diasporic feminist film-makers, 'travel' takes on a very different set of 'looking relations'. She shows how 'black American, British and Asian women traveling on film and with cameras' have established very different 'inter-gender' and 'inter-racial looking' relations in the 1980s and 1990s. Kaplan claims that '[m]any of these film makers turn the gaze back on whites, imagine a world in which whiteness is irrelevant, or begin thinking differently about inter-racial looking – imagining it as a process, a relation rather than a gaze' (1997: 15). Kaplan identifies a number of women film-makers whose work has been pivotal in advancing debates in these areas, including Julie Dash, Clare Denis, Pratibha Parmar, Hu Mei, Yvonne Rainer, Alison Aders and Trinh T. Minh-ha among others.

The work of these film-makers is too extensive to be comprehensively covered here and their work can be seen to have particular resonance for the culture they are writing out of or in which they are 'travelling'. Kaplan shows how some 'film makers (e.g. Trinh, Parmar, Denis) at times literally travel with their cameras; others (e.g. Dash, Rainer, Anders, Denis) "travel" within their own cultures, in the sense of moving out to imagine other identities, the struggle of other "Others"' (ibid.: 16). Films such as Claire Denis's *Chocolat* which locates the story in postcolonial Africa with flashbacks to 1950s French colonialism suggest possibilities in which both imperial and male gazes can be contested and raise opportunities for a reworking of postcolonial concepts such as Homi Bhabha's 'ambivalence' in relation to the colonial gaze.

Trinh T. Minh-ha's pioneering work in film combines a number of theoretical dimensions and practices. Her work addresses 'how we can "know" the other' and combines postcolonial, post structural and feminist theoretical dimensions:

Trinh T. Minh-ha is one film maker who has struggled in her theories and practices in film, writing, photography and music ... to work out from the level of subjectivity, not from that of broad abstractions. Perhaps more than any ... Trinh focuses on 'how to make one-self a "subject" within struggles against the State and make women's concerns central; how to link the specificity of one's particular context and struggle with those of women in different natural, cultural and geographical locations'.

(ibid.: 196)

Her work, in whatever form it takes, literary, visual, filmic, addressing cultural and contextual specificities, aims to destabilize and deconstruct 'the apparently secure positions that mainstream western culture has established for itself ' (ibid.: 197). In addressing these dimensions in her essay (1995) and in her film *Reassemblage*

> she challenges previous constructions of inter-racial looking relations, which, ... begin with the subject-object structure, but come into particular tension in regard to how western thought has constructed the relation so as to emphasize people of color as the deplored 'object'... What Trinh does, however, is begin to move toward another conceptualizing of inter-racial looking relations. She aims to practice from a place beyond the usual subject-object western binary by moving toward the notion of multiple 'I's' confronting 'multiple I's' in the Other'
>
> (Kaplan, 1997: 199)

The work of these feminist film-makers counters the framing of inter-gender and inter-racial looking relations in terms of Western binary models based on the 'male and imperial gaze'. Their work deconstructs westernized conceptions of representation and identity and establishes women of colour as artists and cultural producers.

The link between the 'male gaze' and the 'imperial gaze' has been highlighted in Kaplan's work, she also shows how they 'collide and conflict depending on the specificities of context' and she points to the need for an understanding of the links between these gazes and how national identities are constructed.

The positioning of women within this conception of the 'national imaginary' is a problematic one. Homi Bhabha discusses the issue of nation as an 'imagined community' in much the same way that Benedict Anderson does, and specifically in terms of his position as a 'postcolonial Indian/British citizen'. Bhabha provides an analysis of the relationship between travelling and issues of nation, particularly in relation to confronting Britain's imaginary of itself, captured in its 'imagined communities' in which he is not included. However, Bhabha's analysis has no space for a conceptualization of gender within 'the imagined community' and it is Kaplan who shows how diasporic women film-makers such as Pratibha Parmar, Gurinder Chanda and Ngozi Ohwurah frame a different conception of the 'British imagined community' which has no place for them.

Conclusion

Shohat states that the globalizing aspects of both colonial and cultural processes oblige 'the cultural critic to move beyond the restricting framework of the nation-state'

(1997: 207). She also notes that: 'In the postcolonial context of a constant flux of peoples, affiliation with the nation state becomes highly partial and contingent' (ibid.: 195). Transculturalism and transnationalism require a reconceptualization of representation, subjectivity and identity which diasporic feminist film-makers have gone some way to addressing in their reframing of cultural and filmic discourses. This chapter has attempted to explore how discourses on transnationalism and transculturalism have shown both 'place-bound' and 'disciplinary-bound' concepts of subjectivity, representation and identity to be an inadequate way of representing new cultural and ethnic identities on the global stage. The interdisciplinary matrix of cultural studies including feminism, postcolonialism, postmodernism, critical ethnography, film, literature and cultural politics have been shown to produce a dynamic interplay of epistemological and representational discourses more reflective of the transnationalization of genders, classes, ethnicities, and publics which frame the contemporary social world.

Notes

1 I am grateful to McKenzie Wark for this concept. See Wark (1992).
2 See Graeme Turner (1992b).

References

Ahmed, L. (1992) *Women and Gender in Islam: Historical Roots of a Modern Debate*. New Haven, CT: Yale University Press.

Ashcroft, B., Griffiths, G. and Tiffin, H. (eds) (1995) *The Post-Colonial Studies Reader*. London: Routledge .

Bhabha, H. (1984) 'Of Mimicry and Man: The Ambivalence of Colonial Discourse', *October* 28: 125–33.

Bhabha, H. (1985) 'Signs taken for wonders: questions of ambivalence and authority under a tree outside Delhi, May 1817', *Critical Inquiry*, 12(1): 144-65.

Bhabha, H. (1991) 'The postcolonial critic - Homi Bhabha interviewed by David Bennett and Terry Collits', *Arena*, 96: 47–63.

Bhabha, H. (1994) *The Location of Culture*. London: Routledge.

Brooks, A. (1997a) *Postfeminism: Feminism, Cultural Theory and Cultural Forms*. London: Routledge.

Brooks, A. (1997b) 'The politics of postmodernism and popular culture. Angela McRobbie: postmodernism and popular culture', *Discourse: Studies in the Cultural Politics of Education*, 18(1): 171–80.

Brooks, A. (2006) *Gendered Work in Asian Cities: the New Economy and Changing Labour Markets*. Aldarshot: Ashgate.

Bulbeck, C. (1998) *Re-Orienting Western Feminisms: Women's Diversity in a Postcolonial World*. Cambridge: Cambridge University Press.

Chow, R. (1993) *Writing Diaspora*. Bloomington, IN: Indiana University Press.

Clifford, J. (1992) 'Travelling cultures', in L. Grossberg, C. Nelson and P.Treichler (eds) *Cultural Studies*. London: Routledge.

Curti, L. (1996) 'Between two shores', in I. Chambers and L. Curti (eds) *The Post-colonial Question*. London: Routledge.

Derrida, J. (1978) *Writing and Difference*. London: Routledge and Kegan Paul.

Dirlik, A. (1993) 'Introducing the Pacific', in A. Dirlik (ed.) *What Is in a Rim? Critical Perspectives on the Pacific Region Idea*. Boulder, CO: Westview Press.

Dirlik, A. (1999) 'Globalism and the politics of place' in K. Olds, P. Dicken, P.F. Kelly, L. Kong and H.W. Young (eds) *Globalization and the Asia-Pacific*. London: Routledge.

During, S. (1993) The Cultural Studies Reader, New York/London: Routledge.

Emberley, J.V. (1993) *Thresholds of Difference: Feminist Critiques, Native Women's Writing, Postcolonial Theory*, Toronto: University of Toronto Press.

Featherstone, M. (1990) 'Global culture: an introduction', *Theory, Culture and Society*, 7: 1–14.

Frankenberg, R. and Mani, L. (1993) 'Crosscurrents, crosstalk: race, "postcolonial" and the politics of location', *Cultural Studies*, 7(2): 292–310.

Gilroy, P. (1987) *There Ain't No Black in the Union Jack*. London: Hutchinson.

Gilroy, P. (1992) 'Cultural studies and ethnic absolutism', in L. Grossberg, C. Nelson, and P. Treichler (eds) *Cultural Studies*. London: Routledge.

Gilroy, P. (1993) *The Black Atlantic: Modernity and Double Consciousness*. London: Verso.

Gole, N. (1996) *The Forbidden Modern: Civilization and Veiling*. Ann Arbor, MI: University of Michigan Press.

Gole, N. (2002) 'Islam in public: new visibilities and new imaginaries', *Public Culture* 14(1): 173–90.

Gunew, S. and Yeatman, A. (eds) (1993) *Feminism and the Politics of Difference*. NSW: Allen and Unwin.

Hall, C. (1996) 'Histories, empires and the post-colonial moment', in I. Chambers and L. Curti (eds) *The Post-colonial Question*. London: Routledge.

Hall, S. (1991) 'The local and the global: globalization and ethnicity', in A.D. King (ed.) *Culture, Globalization, and the World System: Contemporary Conditions for the Representation of Identity*. London: Macmillan.

Hall, S. (1992a) In discussion with James Clifford, printed as Appendix to J. Clifford (1992), 'Travelling Cultutes', in L. Grossberg: C. Nelson and P. Treichler (eds) *Cultural Studies*. London: Routledge.

Hall, S. (1992b) 'Cultural studies and its theoretical legacies', in L. Grossberg, C. Nelson, P. Treichler (eds) *Cultural Studies*. London: Routledge.

Hall, S.(1992c) 'The question of cultural identity', in S. Hall, D. Held and T. McGrew (eds), *Modernity and its Futures*. Cambridge: Polity Press.

Hall, S. (1993) 'Minimal selves', in A. Gray and J. McGuigan (eds) *Studying Culture: An Introductory Reader*. London: Edward Arnold.

Hall, S. (1996) 'When was the "post-colonial"? Thinking at the limit', in I. Chambers and L. Curti (eds), *The Post-colonial Question*. London: Routledge.

Harvey, D. (1989) *The Condition of Modernity*. Oxford: Basil Blackwell.

Hooks, b. (1992) 'Representing whiteness in the black imagination', in L. Grossberg, C. Nelson and P. Treichler (eds) *Cultural Studies*. London: Routledge.

Irigaray, L. (1985) *This Sex Which Is Not One*. Trans. C. Porter. Ithaca NY: Cornell University Press.

Kaplan, E.A. (1997) *Looking for the Other: Feminism, Film and the Imperial Gaze*. London: Routledge.

Lewis, R. (1996) *Gendering Orientalism: Race, Femininity and Representation*. London: Routledge.

McClintock, A. (1995) *Imperial Leather: Race, Gender and Sexuality in the Colonial Context*. London: Routledge.

McRobbie, A. (1994) *Postmodernism and Popular Culture*. London: Routledge.

Mercer, K. (1990) 'Welcome to the jungle: identity and diversity in postmodern politics', in J. Rutherford (ed.) *Identity: Community, Culture, Difference*. London: Lawrence and Wishart.

Morris, M. (1988a) *The Pirate's Fiancée: Feminism, Reading, Postmodernism*, London and New York: Verso.

Morris, M. (1988b) 'Things to do with Shopping Centres' in Sheridan, S. (ed) *Grafts: Feminist Cultural Criticism*, London: Verso.

Morris, M. (1991) 'Reply to Graeme Turner', *Meanjin*, 50(1).

Morris, M. (1992a) 'Afterthoughts on "Australianism"' *Cultural Studies*, 6(3): 468–75.

Morris, M. (1992b) 'On the beach', in L. Grossberg, C. Nelson and P. Treichler (eds) *Cultural Studies*. London: Routledge.

Nagata, J.A. (1994) 'How to be Islamic without being an Islamic state', in A. Ahmed and H. Donnan (eds) *Islam, Globalization and Postmodernity*. London: Routledge.

Nonini, D. and Ong, A. (1997) 'Chinese transnationalism as an alternative modernity', in A. Ong and D. Nonini (eds) *Underground Empires: The Cultural Politics of Modern Chinese Transnationalism*. London: Routledge.

Olds, K., Dicken, P., Kelly, P.F., Kong, L. and Yeung, H.W. (eds) (1999) *Globalization and the Asia-Pacific*. London: Routledge.

Ong, A. (1987) *Spirits of Resistance and Capitalist Discipline: Factory Women in Malaysia*, Albany: Suny University Press.

Ong, A. (1990) 'State versus Islam: Malay families, women's bodies and the body politic', *American Ethnologist*, 17(2): 28–42.

Ong, A. (1997) 'Chinese modernities: narratives of nation and of capitalism', in A. Ong and D. Nonini (eds) *Underground Empires: The Cultural Politics of Modern Chinese Transnationalism*. London: Routledge.

Ong, A. (1999) *Flexible Citizenship: The Cultural Logics of Transnationality*. Durham, NC: Duke University Press.

Ong, A. and Nonini, D. (eds) (1997) *Underground Empires: The Cultural Politics of Modern Chinese Transnationalism*. London: Routledge.

Ong, A. and Peletz, M.G. (eds) (1995) *Bewitching Women and Pious Men: Gender and Body Politics in Southeast Asia*. Berkeley, CA: University of California Press.

Parry, B. (1995) 'Problems in current theories of colonial discourse', in B. Ashcroft, G. Griffiths and H. Tiffin (eds) *The Post-colonial Studies Reader*. London: Routledge.

Rosaldo, R. (1988) *Culture and Truth: the remaking of social analysis*, Beacon: Beacon press.

Said, E. (1978) *Orientalism*, London: Routledge.

Said, E. (1983) 'Traveling theory', in *The World, the Text and the Critic*. Cambridge, MA: Harvard University Press.

Said, E. (1985)'Orientalism reconsidered', *Cultural Critique*, 1: 98–107.

Said, E. (1986) 'Intellectuals in the post-colonial world', *Salamagundi*, 70(1): 45–64.

Shohat, E. (1997) Post-Third Worldist Culture: Gender, Nation and the Cinema, in M.J. Alexander and C.T. Mohanty (eds) *Feminist Genealogies, Colonial Legacies, Democratic Futures*, New York/London: Routledge.

Spivak, G. C. (1985a) 'Can the subaltern speak?: Speculations on widow sacrifice', *Wedge*, 7(8): 120–30.

Spivak, G.C. (1985b) 'Three women's text and a critique of imperialism', *Critical Inquiry*, 12(1): 43–61.

Spivak, G.C. (1985c) 'Three Women's Texts and a Critique of Imperialism', *Critical Inquiry* 12(1): 43–61.

Stivens, M.(1998) 'Sex, gender and the making of the new Malay middle classes', in K. Sen and M. Stivens (eds) *Gender and Power in Affluent Asia*. London: Routledge.

Stivens, M. (2000) 'Re-inventing the "Asian family", "Asian values", globalization and cultural contest in Southeast Asia', paper given at the Conference on Families in the Global Age, National University of Singapore, 4–6 October, Singapore.

Stratton, J. and Ang, I. (1996) 'On the impossibility of a global cultural studies', in D. Morley and K.H. Chen (eds) *Stuart Hall: Critical Dialogues in Cultural Studies*. London: Routledge.

Suleri, S. (1995) 'From "Women skin deep: Feminism and the postcolonial condition"' *Critical Inquiry*, 18(4), Summer 1992, in B. Ashcroft, G. Griffiths and H. Tiffin (eds), *The Post-colonial Studies Reader*. London: Routledge.

Terry, L. (1995)"Not a postmodern nomad": A conversation with Stuart Hall on race, ethnicity and identity', *Arena Journal*, 5: 51–70.

Trinh, T. Minh-ha (1988a) 'Reassemblage: sketch of a soundtrack', *Camera Obscura*, 13–14: 105–12.

Trinh, T. Minh-ha (1988b) 'Not you/Like you: post-colonial woman and the interlocking questions of identity and difference', *Inscriptions*, 3(4): 71–79.

Trinh, T. Minh-ha (1989) *Woman, Native Other: Writing, Postcoloniality and Feminism.* Bloomington, IN: Indiana University Press.

Trinh, T. Minh-ha (1991) *When the Moon Waxes Red: Representation, Gender and Cultural Politics.* London: Routledge.

Trinh, T. Minh-ha (1995a) 'No master territories' in B. Ashcroft, G. Griffiths and H. Tiffin (eds) *The Post-Colonical Studies Reader.* London: Routledge.

Trinh, T. Minh-ha (1995b) 'Reassemblage (text)', in S. MacDonald (ed.) *Screen Writings.* Berkeley, CA: University of California Press .

Turner, G. (1992a) 'Of rocks and hard places: the colonized, the national and Australian cultural studies', *Cultural Studies*, 1(3): 424–32.

Turner, G. (1992b) '"It works for me": British cultural studies, Australian cultural studies, Australian film', in L. Grossberg, C. Nelson and P. Treichler (eds) *Cultural Studies.* London: Routledge.

Wark, M. (1992) 'Speaking trajectories: Meaghan Morris, antipodean theory and Australian cultural studies', *Cultural Studies* 6 (3): 433–48.

West, C. (1990) 'The new cultural politics of difference', in R. Ferguson, M. Gever, Trinh, T. Minh-ha, and C. West (eds), *Out There: Marginalization and Contemporary Cultures.* Cambridge: MIT Press.

Wilson, R. and Dirlik, A. (eds) (1994) 'Asia/Pacific as space of cultural production', Special issue of *Boundary*, 2(21): 1.

Yegenoglu, M. (1992) 'Supplementing the Orientalist lack: European ladies in the harem', *Inscriptions 6, Orientalism and cultural differences.* pp. 45–58.

CHAPTER ELEVEN

Feminist Knowledge and Socio-Cultural Research

Ethnomimesis, feminist praxis and the visual turn

Maggie O'Neill

Introduction

This chapter explores cultural sociology in practice by focusing upon the author's participatory action research with female sex workers. An interpretive feminist account of women's life histories, rooted in immersion in the feeling worlds of participants is represented through fragments of women's narratives, live art and photography. This approach is defined as 'ethno-mimesis', and is rooted in four key concepts: (1) the inter-relation between feminist thought and practice/praxis involving a methodological process of immersion, interpretation, commentary and criticism; (2) the importance of critical feminist theory; (3) interpretive ethnography as a way of understanding women's lived experiences, especially the development of critical standpoint epistemologies; and (4) cultural sociology as praxis – as transformative.

Through cultural sociology in practice (as praxis) sociologists can better understand the socio-cultural-political (macro) relations and inter-relations, and the multiple (micro) 'realities' we might want to transform. Accessing and documenting lived experiences in a reflexive, critically aware way can lead us to a better understanding of psychic processes and socio-cultural structures and processes. This knowledge in turn can help us to develop transformative possibilities through conducting participatory action research (PAR).

The author's concept of 'ethno-mimesis' is defined in this chapter through a combination of participatory action research and participatory arts informed by the work of Adorno and Benjamin. Ethno-mimesis draws upon 'feeling forms' such as photographic art, performance art and life story narratives, and engages dialectically with lived experience through critical interpretation, towards social change. In the Chapter, two examples of ethno-mimesis are introduced and discussed as cultural sociology in practice.

Feminism, Cultural Sociology and Prostitution

Western feminisms can be charted through a trajectory that begins with concerns about sex and gender, nature and culture; through concerns with racial or sexual exclusion and emergent theories of power, and gender in constituting the subject (Hemmings and Brain 2003: 21). The intersection between feminism and postmodernism developed out of critiques of Enlightenment and modernism, structuralism and psychoanalysis. Linda Nicholsen (1990) states that the postmodern turn has been an important one for feminist scholars, signified by diversity, difference, plurality, and multiple voices. Freed from the need to root feminist politics in identification, vanguard parties, purity or mothering, we can instead embrace the possibilities of multiple and contradictory aspects of our individual and collective identities. Taking a historiographic approach, Hemmings and Brain in a most interesting article reflect on the idea that the feminist 1970s shaped the feminist present. 'In this historiographic approach we join other writers in thus understanding the past as imaginatively taking place in the present, and as securing the means of the present' (2003: 11).

The feminist trajectory can be compared with the emergence of cultural studies. 'Cultural studies designates a wide-ranging and expanding domain of research-questions concerning processes and structures of sense-making and, more specifically, the way in which "sense" becomes "lived" in practices of everyday life' (van Loon, 2000).

Cultural studies is eclectic in its use of various theoretical infrastructures, research questions and methodologies (McGuigan, 1997). Van Loon identifies a set of historical trajectories through which 'cultural studies' has evolved in the UK, North America and Australia. First, the origins of cultural studies and the importance of Marxism is rooted in the work of *Raymond Williams* and *Richard Hoggart* in the 1950s. Their work gave rise to such questions as – under what conditions did reading or making books, watching or making films matter? Second, ethnography has emerged as an effective and popular approach to researching cultural processes. Third, an important distinction between *culturalism* and *structuralism* was made by Stuart Hall (found in Bennet et al., 1982) that was to be conceptually foundational for the emergent cultural studies. Finally, the importance of the *'linguistic turn'* (Alasuutari, 1995: 24) in cultural studies. For Van Loon (2000), this 'has produced a sensitivity to culture as an ensemble of sense-making practices that demand a dialogic and reflexive engagement'.

Feminisms and cultural studies share a methodological and epistemological focus upon a primarily phenomenological approach to understanding the processes and practices of our socio-cultural worlds, and the everyday lived experiences and meaning – making practices we engage in. Although there is an explicit interest and focus on the transformative possibilities of feminism and cultural studies, very few texts identify PAR as a method/methodology. For me, the emergence of postmodernism and the cultural turn in sociology was pivotal and best expresses my engagement with issues of gender, power, knowledge, class, race, sexuality, and social structures, both empirically/methodologically and theoretically. Feminist research is inherently linked to action. My earlier work on feminist aesthetics looked to develop an understanding of the foundations in social life for a feminist aesthetics of modernism rooted in an analysis of the transformative, liberating potential of women's art. Examples of empirical feminist research that have been major influences are the work by Maria Mies with women in Cologne, India and Holland, and Jalna Hanmer and Sheila Saunders' community action work in Leeds on violence against women and the photo therapy work of Jo Spence and Rosy Martin.

Contemporary literature on prostitution can be interpreted as following the conceptual trajectory of feminist thought and analysis linked to modernity, postmodernity and the shifts and transformations taking place in the 1960s but rooted in much earlier social and cultural changes. Feminist theorists have engaged with discourses on prostitution and health, the law, prostitutes' rights and activism (McLeod, 1982; Phoenix, 1999; West, 2000; Campbell and O'Neill, 2006). Historical analyses focus upon the relationships between women working as prostitutes and the state, working-class communities and the regulation of the body (Finnegan, 1979; Walkowitz, 1980; Corbin, 1987; Roberts, 1992). Sex tourism, consumption and feminist debates on power, rights and knowledge (Truong, 1990; O'Connell-Davidson, 1998; Bishop and Robinson, 1997; Kempadoo and Doezema, 1998) add important challenges to debates that have focused on binary distinctions between good and bad girls in the literature and public imagination (Nagle, 1997).

Participatory Action Research: Critical Theory in Praxis

At an international conference, Academic Knowledge and Political Power, organized by Richard Harvey Brown at the University of Maryland, Department of Sociology, 20–22 November 1992, I was introduced to the work of Orlando Fals Borda and William F Whyte as Richard saw parallels in my paper with participatory action research. My paper at the conference focused upon two years of fieldwork with sex workers, epistemologically underpinned by my sociological approach – critical theory as feminist praxis. Following this introduction to PAR, I embarked upon a process of assimilating and using the methodology in my work with marginalized groups – sex workers, communities affected by prostitution and asylum seekers and refugees.[1] This research and accompanying publications stress three major themes in my empirical work. First, the importance of stories and storytelling. Second, the importance of alternative ways of re-presenting these stories in visual/artistic form. I am interested in the ethno-mimetic re-presentations and in exploring the language like quality of art. Third, the importance of working with people as subjects through PAR. PAR is a social research methodology, which includes the stereotypical subjects of research as co-creators of the research. It creates a space for the voices of the marginalized to become involved actively in change or transformation.

Participatory action research is little used in the UK. Rarely will it get a mention in research methods texts, other than in the literature on development, and it is most prevalent in countries of the South, North and South America, and India (see Laws et al., 2003). Fals Borda (University of Columbia, Bogotá) and William Foote Whyte (USA) are key proponents of PAR.

PAR is rooted in principles of inclusion (engaging people in the research design, process and outcomes); participation; valuing all local voices; and community-driven sustainable outcomes. PAR is a process and a practice directed towards social change with the participants; it is interventionist, action-oriented and interpretive. PAR involves a commitment to research that develops partnership responses to developing purposeful knowledge (praxis); includes all those involved where possible, thus facilitating shared ownership of the development and outcomes of the research; uses innovative ways of consulting and working with local people and facilitates change with communities and groups.

Given the relative demise of action and activism over the past two decades and the closing down of spaces for public resistance under the auspices of Thatcher, Major and Blair governments, this research method provides a potentially powerful tool for resistance and a platform for civic participation – a critical theory in practice. This is akin to Smith's thesis (drawing upon Laclau and Mouffe) that 'radical democracy is the best route towards social change for the Left Today' (Smith, 1998: 6), and fosters 'a democratic politics that aims at the articulation of the various different struggles against oppression. What emerges is the possibility of a project of radical and plural democracy' (Smith, 1986: 328).

Fals Borda defines PAR (it emerged in the 1970s) as anticipating postmodernism for PAR drew on a range of conceptual elements to guide fieldwork 'Marxism, phenomenology, and classical theories of participation, including action' (1999: 1) and yet went beyond them. Fals Borda defines PAR as *vivencia* (life experience akin to Husserl's *Erfahrung*) 'necessary for the achievement of progress and democracy and as a complex of attitudes and values to give meaning to our praxis in the field' (Fals Borda, 1999: 17).

Interpretive Ethnography and Standpoint Epistemologies

In a recent paper (O'Neill et al., 2002), I argued that the self-reflexivity inherent in the ethnographic process, alongside the crisis in ethnography and the 'linguistic' and 'cultural turn' in socio-cultural theory has led to demands for experimentation in the representation of ethnographic data, especially in relation to gender and race (see Trinh, 1991; Ugwu, 1995). Drawing upon the work of Adorno and Benjamin, I argued that alternative re-presentations of ethnographic work can create multivocal, dialogical texts that can make visible emotional structures and inner experiences which may 'move' the audience through what can be described as 'sensuous knowing' or mimesis (Taussig, 1993).

Ethno-mimesis as critical feminist praxis[2] is reflexive and phenomenological but it is also critical and looks to praxis, as in the theatre work of Boal (1979) and Mienczakowski (1995); the socio-cultural research of Fals Borda (1988); or the filmic work of Trinh (1989, 1991). Alasuutari, Gray and Hermes tell us that hybrid theorizing and reflexivity are crucial to better understand contemporary culture and society, especially when we consider the ways in which such hybrid research can 'understand culture as a process of meaning making, and to give attention to the power relations that set boundaries to those processes' (1998: 9).

Standpoint epistemologies as articulated by early proponents such as Sandra Harding (1991), Patricia Hill-Collins (1990), Dorothy Smith (1989), and Hilary Rose (1983) pose a challenge to and resist orthodox scientific empiricist ways of practising research. Indeed, for Harding, standpoint feminism is 'a moral and political act of commitment to understand the world from the position of the socially subjugated' (1986: 149). It involves a process of developing better knowledge of the social, and of culture as a process of meaning making, from direct engagement with people.

The work of Trinh (1991) further developed this process for, in undoing the realist ethnography project, she seeks to show that there is no single overriding vision of the world but rather multiple realities, multiple standpoints, and multiple meanings. Such reflexivity led to the acknowledgement that the 'real' world can still be recovered through ethnographic work, through a postmodern 'multinational, multicultural gaze that probes, yet goes beyond local markets while it remains anchored in the interactional experiences of the reflexive ethnographer' (Denzin, 1997: 19). What Denzin (1997) and Alasuutari, et al. (1998) call 'hybrid texts' are emerging; these are outcomes of research that engage with alternative forms of representation, be it visual, performative, or literary/poetic.

In this chapter, hybrid methodologies are illustrated in the author's ethnnographic, participatory action research work with women working in the sex industry and communities affected by prostitution; and the re-presentation of ethnographic work through photographic work and live art/performance. The re-presentation of the author's ethnographic work through live art/performance was undertaken with Sara Giddens. The work with sex workers, communities and young people was undertaken in collaboration with Rosie Campbell. This hybrid form is defined as ethnomimesis; the mimetic re-telling of life stories in visual, artistic form and a focus upon the transformative, change causing gesture involved in participatory action research.

Participatory action research seeks to understand the world from the perspective of the participants. Fals Borda quotes what Agnes Heller termed 'symmetric reciprocity' as a key tension in PAR, in order to arrive at a 'subject–subject horizontal or symmetric relationship' (Fals Borda, 1999: 13). Additionally, recognizing this symmetry involves developing what Gramsci called 'good sense' and, achieving authentic 'participation'. This necessarily involves reporting or communicating results/findings in ways that are understandable to the participants. A key aspect is praxis as purposeful knowledge involving interpretation, action, and transformation.

At every phase of the PAR model there is the possibility for change. PAR can validate the experiences of the participants and also of grassroots knowledge. In the process of involving participants as co-researchers, this validation is transformed into constructive and creative responses for them and their communities. Outcomes of participatory research can inform, educate, remind, challenge and empower both those involved and the audiences of the research outcomes. Outcomes can be print based or performance based, or art/exhibition based. The combination of popular knowledge and academic knowledge can create change. Fals Borda tells us that 'popular knowledge has always been a source of formal learning. Academic accumulation, plus people's wisdom, became an important rule for our movement' (1999: 7).

The inter-relationship between research and praxis is fraught with tensions. Renewed methodologies which incorporate the voices of citizens through scholarly/ civic research as participatory research not only can serve to enlighten and raise our awareness of certain issues but can also produce critical reflexive texts which may help to mobilize social change. Ethno-mimesis as critical praxis seeks to speak in empathic ways with the participants in the research, re-presented through the performance text in ways that counter valorizing discourses, and the reduction of the Other to a cipher of the oppressed/marginalized/exploited.

Critical Feminist Theory and Ethnomimesis

'Critical theory' emerged from Western Marxism and its most famous proponents were the Frankfurt School, especially Theodor Adorno and Walter Benjamin. The work of Adorno and Benjamin are inextricable connected (Weber-Nicholsen, 1993; 1997; 1999; O'Neill, 1999; 2002). I have argued elsewhere that Adorno has proved useful to feminists because he illuminated the contradictory nature of sexual and social oppression (see Benjamin, J; Braidotti, 1994; Weber-Nicholsen, 1997; Battersby, 1998; O'Neill, 1999). For Shierry Weber-Nicholsen (1997), the importance of Adorno's usefulness for us today is his focus on the role of the subject and subjective experience, particularly the imaginary and imagination. In the words of Buck-Morss, 'His was a negative anthropology; and its knowledge was to keep criticism alive' (1977: 186). Adorno was an outstanding social and cultural theorist, member of the Frankfurt School, and Professor of Sociology and Philosophy at the University of Frankfurt. His work is notoriously difficult to understand. Adorno refused to simplify his ideas into the conversational form of everyday language and 'demanded of the listener not mere contemplation but praxis' (see Jay 1984: 11). Robert Witkin concludes his book on *Adorno and Music* as follows: 'No one has done more to persuade us of the moral dimension of all cultural construction and of the sociality that is the basis of anything truly creative and liberative' (1998: 200).

The usefulness of Adorno's oeuvre is that his work gives voice to the critical, moral, creative potential of non-identity thinking, *Kulturkritik*, and the social role of art in dialectical tension with the role of subjective experience, within the context of a social world marked by identity thinking and instrumental reason. Thinking against the grain through what he termed 'micrology' using 'non-identity thinking' and '*Kulturekritik*', Adorno's critical theory inspired my critical feminist theory and ethnographic work with sex workers and other marginalized groups. Adorno famously said, 'The splinter in your eye is the best magnifying glass' (1978: 50) and for Walter Benjamin, a fragment of a story of a life can tell us so much more than one hundred pages of information about a life.

Focusing upon the small scale, the minutiae of life can often surprise, inspire and throw light on broader social structures and processes.

Following Adorno, 'mimesis' does not simply mean naïve imitation, or mimicry, but rather feeling, sensuousness, spirit – a sensuous knowing. The concept of mimesis (as sensuous knowing) must be understood in tension with what Adorno calls 'constructive rationality', reason, instrumental rationality, the 'out there' sense of our being in the world. Taussig understands mimesis as 'both the faculty of imitation and the deployment of that faculty in sensuous knowing' (1993: 68).

By re-presenting ethnographic data (life story interviews) in artistic form (via ethno-mimesis) we can access a richer understanding of the complexities of lived experience which can throw light on broader social structures and processes. Such work can also reach a wider population, beyond academic communities, facilitating understanding/interpretation and, maybe, action/praxis in relation to certain social issues.[3] The multiplicity of oppression and fractured notion of 'woman', challenges from postcolonial and Third World feminisms, queer theory, and the performative nature of sexual identity help to map out the ongoing production of feminist theory and practice. Experimentation in the handling and disseminating knowledge production has led to a range of possible ways of visualizing feminist praxis.

Interpretive Ethnography and Women's Lives: Visualizing Feminist Praxis

Hillis Millar draws upon Walter Benjamin's work to illustrate

> how works of art bring something new into the world rather than reflecting something already there. This something new is constitutive rather than being merely representational or, on the other hand, reveals something already there but hidden. Works of art make culture. Each work makes different the culture it enters. (1992: 151).

Figure 11.1 Stills from the video of the performance 'Not all the time ... but mostly ...'

Exemplar 1: Not all the time … but mostly …

This example involved collaborating across disciplines and genres drawing upon ethnographic research with sex workers *and* performance art/live art. A video/live art performance, *Not all the time … but mostly …* was developed by the team and performed by Patricia Breatnach, choreographed by Sara Giddens, with soundscape by Darren Bourne and video produced by Tony Judge. The video/live art performance was a response to transcripts of interviews with women working in prostitution and fuses dance, text, sound and video. A trilogy of work was eventually developed. Sara and Patricia interpreted and created a live art performance that was captured first on video with Darren's soundscape; then a live performance emerged using the video too; a second (and final) live performance was later developed and photographs from this performance were later exhibited.[4]

The research team involved two sociologists, a video maker, a sound artist, a dancer/live artists and a performing arts lecturer and choreographer. The work was shown to a sex worker project for responses and feedback. Following this, the team organized public performances and the exhibition. Methodologically, the intention was to run a pilot project in order to explore the possibilities for developing alternative re-presentations of ethnographic data as 'ethno-mimesis'.

In a recent book, Emmison and Smith (2000) suggest that the problems in connecting visual research to social scientific enquiry lie in the tendency to use visual materials as merely illustrative, archival, rather than giving them a more analytical treatment. They argue that 'we live in a massively visual society, and researchers should become more reflexive about the visual; more methodologically skilled within it; and indeed, that this should enhance the quality of our research' (ibid.: x). They claim that social science has privileged verbal forms of communication over visual communication, despite the fact that the 'visual' is 'a pervasive feature not only of social life but of many aspects of social enquiry as well' (ibid.: 2). This, they argue, is largely due to the fact that sociology as a discipline has not encouraged visual exploration of society and, with the removal of the body in social theory (see Turner, 1984), so too went the eye (Emmison and Smith, 2000: 13). Emmison and Smith's aim in the book is to propose analytical frameworks for investigating visual data that include: (1) the generation of photographic stills through ethnographic work; (2) the analysis of media products; (3) the analysis of practices of visualization (using diagrams, sketches in research and dissemination); and (4) video recordings of 'naturally occurring social interaction' (ibid.: 25).

I am most interested in their focus upon phenomenological analyses and use of the visual. What I define as ethno-mimesis is a phenomenological, hermeneutic mode of exploring, analysing and seeking to transform social and sexual inequalities through artistic re-presentations of ethnographic research. Such an approach takes us beyond the four major methodological frameworks outlined by Emmison and Smith. Ethno-mimesis as performative praxis is reflexive and phenomenological but it is also critical and looks to praxis. The immediacy and directness of live art, its potential to move and, in the words of Catherine Ugwu, its 'resistance to categorisation and containment, along with its ability to surprise and unnerve, makes live art's impact so far-reaching' (1995: 9). Performance art could be described as an exemplar of anti-identitarian thinking. The audiences are able to re-engage in interpretation at every performance; they do not just receive information but have to actively engage in meaning making through the process Adorno identifies as: coming to know a work of art, via a process of immersion in the performance; identification and subsequent distancing; and finally critical reflection. In earlier work, I have argued that through art works – performing arts/live arts, painting, poetry, literature, photography – we are able to get in touch with our 'realities', our social worlds and the lived experiences of others, in ways which demand critical reflection. This is an active process involving immersion, interpretation, commentary and criticism.

The live art performance of *Not all the time ... but mostly ...* as ethno-mimetic text engages with people as human beings, not as 'stand-in political subjects', and in so doing re-presents the ambivalence of prostitution, and the situation of the women involved, located as they are between and within discourses of good and bad women. Moreover, our potential 'feeling involvement' in the ethno-mimetic text erupts from the tension between the mimetic (sensuous knowing) and the rational/constructive moments in the interplay between movement/performance/motifs and narrative voice. An evocative tension is created between what is played out on screen (or live) and the relationship the viewer or audience has with the 'performance'. One is left feeling in some cases 'stunned', but in others able to grasp reality in its 'otherness'; 'feel' emotional structures and inner experiences; experience the traces of the 'prostitutes' 'work' within the context of a life, albeit for some a damaged life. In this sense the ethno-mimetic text is able to 'say' the 'unsayable', the 'outside of language' and undercut identity/identitarian thinking creating potentially space for genuine 'felt' involvement which demands critical reflection.

Exemplar 2: Safety soapbox

This second example emerged from research (with Rosie Campbell) in the West Midlands in 2000–2002.[5] A combination of 'Participatory Action Research' (PAR)[6,7] and 'Participatory Arts' (PA) was used to consult sex workers and communities affected by prostitution and included the following three groups: sex workers; residents; and young people resident in the 'red light' area, with a view to developing strategic local responses to prostitution. The research team was made up of the researchers from Staffordshire and Liverpool Hope University and co-researchers who were local residents. Alongside the usual ethnographic work and focus group interviews, the research team organized art workshops with residents in the red light area; young people who are resident in the 'red light' area; and women working on street. All produced artforms to express their views, experiences and ideas for addressing the complex issues of prostitution in residential areas. This work was funded by Walsall South Health Action Zone and facilitated by Walsall Community Arts and Walsall Youth Arts.

In the process of conducting consultation research, the researchers became aware very quickly that 'safety' was a pressing issue for all three groups. Sex workers are very vulnerable to violence, assault, verbal abuse and in some cases murder (see O'Neill, 2001; Kinnell, 2006, 2001). Young people and older residents expressed their fears and insecurities about: harassment from kerbcrawlers; lack of safety on streets, especially after dark; and fear of crime linked to drug cultures, and drug dealing. The three groups attended arts workshops facilitated by Kate Green (freelance arts worker with Walsall Youth Arts) and produced visual re-presentations through a combination of PA and PAR.

The collaboration across the groups aimed to: challenge stereotypes; create a space for the voices of those living in the 'red light area'; develop artistic forms for re-presenting their experiences; and facilitate ideas for change.

The main themes emerging from the workshops were: the development of participatory action research and processes of community development and governance; the vital role of the arts in processes of social regeneration and inclusion (sex workers are not usually consulted about safety in the areas they live and work in, despite the endemic levels of violence against them); and the role of creative inclusion in facilitating spaces for the voices of local people.

The main outcomes of the collaboration were: some changes in local policy (see www.safetysoapbox.com); an exhibition launched at The New Art Gallery in Walsall and the Big Issue ran an article on the exhibition and research project; an understanding of the role of the arts in research (cultural sociology) with communities, especially in relation to cultural diversity and the generation of praxis as purposeful knowledge; and creative ways of working with people to consult and make visible their concerns and ideas for change.

Purposeful knowledge as praxis emerged from a combination of PAR and PA (as ethno-mimesis) and focused attention upon the standpoints of the people concerned promoting 'thick' descriptions of lived cultures and helping audiences to better understand complex issues and lived experiences. Purposeful knowledge can also alter attitudes, policy and practice. Dialogic texts can help the de-construction of stereotypes of 'otherness' thus challenging the stereotype of the 'prostitute' (we prefer the term sex worker) in the public imagination.

Cultural Sociology as Praxis:
Creative Inclusion and Cultural Change

Over a period of ten months the research team met and interviewed agencies and residents, and also conducted interviews and ethnographic outreach with women and young women working both on and off street in Walsall.

The researchers took the view that residents and sex workers are the 'experts' in the local area; and through processes of consultation and inclusion of residents and sex worker voices we can work in partnership with statutory and voluntary agencies and dedicated sex work projects to reach a pragmatic strategic response to better 'manage' prostitution in the Walsall South HAZ area. In this section the findings from our work with residents and sex workers are identified and re-presented through visual ethno-mimetic texts.

> Prostitution affects my life and my children. I go home and there it is, all week-end, there is no escape, no rest.
>
> (A resident in O'Neill and Campbell, 2001)

Figure 11.2 'If this is what our children see'

In 1995, Benson and Matthews completed a survey of vice squad activity in the England. They found that:

> Vice units explained that the main complaints from the public were general problems of noise and disturbance associated with street prostitution. In some areas, there were moral issues related to the fact that the working women were openly selling sexual services, but for the most part residents were concerned primarily with noise, litter and the activities of kerb crawlers particularly in rela-tion to the harassment of local female residents.

Responses of residents fit broader concerns documented nationally, such as noise from kerbcrawlers, and the slamming of car doors; litter such as condoms and dis-carded syringes; increases in traffic; intimidation of residents and fear of reprisals and victimization; increase in criminal activities such as drug dealing, pimping, and robbery; disregard for private or communal property; and male residents solicited by sex workers. Webster provides a vivid account of the area where he lives:

> At night the Green takes on an altogether different character. Fast food eateries and Balti restaurants stretch up ... Road. Groups of men hurry home from the mosque. Women standing on corners peer questioningly into the windows of cars cruising through or ask male pedestrians if they want 'Business'. The speed bumps – *Sleeping policemen* – ensure that essentially all drivers become kerb crawlers, and the humps raise the eye line of inadvertent drivers so that they have to meet the gaze of the women eye to eye. (in O'Neill et al., 2003)
>
> The big problem for our community is that soon after the dark our sister and daughter wouldn't go and walk on the road because the people passing are shouting, Are you in business?' I feel shame for us when this happens. I wouldn't like my daughter or my sister or my wife to walk round this area after the dark because, you know, you don't know who's approaching them.

(Resident at Focus Group 1)

The majority were also concerned about how the women and young women involved are personally affected and this included routes in to prostitution and the impact of pimping.

Figure 11.3   'Glad it's not me'

The pimps were described as a hidden mafia. The young people at the workshops showed a great deal of understanding about the complexity of the issues. On the subject of pimps, they said: 'the pimps are disrespectful ... they disrespect women and take their money'; 'they protect them ... they watch out for them ... for the pimps it's an easy way to get money' (O'Neill et al., 2002: 152).

They also expressed awareness and understanding of the situation for women working on street.

> They should be safe ... there should be support and somewhere to go. ... They watch you, the dirty perverts. I've lived here eight months now and I am used to it ... it doesn't bother me ... but prostitutes have to work somewhere ... they are always going to be there.
> It isn't their fault and it's up to them what they do, but it isn't very nice when we get seen as a prostitute.

> (O'Neill et al., 2002: 152)

Sex workers

The key issue that emerged with the work with women working on and off street focused upon safety, and the endemic levels of violence against them.

> One bloke tried to ammonia me ... he was telling me I was going to give him a blow job for a fiver ... he drove past and squirted ammonia at me ... it went in my hair and down my coat luckily.

> (ibid.: 152)

For many women, protection of their families was key. They did not want their children to know what they do and so lead double lives. This is experienced as very stressful. For other women, attempts to do something else were frustrated by people's attitudes towards them, and the fact that as a 'common prostitute' you have a criminal record. Attempts at change for some women were also frustrated by lack of self-esteem, economic necessity, drug use, and homelessness caused by fleeing violence at home.

The main themes emerged as a wish to be seen as ordinary and avoid derogatory stereotypes; fear of violence; dangers of street work; health issues; problematic punters; attempts to escape; and the effect of fines. A local woman was very anxious not to be identified because of her desire to protect her children from the knowledge of what she does.

> I'm just an ordinary mum now when I go to the school, but what would they think if they knew? ... I'm a mum; I'm just like everybody else ... I'm really paranoid about the kids; I worry about them all the time.

> (ibid.: 153)

The problems of leading double lives and experiencing prejudice from others is also relevant here:

> People see women involved in prostitution as weird, perverse, not ordinary people ... I think they think we've got two heads and are all nymphomaniacs.
>
> (ibid.: 153)

Figure 11.4 'Look behind the mask'

Overwhelmingly, the pivotal issue emerging in our research (and in my previous research over the past 13 years) is how susceptible sex workers are to violence from clients/punters/customers as well as passers-by, and how few rights they have as a 'common prostitute':

> They think you've got no rights. In the papers, it will say 'a prostitute' has been murdered. Does it matter that she's a prostitute, she's dead – she is a woman too.
>
> (ibid.: 154)

Women felt also that it was much safer to work indoors than outdoors and that there were greater risks and dangers with street prostitution:

> You don't see the dangers on the street until something happens.
>
> Nine out of 10 times you can always sus them out ... 'dodgy punters' ... you might have seen them before in the area.
>
> (ibid.: 153)

Another key issue that emerged was the importance given to condom use:

> At the end of the day you've got to go home and kiss your kids – no sex without condoms. Is that bit extra worth your life? Always wear condoms.

(ibid.: 154)

The group felt that some of the images that emerged could be used as public health leaflets promoting safety and sexual health. One woman's 'tips of the trade' artwork is a particularly striking image that would be useful for women and safe sexual health/peer education projects. This is also a way of educating clients, many of whom ask for unprotected sex.

Some women also talked about other 'options' and exiting sex work. One woman went for careers advice mentioning her criminal record – the woman advising her was very unprofessional and insensitive. 'She might as well have said to the whole room, she's been a prostitute. You just get fed up with it when your older, you just don't want it.' This woman talked about splitting off sex in work, and work generally from home and the rest of life. She wants to move out in two years but wants to start thinking about what she wants to do and undertake some training for another job. 'It's hard to get out, I've done nothing else really' (ibid.: 154)

EMPLOYMENT HISTORY
(Please list in order the organisations for which you have worked).

Name and address of current employer:	Please summarise the main duties of the post
self	customer satisfaction negotiating prices communication skills advertising
Post held: **sex worker**	Date started: **1995** Until: **2002/3**

Salary:	Period of notice:	OR	Reason for leaving (if applicable)
£500 - 1000/wk	?		

PREVIOUS POSTS

From Month/ Year	To Month/ Year	Name and Address of Employer	Post Held	Salary	Reason for leaving
93 - 94		Posh Hotel	2nd chef	£110/wk	career change
94 - 95		Local council	admin officer	£100/wk	seeking more money

FURTHER INFORMATION:
Please use this section to provide evidence that you possess the skills and experience required for this post.

(Please use additional sheets if necessary)

Despite what you may think about my current employment I feel that you need to value me as a whole person with a range of positive skills gained often working in difficult circumstances. Your prejudices should not hinder me from progressing with my life and with my future plans to move forward.

Figure 11.5 'Job application'

Research Recommendations from the Collaboration of PA and PAR

The research that took place through the arts workshops and combining PAR and PA let to a range of recommendations, some of which have been carried through. The team agreed that there is a need for agencies and funders to support community arts initiatives which continue to give voice to local concerns regarding safety and consult people about solutions. It was also agreed that a combination of socio-cultural research and community arts can be used to evaluate change and a long-term arts consultation/evaluation project could be developed. It was also felt that research should continue to support initiatives that challenge stereotypes, explore issues, and also inform and educate young people about the dangers of prostitution. The Arts can be shown to build self-esteem, and therefore it makes sense to commission more arts projects which offer opportunities to all young people to develop their creative potential and enable them to make positive choices. Cultural opportunities and cultural industries, arts-based training could also be tailored to the needs of sex workers. This would give the two groups marketable arts skills and be integrated into a programme of alternative options – initiatives developed from a grass roots drop-in in collaboration with sex worker projects, local colleges and community arts.

Together the three groups wanted to see the following recommendations actioned:

- Stop kerbcrawlers harassing women and young people.
- Address prostitution and kerb crawling so children can 'retain innocence and be safe'.
- Create a tolerance zone and allow women to work off street.
- Improve safety on street: street lighting and more police in evidence.
- Change the law. 'The police can't physically do any more.'
- Improve support for drug and alcohol problems.
- Address the issue of pimps and pimping.
- Address violence against women.
- Provide support and options to women working on street.
- Acknowledge women working as prostitutes as ordinary women – as human beings – as mothers and daughters. Work together to create change!

Conclusion

Through a combination of socio-cultural research (cultural sociology); lived experience (life stories); and practice/praxis (live art and photographic forms) defined as ethno-mimesis, this chapter has explored (with a view to developing better understanding across the widest possible audience – lay and academic) some of the key themes and issues evolving from feminist research with sex workers and communities affected by prostitution. Renewed methodologies which incorporate the voices of citizens through scholarly/civic research as participatory research not only can serve to enlighten and raise our awareness of certain issues, but can also produce critical reflexive texts that may help to mobilize social change. The emphasis is upon methodologically and theoretically extending the legacy of phenomenology through a hermeneutic, reflexive understanding in co-operation with the stereotypical subjects of research working together across genres (socio-cultural research/arts/community development), and in the process developing hybrid texts generated from ethnographic research (fieldwork/life history interviews/ in co-operation with community development) and re-told through artistic re-presentations. This renewed methodology is embedded within critical theory as feminist praxis – for our task is not just to understand the world but also to seek to change it, by addressing and challenging sexual and social inequalities *with* the 'stereotypical subjects' of research. We can do this not only with words, but also with images, visual re-presentations, with ethno-mimetic texts, through cultural sociology in practice.

Notes

1 See 'Global refugees: ethno-mimesis as performative praxis', with Bea Tobolewska, in J. Rugg, and D. Hinchcliffe (eds) (2002) *Divers (C)ities: Recoveries and Reclamations*. Intellect Press: Bristol and Portland, Oregon, USA. 'Global refugees: citizenship, power and the law' in *Law, Justice, and Power: An Impossible but Necessary Relationship*. S. Cheng (ed.) University of California at Irvine: Univesity of California Press, 2003. See also the special section in *Sociology*, 'Global refugees: towards a sociology of exile, displacement and belonging', Spring 2003, 37.

2 See Hillis Millar's excellent book *Illustration* (1992) for a thorough account of the development and role of cultural studies as 'performative praxis'.

3 For example, funded by the AHRB the author conducted PAR with 'refugees' from Bosnia-Herzegovina, and together with community arts and community development we facilitated the re-presentation of life history narratives in photographic form (by the people themselves as co-creators of the research) for exhibition in 1999–2001. 'Global Refugees: the Bosnians in Nottingham – past, present and future' was accessed by a relatively wide audience in the Bonnington Gallery, Nottingham, and also discussed in local newspaper articles. The latter served to re-present the Bosnian community in ways that challenged negative stereotypes of 'refugees' and presented their stories of resistance, loss and exile in creative, informative ways, thus validating their voices and creative reconstructions/ re-presentations of their lives before the war, through the war and now living in the UK. This work was able to help a wider population than might ordinarily access the ethnographic research data to see and better understand the experiences of displacement, loss, 'longing' and re-settlement in the UK which is part of the experience of being in exile, a refugee, an asylum seeker. The ethnographic research was developed in collaboration with the Bosnian Association, Nottingham, City Arts Nottingham and the City Council Community Development. The latest work including PAR with an Afghan community in London was exhibited with the Bosnian work at Watermans Multi-media Centre, High St, Brentford, in November and December 2002.

4 This was presented at the BSA in Edinburgh 1998 and published as a visual essay in *Feminist Review's* special edition *Sex Work-Reassed*, October 2000.

5   Funded by Walsall South HAZ, we developed consultation research on prostitution in the West Midlands. Seedfunding was included in the tender bid for arts-based consultation and inclusion of residents and more marginalized groups. The community arts team (represented on the steering group for the research) raised funding to enable the arts aspect of the research to be developed. Thanks go to Mark Webster, Walsall Community Arts, for following this up and being such a staunch supporter of the work and to Walsall Youth Arts and Kate Green. See www.safetysoapbox.com

6   A small group of community co-researchers (local residents) came forward to work on the project and were trained in focus groups methods and participated in the ethnographic work too; a larger group acted as a steering group (agency representatives, including police, health authority, social services, local councillors, sex work projects and various voluntary and statutory support agencies).

7   PA has its roots in social and cultural movements that aim to create opportunities for people to have access to the means to participate in the processes that generate culture. Sometimes described through the concept of cultural democracy, it is a fundamental principle governing community arts and local authority cultural strategies. PA provides a unique way of consulting people especially marginalized, hard-to-reach groups, it is non-threatening, non-hierarchical and results are presented in a way which reflects the richness of opinions and ideas (see Webster, 1997).

References

Adorno, T. (1978) *Minima Moralia: reflections from a Damaged Life*. Trans. E,. F. N. Jephcott. London: Verso.

Adorno, T. (1984) *Aesthetic Theory*. Trans C. Lendhart. London: Routledge.

Alasuutari, P. (1995) Researching Culture: qualitative method and cultural studies, London: Sage.

Battersby, C. (1998) *The Phenomenal Woman*. Cambridge: Polity.

Benjamin, J. (1993) The Bonds of Love: Psychoanalysis, feminism and the politics of domination, London: virago.

Bennet, Martin, Mercer, and Woollacot, (eds) (1982) *Culture, Ideology and Social Process*. Milton Keynes: Open University Press.

Becker, H.S., McCall, M.M., Morris, L.V., and Meshejian, P. (1989) 'Theatres and communities: three scenes', *Social Problems*, 36(2): 93–8.

Benjamin, W. (1992) *Illuminations*. London: Fontana Press.

Benson, C. and Matthews, R. (1995) *National Vice Squad Survey*. Middlesex: University, centre for Criminology.

Bishop, R. and Robinson, L. (1997) Night market: Sexual Cultures and the Thai economic miracle, New York and London: Routledge.

Boal, A. (1979) *Theatre of the Oppressed*. London: Pluto 1979.

Braidotti, R. (1994) *Nomadic Subjects*. New York: Columbia University Press.

Buck-Morss, S. (1977) *The Origin of Negative Dialectics: Theodor W. Adorno, Walter Benjamin and the Frankfurt Institute*. Brighton: Harvester Press.

Campbell, R. et al. (1996) *Street Prostitution in Inner City Liverpool*. Liverpool Hope University, Deanery of Hope in the Community.

Campbell, R. and O'Neill, M. (eds) (2006) *Sex Work Now*. Cullompton, Devan: Willan.

Corbin, A. (1987) 'Commercial sexuality in nineteenth century France: a system of images and regulation', in C. Gallagher and T. Laquer (eds) *The Making of the Modern Body: Sexuality and Society in the Nineteenth Century*. Berkeley, CA: University of California Press.

Denzin, N. (1997) *Interpretive Ethnography: Ethnographic Practices for the 21st Century*. London: Sage.

Emmison, M. and Smith, P. (2000) *Researching the Visual*. London: Sage Publications.

Evans, J. and Hall, S. (eds) (1999) *Visual Culture: The Reader*. London: Sage Publications.

Fals Borda, O. (1988) *Knowledge and People's Power: Lessons with Peasants in Nicaragua, Mexico and Colombia*. New York: New Horizons Press.

Fals Borda, O. (1999) *The Origins and Challenges of Participatory Action Research.* Center for International Education, University of Massachusetts at Amherst.

Finnegan, F. (1979) *Poverty and Prostitution: A Study of Victorian Prostitutes in York.* Cambridge: Cambridge University Press.

Geertz, C. (1983) *Local Knowledge: Further Essays in Interpretative Anthropology.* New York: Basic Books.

Harding, S. (1986) *The Science Question in Feminism.* Milton Keynes:Open University Press.

Harding, S. (1991) *Whose Science? Whose Knowledge? Thinking from Women's Lives.* Milton Keynes: Open University Press.

Hillis Millar, J. (1992) *Illustration.* London: Reaktion Books.

Jay, M. (1984) Adorno, London: Fontana.

Kempadoo, K. and Doezema, J. (1998) *Global Sex Workers: Rights, Resistance and Redefinition.* London: Routledge.

Kinnell, H. (2006) 'Murder made easy: the final solution to prostitution?' in Campbell, R. and O'Neill, M (eds) Sex Work Now, Cullompton, Devon: Willen.

Mienczakowski, J. (1995) 'The theater of ethnography: the reconstruction of ethnography into theater with emancipatory potential', *Qualitative Enquiry*, 1(3): 360–75.

Laws, S. et al. (2003) *Research for Development.* London: Save the Children and Sage.

McGuigan, J. (1997) *Cultural Methodologies.* London: Sage.

McLeod, E. (1982) *Women Working: Prostitution Now.* London: Croom Helm.

Nicholsen, L. (1990) *Feminism/Postmodernism.* London: Routledge.

O'Connell-Davidson, J. (1998) Prostitution, Power and Freedom, Cambridge: Polity.

O'Neill, M. (ed) (1999) *Adorno, Culture and Feminism.* London: Sage.

O'Neill, M. (2001) *Prostitution and Feminism: Towards a Politics of Feeling*, Cambridge: Polity Press.

O'Neill, M. (2002) 'Adorno', in L. Ray, and A. Elliott, *Key Contemporary Social Theorists.* Oxford: Blackwell.

O'Neill, M. and Campbell, R. (2001) *Working Together to Create Change: Walsall Prostitution Consultation Research.* Staffordshire University and Liverpool Hope University.

O'Neill, M., Campbell, R. and Webster, M. (2002) 'Prostitution, ethno-mimesis and participatory arts: processes and practices and inclusion', in J. Swift, and T. Daves, (eds) *Disciplines, Fields and Change in Art Education, vol. 3. Art Therapy, Psychology and Sociology.* ARTicsle Press UCE.

O'Neill, M. and Giddens, S. (2001) 'Not all the time … but mostly …' *Feminist Review: Sex Work Reassessed*, 67: 109–11 (plus inserts.)

O'Neill, M., McDonald, M., Webster, T., Wellik, M. and McGregor, H. (1994) 'Prostitution, feminism and the law', in *Rights of Women.* London: Rights of Women Collective.

Pheonix, J. (1999) *Making Sense of Prostitution Today.* London: Macmillan.

Roberts, N. (1992) *Whores in History.* London: HarperCollins.

Smith, A. M. (1986) Laclau and Mouffe: the radical democratic imaginary, London and New York: Routledge.

Smith, A.M. (1998) *Laclau and Mouffe: The Radical Democratic Imaginary.* London: Routledge.

Taussig, M. (1993) *Mimesis and Alterity.* London: Routledge.

Trinh, T. Min-Ha (1989) *Woman, Native, Other: writing postcoloniality and feminism*, Bloomington and Indianapolis: Indiana University Press.

Trinh, T. Minh-ha (1991) *When the Moon Waxes Red.* London: Routledge.

Truong, T. (1990) *Sex, Money and Morality: prostitution and Tourism in South East Asia*, London: Zed books.

Ugwu, C. (1995) 'Keep on running: the politics of Black British performance', in *Let's Get it On: The Politics of Black Performance.* London: ICA, and Seattle Bay Press.

Weber-Nicholsen, S. (1993) 'Walter Benjamin and the aftermath of the aura: notes on the aesthetics of photography', in *Antioch Community Record*, February 12th 1993 – personal communication from the author.

Weber-Nicholsen, S. (1999) 'Adorno, Benjamin and the aura: an aesthetics for photography', in M. O'Neill, *Adorno, Culture and Feminism.* London: Sage.

Weber-Nicholsen, S. (1997) *Exact Imagination/Late Work: On Adorno's Aesthetics*. Cambridge, MA: MIT press.

Walkowitz, J. (1980) *Prostitution and Victorian Society*. Cambridge: Cambridge University Press.

Webster, M. (ed.) (1997) *Finding Voices, Making Choices: Creativity for Social Change*. Nottingham: Educational Heretics Press.

Witkin, R. (1974) *The Intelligence of Feeling*. London: Heinemann.

Witkin, R. (1995) *The Social Structure of Art*. Cambridge: Polity Press.

Whyte, W.F. (1989) 'Advancing scientific knowledge through participatory action research' *Sociological Forum*, 4(3): 367–85.

Acknowledgements

Safety Soapbox images with kind permission of Kate Green, Walsall Youth Arts.

Not all the time … but mostly images with kind permission of Sarah Gidden and Tony Gudge.

CHAPTER TWELVE **Popular Music**
●●●●●●●●
Eamonn Carrabine

Elvis Costello once famously insisted that writing about music was like 'dancing about architecture' (Goddard, 2002: 9). His point is that words can never fully capture the electrifying rush and emotional punch that a great pop song can deliver. While a common objection among fans, journalists and performers is that attempts to analyse music often fail to grasp what makes the sound so important in the first place,[1] explaining why popular music can have such a powerful impact in our daily lives is one of the central tasks of cultural analysis and one that has a rich theoretical legacy. A core theme in this critical literature on popular music is a tension between describing the music industry as a constraining, exploitative and manipulative machine while perceiving the audience as active, autonomous and creative in its use of the texts manufactured by capitalist enterprise. At its extremes this can be thought of as equating production with domination and consumption with freedom, which reflects tensions between 'mass culture' and 'postmodern' discussions of popular culture more generally and documented elsewhere in this book, but also finds expression in journalistic accounts of hackneyed struggles between 'the Man' and 'the Kids'.

As we will see, one of the problems with this characterization is the assumption that the relationships between production and consumption are direct and straightforward. They are, of course, neither. The industry does not have the power to control which music will be made nor determine its popularity, while the audience has little say in deciding which products will be on display in high street mega-stores. In this chapter, I discuss the three major approaches to popular music found in cultural theory and argue that a continuing failure in the literature is to isolate the analysis of production, text and audience from each other in ways that militate against synthesis and simplify, or simply ignore, questions surrounding power.

First, the critical theory of Theodor Adorno (1991), who maintained that a 'culture industry' produced standardized popular music that deceived listeners through 'pseudo-individualization' and manipulated their desires, has left a major legacy in the field with many studies continuing to examine the organizational dynamics of the music industry in a political-economic context of profit maximization. Second, the cultural critic Roland Barthes (1977a) has done much to shift the textual study of popular music away from the traditional concerns of musicologists (who tend to concentrate on evaluating the technical qualities of harmonic, melodic and rhythmic structures in selected compositions) onto semiotic questions of representation and meaning, as well as emphasizing the pleasures of the text. Third, Antonio Gramsci's (1971) neo-Marxist argument that there is a constant struggle for hegemony, the battle to win 'total social authority' by the ruling classes over subordinate groups, has influenced much of the scholarship on musical subcultures and fandom by emphasizing the ways in which acts of consumption can create oppositional cultures through challenging the status quo. The key site articulating Gramsci's position has been the Centre for Contemporary Cultural Studies at the University of Birmingham in the 1970s through its classic work on youth subcultures.

Before the discussion can properly begin, it is important to recognize that most authors writing in the field tend to distinguish popular music from folk and classical music as it 'developed historically in and through the mass media' (Toynbee, 2000: xix). While definitional disputes continue to be significant in the literature, not least since there are conflicting meanings generated by the very notion of 'popular', in this chapter, the term popular music will be used to refer to mass-produced music with a large audience in mind and includes such genres as dance, hip-hop, pop, as well as rock, which has tended to receive most sociological attention (the ground-breaking study is Frith, 1983). Nevertheless, it is this refusal to be defined that helps to give popular music its cultural vitality.

Production

Adorno and the culture industry

It is difficult to exaggerate the importance of Theodor Adorno's uncompromising thinking on popular music as a product of a monolithic 'culture industry'. For instance, it has been argued that 'Adorno's is the most systematic and most searing analysis of mass culture and the most challenging for anyone claiming even a scrap of value for the products that come churning out of the music industry' (Frith, 1983: 44). As we have seen in other chapters, Adorno's ideas on popular music were not only part of a broader reworking of Marxist philosophy at the University of Frankfurt, and then in exile following the Nazi seizure of power in the 1930s, but were also only a minor element in his attempt to develop a general aesthetics of music (Paddison, 1993).

His early critique 'On Popular Music', originally published in 1941, which establishes these themes, has three main targets. First, he argues the 'fundamental characteristic of popular music' is 'standardization' (Adorno, 1941: 302). He insists that the product is standardized from the overall range of songs on offer all the way down to the specific details of the tunes and he explains that the 'beginning of the chorus is replaceable by the beginning of innumerable other choruses' (ibid.). Moreover, this 'part-interchangeability' is little different to the production processes found in other mass consumer goods. For instance, the mass-produced car has been used to describe Adorno's point 'as virtually any mechanical part from any 1956 Cadillac Eldorado (e.g. a carburettor) can be substituted for any other 1956 Eldorado without disturbing the functional unity of the overall mechanism' (Gendron, 1986: 20). Adorno (1941: 306) goes on to argue that once a successful formula is hit upon, it is exploited to commercial exhaustion, culminating in 'the crystallization of standards' and stunting innovation. In order to disguise standardization, the music industry makes claims to originality and product variation through what Adorno terms 'pseudo-individualization', by which he means the ways that cultural objects of mass production are endowed 'with the halo of free choice'. The second target of his critique is that popular music induces passive listening in order to maintain a 'hold on the masses' (ibid.: 309). In certain key respects his argument is a polemic against Walter Benjamin's (1936) optimistic reading of the emerging media technologies in his essay, 'The work of art in the age of Mechanical Reproduction'. Benjamin's position is that the technology of the mass media had changed the relationship of the masses to art and opened up exciting new and more democratic possibilities, as creation had now become a collective rather than an individual process. For instance, while traditional art required appreciation through an almost fierce concentration of effort on the 'aura', the new media forms are consumed in a distracted manner, which has the potential to challenge traditional, conservative forms of authority. In contrast, Adorno's (1941: 310) more despairing view is that listeners 'are distracted from the demands of reality by entertainment which does not demand attention'. The 'strain and boredom' of work 'lead[s] to avoidance of effort' in leisure time and the 'impossibility of escape causes the widespread attitude of inattention toward popular music' (ibid.: 311). The debate between Adorno and Benjamin continues to be important in studies of popular music. For instance, it has been argued that from Adorno 'come analyses of the economics of entertainment', while it is further claimed that Benjamin laid the ground for analyses of how youth subcultures 'create cultures in their acts of consumption' (Frith, 1983: 57, emphasis in original).[2]

The third critical point is that popular music is a form of 'social cement' that binds listeners into subordination through inducing two different forms of 'psychical adjustment': 'the 'rhythmically obedient' type and the 'emotional' type' (Adorno, 1941: 311–12). This distinction is developed from arguments initially made in a 1938 essay, 'On the Fetish Character in Music and the Regression of Listening' (in Adorno, 1991), where he claims that popular music audiences regress to a submissive state and can be manipulated just as easily by fascist dictators as capitalist corporations. The first type is the person who blindly dances along with the crowd to the rhythm of their own oppression. As he disdainfully puts it, dancers 'affirm and mock their loss of individuality' (Adorno, [1938] 1991: 53). The second type is an alienated and obsessive individual who sentimentally wallows in music 'in order to be allowed to weep' (Adorno, 1941: 313).

Adorno's thinking, as the reader might by now have suspected, is not without its problems. Although there is something unsettling about these derisory characterizations, which I discuss below, it is important to recognize that at the time he was formulating his ideas in the 1930s and 1940s, the sound of big band jazz filled the airwaves, charts and dance halls where the flamboyant dance the jitterbug had replaced the Charleston as the latest style attracting moral condemnation, while the Tin Pan Alley songwriting system that had been dominant since the early 1900s was 'characterised by simple rhyming formulas and harmonies' (Shuker, 2001: 19). However, up until his death in 1969 Adorno continued to equate popular music with Tin Pan Alley sounds and ignored, among other things, rock 'n' roll in the mid-1950s, Beatlemania in the early 1960s and the counter-culture movement of the late 1960s. (Adorno, 1976). This lack of attention to his own historical and social location partly explains Adorno's difficulties in addressing cultural change in music making, 'as he continued to value a particular and very specific form of popular music' (Longhurst, 1995: 13).

For many contemporary authors Adorno's characterization of a monolithic culture industry, elitist denial of the aesthetics of popular music, and his condescending accounts of the uses of popular music have all been roundly and routinely criticized. For instance, Jason Toynbee (2000: 6) largely accepts Adorno's arguments against standardization and pseudo-individualization, but goes on to state that the two terms are actually key aesthetic attributes of popular music: deliberate repetition and subtle variation. The problem is that Adorno cannot appreciate them. In other words, 'he can see funk but he can't hear it' (Toynbee, 2000: 6). The general response to Adorno's pessimism has been to broadly agree with his diagnosis of the organization of mass cultural production, while ignoring the complexities of his aesthetic theory of music and thoroughly rejecting his account of passive consumption (Frith, 1996: 13). The main failing is his inability to think through the relationships between production and consumption as he reduces complex social processes down to simple psychological responses. Adorno's view is that how the music is produced determines its meaning and significance for an undiscriminating mass audience. In contrast, Benjamin's more optimistic argument that meaning is derived through consumption has proved to be the more influential account. Nevertheless, Adorno's point that modern capital is burdened by the problem of overproduction and works to create false needs has left a lasting legacy and helped to academically legitimize studies of popular music, which I now discuss.

Corporate control and artistic creativity

A particularly good example of this legacy is Steve Chapple and Reebee Garafalo's (1977) account of how capitalist corporations have turned popular music into a commodity (Harker, 1980; and Wallis and Malm, 1984; others include Eliot, 1989; Goodman, 1997). While these authors share Adorno's insistence on examining the economic base of pop, they do not dismiss the music and are aware of its subversive potential among youth movements. Nevertheless, Chapple and Garafalo (1977) stress that throughout the twentieth century only a handful of companies have been responsible for the majority of recorded music manufactured and distributed in the United States. They estimate that between five and eight companies have made and distributed 70 per cent of the music available since the end of the nineteenth century, while it has more recently been calculated that six major companies[3] have come to dominate the global music market in the 1990s by controlling the means by which 80 to 85 per cent of the recordings sold are produced, manufactured and distributed (Negus, 1996: 51).

Chapple and Garafalo's (1977: 300) central point is that this concentration of ownership among a few major companies has enabled capitalist corporations to 'colonize leisure' and that the music business has become 'firmly part of the American corporate structure'. Their conclusion then is that any critical possibilities in popular music are absorbed and exploited by the corporations. This point is developed in Nelson George's (1988) critical discussion of the impact of a white dominated industry on the music and cultural identities of black performers. He argues that the industry has been directly responsible for transforming black forms of expression into a commodity and turning the sounds into bland, predictable, apolitical genres from the late 1960s. Like Chapple and Garofalo, he argues that forms of music lose their radical edge when they are co-opted by the music business. He states this unequivocally:

> black culture, and especially R and B music, has atrophied. The music is just not as gutsy or spirited or tuned into the needs of its core audience as it once was. Compare the early Aretha Franklin to Whitney Houston. Franklin's music always relied heavily on the black inner-city experience, and especially on the black church. When she forgets that, she stumbles. Houston is extremely talented, but most of her music is 'color-blind,' such a product of eighties crossover marketing, that in her commercial triumph is a hollowness of spirit that mocks her own gospel roots.
>
> (George, 1988: xiv)

This passage clearly illustrates the impact of standardization and 'integration' on artistic creativity and cultural identity – though hip hop would come to define the anger and disillusionment rendered by economic marginalization and urban apartheid experienced for a generation of black and white youth (Rose, 1994). The alienation at the heart of America's race relations is also captured in Naomi Klein's (2000: 76) discussion of Tommy Hilfiger's marketing strategy as it is based on 'selling white youth on their fetishization of black style, and black youth on their fetishization of white wealth'.

Another way of analysing popular music is through looking at the actual production processes themselves, and a number of writers point to the complexity and contested nature of cultural production. It is far from the case that music simply turns up as mass industrial product, rather 'it is the outcome of intense competition and struggle between, for example, record companies and musicians, radio stations and music publishers, disc jockeys and club owners' (Toynbee, 2000: xvi). One of the most important discussions of the social production of music is Howard Becker's (1963) classic account of the culture of jazz musicians and their desire to be perceived as artists rather than slaves to commercial imperatives. More recently, Georgina Born (1993) has attempted to psychoanalytically theorize the subjective drives towards mass popularity through the notion of a 'global imaginary', which has for cultural producers both aesthetically powerful and socially seductive psychic qualities that cannot be condensed down to economic forces alone. She explains:

> Aesthetically, because of the pleasures and skills involved in 'hitting upon' the next transformation of extant mainstream genres. Socially, because of the pleasures – derived from the phantasy in play – of aligning around a cultural product a vast, diverse and unknowable international community of connoisseur-fans: a phantasy of social and cultural power which is at once both utopian and omnipotent ... In short, neglecting these internal yet very real components of the psychic investment of producers risks reducing cultural production to a set of banal economistic and institutional forces.
>
> (Born, 1993: 237–8)

These arguments have been developed by David Hesmondhalgh (1999) in his discussion of the difficulties faced by two independent record labels, Creation and One Little Indian, and their controversial partnerships with major corporations (Sony and PolyGram) in the 1990s. The two prevailing discourses among fans, musicians and journalists were that they had 'sold out' for financial gain, through abandoning previously held political and aesthetic convictions of artistic autonomy over commercial exploitation. The second, more generous view was that the two independents had 'burnt out' as it was only a matter of time before the human and financial resources run out. Instead, he argues the post-punk sensibility has a deep ambivalence over 'being different but also being popular' (Hesmondhalgh, 1999: 52). In the end, it proved to be impossible to reconcile the contradiction:

> 1990s indie as a whole was marked by nostalgia, political conformity, aesthetic traditionalism, a notion of personal and professional success indistinguishable from the aspirational consumerism of much of the rest of British society and a lack of interest in changing the social relations of production. Whatever the limits and contradictions of late 1980s indie, it at least offered a critique.
>
> (ibid.: 56)

His conclusion confirms what will by now be a familiar theme in the literature – artistic creativity eventually becomes compromised by corporate control; though crucially he recognizes that the political-aesthetic consequences were not simply a result of economic-institutional forces but were powerfully mediated by subjective drives to make the music matter to a large audience. Nevertheless, it is important to remember that while the Blur and Oasis playground rivalry revealed much about the continuing class divide in 1990s Britain, Pulp's Jarvis Cocker actually went on to define the problem in 'Common People' and then later satirize Britpop's obsession with youth in 'Help the Aged' (Mulholland, 2002: 378).

The most sustained attempt to think through and empirically analyse the relationships between commerce and creativity lies in Keith Negus's (1992; 1999) detailed examination of the music industry. One of his key findings is that there is much uncertainty among business executives, fans, musicians and journalists over what type of music is going to be commercially successful. In many ways this demonstrates both the power of the audience, because the industry cannot predict the popularity of music nor can it control the way it is used, and the specific problems posed by overproduction. For instance, Simon Frith (1983: 101) estimated that 80 per cent of the recordings made by the industry in any year are never bought or even heard by an audience (though the small proportion that do sell well cover their own costs many times over and thereby cover the more general costs as well). Because the market is inherently uncertain,[4] the companies have developed a number of strategies to deal with the risk. One way of managing uncertainty is to spread the risk across a wide range of different titles to develop a 'repertoire'. In fact, Nicholas Garnham (1990: 161–2, emphasis in original) makes the crucial, but seldom made, point that *'cultural distribution, not cultural production, ... is the key locus of power and profit'.* Consequently all the major record companies own large distribution divisions to make money and manage risk (Toynbee, 2000: 16).

A further strategy that has been developed to deal with this uncertainty involves establishing a series of aesthetic judgements and commercial hierarchies, so that particular types of music are prioritized over others with artists struggling for position in a broader set of social, economic and political constraints. For instance, at the time Negus (1992) was conducting his research in the late 1980s and early 1990s, he found that white, male, guitar-dominated bands were being prioritized as long-term commercial propositions, while, in contrast, soul and dance music was being treated in a less strategic and more *ad hoc* manner. The effect of this was that rock was prioritized over soul, albums over singles, live guitar bands over studio-based keyboard groups. In his more recent work, Negus (1999) examines how the major record labels companies use corporate strategies to exert control and enforce accountability through 'portfolio management' across a diverse range of genres (such as rap, country and salsa) while distribution divisions construct an imagined consumer and various 'cultural intermediaries' (Bourdieu, 1986) act as significant taste makers in the promotion of particular artists and styles of music.

This work, however, is not without its critics. One uncharitable view is that Negus 'quietly absorbs the terminology (of the industry and the Harvard Business School) and its ideological premises and implications into his discourse' (Harker, 1997: 73). This classic Marxist critique strongly indicates how attempts to pit 'political economy' against 'cultural studies' not only continues to simplify the relationships between culture and economy but also marginalizes the active role played by musicians and record company staff in attempting to change cultures of production. In other words, a more nuanced understanding of organizational power is needed here that can overcome the determinism of classic political economy approaches while acknowledging that there are very real structural constraints that limit and enable certain kinds of action. Nevertheless, it is certainly the case that the work of Hesmondhalgh and Negus evades confronting the schisms between the micro-process of meaning they skilfully portray and the macro-conditions of economic control they largely ignore.

These divisions reflect long-standing tensions between sociologies of the media, which tend to analyse the economic determinants that produce culture, and cultural studies approaches that build on ethnographies of media professionals to question 'top-down' models of ideological power. As we will see, this tension pervades studies of popular music and this chapter will argue that an attempt to integrate the positions is long overdue.

Meaning

Roland Barthes and the critique of production

The chapter now turns to a consideration of the ways in which popular music creates meaning. Particularly influential here is the work of the French cultural critic Roland Barthes and his attack against authorship as the privileged source of textual meaning. His overall significance to cultural theory rests in the way he reveals how images, sounds and texts contain codes and practices that shore up myths which serve to render particular values (often bourgeois) as possessing a natural, universal and eternal meaning. He argues that 'myth has the task of giving an historical intention a natural justification, and making contingency appear eternal' (Barthes, 1957: 142). While his other target came to be the futility of the form of literary criticism which claims that the full meaning of a text is to be found in discovering the motivations of the author behind the work, an enterprise that he would subsequently condemn through famously announcing 'The Death of the Author' (Barthes, 1977a). This introduces the important point: the price to pay for the author's demise is at the light expense of the birth of the reader. While Barthes (ibid.: 148) is aware that this does not mean a simple championing of 'reader's rights', his work is useful for demonstrating how cultural theory has shifted from a structuralist concern with the ideological functions of texts to a post structuralist recognition that socially positioned audiences interpret texts in a multiplicity of ways that can wildly diverge from the author's intentions (which goes further in Jacques Derrida's (1976) notion of deconstruction that emphasizes the inherent instability of meaning). Simultaneously, he introduced another feature of reading that had long been ignored in cultural and literary criticism: pleasure.

In some respects, Barthes's arguments echo classic sociological critiques of individualistic accounts of human life in which the creative artist is one important ideological strand. Jeremy Tanner (2003: 67, emphasis in original) has explained how the 'dominant idea of the artist in the modern west imagines an isolated *creator*, who produces works of art as an expression of a unique individual *aesthetic* vision' has been heavily critiqued. Instead, sociologists have tended to concentrate on 'cultures of production' by following Howard Becker's (1982: x) influential examination of 'art worlds', which he has defined as 'the network of people whose cooperative activity, organized via their joint knowledge of conventional means of doing things, produce the kind of artwork that the art world is noted for'. The idea that art is a form of collective action is taken further in Pierre Bourdieu's (1993a; 1996) sociology of artistic production where more structural concepts (like 'fields', 'positions' and 'habitus') are introduced to grasp 'the whole set of relationships ... *between the artist and other artists,* and beyond them, the whole set of agents engaged in the production of the work, or, at least, of the *social value* of the work (critics, gallery directors, patrons, etc.)' (Bourdieu, 1993b: 97, emphasis in original).

These are important arguments and I now turn to how they have been taken up in studies of popular music. In Toynbee's (2000) account of musical creativity, he begins by warmly endorsing Barthes's critique as the author cult can be found across music publishing: from breathless biographies through to heavier treatments of the life and work of established performers and greats from the past. As he puts it:

> The 'Author-God' characterized by Barthes is a real social institution, and one which needs to be attacked not just in high art, but also in those areas of popular music which have imported it. I am thinking mainly of jazz and rock where the author cult has been renewed with a vengeance. Many of those biographies ... fall into the trap of hearing music as an expression of the soul or psyche of the complex/sensitive/tortured/heroic artist. Moreover this is almost invariably a great *man* approach which celebrates masculine energy and drive, and conflates these qualities with creativity.
>
> (ibid.: emphasis in original)

Instead he characterizes popular musicians as mediators who exchange sounds, styles and forms. They do not generate music from within. Rather their materials are located outside in the 'field of the social' (ibid.: xv). I will return to the gendering of meaning below for I now turn to another area in which Barthes has been influential.

Barthes's (1977b) essay, 'The Grain of the Voice' is generally regarded as the work that laid the ground for a textual study of pop music. Traditionally, musicology has rested on examining the internal coherence of compositions in terms of rhythm, harmony and melody and has generally ignored pop music. In this essay he complains that music critics are obsessed with adjectives. This 'intimidation of detail' actually serves to prevent an adequate understanding of the text. In order to grasp the meaning of a musical experience he argues that we ought to dispense with trying to capture the minutiae but instead respond directly to its 'surface' – the 'grain' of the voice as expressed in the 'materiality of the body' (ibid.: 294–5). In his view, some singers are able to produce the pleasures of *jouissance* in the audience. As Brian Longhurst (1995: 173) explains, this is a difficult term to translate from French, but it can be contrasted with *plaisir. Plaisir* refers to structured feelings and pleasures, where *jouissance* is like the bliss experienced in sexual orgasm. To put it simply, Barthes's overall argument is that we enjoy some singers because of the physical pleasures they provoke.

The implications of this view are captured in the following passage, which, while discussing rock, can be extended to other genres:

The pleasures of rock texts (combinations of words and music) has always derived from the voluptuous presence of voices, and rock fans, unlike high art aestheticians, have always known that music's sensual truth isn't dependent on rules of expression. We respond to the materiality of rock's sounds, and the rock experience is essentially erotic – it involves not the confirmation of self through language (the mode of bourgeois aesthetics, always in control), but the dissolution of the self in *jouissance.*

(Frith, 1983: 164)

Frith (1988: 120–1) has developed these arguments to suggest that future textual analysis of music meaning should take three possible directions. First, studies should not simply restrict themselves to analysing lyrics, which had become by then a common feature of pop musicology, but need to pay attention to the way the song is sung, as this mediates what the singer means to an audience. Second, accounts of pop music need to situate songs within their respective genres as 'different people use different music to experience (or fantasize) different sorts of community; different pop forms (disco, punk, country, rock, etc.) engage their listeners in different narratives of desire' (ibid.: 121). Third, detailed attention needs to be given to how songs work – how the words themselves function as rhythm and sound. While studies in the last decade or so have shown a greater attentiveness to these issues (good examples include Walser, 1993; Born, 1995; van Leeuwen, 1999; Brackett, 2002), it remains the case that the specific ways in which music communicates meaning has not yet been fully addressed in relation to questions of social power, cultural value and historical change.

Moreover, anyone who has an interest in popular music will recognize this preoccupation with the particular 'grain' of a vocalist – the distinctive and idiosyncratic way a voice communicates. For instance, I am with Nelson George (1988) and his preference for early Aretha Franklin over anything by Whitney Houston, while John Lennon singing even the lamest of his post-Beatles material moves me in ways that Elvis Costello, save for one or two performances, cannot. This is partly because I think Houston and Costello are trying too hard. It is also clear that each genre has its own set of established conventions. Whether these be 'the sentimental country whine, the fey mournful plead of alternative rock, the snarling macho sneer of hard rock, the street wise assertiveness of rap or the soft sincerity of the singer-songwriter' (Negus, 1992: 90). Yet for artists, critics, fans and record company staff alike what is often the most emotionally involving voice is the one that transcends simple genre conventions to produce a distinctive grain. However, the vocalists I have just mentioned are not simply singers. They are pop stars. And I now turn to the ways in which stars not only generate musical meaning but also operate as lucrative trademarks to maintain sales for the culture industries.

The star system and gendering meaning

Ultimately it is stars – not songs or even records – who are the most fascinating commodities produced by the music business. In his pioneering work on film stars, Richard Dyer (1982; 1991) makes the point that the construction of a star's image incorporates representations of him or her across a vast range of media and contexts, to the extent that the appearance of a star in a film has a signifying function that goes well beyond the character they play. These arguments have been developed in discussions of pop stardom. For instance, Longhurst (1995: 185) suggests that 'a new record by Madonna may be seen in the context of the various meanings of Madonna, and not as, for example, another dance or disco hit'.

Record company marketing strategies have long depended on the creation of performers who can guarantee sales to manage the uncertainties posed by over production discussed earlier. For instance, it has been argued that 'the importance of stars for *all* sales means that papers will publicize them as much as they can, radio stations play their latest records as soon and as often as possible, magazines litter their pages with their pictures' (Frith, 1983: 135, emphasis in original). Moreover, the star system lay behind the development of a rock aristocracy in the 1960s, who were then able to redefine the commercial terms of music making. This process has been described in the following way:

> Rock musicians, in response to what they saw as the increasing commercialization of music during the 1960s, sought to distinguish themselves from this trend by emphasizing the internal convictions of the *artist* as opposed to the external trappings of style. In opposing stylistic manipulation, musicians returned to 'sincerity', a previous criterion of the star, manifested by a commitment to counterculture values and the themes of nineteenth-century romanticism, from the communication of higher spiritual values like 'love' (Shelley, Donovan, Jefferson Airplane) to the exaltation of decadence (Baudelaire, Velvet Underground, the Doors).
>
> (Buxton, 1983: 436–7, emphasis in original)

Although this is quite a romantic reading of the motives of late 1960s rock stars, it does illustrate how one of the key qualities of stardom, 'sincerity', was sought in order to legitimize the public identity of the artist in response to changing aesthetic and cultural contexts. Other defining adjectives include 'genuine', 'integrity', 'real', 'direct', 'spontaneous' and 'immediate', which taken together suggest that authenticity is the key dynamic making the star phenomenon work (Dyer, 1991). Although it is important to emphasize that audiences are acutely aware of the ways in which artists are packaged as commodities, the central irony is that 'in the very same breath as audiences and producers alike acknowledge stars as hype, they are declaring this or that star as the genuine article' (ibid.: 70).

For some commentators, the boom in dance music in Britain since the late 1980s has powerfully challenged the dominance of the mainstream recording industry in important ways. It is often said, for example, that the lack of a star system within dance music offers a politics of anonymity that enables 'the music itself' to speak rather than the 'image' of a performer, while the use of digital technologies has democratized music making and made possible the rise of the 'bedroom studio' (Hesmondhalgh, 1998). In fact, this apparent lack of concern with authorship reveals much about how meanings are organized within genres. Will Straw (1991) has argued that dance music cultures have always been less troubled by issues over performer identity than other music cultures, such as alternative rock (which enshrines specific forms of connoisseurship of a relatively stable rock canon as vital to participating in the culture). This lack of interest among dance audiences for such rockist values as authenticity, sincerity and integrity reflects a preference for other qualities such as immediacy and sensuality, but also a pleasure in secrecy and obscurity, which began with Northern Soul enthusiasts in the 1970s and continues in 'post-house dance music' where the highest degree of credibility is attached to the 'white label' 12-inch vinyl single – a record devoid of any details over who actually made it (Hesmondhalgh, 1998: 238; see also Straw, 2002; Huq, 2002).

Nevertheless, Hesmondhalgh (1998) has identified a number of features of the British dance music industry that caution against characterizing it as a radical challenge to dominant culture industry practices. First, the dance music industries rely heavily on the success of crossover hits and compilation albums, which are usually sold on the basis of a sub-genre or connected to a well-known DJ. For instance, Rupa Huq (2002: 97) argues that magazines like 'Muzik, Mixmag and Ministry, implicitly aimed at men, contain lifestyle articles and personal profiles on 'name' DJs alongside articles of a more technical nature for the aspiring bedroom DJ'. Second, the close ties between the independents and their corporate partners through a range of distribution, licensing, financing and ownership deals during the 1990s suggest that the majors have acted quickly and flexibly to incorporate the subcultural credibility of independents into their operations. Third, the more established sections of dance music industry are keen to see the development of a star system in order to deal with the inherent risks in the business. For instance, over the last decade or so many dance music acts have become 'serious' album artists and have taken on the industrial trappings of rock acts, while the development of brand names for the packaging of compilations has steadily diluted the politics of anonymity associated with dance culture.

Another significant approach is to examine the historical development of particular cultural forms and how they construct meanings. One influential account of this kind of textual analysis is Simon Frith and Angela McRobbie's article on 'Rock and Sexuality', which was written in 1978 (reprinted in Frith and McRobbie, 1990). They argue that rock music cannot be analysed as either simply a product of the culture industry or as a form of consumption by different audience groups, such as the young. Instead they propose that rock's meanings, especially in the construction and representation of sexuality, are more complex than these general accounts allow. Their suggestion is that the male domination of the music industry leads to very particular representations of masculinity in contemporary pop music. They identify two main types of pop music, which they label 'cock rock' and 'teenybop'. Cock rock is defined as music making which displays an explicit, raw and often aggressive expression of male sexuality, whereas teenybop is consumed mainly by girls, and the idol's image is based on vulnerability, self-pity and need.

Their argument is that these textual and performance types connect to different audiences. Boys, as the main consumers of cock rock, are active. They attempt to follow guitar-playing idols by forming bands and collectively go to rock concerts. In contrast, the female fans of the teenybopper are relatively passive and consume as individuals through forms of 'bedroom culture': 'as the music to which girls wash their hair, practise makeup, and daydream' (Frith and McRobbie, 1978: 381). While they did recognize that teenybop idols can be used in different ways by girl audiences as a form of collective appropriation and resistance to school norms, Frith (1985) was quick to acknowledge the problems in their argument. In particular, he concedes that they 'confused issues of sex' with 'issues of gender' (ibid.: 420) and while the distinctions drawn between teenybop and cock rock now seem rather crude, the assumptions that underpin them continue to inform popular music practice. Boyzone and Oasis, for instance, gained much of their cultural currency from these styles of presentation in the mid-1990s, while the *Pop Idol* formula trades on the audience's identification with a future 'star' in the manufacturing process.

Sheila Whiteley (2000), in her discussion of the Spice Girls, also notes some important continuities in the packaging of the group with earlier teenybop idols, but contends that they also did much to shape and construct for their pre-teen and teenage fans an understanding of difference in a multicultural Britain. It was highly significant that each of the Girls had a different image and distinct personality, which contributed to the impression that brash individuality rather than blank conformity could be achieved in a group setting. While many dismissed 'girl power' as 'cartoon feminism', she concludes that they did make 'a difference, not least in being the first mixed-race all-girl vocal group to front the tensions between individuality and collective identity that are intrinsic to both 1990s' feminism and pop music' (ibid.: 227). In contrast, Steven Miles (1998: 123) argues that the Spice Girls phenomenon resulted from a slick combination of relentless marketing, catchy tunes and overt sexuality so that girl power ultimately justifies the continuing 'commodification of female sexuality and the prioritization of image over substance'. What these issues of meaning pose, perhaps more than anything else, is that they cannot be divorced from questions of audience interpretation and it is to such matters that I now turn.

Audience

The Birmingham Centre and the subcultural tradition

Up until recently studies of popular music audiences have overwhelmingly concentrated on youth subcultures. Of course, the fact that the music itself has been targeted at the youth market since the 1950s suggests that there are strong historical reasons for this. Moreover, for many, the defining feature of popular music lies in its radical potential to articulate youthful rebellion against authority figures. Whether this focus on youth remains the most fruitful for future research on popular music audiences will be discussed below. Nevertheless, it is important to emphasize that the key resource for subcultural accounts of popular music has been the work associated with the Centre for Contemporary Cultural Studies (CCCS) at the University of

Birmingham in the 1970s. For theorists working at the CCCS, the music and style of the various spectacular youth subcultures, such as teddy boys, mods, rockers, skinheads and punks, signified fractions of working-class resistance to the structural changes occurring in post-war Britain. In particular, a Gramscian understanding of class domination and opposition is mobilized in an effort to assess whether subordinate groups are incorporated into the dominant ideology.

Phil Cohen's (1972) article was an early instance of this work and proved to be a highly influential account of the emergence of 'mods' and 'skinheads' in the East End of London during the 1960s, as he offered a distinctive class analysis of the destruction of working-class community as a consequence of economic changes that were drastically restructuring social relations in the area. The Birmingham Centre refined this approach by explicitly drawing on Gramsci's (1971) work to locate subcultures not just in relation to parent cultures, but in a fully theorized understanding of class conflict. The conceptual framework is detailed in the chapter 'Subcultures, cultures and class' (Clarke et al., 1976) from the collection *Resistance through Rituals* (Hall and Jefferson, 1976). The various post-war working-class youth subcultures discussed in the book are seen as movements that win back space, through issuing challenges to the status quo. However, these are not political solutions. Resistance is played out in the fields of leisure and consumption, rather than in the workplace. For Clarke et al. (1976), a key consequence of resistance through rituals and symbols is that they ultimately fail to challenge the broader structures of power. However, few of the essays in the collection explicitly address how music is used by subcultures, partly because the concept itself has its roots in the sociology of deviance and studies of youth delinquency. Instead the most detailed accounts from the Birmingham Centre on this question can be found in the work of Paul Willis (1978) and Dick Hebdige (1979).

In Paul Willis's (1978) study of hippies and motor-bike boys in his book, *Profane Culture*, he develops a class-based analysis of popular music's social significance. He interprets the different ways music is used by working-class motorcycle boys and middle-class hippies in terms of their contrasting structural locations. In constructing these arguments he draws on the anthropologist Claude Lévi-Strauss's (1966) concept of homology to describe the symbolic fit between the values and life-styles of a group, its subjective experiences and the musical forms it uses to express its primary concerns. What he demonstrates is that, contrary to popular images, which present subcultures as lawless mobs, the internal structure of any subculture is characterized by extreme orderliness. The key implication is that subcultures are structured so that different aspects of the lifestyle fit together to form a whole. For example, he argues that it was no accident that the motor-bike boys liked early rock 'n' roll singles, whereas the hippies preferred album-based progressive rock. Rock 'n' roll music matched the restlessness and mobility of the motor-bike boys. In contrast, there is a different homology in the hippie subculture, which is expressed in the fit between an alternative value system, hallucinogenic drugs and progressive rock albums.

Dick Hebdige's (1979) *Subculture: The Meaning of Style* is essentially a textual reading of various post-war youth subcultures using the methods of structuralism and semiotics to account for the meanings of youth style. For instance, he uses Barthes's (1977a) discussion, 'The rhetoric of the image' to analyse the meaning of style. In this essay, Barthes draws a contrast between the 'intentional' advertising image and the apparently 'innocent' news photograph. Both are, in fact, complex articulations of specific codes and practices, but the news photo appears more 'natural' and less loaded than an advertisement. Hebdige (1979: 100–1) uses this distinction to point out the difference between subcultural and normal styles. For example, the conventional outfits worn by the 'average man and woman in the street' contain a whole range of messages that display such matters as class, status, and so forth. But the crucial point is that they appear natural or normal in contrast to the spectacular subcultural styles. Moreover, these are obviously fabricated and display their own codes, for example, the punk's ripped t-shirt demonstrates that such matters have been thought about rather than just thrown together. In this they go against the grain of the mainstream culture. Hebdige (ibid.: 102) argues that the 'point' of all the spectacular subcultural styles is to communicate difference from the mainstream while sustaining a common group identity.

One especially important defining feature of subcultural groups, which distinguishes them from other cultural formations, is the way in which commodities are used. They are all cultures of conspicuous consumption. Hebdige uses the anthropological concept of bricolage to indicate how various commodities are subverted through processes of improvisation and innovation. For example, he indicates how the Mods transformed the motor scooter from an ultra-respectable means of transport into a menacing symbol of group solidarity. In the same manner of improvisation, Union Jacks were cut up and turned into tailored jackets, or put in the back of parkas. Nevertheless, while Hebdige argues that subcultures resist the dominant order, they do so only indirectly. Often, however, forms of subcultural expression are incorporated back into the dominant social order through two main routes. First, there is the 'commodity form', which involves the 'conversion of subcultural signs (dress, music, etc.) into mass-produced objects' (ibid.: 94). It is the means by which 'the Other can be trivialized, naturalized, domesticated' or 'transformed into meaningless exotica' (ibid.: 97). Second, there is the 'ideological form' of incorporation through 'the "labelling" and re-definition of deviant behaviour by dominant groups – the police, media, the judiciary' (Hebdige, 1979: 94), which involves the social control of subcultural groups.

Although difficulties in the CCCS approach were quickly realized, it is important to emphasize that it has cast an influential spell over subsequent work in the field. Much of the writing on rave culture, for instance, in the 1990s clearly remained committed to analysing the more spectacular dimensions of youth consumption and to use this as the means of commenting on the situation of young people in general (see, for example, Melechi, 1993). Nevertheless, an early and very useful critique is contained in Gary Clarke's (1981) discussion, in which three specific problems are identified. First, there is no consideration of the dynamic nature of subcultural membership as 'we are given little sense of what subcultures actually *do*, and we do not know whether their commitment is fulltime or just, say, a weekend phenomenon'.

Second, the theory rests on the assumption that the rest of society is 'straight' and 'incorporated in a consensus'. Third, the analysis elevates 'a vague concept of style to the status of an objective category' (Clarke, 1981: 178). These are formidable criticisms and there is a clear sense that what troubles Clarke is the elitism of subcultural theory. By setting up a distinction between an active subculture and a passive mainstream, the practices of the vast majority of people who actually listen to popular music are dismissed with a condescension that recalls Adorno's more disparaging comments. Moreover, as others pointed out, the constant preoccupation with class meant that gender and ethnicity were effectively ignored in the subcultural tradition.

Contesting traditions

The almost exclusive focus on white working-class young men was first challenged from within the CCCS approach by Angela McRobbie and Jenny Garber (1976). In this paper they argued that because girls are subjected to much stricter parental control of their leisure time they have developed alternative strategies of winning back space through the bedroom-centred teenybopper culture. Subcultural theorists had completely ignored the consumption of music in the home, preferring the action of the street to the tedium of everyday life. Angela McRobbie (1980) subsequently developed an influential feminist critique of subcultural theory for its uncritical masculine agenda and persuasively maintained that

> while the sociologies of deviance and youth were blooming in the early seventies, the sociology of the family was everybody's least favourite option … No commentary on the hippies dealt with the countercultural sexual division of labor, let alone the hypocrisies of 'free love'; few writers seemed interested in what happened when a mod went home after a weekend on speed.
>
> (ibid.: 68–9)

In her later work on the sexual politics of dance, she argued that dancing 'carries enormously pleasurable qualities for girls and women which frequently seem to suggest a displaced, shared and nebulous eroticism rather than a straightforwardly romantic, heavily heterosexual "goal-orientated drive"' (McRobbie, 1984: 134). She has also discussed the opportunities rave culture has afforded young women for creating new identities as well as examining the place of popular music in magazines aimed at young girls, like *Just Seventeen*, in relation to debates on postmodernism (McRobbie, 1994). Her overall approach is driven by the insistence that the cultural life of young women is structured in different ways from that of boys and thereby raises the crucial point that gender divisions mediate the consumption and meaning of popular music.

While it is fair to say that gender issues had been marginalized in the CCCS approach to subcultural theory, considerations of 'race' did occupy an important place in the Centre's work.[5] For instance, Hebdige (1979: 45) was keenly aware that across 'the loaded surfaces of British working-class youth cultures, a phantom history of race relations since the War' has been played out. Paul Gilroy (1987) has developed some of the

CCCS themes to explore the relationships between race and class in contemporary Britain and includes an extensive discussion of how black music contributes to a cultural diaspora. As he puts it, the task is 'to suggest why Afrika Bambaataa and Jah Shaka, leading representatives of hip-hop and reggae culture respectively, find it appropriate to take the names of African chiefs distinguished in anti-colonial struggle, or why young black people in places as different as Hayes and Harlem choose to style themselves the Zulu Nation' (Gilroy, 1987: 156). In Gilroy's (1993) later work he examines how the *Black Atlantic*, his term for the African diaspora, binds together the black people of Africa, the Americas, the Caribbean and Europe in a long history of intercultural connection to develop an alternative account of modernity.

Gilroy's arguments have also been taken up by scholars concerned with how new forms of cultural identity are sustained in metropolitan contexts. One influential study is Steve Jones's (1988) discussion of *Black Youth, White Culture*, which contains a rich ethnography of young people's identity formation in Birmingham. Particularly significant is the way in which reggae provides a site where dialogues between black and white youth can occur. He argues that:

> They are visible everywhere in a whole range of cross-racial affiliations and shared leisure spaces; on the streets, around the games machine, in the local chip shop, in the playgrounds and parks, right through the mixed rock and reggae groups for which the area has become renowned.

> (ibid.: xiv).

More recently Les Back (1996) has analysed how new identities are emerging within hybrid forms of musical and cultural expression. Especially important to his argument is the development of London's jungle scene as he explains that:

> Jungle demonstrates a diaspora sensitivity that renders explicit the Jamaican traces within hip hop culture along with a radical realignment of national images. Black, white and Asian junglists all claim that the music uniquely belongs to Britain, or more specifically that jungle is a 'a London somet'ing' ... The nascent patriotism found in jungle is all the more surprising given that the genesis of the scene was in some part due to a hardening of racism within rave, combined with a racially exclusive door policy in London clubs.

> (ibid.: 234).

Clearly much of this work continues to be influenced by the CCCS subcultural approach, albeit through the lens of multicultural politics. Others, however, have been much more critical of the Centre's overall thinking.

Sarah Thornton's (1995: 8) case study of British rave clubs in the late 1980s and early 1990s is an explicit attempt to offer a 'post-Birmingham' analysis of youth culture in a number of important ways. Her definition of club cultures is based on the understanding that clubbers form specific 'taste cultures', which enables her to examine the role of 'distinction' in three spheres: 'the authentic versus the phoney, the "hip" versus the "mainstream", and the "underground" versus the "media"' (Thornton, 1995: 3–4). Her arguments build on Bourdieu's (1986) discussion of the relationships between taste and social structure and she influentially argues that club cultures trade in 'subcultural capital' in which 'hipness' is the key commodity. In doing so she moves beyond a simple division between mainstream incorporation and subcultural resistance. For while vague opposition might be how many members of youth subcultures characterize their own activities, she cautions against taking youthful discourses at face value as subcultural ideologies are not innocent accounts of the way things really are. Instead they are ways of imagining what their own and other social groups are like.

The performance of distinctions serves to mark out cultural hierarchies and can be an alibi for subordination. It is no coincidence that the terms used by clubbers to denigrate the mainstream are highly gendered, such as 'Techno Tracy' and 'Handbag House'. She further insists that these terms should not 'be confused with actual dance culture of working class girls' as the 'distinction reveals more about the cultural values and social world of hardcore clubbers' (Thornton, 1997: 205) and she goes on to quote Bourdieu's (1990: 132) point that 'nothing classifies somebody more than the way he or she classifies. These activities suggest that what is at stake is a more conformist jockeying for status rather than any alternative gestures of defiance and the continuing salience of class and gender in young people's lives.

Another study of popular music audiences that marks a break with the CCCS approach is Wendy Fonarow's (1996; 1997) analysis of the spatial distribution of indie gigs. Her work combines the Chicago School's sociology through examining the spatial zoning at well-attended concerts with Erving Goffman's (1963) attentiveness to conduct in public places through revealing how social interactions and spatial distribution are regulated by age. She identifies three zones that regularly appear. Zone one is 'the pit'. It is the area closest to the stage and is the most densely packed where diving from the stage and other forms of immediately frantic action like 'pogoing, slamming, moshing, and the shaking of heads' take place (Fonarow, 1997: 361). In this zone are the youngest members of the audience – their ages ranging from about 14 to 21. The second zone begins a quarter of the way back into the venue and extends to the back of the floor area. It is the most static. Here fandom is expressed through 'aural connoisseurship and the undivided attention given to the performers' (1997: 366). The third zone is at the back of the venue and is normally where the bar is. It is not only the place where participants move to if they do not like the band but it is also the domain of music industry professionals (agents, managers, journalists, promoters, musicians and record company staff).

Fonarow's argument is that individuals in each zone claim that their own location is the best and deride other zones. For instance, even though professionals[6] are at the furthest spatial distance, their social proximity means that they 'privilege their spectatorship over that of the "punters", the paying customers, through their access to the band' (1997: 367) whereas the young fans in zone one would claim they have a greater emotional connection while regarding the other areas as boring and lacking atmosphere. Her work importantly demonstrates how music audiences are not homogenous, in the subcultural sense, but are instead a 'body of organized and contested spectatorships' (ibid.: 368). While both Fonarow and Thornton offer important advances over the CCCS approach, there is a significant sense in which they remain committed to analysing the more spectacular dimensions of popular music consumption, especially among the young.

In recent years there are signs of an increasing dissatisfaction with the neglect of the 'ordinary' and continuing obsession with youth culture. For instance, Hesmondhalgh (2002) convincingly argues that a youth-centred approach has long outlived its usefulness, but can only single out three studies that attempt to connect music consumption to the rhythms of everyday life. These are Crafts et al.'s (1993) collection of interview transcripts in *My Music;* DeNora's (2000) account of how music is a device of social ordering in *Music and Everyday Life;* and Bull's (2000) discussion of Walkmans and the aestheticization of urban experience in *Sounding Out the City.* Likewise, Carrabine and Longhurst (2002) have argued that it is the dynamic between the ordinary and extraordinary that demands attention in future research on consumption in everyday life to overcome partial and selective accounts of cultural practice.

Some of these issues are addressed in Andy Bennett's and Keith Kahn-Harris's (2004) edited collection *After Subculture,* but as the subtitle indicates, *Critical Studies in Contemporary Youth Culture,* the focus remains on the young and thus ignores the ways in which popular music is consumed outside of youth cultural practice. In addition, there remains a 'continuing assumption that a girl or a boy with an ostentatiously pierced body is being more "resistant" to dominant culture than if they were, say, to join a radical political organization or even, come to that, a choir' (Frith, 2004: 176). Clearly the subcultural terrain is in need of greater revision than has thus far been attempted. While recent ethnographic accounts of music audiences can offer sophisticated hermeneutic modes of interpretation, this tends to be at the expense of situating the findings in a broader context of material relations of power. In important respects, these difficulties echo the problems already discussed in relation to the conflicts between cultural studies and political economy approaches to culture.

Conclusion

This chapter has outlined a number of different approaches in the cultural analysis of popular music. Inevitably it has barely scratched the surface of what is a dynamic and lively area of study. However, as will now be obvious, writers have tended to concentrate on specific aspects of music production, textual meaning or subcultural consumption at the expense of a detailed consideration of the relationships between them. This 'production–text–consumption' framework is now regarded as the definitive basis of organizing the literature and versions of it can be found in most recent discussions of the material (Longhurst, 1995; Negus, 1996; Shuker, 2001). For instance, it has been argued that 'popular music texts can be analyzed as institutionally produced commercial commodities that function as cultural artefacts inscribed with meanings which are then consumed and interpreted by fans and audiences'

(Herman et al., 1998: 4). Nevertheless, problems remain over how these three domains of analysis might be integrated. It is still the case that while most authors in the field acknowledge that production and consumption are interrelated, far fewer have attempted to fully theorize the complex processes condensed under these terms and consider how they might be related.

Much of the textbook commentary implies that the various approaches can be simply bolted together to form a satisfactory resolution of the problem. However, as this chapter has indicated, there are intense disagreements and fundamental differences over how the same domain ought to be approached that undermines any crude synthesis of incompatible positions. Nevertheless, there are sufficient points of convergence that can open up a space for dialogue between competing positions. Two important studies that do attempt to draw together the different traditions are Goodwin's (1993) study of MTV and du Gay et al.'s (1997) account of the Sony Walkman – though crucially the two accounts restrict themselves to analysing a distinctive medium as a window to explore the complexities of cultural practice. Ultimately, few would doubt that the sounds, styles and images surrounding popular music need to be situated in historical and economic context. Of course, the difficulties lie not in keeping production, text and consumption artificially distinct, but by bringing them together in a convincing synthesis that recognizes that neither a focus on micro-processes of consumption and everyday life – or macro-contexts of production and institutional analysis – is likely to capture, on their own, the rich meanings generated by popular music. It is to such matters of integration that future work in cultural theory might best be directed.

Notes

1   An example of this is provided by Costello himself on the voluminous liner notes to a recent CD reissue of his *Get Happy!!* (1980/2003) album where he explains that the track 'Black and White World' drew upon 'the narrative style of a Ray Davies song while the final recording was based on a Pete Thomas drum pattern which owed something to the style of Little Feat employed on "Cold, Cold, Cold"'. This revelation led one reviewer to complain that such detail 'adds nothing to the pure enjoyment of the song while taking plenty away' (Wilde, 2003: 133).

2   Simon Frith is rather overstating Benjamin's impact here. Arguably, Gramsci (1971) has had a much greater influence on studies of youth subcultures (Carrabine and Longhurst, 1999: 126–7). Nevertheless, the debate between Adorno and Benjamin continues to be a major influence on cultural theory more generally.

3   The six major companies are Bertelsmann Group (BMG), EMI Music, MCA Music Entertainment, PlayGram Records, Sony Music Entertainment and Warner Music (McDonald, 1999: 94). Each of these companies are parts of other larger multinational companies with headquarter bases in Britain (EMI), Germany (BMG), Japan (MCA and Sony), the Netherlands (PolyGram) and the United States (Warner). Up until the Time–Warner merger in 1989, the Bertelsmann Group which, although maintaining a low corporate profile, was the largest media conglomerate (Negus, 1992: 2). Recent years have seen increased rumours of mergers and acquisitions in the entertainment industry in response to fears over digital piracy (from CD copying and Internet file sharing), the virtual collapse of single sales and supermarkets offering substantial discounts on a narrow range of chart and MOR albums. By

1996, 'the term "Asda artist" was coined to describe titanic product-shifters such as Mariah Carey and the Lighthouse Family' by industry insiders who 'were encouraged to sign only the most conservative, supermarket-friendly acts' (Cavanagh, 2001: 683). However, figures released by the British Phonographic Industry indicate that sales for albums hit a peak of 228.3 million at the end of June 2003 – almost 3 percent up on 2002 and marks the fifth consecutive year that album sales have topped 200 million in the UK (http://www.guardian. co.uk/arts/netmusic/story/0,13368,1020971,00.html, accessed 24 September 2003). Clearly, the continuing success of album sales challenges the industry's bleak picture of the digital age and illustrates their continuing ignorance of how records are actually used. Like the home tapers in the 1970s and 1980s, the present-day 'CD burners' are more often than not fans who circulate illegal copies among a small network of enthusiasts. This constituency then go on to buy more albums than anyone else!

4 The biggest fear is 'not that any particular record won't sell but that *none* of their releases will hit' (Frith, 1983: 102, emphasis in original).

5 The collectively authored *Policing the Crisis* (Hall et al., 1978) is the most wide-ranging discussion as it explores the moral panic that developed in Britain in the early 1970s over the phenomenon of mugging and it demonstrates how black youth became a scapegoat for all the social anxieties produced by the changes to an affluent, but destabilized society.

6 Fonarow (1996, 1997) gives a number of insights into the complex and hierarchical system of status markers at the gigs for industry personnel. For instance, there is an elaborate system of guest passes (guest, after party, photo, all access, and laminate), each with different levels of access and prestige. Moreover, where one places a pass is also a marker of status – 'overt pass display is considered a sign of a novice', while professionals will 'discreetly place passes on the inside of a jacket or in a back pocket' (Fonarow, 1997: 367).

References

Adorno, T. ([1941] 1990) 'On popular music', in S. Frith and A. Goodwin (eds) *On Record*. London: Routledge.

Adorno, T. (1976) *Introduction to the Sociology of Music*. New York: Seabury Press.

Adorno, T. (1991) *The Culture Industry: Selected Essays on Mass Culture*, London: Routledge

Back, L. (1996) *New Ethnicities and Urban Culture: Racisms and Multiculture in Young Lives*. London: UCL Press.

Barthes, R. (1957/1993) *Mythologies*, London: Village.

Barthes, R. (1977a) *Image–Music–Text*. London: Fontana.

Barthes, R. ([1977b] 1990) 'The grain of the voice', in S. Frith and A. Goodwin (eds) *On Record*. London: Routledge.

Becker, H. (1963) *Outsiders: Studies in the Sociology of Deviance*. New York: Free Press.

Becker, H. (1982) *Art Worlds*. Berkeley, CA: University of California Press.

Benjamin, W. ([1936] 1973) 'The work of art in the age of Mechanical Reproduction', in *Illuminations*. London: Fontana.

Bennett, A. and Kahn-Harris, K. (2004) *After Subculture: Critical Studies in Contemporary Youth Culture*. Basingstoke: Palgrave Macmillan.

Born, G. (1993) 'Against negation, for a politics of cultural production: Adorno, aesthetics, the social', *Screen*, 34 (3), 223–42.

Born, G. (1995) *Rationalizing Culture*. Berkeley, CA: University of California Press.

Bourdieu, P. (1986) *Distinction: A Social Critique of the Social Judgement of Taste*. London: Routledge.

Bourdieu, P. (1990) *In Other Words: Essays Towards a Reflexive Sociology*. Cambridge: Polity.

Bourdieu, P. (1993a) *The Field of Cultural Production*. Cambridge: Polity.

Bourdieu, P. ([1993b] 2003) 'But who created the creators', in J. Tanner, (ed.) *The Sociology of Art: A Reader*. London: Routledge.

Bourdieu, P. (1996) *The Rules of Art*. Cambridge: Polity.

Brackett, D. (2002) '(In search of) musical meaning: genres, categories and crossover', in D. Hesmondhalgh and K. Negus (eds) *Popular Music Studies*. London: Arnold.

Bull, M. (2000) *Sounding Out the City*. Oxford: Berg.

Buxton, D. (1983) 'Rock music, the star system, and the rise of consumerism', in S. Frith and A. Goodwin (eds) *On Record*. London: Routledge.

Carrabine, E. and Longhurst, B. (1999) 'Mosaics of omnivorousness: suburban youth and popular music', *New Formations,* 38: 125–40.

Carrabine, E. and Longhurst, B. (2002) 'Consuming the car: anticipation, use and meaning in contemporary youth culture', *Sociological Review,* 50 (2): 181–96.

Cavanagh, D. (2001) *The Creation Records Story: My Magpie Eyes are Hungry for the Prize*. London: Virgin.

Chapple, S. and Garafalo, R. (1977) *Rock 'n' Roll is Here to Pay: The History and Politics of the Music Industry*. Chicago: Nelson Hall.

Clarke, G. ([1981]1997) 'Defending ski-jumpers: a critique of theories of youth subcultures', in K. Gelder and S. Thornton (eds) *The Subcultures Reader*. London: Routledge.

Clarke, J., Hall, S. Jefferson, T. and Roberts, B. (1976) 'Subcultures, cultures and class', in S. Hall and T. Jefferson (eds) *Resistance through Rituals: Youth Subcultures in Post-war Britain*. London: Routledge.

Cohen, P. (1972) 'Subcultural conflict and working class community', *Working Papers in Cultural Studies,* 2, Spring: 5–52.

Crafts, S., Cavicchi, D. Keil, C. and the Music in Daily Life Project (1993) *My Music*. London: Wesleyan University Press.

DeNora, T. (2000) *Music in Every Life*. Cambridge: Cambridge University Press.

Derrida, J. (1976) *Of Grammatology*. Baltimore, MD: Johns Hopkins University Press.

Du Gay, P., Hall, S., Janes, L., Mackay, H. and Negus, K. (1997) *Doing Cultural Studies: The Story of the Sony Walkman*. London: Sage.

Dyer, R. (1982) *Stars*. London: British Film Institute.

Dyer, R. (1991) 'A star is born and the construction of authenticity', in C. Gledhill (ed.) *Stardom: Industry of Desire*. London: Routledge.

Eliot, M. (1989) *Rockonomics: The Money Behind the Music*. New York: Franklin Watts.

Fonarow, W. (1996) 'Spatial distribution and participation in British contemporary musical performances', *Issues in Applied Linguistics,* 7 (1): 33–43.

Fonarow, W. (1997) 'The spatial organization of the indie music gig', in K. Gelder and S. Thornton (eds) *The Subcultures Reader*. London: Routledge.

Frith, S. (1983) *Sound Effects: Youth, Leisure and the Politics of Rock*. London: Constable.

Frith, S. ([1985] 1990) 'Afterthoughts', in S. Frith and A. Goodwin (eds) *On Record*. London: Routledge.

Frith, S. (1988) 'Why Do Songs Have Words', in *Music for Pleasure: Essays in the Sociology of Pop,* Cambridge: Polity.

Frith, S. (1996) *Performing Rites: On the Value of Popular Music*. Cambridge, MA: Harvard University Press.

Frith, S. (2004) 'Afterword', in A. Bennett and K. Kahn-Harris *After Subculture: Critical Studies in Contemporary Youth Culture*. Basingstoke: Palgrave Macmillan.

Frith, S. and McRobbie, A. ([1978] 1990) 'Rock and sexuality', in S. Frith and A. Goodwin (eds) *On Record*. London: Routledge.

Garnham, N. (1990) 'Public policy and the culture industries', in *Capitalism and Communication: Global Culture and the Economics of Communication*. London: Sage.

Gendron, B. (1986) 'Theodor Adorno meets the cadillacs', in T. Modleski (ed.) *Studies in Entertainment: Critical Approaches to Mass Culture*. Bloomington: Indiana University Press.

George, N. (1988) *The Death of Rhythm and Blues*. London: Omnibus Press.

Gilroy, P. (1987) *There Ain't No Black in the Union Jack*. London: Hutchinson

Gilroy, P. (1993) *The Black Atlantic: Modernity and Double Consciousness*. London: Verso.

Goddard, S. (2002) *The Smiths: Songs That Saved Your Life*. London: Reynolds and Hearn Ltd.

Goffman, E. (1963) *Behavior in Public Places*. New York: Free Press.

Goodman, F. (1997) *The Mansion on the Hill: Dylan, Young, Geffen, Springsteen and the Head-On Collision of Rock and Commerce*. New York: Time Books.

Goodwin, A. (1993) *Dancing in the Distraction Factory: Music Television and Popular Culture*. London: Routledge.

Gramsci, A. (1971) *Selections from the Prison Notebooks*. London: Lawrence and Wishart.

Hall, S. and Jefferson, T. (eds) (1976) *Resistance Through Rituals: Youth Sub-Cultures in Post-War Britain*. London: Hutchinson.

Hall, S. Critcher, C., Jefferson, T., Clarke, J. and Roberts, R. (1978) *Policing the Crisis: Mugging, the State and Law and Order*, London: Macmillan.

Harker, D. (1980) *One for the Money: Politics and Popular Music*. London: Hutchinson.

Harker, D. (1997) 'The wonderful world of IFPI: music industry rhetoric, the critics and the classical Marxist critique', *Popular Music*, 16 (1): 45–79.

Hebdige, D. (1979) *Subculture: The Meaning of Style*. London: Methven.

Herman, A., Swiss, T. and Sloop, J. (1998) 'Mapping the beat: spaces of noise and places of music', in T. Swiss, J. Sloop and A. Herman (eds) *Mapping the Beat: Popular Music and Contemporary Theory*. Oxford: Blackwell.

Hesmondhalgh, D. (1998) 'The British dance music industry: a case study of independent cultural production', *British Journal of Sociology*. 49 (2): 234–51.

Hesmondhalgh, D. (1999) 'Indie: the institutional politics and aesthetics of a popular music genre', *Cultural Studies*, 13(1): 34–61.

Hesmondhalgh, D. (2002) 'Popular music audiences and everyday life', in D. Hesmondhalgh and K. Negus (eds) *Popular Music Studies*. London: Arnold.

Hesmondhalgh, D. and Negus K. (eds) (2002) *Popular Music Studies*. London: Arnold.

Huq, R. (2002) 'Raving not drowning: authenticity, pleasure and politics in the electronic dance scene', in D. Hesmondhalgh and K. Negus (eds) *Popular Music Studies*. London: Arnold.

Jones, S. (1988) *Black Youth, White Culture: The Reggae Tradition from JA to UK*. London: Macmillan.

Klein, N. (2000) *No Logo*. London: Flamingo.

Lévi-Strauss, C. (1966) *The Savage Mind*. London: Weidenfield and Nicholson.

Longhurst, B. (1995) *Popular Music and Society*. Cambridge: Polity.

McDonald, P. (1999) 'The music industry', in J. Stokes and A. Reading (eds) *The Media in Britain: Current Debates and Developments*. London: Macmillan.

McRobbie, A. ([1980] 1990) 'Settling accounts with subcultures: a feminist critique', in S. Frith and A. Goodwin (eds) *On Record*. London: Routledge.

McRobbie, A. (1984) 'Dance and social fantasy', in A. McRobbie and M. Nava (eds) *Gender and Generation*. London: Macmillan.

McRobbie, A. (1994) *Postmodernism and Popular Culture*. London: Routledge.

McRobbie, A. and Garber, J. (1976) 'Girls and subcultures', in S. Hall and T. Jefferson (eds) *Resistance Through Rituals: Youth Sub-cultures in Post-War Britain*. London: Hutchinson.

Melechi, A. (1993) 'The ecstasy of disappearance', in S. Redhead (ed.) *Rave Off: Politics and Deviance in Contemporary Youth Culture*. Aldershot: Avebury.

Miles, S. (1998) *Consumerism – as a Way of Life*. London: Sage.

Mulholland, G. (2002) *This is Uncool: The 500 Greatest Singles since Punk and Disco*. London: Cassell Illustrated.

Negus, K. (1992) *Producing Pop: Culture and Conflict in the Popular Music Industry*. London: Arnold.

Negus, K. (1996) *Popular Music in Theory*. Cambridge: Polity.

Negus, K. (1999) *Music Genres and Corporate Cultures*. London: Routledge.

Paddison, M. (1993) *Adorno's Aesthetics of Music*. Cambridge: Cambridge University Press.

Rose, T. (1994) *Black Noise: Rap Music and Black Culture in Contemporary America*. Hanover: Wesleyan University Press.

Shuker, R. (2001) *Understanding Popular Music*. London: Routledge.

Straw, W. (1991) 'Systems of articulation, logics of change: communities and scenes in popular music' *Cultural Studies*, 5 (3): 368–88.

Straw, W. (2002) 'Value and velocity: the 12-inch single as medium and artefact', in D. Hesmondhalgh and K. Negus (eds) *Popular Music Studies*. London: Arnold.

Tanner, J. (2003) 'The social production of art', in J. Tanner (ed.) *The Sociology of Art: A Reader.* London: Routledge.

Thornton, S. (1995) *Club Cultures: Music, Media and Subcultural Capital.* Cambridge: Polity Press.

Thornton, S. (1997) 'The social logic of subcultural capital', in K. Gelder, and S. Thornton (eds) *The Subcultures Reader.* London: Routledge.

Toynbee, J. (2000) *Making Popular Music: Musicians, Creativity and Institutions.* London: Arnold.

Van Leeuwen, T. (1999) *Speech, Music and Sound.* Basingstoke: Macmillan.

Wallis, R. and Malm, K. (1984) *Big Sounds from Small Countries.* London: Constable.

Walser, R. (1993) *Running with the Devil.* Hanover: Wesleyan University Press.

Whiteley, S. (2000) *Women and Popular Music: Sexuality, Identity and Subjectivity.* London: Routledge.

Wilde, J. (2003) 'High fidelity', *Uncut,* 77, Oct: 132–3.

Williams (1983) *Keywords: A Vocabulary of Culture and Society,* 2nd edn. London. Fontana.

Willis, P. (1978) *Profane Culture.* London: Routledge and Kegan Paul.

CHAPTER THIRTEEN

Cultural Citizenship

Questions of consumerism, consumption and policy

Nick Stevenson

The idea of 'cultural' citizenship is progressively developing in a field of overlapping concerns that seeks to locate normative values within the cultural sphere. Cultural citizenship's central question is, how does the operation of 'culture' effect notions of justice and 'difference' within a post-modern and post-national world? Typically, these ideas join together notions of corporate and cultural power, the possibility of resistance, the unequal distribution of material and cultural resources and attempts to reconcile questions of community with those of plurality and difference. Cultural citizenship marks out an interdisciplinary area of concern with its main contributors coming from sociology, political theory, cultural studies and geography. These developments arguably bring together previously falsely segregated debates and questions in new and exciting ways. Here I aim to discuss what I shall call a 'common' cultural citizenship in terms of questions of consumerism, consumption and cultural policy. If we are to appreciate the relevance of questions of justice and recognition to the cultural sphere, it is arguably in these contexts such values will need to take hold. While issues of cultural citizenship can be pursued in other ways, these debates have been chosen, given that they connect to some of the central concerns of sociology and cultural studies.

Cultural Citizenship

T.H. Marshall (1949; reprinted in Marshall and Bottomore 1992), as is well known, was concerned with the historical development of civil, political and social rights in the British national context. Marshall drew attention to the contradiction between the formations of capitalism and class, and the principle of equality enshrined within a common citizenship. Such a view of citizenship was hardly surprising, given that Marshall was writing just before the end of the Second World War, a time where identity and social conflicts were dominated by class. The setting up of the welfare state, the possibility of full male employment, the nuclear family, the dominance of the nation-state and the separation between an elite literary culture and a popular mass culture all inform his dimensions of citizenship. More recently a number of writers have sought to rehabilitate notions of citizenship. In this context, citizenship studies have revived a notion of political community set against the economic reductionism of the Left and the market individualism of the Right (Ignatieff 1991). From the 1980s citizenship has provided the focus for a series of debates connecting the role of new social movements (Stevenson 2001), social welfare (Roche 1992), feminism (Lister 1997) and broader questions of social responsibility and obligation (Dahrendorf 1994). Current theorizing in citizenship therefore seeks to remoralise political debates in a way that is critical of rights-based liberalism, New Right market atomism and Left cynicism (Kymlicka and Norman 1994).

The concern here is not only with a politics of the possible, but also with how questions of justice might be pursued within less than favourable conditions. Further, there has also been a growing concern within the literature that notions of citizenship need to be revised due to the impact of cultural questions. Many have argued that Marshall's initial framework poorly appreciates the conflicts of identity and globalising features that are reshaping the operation of citizenship (Turner 1994; Isin and Wood 1999). Claims to citizenship are having to operate in a political context Nancy Fraser (1997) has accurately described as post-socialist. Citizenship has become a progressive force in the face of socialism's collapse as a credible alternative, a resurgent economic liberalism, and the enhanced struggle for recognition and difference on the part of 'minority' communities.

Yet how to achieve wide participation in questions of genuinely communal concern is at the heart of our discussion. As Ruth Lister (1997) argues, Marshall's liberal idea of citizenship needs to be supplemented with a more republican emphasis upon participation within the political process. For Raymond Williams (1962) this was the possibility of achieving a genuinely participative and educative democracy. Cultural citizenship, as opposed to mainstream understanding of citizenship, should be concerned with both having access to certain rights and the opportunity to get your voice heard, in the knowledge that you will have the ear of the community. As Cohen and Arato (1992) argue democracy is maintained through formal institutions and procedures, and through the generation of an active and communicative civil society. Here, rights of communication and dialogue have a necessary priority over all other social and economic rights. That is, whereas Marxism has criticised capitalist societies for instituting mere bourgeois rights and liberalism has sought to remain agnostic in respect of the lifestyle choices of its citizens, a politics based upon a communicative civil society takes us in a different direction. Civil society should 'institutionalise' the everyday practice of democratic communication. A politics of 'cultural' citizenship is concerned with how we might foster free and equal forms of participation within political and cultural processes and institutions. For Habermas (1990) the idea of discourse ethics is based upon the notion that the rightness or the justness of the norms we uphold can only be secured by our ability to give good reasons. In turn, these norms are considered valid if they gain the consent of others within a shared community. The political and cultural question becomes how to promote genuinely cosmopolitan definitions, practices and understandings of public space?

An institutional definition of civil society (usually made up of relatively independent organizations likes churches, trade unions, schools, and the media), however, does not go far enough. Arguably Habermas's analysis of citizenship stops short of an investigation into the ways in which civil society has become historically and culturally constructed. That is, while he correctly emphasises the normative importance of rights for fostering civic solidarity, he understates the cultural dimensions of what he calls a 'cosmopolitan consciousness' (Habermas 2001: 112). It has been the strength of cultural studies and post-structuralism in that they have been able to highlight the ways in which civil society becomes coded through a multiplicity and often antagonistic discourses (Mouffe 1993). Further, that cultural understandings of citizenship are concerned not only with 'formal' processes such as to who is entitled to vote and the maintenance of an active civil society, but with whose cultural practices are included and excluded. That is with who is silenced, marginalized, stereotyped and rendered invisible. As Renato Rosaldo (1999: 260) argues, cultural citizenship is concerned with 'who needs to be visible, to be heard, and to belong'. What becomes defining here is the demand for the recognition of difference and cultural respect. Whereas liberalism commonly recognises that a political community can generate disrespect by forms of practical mistreatment (torture or rape) and by withholding formal rights (civil, political and social), notions of cultural citizenship point to the importance of questions of hierarchy and disrespect. That is, cultural citizenship is concerned with 'the degree of self esteem accorded to his or her manner of self-realisation within a society's inherited cultural horizon' (Honneth 1995: 134). Our question is how to balance claims to justice and recognition in the context of contemporary commercial and public cultures. I now intend to pursue these issues by investigating the ways that consumerism and consumption has sought to rework our understandings of citizenship.

Consumer Culture and the Death of Citizenship

In this section I aim to explore the relationship between consumerism and citizenship. In doing so, I want to build upon and establish a more complex relationship between these terms than currently appears to be available. We need to avoid polarising the debate between two of the perspectives prevalent within the literature. The first is that consumerism merely undermines the practice of citizenship. Such arguments posit that the declining fortunes of Western democracies are tied to a culture of 'contentment' amongst the middle-class population, or that a substantial aesthetic and political culture is currently swamped by synthetic commercialism. The argument here is that practices of democratic engagement have been replaced by visits to shopping malls, channel hopping and the culture of cool interactivity to be found on the web. As we shall see, such views have a certain persuasive logic, but remain blind to the ways in which the practice of citizenship may have changed within contemporary societies. The other view, which I aim to consider here, is that consumerism provides a new basis for the practice of citizenship largely unappreciated by mainstream political parties and more traditional frames of analysis. This view would argue that the popularity of consumerism amongst 'ordinary people' speaks of a popular democratic revolution waiting to happen. Again, such a view opens interesting dimensions into the debate, while being insufficiently appreciative of the ways in which consumer societies undermine the quest for justice. My argument is that we need not make a choice between either perspective.

The American social critic Daniel Bell (1976) has identified some of the historical and cultural transformations and contradictions that led to the emergence of a consumer society. The most evident contradiction within capitalism today being the division of the economic structure (based upon efficiency and functional rationality) and the cultural sphere (oriented around the aesthetic point of view and the pursuit of diverse life-styles). Bell argues that capitalism was built upon a culture of self-discipline and hard work that became opposed by modernist avant-garde movements that propagated a desire for the new and anti-bourgeois sentiments more generally. The culture of modernism was guided by the principles of life-style experimentation and innovation which sought to critique the restrictive nature of the common culture of capitalism. For Bell there are clear links between the more expressive culture originally propagated by artistic movements and what he calls the 'consumptive ethic'. Today the culture of the modernist avant-garde, on this reading, constitutes rather than opposes bourgeois culture. The war between the culture of self-expression and the conservative disciplines of hard work is over. The ideals of the Protestant ethic (saving, industriousness and thrift) have been displaced through the operation of the free market and the celebration of new consumer freedoms. The rise of consumer culture has been built upon the displacement of the forms of self control exhibited by smaller, less commercially defined communities. The new capitalism, built upon mass marketing, rising standards of living and the expansion of debt and credit, destroys the ability to defer gratification and replaces it with hedonism.

The contemporary author who has extended these arguments the furthest is Zygmunt Bauman. For Bauman (1998), we have moved from a producer to a consumer society. A producer society became defined through capitalism's requirement for an ever expanding supply of labour, collective provision, security through the welfare state, the disciplines of the work ethic and a collective concern for the poor. Under the rubric of consumer society, however, the duties of citizenship and the disciplines of work have become undermined by the desire of consumers to make individualised choices within the market place. The consumer is easily excitable, quickly bored, has few substantial commitments, and values individual choice above everything else. The consumer, in terms of citizenship, is guided by aesthetics rather than ethics, and is not so much concerned with political ideology as by an individualised 'right to enjoy, not a duty to suffer' (Bauman 1998: 31). The ability to be able to make different kinds of pleasurable choice then becomes the dominant principle, or what Castoriadis (1997) called, 'social imaginary' amongst those who are not currently excluded from the labour market. The language and duties of citizenship, in this context, become overrun by the seductive rather than the disciplinary logics of consumer society.

Crucially, support for the welfare state becomes run down through the privatisation of 'individual' insurance, a refusal to pay high taxes, and the progressive criminalisation of the poor. The de-politicisation of the vast majority of society, those living under the pleasurable engagements of consumption, has converted 'the poor' into society's new 'other'. Despite occasional 'carnivals of charity' (witnessed through mass mediated appeals) the poor become simultaneously 'air-brushed' out of sight and demonised within our culture. In an age of flexible capitalism, the poor no longer act as a reserve army of labour and are better seen as the waste products of consumer society. We live in a world dominated by a huge consumer fun house that has little use for ideological debate or the most obvious losers of the economic system. The under-class in a society of post-ideological consumerism is the new enemy to be kept outside of the places and spaces where the affluent enjoy themselves. Bauman reminds us that if we are to consider the question of politics within consumer societies we can only do so if we acknowledge the link between a culture of pleasurable consumption and the progressive polarisation of advanced capitalist societies.

Similarly, Ritzer (1999) has argued that the development of new means of consumption (malls, the internet, the privatization of public space, catalogs etc) has increased the number of opportunities to consume within modern society. This has led overdeveloped Western societies into a condition of hyperconsumption. Increasing levels of personal debt, expansion of credit systems, and a decline in the level of saving and the spread of American style consumption patterns fuel contemporary consumption across the globe. The increasing spread of sanitised and homogenous practices of consumer behavior is however masked by entertaining forms of distraction and simulation that have become progressively utilised to hide from consumers the ways in which they are being duped and exploited. Through the use of spectacles, simulated events or celebrity endorsement consumers are being entertained while they shop. This creates the sense of consumption as fun. Yet Ritzer argues that while consumers may resist such suggestions the only real winners from this situation are the profit margins of global corporations.

Bauman's and Ritzer's political vision, which is arguably an extension of some of Daniel Bell's arguments, offers little prospect of 'repoliticising' consumer society other than through the recovery of more substantive ethical visions. For Bauman (1999), and indeed many others, the citizen has become the consumer. Once the market and pleasures of consumption gain precedence over our shared abilities to act within the public sphere then we know that citizenship is withering on the vine. The market leaves each of us to pursue our own individualised version of the good life, whereas citizenship requires public forms of deliberation and shared concerns. That is, citizenship requires a republican ideal that puts active engagement and the common good at the heart of society. The pleasures of consumption, the declining power of nation-states, privatization of common resources and rituals, increased mobility and short-term contracts, and market uncertainty all undermine the pursuit of a common citizenship. A new republicanism is however only possible once people are free from uncertainty and the threat of poverty. It is the recovery of social solidarity through a basic income (guaranteed to all irrespective of capacity to work) and new global republican institutions that stand the best chance of recovering the ethical life. The aim here being to reintroduce the possibility of other styles of living other than one of hyperconsumption. Arguably, this only becomes possible in a society that has not only become more just through the reduction of inequality, but has also become more stable and less uncertain and fearful. Such a society would need to introduce a substantial amount of social equality rather than simply expanding the equality of opportunity. Citizenship would need to embrace substantive social rights (not merely cultural rights), promote the possibility of active citizenship, and help devise public places that enabled people to rub shoulders with people who were unlike themselves. That is, as David Miller (1997) has proposed, a society where citizens have few meeting points with each other will find it difficult to sustain solidarity across status and class divisions. Again a republican citizenship would require both the reduction of material inequality and more convivial common public places. The concern here is that those that can afford to do so will permanently withdraw from public places and institutions into more exclusive environments. Without more substantive features, expecting citizens to consume less and deliberate more consumerism will continue to dominate over citizenship.

Consumer Culture as Citizenship

In certain circles it has been precisely the 'demonising' of consumer society that has led to the marginalisation of progressive political forces. In Britain, a number of fresh perspectives around the journal *Marxism Today* during the 1980s sought to rethink the Left's response to consumerism. These voices sought, in the language of the time, to reject a form of Left moralism, and to engage with the ways in which consumer society had sought to create a new popular common sense. These viewpoints were tied to the analysis of a particular political terrain that saw the exclusion of Left governments from political power throughout most of the 1980s. While this is not the place to review the success or failure of such 'rethinking', a number of more populist ways of viewing consumption became evident within this literature. Such perspectives, I shall argue, continue to have relevance for the links between consumption and citizenship.

Particularly important here was the analysis by Stuart Hall (1988) of Thatcherism as a political and cultural hegemonic project. Thatcherism was of special interest due to the way that it sought to construct a new common sense within civil society. For example, Hall sought to uncover the ways in which Thatcherism connected with and constructed a popular view that the market could be experienced as a domain of freedom. The state in such a view was represented as bureaucratic and repressive whereas the market was the domain of choice and autonomy. While Hall has been criticised for overstating the ideological success of Thatcherism, his genius lay in the claim that such a view was not wholly illusory and that the Left had much to learn from this perspective (Stevenson 2002).

Frank Mort (1989) argued in similar terms that a politics around consumption was as much about culture and language as economic policy. Consumption throughout the eighties becomes associated with an array of popular images including Yuppies and the affluent working-class (popularised by comedian Harry Enfield's 'Loadsa money'). In this respect, Thatcherism had succeeded in translating 'policy into the popular aspirations' (Mort 1989: 164). The problem for Left social democratic parties was that they were widely seen as the party of production rather than consumption, and at worst were perceived as seeing the desire to consume as morally debilitating. The reorientation of capitalism around life-style niches and a heavier emphasis upon design actually interconnected with a number of new social movements articulating a politics around cultural difference and less stable social identities. Hence the politics of consumption and the development of new social movements have many connecting points not always appreciated by the kinds of moralising prevalent within certain sections of the Left. Social movements and consumer campaigns are mutually dependent upon the operation of powerful codes and the transmission of knowledge. That is the proliferation of consumer information, codes about responsibility and risk, and complex understandings of identity are the shared concerns of consumer cultures and a range of social movements. How the rules of normality are established, what is considered 'other', who has the power to determine what everyone is talking about are the shared concerns of consumer culture and social movements alike (Melucci 1985). Further, new forms of politics are more dependent upon images, spectacles and making an impact generally within the media just as are advertising campaigns for new products (Crook 1992). Yet there are also dangers in pushing this argument too far. Many 'new' social movements are critical of the distribution of resources within society and have concerns that cannot be restricted to 'merely' cultural questions (Butler 1998). Such a reading would cancel many concerns evident within green, peace and Third World movements about the long term effects of capitalist growth and sustainability (Habermas 1981). These qualifications aside, new consumer environments and some of the new social movements do seem to share an emphasis upon spectacle, fun and pleasurable forms of identification.

Further, Mica Nava (1992) has argued that the political Left has continued to ignore the progressive possibilities of a politics of consumerism. A common masculinist assumption that 'real' politics goes on within the government or the work place has ignored new sites of activism within consumption. Nava, in this context, draws attention to the rise of ethical consumption, consumer boycotts, and increased forms of ecological awareness amongst consumers. For example, in Britain we have witnessed consumer militancy in respect of Shell oil's desire to dump old oil rigs, Barclays bank's support of apartheid and more recently GM foods (Vidal 1999).

Daniel Miller (1997), taking this argument further, has suggested that while politics is experienced as being hierarchical and bureaucratic, the practice of shopping can be an empowering experience. Both Nava and Miller suggest that we see shopping as a daily election whereby consumers, who wield considerable power, make daily ethical choices in terms of the goods they purchase and the way they inhabit public and private space. Indeed, argues Miller, a focus upon consumption, rather than citizenship, might under this reckoning reconnect questions of welfare and consumption? By this Miller does not mean abandoning citizenship (although its rights focus gives it a legalistic orientation), but a rejoining of consumption and welfare that sees them as equally important moral domains for the distribution of social goods. Such a switch would recognise the moral and ethical concerns involved within shopping, while refusing a certain masculine logic that sees it as a peripheral activity. It matters greatly if we can afford a balanced diet, how safe the food is in the supermarket, and whether mobile phones cause cancer.

Some of these points are well made. It is undoubtedly the case that consumption is the place where politically marginalised groups (including gays, lesbians, young people and women) have sought to forge an identity. Put in terms of 'cultural' citizenship, consumption is one of the key places in the modern world where the 'right to be different' is pursued. Where Bauman's argument is perhaps at its weakest is the recognition that this domain for many people is not experienced as either as post-ideological or as atomised as he describes. The perspectives outlined above suggest that while the relatively affluent have been the main beneficiaries of the expansion of consumptive practices, such spaces and places have helped inform 'new political agendas' that cannot be derived from a reformulated class politics. However, what is noticeable, particularly in retrospect, about the 'New Times' arguments is that they fail to raise substantive ethical and moral arguments in respect of equality and fairness. This is a major weakness in a society that has witnessed the exaggeration of wealth differences accompanying the spectacle of consumption. Accepting the legitimacy and complexity of popular pleasures, while protesting against material and cultural exclusion, seems like a line worth holding.

The cultural patterns of the above discussions are suggestive about the connection between citizenship and consumerism in a number of ways. Firstly, that 'political questions' are very much part of contemporary commercial cultures. Commercial and aesthetic cultures, in contemporary society, continue to simultaneously raise and obstruct issues that can be related to the cultural nature of citizenship. Many marginalised groups have searched for an identity through a commercial culture not only because other more 'political' avenues have been blocked, but because it has come to signify, increasingly within our culture, a domain of pleasurability and identification. This means that the politics of citizenship and questions of consumption cannot be opposed in any straightforward way. However, it remains the case that while consumption may raise 'ethical' questions, it only does so by being connected to more formal citizenship criteria of rights, obligations and social exclusion. That is, we may become concerned as to the effects consumerism is having upon the distribution of goods, how excluded groups are represented in tabloid newspapers, or levels of ecological and environmental destruction, but this is only made possible due to the fact that they have already been raised as political/moral issues. In other words, no matter how pleasurable and ethically complex, shopping cannot replace the dimensions of citizenship. Indeed such an argument in the current climate is not only dangerous but highly irresponsible. While shoppers are invited to buy or boycott a particular product, citizens should seek to raise questions as to the political context of production and consumption. Participatory notions of citizenship will seek to politicise and thereby transform the horizons of consumers/citizens through shared processes of deliberation. Citizenship, by giving voice to a diversity of concerns, seeks to modify the identities of those participating within a common dialogue (Mouffe 1993). This moves the focus of attention away from our relationship with sets of products while seeking to politicise diverse global networks of production and consumption. Such a logic is poorly captured by our ability to say 'yes' or 'no' to consumer products. Further, if our politics is purely based around shopping then this can only further benefit the already rich and powerful. Firstly, such a vision suggests that democractic politics is no longer able to offer any protection against the market, which it was able to do over the course of the twentieth century with the setting up of the welfare state. Secondly, to base politics around purchasing decisions obviously privileges those with most money and power. We obviously need to be careful to deconstruct overly masculinist assumptions in respect of consumption, however, this should not be allowed to end with the cancellation of meaningful forms of politics.

Questions of Cultural Capital

The problem with the discussion so far is that our analysis of culture has been preoccupied with either the production or reception of commodity culture. Those who are concerned that the market will convert citizens into consumers had little to contribute on the reception of culture, whereas those who highlight the aesthetics of reception tend to neglect production side questions (Lash 1993). By far the most sophisticated attempt to link these questions while offering an understanding of culture and consumption that is linked to frameworks of power and domination is offered by the French sociologist Pierre Bourdieu. In the context of our discussion, Bourdieu's (1984) key insight is what he calls the arbitrariness of culture. By this he means that there is no intrinsic reason why upper class tastes, aesthetic preferences and cultural judgments should be taken as indicative of high culture. That is the love of abstract art, classical music and other cultural styles function as a form of social distinction. What a society takes to be innovative, creative and culturally valuable is largely determined by the social structure. Hence, apparently disinterested practices like the appreciation of a fine wine, a visit to an art gallery or indeed a preference for Stravinsky over Chopin are used to gain what Bourdieu calls cultural capital.

For Bourdieu the social world is structured by different forms of capital which are accumulated, gained and lost in a number of different social fields. While fields are the sites of constant social struggle they are also the places that distribute and determine access to different kinds of capital. The economists and crude Marxists are mistaken in that they can only account for a narrow set of motivations that immediately lead to the pursuit of money and wealth (economic capital). Such a definition of capital ultimately colludes with artists and intellectuals who have sought to mystify their practices by presenting them as either the pure pursuit of art or knowledge. Indeed, Bourdieu's (1996) work traces through the historical emergence of a bohemian view of art that opposed both the industrial bourgeoisie and so called bourgeois art while developing an aristocratic attitude towards consumption and sexuality. The development of 'art for arts sake' as the authentic value of artistic and cultural production helped develop a number of paradoxical attitudes towards the production and consumption of culture. Firstly, the bohemians suspicion of immediate market success meant that artistic success was secured through commercial failure. Further, the ideology of commercial disinterestedness favoured those who had inherited economic capital. In other words, economistic analysis fails to understand the 'profit', 'capital' and 'status' that were attributable to those who developed new aesthetic lifestyles.

Cultural capital in Bourdieu's (1986) analysis can exist within three forms. The first form of cultural capital exists within an embodied state, or what Bourdieu also describes as the habitus. The habitus is a set of cultural dispositions which are passed on through the family and become literally second nature. These embodied dispositions become a way of speaking, standing, walking, thinking and feeling. The habitus is largely structured through the opposition of different cultural characteristics found in different social classes. While the habitus can become transformed by entering into a different field, or more generally through social mobility, it molds the body in ways that are largely unconscious but relatively durable. Yet by virtue of the habitus individuals become predisposed towards certain cultural preferences and tastes. Hence it makes a good deal of sense to talk of consumer lifestyles in terms of both cultural and economic capital. That is, those who are able to define taste, vulgarity and discernment impose these definitions on subordinate groups. For Bourdieu (1984) it was the new petit bourgeoisie (school teachers, artists, academics etc) whose aesthetic lifestyles meant that they became the new arbiters of good taste. That is, those who are high in cultural rather than economic capital determine taste. The new petit bourgeoisie were able to distinguish themselves from industrialists (high in economic but low in cultural capital) and the working-class (low in both economic and cultural capital) by seeking to expand the autonomy of the cultural field. Whereas the transmission of cultural capital through the body is the most efficient given its hereditary nature it can also be reproduced through material objects. That is, cultural capital can exist in an objectified state through art collections, musical instruments, objects of art and jewellry. Finally, we can also talk of cultural capital in a third sense, that is, the institutional confirming of educational qualifications. This confers on the holder a legally guaranteed amount of cultural respect and level of cultural competence. These three forms of cultural capital can of course all be converted into economic capital. In this sense Bourdieu is able to talk of the symbolic as well as the material profits due to its relative scarcity from which its holders are able to profit.

In addition to economic and cultural capital we can also talk of social capital. Social capital depends upon the networks and connections that an individual is able to maintain. If you like: if economic capital is what you have, cultural capital is what you know, social capital is whom you know. In this respect, social capital in part depends upon active forms of sociability that sustain relations of either friendship or acquaintance. However, despite these different types of capital Bourdieu has consistently maintained that economic capital (in the final analysis) is at the root of the other forms of capital. That is, the power and privilege that access to different forms of capital reproduces class distinction. Hence consumption, leisure and lifestyle patterns become important given the extent to which they link into economic, cultural and social capital.

More recently, Bourdieu and Darbel (1991) have sought to link these concerns to the cultural capital necessary to visit a museum or art gallery. These institutions were chosen as they are often (although not always) free at the point of access and emphasise a form of cultural self-exclusion. That is, the study concludes, that the best predictor of whether or not you are likely to attend a formal gallery or exhibition is family background and educational qualifications. Working-class people who lack the necessary cultural capital to make works of art meaningful are forced to make sense of them through more restricted repertoires of interpretation. Working-class visitors then are 'condemned to see works of art in their phenomenal state, in other words as simple objects' (Bourdieu and Darbel 1991: 45). Those without the appropriate cultural capital complained of feeling out of place, were in constant fear of revealing their lack of knowledge and displayed most interest in art (like furniture) that had an obvious social function. Educational institutions that only sought to transmit a limited understanding of artistic works compounded this lack of affinity with the world of art. Familiarity then with a wide range of artistic and aesthetic practices was more often transmitted by the bourgeoisie family. For Bourdieu, then, a cultural democracy (or in our case cultural citizenship) can only be achieved by educational institutions seeking to make up for the lack of cultural capital available within the working-class family. Cultural equality for Bourdieu cannot be sought by either celebrating a working-class populism or by leaving artistic taste to the private discernment of individuals. Unless educational resources make some attempt to reverse the flow of cultural capital transmitted in the home then the end result will be enhanced forms of cultural inequality. Hence populist strategies which either seek to convert working-class culture into the curriculum or seek to create more opportunities for working-class children to visit gallery's are unlikely to have much effect. The question is not so much crude populism, rather the transmission of aesthetic taste proceeds by habit, learning and exercise. Bourdieu and Darbel (1991) powerfully argue that the only way to short circuit assumptions of working-class barbarism is to disrupt the idea that taste is naturally rather than socially reproduced. An inclusive cultural citizenship requires the intensification of the presence of the school within working-class people's cultural lives.

Yet it might be objected if the dominant culture is 'arbitrary': why should dominant institutions seek to intensify rather than reform the cultures it socially reproduces? This is because while the artistic avant-garde has historically pursued a strategy of distinction it has also historically preserved a sense of cultural autonomy against the market place. While the idea of 'art for arts sake' is mystificatory in that it hides the symbolic dividend of bohemian life-styles, its mythology has preserved ideas of artistic creativity against the market place. The democratisation of art cannot be pursued through its commercialisation. The invasion of the market into the cultural domain will inevitably 'cheapen' the value of the work, and undermine the inevitably specialised knowledge and experience necessary to produce and experience the work of art (Crook 2000). Hence Shusterman (1992) has argued that while Bourdieu has exposed the hidden economy of the disinterested aesthetic of high culture he remains so enchanted by its myth he retains hostility to popular art. This means the creativity evident within popular forms such as rap music, the working-class novel, and diverse forms of youth culture or alternative art forms like Pop Art are neglected by Bourdieu (Fowler 1997). Arguably, these questions become particularly pressing once we consider the relationship between the market, popular culture and cultural policy. Here I shall argue for both a cultural policy that pursues a strategy of equality while continually seeking to deconstruct claims to cultural hierarchy and status. That is, Bourdieu is right to draw attention to the ways in which working-class people commonly exclude themselves from dominant cultural institutions, but mistaken in the way he remains sceptical of the aesthetic merit of much popular forms of cultural expression.

Cultural Policy

The development of debates within cultural policy has been a welcome addition to the number of concerns mapped by cultural studies. These developments have been accompanied by an increasing concern on the part of European, North American and Australian governments in particular to develop substantial cultural policies covering a range of cultural practices. According to Tom O'Regan (2001), we might roughly talk of three ages of cultural policy. The first involved democratic initiatives through arts councils and other publically funded organisations to bring the arts to the people. This approach largely characterised initiatives in the 1950s and 1960s where a variety of cultural policies were developed to overcome social (mainly class based) barriers to high culture. Since the 1970s there has been an increasing amount of questioning as to what counts as 'art' or 'culture'. More inclusive definitions of 'cultural' experience and aesthetic forms of experimentation have sought to encompass more 'popular', community orientated and multicultural definitions. Finally, these trends and directions have increasingly focused question upon question of diversity and identity. Here cultural policy questions increasingly have to take into account the shifting terrain of popular taste and life style (Bennett 1998). Such has been the impact of these developments that many commentators assume that post-modern cultures have eclipsed ideas of the 'high' and the 'popular'. Under post-modern definitions of culture both consumer and artistic cultures talk the language of strategic management, niche marketing, product differentiation and promotion. Within these definitions art has become democratised and commodified. These developments have seemingly brought to an end a long tradition of left-liberalism that sought to redistribute art and culture, rather than question what constituted it in the first place (Mulgan and Wapole 1986).

Particularly striking in the European context has been the development of city based cultural policies. Since the 1980s local strategies sought to diversify the economic base of the city and develop a more cosmopolitan definition of urban civil life. These trends, which build upon post-modern definitions of culture, have seen the decentralisation of cultural policy and the development of more inclusive civic identities. For example, Simon Frith (1993) argues that in the 1980s there was a burst of state intervention in the production of popular music. This included attempts to enhance employment opportunities and grant access, knowledge and relevant technology to previous excluded groups of cultural producers. Yet there is growing concern that more inclusive cultural strategies are being progressively overshadowed by cultural policies that more explicitly target urban regeneration. The neo-liberal need to maximize the economic potential of local cultural industries has meant that more inclusive strategies have become progressively sidelined (Bianchini 1993; Griffiths 1993). That is, while broadening the definition of the 'cultural' had initially inclusive implications attempts to combat social exclusion have progressively given way to the needs of the market. For example, in the North American context Sharon Zukin (1995) has reasonably argued that the rise of symbolic or cultural cities has primarily sought to establish the city as a safe place for cultural consumption, seeking to attract new business and corporate elites into the city. That is, as the city seeks to establish itself as a dynamic place of business, tourism and multiculturalism, it becomes progressively divided as its public places become commodified and under the constant watch of security cameras. As cities become the playgrounds of the affluent classes (or those high in economic, cultural or symbolic capital) they also become places of surveillance and social division.

A 'Common' Cultural Citizenship

Here I aim to develop a normative model of cultural citizenship, and then seek to understand how it might help us with questions of cultural policy. The aim here is to develop a framework for cultural policy that seeks to both deconstruct ideas of high and low culture (that is, problematising which cultures, artifacts, experiences require governing) within a context that both preserves difference against homogeneity while promoting a strategy of equality. As such, my argumentative strategy will be post-modern the extent to which it questions distinctions between 'high' and 'popular' culture, egalitarian in that there is still a need to promote the widest of possible conditions of access to hierarchically organised cultures, and finally democratic in that we need to consider how to promote constructive forms of dialogue and participation across cultural divides. The idea here is that the commodification of culture has provided cultural policy with opportunities (the flourishing of a variety of life styles and the aestheticisation of everyday life) and dangers enforced patterns of social and cultural exclusion. That is, cultural policy as cultural citizenship needs to recognise that the ground that it currently operates upon is historically determined (there seems little point in returning to the benign liberalism of the inter-war period) and will necessarily work within certain limits determined by the wider society.

The idea of a cultural policy based upon democratic citizenship is not a new one. The writing of Raymond Williams in many respects remains a considerable resource from which we can continue to mine many useful ideas. In particular it is the idea of common culture to which I want to return. For many this will seem like an odd choice given the increasing power of the cultural industry and the development of identity politics bringing enhanced forms of fragmentation. Surely better to give up on the idea of a common culture as a homogeneous and repressive ideology that would find few takers outside a few pipe smoking cultural conservatives. Yet if this were what Williams meant by a common culture it would hardly be an idea worth revisiting. For Williams (1989), a common culture had several aspects, but overall it was an instituted culture of dialogue rather than agreement. To be able to talk of a common culture did not mean the possibility of reimagining a fragmented society as one of shared values and aspirations. The *common* element of Williams's argument concerns the ordinary ability of people to contribute, criticise and re-interpret aspects of their culture. Within this process the meanings of 'high' or indeed 'popular' culture are not fixed in stone but require open criticism by members of the community. In particular we need to pay attention to the material conditions and ideologies which aim to exclude different voices from full participation. The second aspect of a *common* culture is the provision of institutions, which transmit the knowledge, skills and resources which allow full participation. Here Williams seems to be saying that it is the most class bound way of thinking which seeks to connect high culture with a privileged minority. Instead works of literature (and other aspects of the culture) need to become openly interrogated through genuinely educated forms of dialogue. This is obviously different from saying Shakespeare is for a minority, but also stops short from blandly saying he's for everyone. Instead, Williams is arguing that a community's self-realisation depends upon 'adequate participation in the process of changing and developing meanings' (Williams 1989: 35). This is not possible without mutually recognising that everyone can participate, and by seeking to secure the material and institutional means that might sustain such participation. In other words, contrary to Bourdieu, full participation does not come by simply providing working-class children with the adequate knowledge of the appropriate repertoires of art criticism. Williams (1989: 36) goes considerably further than this, insisting 'that the culture of a people can only be what all its members are engaged in creating in the act of living'. That is, for Williams, educational institutions not only need to familiarise working-class students with high forms of culture, but to allow them to develop their own arguments and perspectives that might stop well short of traditional forms of reverence. In these terms then Williams (1989: 37) argues that perhaps a 'culture in common' is a better description than the misleadingly titled common culture.

Despite the democratic bent of these ideas we might still object that the pursuit of a culture in common remains an exclusive ideal. Here I want to briefly consider the argument that Williams poorly appreciates the symbolic creativity of popular culture, remaining more of a cultural conservative than he might seem, and that the forms of cultural difference that are likely to exist within a multi-cultural society have finished attempts to construct common cultures. These are both serious objections which are indeed worthy of more extended treatment than I have space to explore here.

It remains the case that despite Williams's sensitivity to questions of class his own cultural ethos was that of a literary critic rather than as a fan of popular culture. This has led many, myself included, to argue that he has a tendency to be overly dismissive of the complexity of consumer culture (Stevenson 2002). If we were looking for a complex textual analysis of popular romances or soap operas we would probably not call on Raymond Williams. Arguably, since Williams's time, cultural studies has done much to extend our appreciation of the complex negotiations that are involved in the everyday consumption of consumer goods. Paul Willis (1990, 1998) has perhaps gone the furthest in claiming that the creative meaning-making of the excluded should be respected rather than reformed by cultural institutions. Here Willis critically contrasts a dominant high culture of traditional artistic practices with a 'common culture' creatively made from everyday consumer culture. Willis maintains that despite arguments from people like Williams who sought to democratise high culture it remains (and is likely to do so) fundamentally detached from the cultural experiences of the vast majority of the population. Instead a democratic and egalitarian cultural policy should seek to empower young people to produce their own cultural forms. Whereas most cultural policy remains focused upon preserving the cultural and aesthetic choices of the educated middle-classes, this needs to be radically reformulated. Willis, as I argued above, wants to argue that working-class young people formulate their cultural experiences through an explicitly commercial culture. Hence cultural policies need to be enacted that enable ordinary forms of symbolic creativity evident within a night at the pub, reading a life-style magazine or listening to a rap artist. That is, the problem is not as cultural elitists of the right and left would argue that young people are consuming the 'wrong culture', but they are restricted by a lack of access to consumer culture. Here Willis advocates the setting up of Cultural Exchanges and Cultural Clubs where symbolic material such as videos and CDs could be swapped and musical and recording material, photographic and video equipment made available for common usage. The key idea being pressed by Willis is not so much inter-cultural dialogue but a determination to provide people excluded from 'educated' culture autonomy as cultural producers and consumers.

The problem with such proposals, according to Jim McGuigan (1997), is they reproduce dominant ideas of consumer sovereignty; that the market is the best provider of cultural goods and individuals the best choosers. The problem with Willis's contribution to policy analysis is that it fails to take account of the power of the market to privilege certain consumers over others, and to help shape and determine certain tastes. While there is much to this criticism, I think Willis could be read as saying that policies are needed to empower young people who might become excluded from the market and give them the confidence to become producers of cultural goods in their own right. These arguments, while populist, remain important in that they deconstruct the assumed superiority of much high culture (is ballet really superior to punk?), and potentially enable some young people access to a wider range of cultural repertoires, thereby expanding cultural literacy. Most music cultures are commercial cultures and I am likely to become experimental in respect of my tastes if I am not overly prohibited by cost. However, if we refer back to Bourdieu's concern about different forms of capital, then we could equally argue that such a strategy could well compound social exclusion. If we remember, it was Bourdieu's concern that a radical cultural policy should enable working-class people to 'appreciate' high art. Willis's proposals then might be criticised in that he simply assumes that for most people visiting art galleries, listening to classical music and reading modernist literature is out of bounds. Willis then actively reproduces the idea of high and popular culture as inevitably disconnected without any bridges between them. Hence, whereas middle-class people may choose between the 'educated' and the 'popular', working-class people are more restricted in the range of repertoires they are able to access. We should be clear that this remains a restriction from full cultural citizenship. Here again, I would return to Williams's idea of a culture in common. Williams (1958) was rightly critical of the idea that high culture belonged to the educated middle-classes, however, Willis reproduces this idea by reinforcing the prejudice that the lower orders are better served by the market and the middle-classes by the art gallery. Williams's radicalism remains in that he correctly perceived such a situation could only be addressed by social and institutional change. The guiding feature of cultural policy for Williams is the ability to be able to promote dialogue across a number of cultural divides, and not the reproduction of class based prejudices about the cultural capacities of the excluded. As Terry Eagleton (1990) has argued, the cultural preferences of excluded and marginalized populations may become reformulated once they have transcended their social condition. While 'culture' may indeed become formed through processes of struggle and oppression it does not mark its producer or consumer with an 'essential' identity.

Many of Raymond Williams's critics have been concerned that the idea of a common culture effectively silences subordinate voices. Williams's politics were mainly concerned with reconnecting questions of class and a literary artistic culture rather than focusing on questions of ethnicity, gender, multiculturalism and sexuality. Indeed there is a growing literature which strongly suggests that Williams can be found wanting on most of these topics and concerns (Jardine and Swindells 1988; Milner 2002). We might argue that the point is not to build a common culture, but to work out ways of empowering marginalised positions within the policy arena. However, recently Bhikhu Parekh (2000) has argued that a multi-cultural society needs a shared common culture fashioned out of diversity. In a multi-cultural society diverse cultures constantly encounter one another and change due to the presence of the other. That Adorno's (1991) arguments in respect of the guardians of culture are no longer acceptable is largely due to a growing awareness of different cultural traditions and practices that fall outside a European avant-guard. However, as Parekh fully recognises, unless we are content to live in a society of cultural apartheid and fragmentation then institutional conditions must be created to foster intercultural dialogue. While a 'common culture' cannot be engineered the opportunities for a common dialogue need to be politically created. Just as Williams argued that the 'national culture' needs to be extended and criticised by working-class voices so Parekh argues similar privileges need to be extended to 'minorities'. Within this process both Williams and Parekh highlight the centrality of cultural and educational institutions. They are both critical of monocultural institutions which aim to impose a collective conformist culture. Yet for Williams the purpose of education was to provide citizens with the educational resources so they would be capable of full cultural participation. This remains a pressing question in a society which has seen illiteracy rates rise in areas of high social exclusion. To achieve a common culture citizens need basic skills so that they are able to write a letter to a newspaper, discriminate between different viewpoints and understand a variety of artistic work. For Wiliams these agendas were blocked by the capitalism and cultural snobbery. Arguably, if basic literacy rates have fallen it is because society no longer requires their participation as workers in the economy and the prejudice against people from poor class backgrounds remains as intense as ever. Alternatively, Parekh places emphasis upon the need to develop a genuinely multicultural system of education that aims to criticise the Euro-centric understandings that pervade educational curriculum. A good education needs to be able to break with specifically 'national' and 'European' understandings of history, the arts and sciences, while building in the experience of minorities into the common narrative of the community. While inspired by different questions both Williams and Parekh place their faith in a common cosmopolitan dialogue where new voices and experiences are brought into the centre of societies dominant self-understandings. That questions of cultural policy have much to contribute in this regard is a position that they would both seek to endorse, while recognising such aims are restricted by wider questions of money and power.

Conclusion

We have seen that ideas in respect of cultural citizenship have sought to balance questions of equality and difference. Here I have sought to stress how we might pursue these questions in respect of the related areas of consumerism and cultural policy. In particular, I have stressed the continued importance of questions of equality in a polity that is increasingly dominated by the demands of neo-liberalism and a number of diverse social movements based upon questions of identity. My argument has been that a genuinely cohesive cultural citizenship can only survive in a context where egalitarian concerns are able to socialise the operation of the market and provide a space to negotiate the expression of difference. This is not to privilege class over other identities, but to recognise the growing forms of social and cultural apartheid that both further polarises questions of difference and increases the dominance of the market. This is likely to be a difficult circle to square for critics and activists alike in a world where such claims are increasingly hard to raise. However, my argument is that the cultural Left urgently needs to find new ways to avoid both celebrating the market or dismissing the different forms of subjectivity that attempt to link questions of ethics and identity. If we can do that, then questions of cultural citizenship might come increasingly to the fore.

References

Adorno, T. (1991) 'Culture and administration', in *The Culture Industry: Selected Essays on Mass Culture*, London: Routledge.

Bauman, Z. (1997) *Post-Modernity and its Discontents*. Cambridge: Polity Press.

Bauman, Z. (1998) *Work, consumerism and the New Poor*, Buckingham: Open University Press.

Bauman, Z. (1999) *In Search of Politics*. Cambridge: Polity Press.

Bauman, Z. (2001) 'Consuming life', *Journal of Consumer Culture*, 1(1): 9–29.

Bennett, T. (1998) *Culture: A Reformer's Science*, London: Sage.

Bianchini, F. (1993) 'Remaking European cities: the role of cultural policies', in F. Bianchini, and Parkinson,M. (eds) *Cultural Policy and Urban Regeneration*, Manchester: Manchester University Press.

Bourdieu, P. (1984) *Distinction*. London: Routledge.

Bourdieu, P. (1986) 'The forms of capital', in J.G. Richardson (ed.) *Handbook of Theory and Research for the Sociology of Education*. New York: Greenwood Press.

Bourdieu, P. (1996) *The Rules of Art; Genesis and Structure of the Literary Field*. Cambridge, Polity Press.

Bourdieu, P. and Darbel, A. (1991) *The Love of Art*. Cambridge: Polity Press.

Butler, J. (1998) 'Merely cultural', *New Left Review*, 227: 33–44.

Castoriadis, C. (1997) *The Imaginary Institution of Society*. Cambridge: Polity Press.

Cohen, L. and Arato, A. (1992) Civil Society and Political theory, Cambridge, MA: MIT Press.

Crook, R. (2000) 'The mediated manufacture of an "avant guarde": Bourdieusian analysis of the field of contemporary art in London, 1997–9', in B. Fowler, *Reading Bordieu on Society and Culture*. London: Routledge.

Crook, S. et al. (1992) *Post-Modernization: Change in Advanced Society*. London: Sage.

Dahrendorf, R. (1994) 'The changing quality of citizenship', in van Steenbergen (ed.), *The Condition of Citizenship*. London: Sage.

Eagleton, T. (1994) *The Ideology of the Aesthetic*. Oxford: Basil Blackwell.

Fowler, B. (1997) *Pierre Bourdieu and Cultural Theory: Critical Investigations*. London: Sage.

Fraser, N. (1997) Justice Interruptus, London: Routledge.

Frith, S. (1993) 'Popular music and the local state', in T. Bennett, et al. (eds) *Rock and Popular Music: Politics, Policies, Institutions*. London: Routledge.

Griffiths, R. (1993) 'The politics of cultural policy in urban regeneration stategies', *Policy and Politics*, 21(1): 39–47.

Habermas, J. (1981) 'New social movements', *Telos*, 47: 33–7.

Habermans, J. (1990) Justification and Application, Cambridge: Polity Press.

Habermas, J. (1993) *Justification and application: Remarks on Discourse Ethics*. Cambridge: Polity Press.

Habermas, J. (2001) *The Postnational Constellation; Political Essays*. Trans. M. Pensky. Cambridge: Polity Press.

Hall. S. (1988) *The Hard Road to Renewal*. London: Verso.

Honneth, A. (1995) *The Struggle for Recognition; The Moral Grammar of Social Conflicts*. Cambridge: Polity Press.

Ignatieff, M. (1991) 'Citizenship and moral narcissism', in G. Andrews, *Citizenship*, Princeton University Press.

Isin, E.F. and Wood, P.K. (1999) *Citizenship and Identity*. London: Sage.

Jardine, L. and Swindells, J. (1989)

Keane, J. (1989) *Democracy and Civil Society*. London: Verso.

Kymlicka,W. and Norman,W. (1994) 'Return of the citizen', *Ethics*, 104: 352–81.

Lash, S. (1993) 'Pierre Bourdieu: cultural economy and social change', in C. Calhoun, E. LiPuma, and M. Postone (eds) *Bourdieu: Critical Perspectives*. Oxford: Blackwell.

Lister, R. (1997) *Citizenship: Feminist Perspectives*. Basingstoke: Macmillan.

Marshall, T.H. and Bottomore, T. (1992) *Citizenship and Social Class*. London: Pluto.

McGuigan, J. (1997) 'Cultural populism revisited', in M. Ferguson, and P. Golding (eds) *Cultural Studies in Question*. London: Sage.

Melucci, A. (1985) 'The symbolic challenge of contemporary movements', *Social Research*, 52(4): 749–87.

Miller, D. (1997) 'Could shopping ever really matter?' in P. Falk, and C. Campbell (eds) *The Shopping Experience*. London: Sage.

Miller, D. (1998) 'What kind of equality should the Left pursue?', in J. Franklin (ed.) *Equality*. London: Institute for Public Policy.

Milner, A. (2002) *Re-Imaging Cultural Studies: The Promise of Cultural Materialism*. London: Sage.

Mort, F. (1989) 'The politics of consumption', in S. Hall, and M. Jacques (eds) *New Times: The Changing Face of Politics in the 1990's*. London: Lawrence and Wishart.

Mouffe, C. (1993) *The Return of the Political*. London: Verso.

Mulgan, G. and Warpole, K. (1986) *Saturday Night or Sunday Morning: From Arts to Industry – New Forms of Cultural Policy*. London: Comedia.

Nava, M. (1992) 'Consumerism reconsidered: buying and power', *Cultural Studies* 5(2) pp. 157–1.

O'Regan, T. (2001) 'Cultural policy: rejuvenate or wither', (professorial lecture), available at: www.gu.edu.au/centre/cmp/.

Parekh, B. (2000) *Rethinking Multiculturalism: Cultural Diversity and Political Theory*. London: Macmillan.

Ritzer, G. (1999) *Enchanting a Disenchanted World: Revolutionizing the Means of Consumption*. London: Sage.

Roche, M. (1992) *Rethinking Citizenship: Welfare, Ideology and Change in Modern Society*. Cambridge: Polity Press.

Rosaldo, R. (1999) 'Cultural citizenship, inequality and multiculturalism', in R.D. Torres, et al. (eds) *Race, Identity and Citizenship*. Oxford: Blackwell.

Shusterman, R.M. (1992) *Pragmatist Aesthetics*. Oxford: Blackwell.

Stevenson, N. (ed.) (2001) *Culture and Citizenship*. London: Sage.

Stevenson, N. (2002) Understanding Media Cultures, London: Sage.

Turner, B.S. (1994) 'Postmodern culture/modern citizens', in van Steenbergen. (ed.) *The Condition of Citizenship*. London: Sage.

Vidal, J. (1999) Power to the People, Guardian newspaper, 7 June.

Williams, R. (1958) *Culture and Society*. London: Penguin.

Williams, R. (1962) Communications, London: Penguin.

Williams, R. (1989) 'The idea of a common culture', *Resources of Hope: Culture, Democracy, Socialism*. London: Verso.

Willis, P. (1990) *Common Culture: Symbolic Work at Play in the Everyday cultures of the Young*. Milton Keynes: Open University Press.

Willis, P. (1998) 'Notes on common culture – towards a cultural policy for grounded aesthetics', *The International Journal of Cultural Policy*, 4(2): 413–30.

Zukin, S. (1995) *The Culture of Cities*. Oxford: Blackwell.

Index